RIDE OF A LIFETIME

The Life and Times of
James Houston

—BOOK TWO—

© James Houston 2023

This book is copyright. Apart from any fair dealing for the purposes of study and research, criticism, review or as otherwise permitted under the Copyright Act, no part may be reproduced by any process without written permission. Inquiries should be made to the publisher.

Published in 2023

Cover design & typesetting by Kate Francis Design
Cover image *The ceiling of Ely Cathedral, Cambridgeshire* by Kev Gregory
Printed by Lightning Source International

RIDE OF A LIFETIME

James Houston

In China in 2004 our group of English teachers from Australia, tutoring lecturers at the Chongqing University of Technology, were each given a Chinese name, based on imitating the sounds of our name to a Chinese ear. I was named *Zhi Hou Min*. When I asked if that meant anything in Mandarin, I was told, after due consideration, that it could mean *'a fast and nimble horse'*.

BOOK TWO
Transformation

1	Sorting out ITEMS	3
2	Girdling the Globe ... *Gratis!*	13
3	(Un)holy Land	17
4	Holy Mountain	25
5	Behind the Iron Curtain	35
6	Picking Theological Brains Worldwide	47
7	To the New World and Beyond	59
8	Reporting In	71
9	Charting New Waters	75
10	Surveying the Broad Meadows	85
11	Family Fortunes	91
12	The Year of Living Dubiously	95
13	Grappling with Theology	103
14	Journey to Parish Ministry	109
15	Up like a bird...Down like a Stone!	115
16	P-Plate Vicar	129
17	Encountering the Chinese Dragon	143
18	A Ripening Harvest	149
19	Seeds Blowing in the Wind	163
20	The Heartache of Parting	175
21	Challenging the Church Establishment	181
22	Battling for Two Asylum Seekers	187
23	'In Journeyings Oft'	197
24	Pilgrimage to Controversy	211
25	To the Cradle of Civilisation	219
26	Nurturing Multicultural Ministries across the Churches	229
27	Family Matters!	239
28	Under the Spell of the Old World	245
29	'Farewell to Old England Forever'	267
30	'A Wilful, Lavish Land'	275
31	Bicultural Parish	281
32	In the Land of the Rising Sun	291
33	Love Affair with Llamas	301
34	The Lure of Cathay	321
35	Old China Hands	333
36	Two Sinophiles on the Loose	351

37	Heart-wrenching Partings	363
38	A New World a-Birthing	371
39	In Search of Meaning	385
40	Core of my Heart	393
	EPILOGUE	411
	BIOGRAPHICAL NOTES	414

We children of the 1930s—*the 'war children'*—are the last link with an Australia now totally gone, having been shaped by the Great Depression experience of poverty and despair, and the wartime experience of fear and threatened invasion by a cruel enemy.

We have been the favoured generation: we escaped any direct involvement in the war but we had the benefit of being formed by the good times, affording us for example the prospect of overseas travel. The aim of that was not only to learn and experience—or to party, which you could have done just as well at home—but to see Australia and yourself in a wholly other light.

—**Writer David Malouf**, also b.1932
in an ABC Radio program
(freely transcribed)

Time is an enormous long river
and I'm standing in it,
just as you're standing in it.

My elders were the tributaries,
and everything they thought and every
struggle they went through,
and everything they gave their lives to and
every song they created
and every poem that they laid down flows
down to me...

And I can reach down into that river and take
out what I need to get through this world.

Bridges from my time to yours.

> —**Utah Phillips,**
> American hobo folk singer

BOOK TWO
Transformation

1
Sorting out ITEMS

Eltham turned out to be a special sort of place, an early rural village in rolling country close to where Diamond Creek runs into the Yarra, 25 kilometres north-east of Melbourne. It is Wurundjeri country with the native name of Nillumbik, now resurrected as the name of the Shire. It boasts a claim to be the green capital of Victoria, and certainly has some strong credentials. In the early 1930s Justus Jörgensen, an artist associated with Max Meldrum, had gathered around him artists, musicians and writers and set up a bushland retreat. It was to grow into *Montsalvat*, an art colony unique in Australia. The rustic complex graces a wooded slope not far from our present home at East Eltham. Its main architectural glory is the Great Hall, authentically modelled on a French *château*, painstakingly built by hand out of materials garnered from demolitions, together with a Gothic gem, the Chapel, and a formal stone water-lily pool with flower-draped arches. European landscape perspectives complete a tranquil, reflective ambiance.

Pioneered by Alistair Knox, a local style of domestic architecture arose in the district, in hand-made mudbrick framed with recycled timber, evident today in many secluded settings around Eltham's forested ridges and glades. Even many of the street names are evocative: Bible Street, Wycliffe Street, Napoleon Street. Our 'rented estate' in Napoleon Street featuring a mudbrick villa and log cabin was 'very Eltham', located on the crown of a ridge high enough for us to spy the tops of the city skyscrapers on the SW horizon. A curious feature of the suburb was a grid of hilly streets fully built up decades earlier but which had never been formally made nor sealed, whether in the name of resisting modernity or because the residents declined to meet their share of the costs. Napoleon Street was one of these, a long thin dirt-track lined by solid modern homes with gardens.

Home among the gumtrees

Though largely cleared, our two-acre lot retained some tall eucalypts and many mature conifers, sloping down to the rear. The house was centrally placed along the street frontage, not far back from the dirt track. It was a rectangular villa, mudbrick, flat-roofed, slate-floored, with a ping-pong table on the wide rear terrace. Inside, the provincial French furniture and farmhouse kitchen made a self-conscious statement, proudly 1930s. Fifty metres away in the grounds stood a real log cabin of untrimmed radiata pine, crammed with shelves of books in English and French, and with a large old desk and a central wood-burning stove. A perfect gentleman's retreat. Since the block only had wire-strand fences we rigged up a long line on the ground, along which Angus could slide his lead till suddenly yanked up short, the illusion of freedom rudely shattered. A whole fauna of insects and tiny creatures regarded the mudbrick house as a natural extension of their habitat, and the nights were punctuated by the possums frolicking on the roof.

The working week soon took on its own rhythm. Chris to be driven to the station for his train/bus ride to La Trobe University, David to Donvale Christian School over the Yarra and beyond, and soon Marjorie found a social worker's position with the Department of Social Security (now Centrelink) at Preston, leaving father alone in his cabin, mulling over the two-year campaign. Before long another member joined our household, Darren Prentice, a country lad studying at La Trobe who became friends with Chris through their membership of the Student Christian Movement. So we were a three-boy household, all of them on the evening meal roster. Nick was still away, in America. We also had snake scares, magpie attacks, and Angus distinguished himself with an amorous escape one night which engendered a litter of gorgeous half-Labrador, half-kelpie puppies.

The ITEMS Project

Working on my project I was to report monthly to the Commission on Community and Race Relations of the Victorian Council of Churches, the State ecumenical body which, unlike its federal parent, included the Catholic Church, though still not the evangelical Churches. While really an employee of the VCC, I was permitted to work from home. The VCC General Secretary, Sister Mary-Lou Moorhead, was squarely behind the project, as was Alan Matheson, then co-leader of the Ecumenical Migration Centre in Fitzroy, nursery of Australian multiculturalism, and also the representatives of the mainline denominations on the Commission, all well versed in theology. After the Public Service I welcomed the novel ambiance of co-operation and goodwill, while enjoying professional freedom to develop the project as I saw fit, but of course seeking guidance on local conditions new to me. I soon realised that Melbourne is a proud city, deferring to no other, and quietly confident of its superiority to its older but brasher neighbour to the north. I gathered it was bad form in Melbourne to mention one's birthplace or *alma mater* as Sydney, while Canberra is quietly dismissed as irrelevant. And of course initially it is disempowering not to be 'in on' the local references in jokes nor the all-important folklore of Australian Rules football (simply called 'football' as if there could be no other). But excellent training in keeping ears open and mouth shut.

Reflecting the guidelines submitted to, and endorsed by the Victorian Government's 150th Anniversary Board, I proposed the minting of the acronym *ITEMS* for my project, to signify *'Intercultural Theological Education in a Multi-faith Society'*. There were five emphases to be pursued:

- to foster a greater awareness, in the theological arena and among the Churches, of the new factor of *cultural diversity* transforming the context for urban ministry;
- to devise and implement an accredited tertiary-level *course in applied cross-cultural theology* in a Melbourne ministry-training seminary;

- to compile, prepare and publish a textbook of cross-cultural theology and mission;
- to encourage in the Churches *an understanding of other world Faiths and nurture inter-faith contact and dialogue*;
- to develop and publish appropriate multicultural study materials for small-group use in the Churches.

As an outsider my first task was to get the feel for the principal denominations in whose vested interests I would be working. The Uniting Church I knew well—or so I thought. But not its divergent character from NSW/ACT, where on union in 1979 the Methodist heritage had more or less prevailed. In Victoria the Presbyterian influence had rather set the tone. Again, student days in the Sydney University Evangelical Union had brought a deal of contact with the Anglican Church but now I learnt what a maverick in world Anglicanism the Sydney Diocese is seen to be for its 'superior' and combative monochrome evangelicalism. By contrast the Melbourne Diocese offers a veritable tapestry of churchmanship, with the balance tilting towards the Anglo-Catholic ('high church') expression. Of the Roman Catholic Church, through my studies in Latin and continental languages I had gleaned a modicum of understanding, updated with face-to-face encounter with Catholic charismatics in Canberra and personal friendships that had mercifully sapped the harsh Protestant bigotry. But what of the Churches of Christ, the Salvation Army, the Quakers (Society of Friends)—not to mention the gaggle of ethnic Orthodox Churches (e.g. Greek, Romanian, Coptic, Antiochian, Armenian, Indian Malankara?

Of course no one knew about all these: each brought their contribution from their own perspective. But I had to shape something universally acceptable and relevant. The task looked more daunting than I had reckoned on, especially when I met the Church leaders with their theological doctorates, while I could cite my profound NSW Methodist Local Preachers' qualifications. *Gulp!*

On the other hand I had not been selected for the task on any other ground than my assumed capacity for expressing the reality of multiculturalism to church educators responsible for training the next generation of clergy. Of that I felt confident, perhaps brashly so. The challenge then was not only to plead the cause with the clergy educators themselves, doubtless uncritically committed to their existing curricula, but also with the ultimate policy makers in the Churches' leadership. But was this merely a routine Public Service approach of identifying and evaluating all the factors involved? But how could I know anything about the factors influencing the minds of church leaders? Yet was this not precisely what Al Grassby had advocated for years with professionals like medicos and lawyers and headmasters and broadcasters? Courage, my lad, in the face of prudence that would cry, '*Desist*'. Just do it!

Initial contact encouraging

Early on I made an appointment with the secretary of the Anglican Archbishop of Melbourne, Rev Dr David Penman. I would start with him for several reasons: though only recently installed ('enthroned'!), he had already become the media's 'go-to man' for his accessibility on Christian social issues. He was knowledgeable and affable, with a PhD in Islamic Studies from Islamabad, Pakistan's capital, and prior experience as a Church Missionary Society worker in Lebanon. He and his missionary wife Jean were New Zealanders, though long resident in Melbourne where he had been director of studies at St Andrew's Hall, the CMS missionary training college, and later Bishop of Melbourne's Western Region. On the retirement of the previous archbishop a long stalemate had supervened because of the near balance of the competing forces in the Diocese. In the end a group of 'concerned Anglicans' had taken out a whole-page ad in The Age calling on the Church to exercise some leadership, and in the ensuing Synod the compromise candidate came up the middle, David Penman, clearly elected as a cleanskin. So he had the moral authority to put his mark upon the Diocese. At an early press conference he announced that in the thrust of his social policies, he 'wanted to be like Jesus'. He was also a democrat, with the common touch: he outraged the traditionalists by suggesting that *Bishopscourt*, the official mansion at upmarket East Melbourne with its extensive olde worlde gardens, be sold and the money used to launch new parishes on the growing fringe of Melbourne. But this was a bridge too far.

His background as an Arabic speaker with a love for the culture, and his experience with clergy training curricula suggested that he could well be open to my approach. Moreover in his public utterances he was already tackling intransigent community issues, among them racial prejudice and cultural diversity.

Anglican recruits—*for a season?*

Over and above all this loomed the factor that, as a family, we had already decided to throw our lot in with the local Anglicans at St Margaret's Eltham rather than with the Uniting Church. On our first Sunday in Melbourne we gravitated to the Uniting Church, only to find the people would be away the following Sunday at a church camp. So next week we went around the corner to the Anglicans, to be intrigued at the mini-majesty of a parish Sung Eucharist from the unfamiliar *Australian Prayer Book*, with hymns and psalms and candles and ritual. In particular it blew Christopher's mind. Tears in eyes, he suggested we keep going there as an antidote to the formlessness of O'Connor. I agreed readily. After all, I had come to Melbourne to be an ecumenical worker. What better place to start than in our own churchgoing? The deal was clinched a couple of days later when the Vicar, Rev. Ron Dowling, turned up at Napoleon Street to welcome us. For the duration we were Anglicans. Or was it the curve of a Shepherd's crook gently redirecting our steps?

Moment of destiny

The meeting with David Penman was literally life-changing. Boggling at the opulence of the 'Palace' (and trying to hide this) I was shown in to the great man's study, like a library but with a massive mahogany desk. A good-looking, prematurely greying man, he stood to receive me with real warmth and motioned me to one of the two armchairs where he joined me. As I made my initial exposition he was all nods and when I finished he stood up before me, saying, "This is a really strategic project, and timely. It's high time all the Churches realised that Australian society is utterly different from the days when clergy training curricula were devised. I can give you an unqualified assurance that this Diocese will collaborate in every possible way. So let's get down to business." Gobsmacked would be too anaemic a term to describe my reaction.

We talked of the unique situation of the Diocese with its two official seminaries, Trinity College in the University of Melbourne with its traditional Anglo-Catholic orientation and Ridley College, the evangelical foundation just up the road. The differing curricula of both needed revision. Why didn't I draft a new subject, perhaps to be made compulsory at both, and requiring practical work in some migrant setting? This could inject a new approach and later, maybe the whole existing curriculum might be reviewed and broadened to reflect more than simply the Anglo-Australian experience of Church. Spoken like a missionary.

We talked on and he offered his personal assistance in any way I needed to get the message across to Melbourne Anglican leaders. He asked me to keep him posted. Then as we were winding up, we stood together and he put his arm around my shoulder and prayed for the success of the project and for me. At that instant my heart was won. I felt like falling at his feet in gratitude. It would also seal my affiliation with the Anglican Church for the rest of my life.

The challenge of building awareness

Where to start? Why not with the most concrete of the four challenges of my task, if conceivably the most exacting: the cross-cultural theology course? But the first step would be to produce a rationale and outline of the whole ITEMS project. Using the resources of the ecumenical movement, then in its heyday, we had 10,000 copies of an introductory brochure printed with the masthead *So many kinds of Australians. Who will minister the grace of God for their needs?* (coyly featuring the photo of a handsomely bearded young dog), and distributed them around local churches all over Melbourne.

Even more strategic however was it to gauge the personal interest of the Heads of Churches in appearing on the ITEMS letterhead as a Reference Panel. My hesitant approach to them bore fruit: to my joy all agreed. The fifteen names appearing in the margin of the letterhead spanned eight Churches and also included a Jewish and a Buddhist leader. Nothing loth, since the funding was coming from the Victorian Government, I followed up with a letter to State Government

House and was rapt when His Excellency the Governor, Sir Brian Murray, agreed to become the Patron of the project. The Office of the Labor Premier, John Cain, also expressed interest, albeit more low-key, and I even sought the blessing of the Opposition Leader, the (later redoubtable) Jeff Kennett. Wow! Maybe the seminary principals might even deign to consider the Project's claims? I was interviewed by the Melbourne Anglican paper *See*, now *TMA [The Melbourne Anglican]*, and the national Anglican paper *Church Scene*, both of them publicising the VCC's sesquicentenary initiative.

Of course this considerable public interest and the responsiveness of the Churches reflect an era, not so far distant, when the great bulk of the general community was willing to identify publicly as Christian (and certainly at the Censuses), although hardly backed by regular church-going (except for the Catholics). Hence an innovative project seeking to encourage ministry candidates to relate more positively to the cultural diversity of the Melbourne population was *per se* newsworthy, attracting interest beyond the Churches.

Autumn 1984 found me pursuing a busy round of appointments at all the city's theological colleges and seminaries. It all amounted to a precipitous learning curve. At the outset the skill required was that of a networker able to relate to a wide range of people varying in temperament and style, though all brilliant intellectuals. In addition to creating goodwill, I was seeking an opening for a novel and experimental approach in theological study—and incidentally, becoming conversant with the highways and byways of Melbourne.

Though theologians may be intellectually adventurous, open to revisiting traditional biblical insights, few at the time had shown much interest in the changing cultural context of the Australian church, not to the point of incorporating any reference to it in their courses. Though their towers are of stone rather than ivory, theological colleges scarcely resonate with the pulse of an ever-changing world. Hence the Churches—in their structure, life and general preoccupation—seemed all too often to evince a disinterest (unawareness?) about the ethnic diversification of their city. Indeed, some Anglican parishes were veritable time capsules of an Australia still unmarked by mass migration.

A historic academic innovation in the making

Back in the log cabin at Eltham as our first Melbourne winter drew on, cosily ensconced by the wood-burning stove, I was drafting the substance of a course to open up the issues confronting the Australian Church through its location within a pluralistic and multicultural society. In my view, the initial challenge facing students would be to develop a genuinely theological understanding of culture, and gain insights into:

- the intrinsic links between religion and culture: is the Gospel merely Western? Discerning the 'pearl of great price' from the oyster shell of culture

- making caring contact with people from varied backgrounds
- unmet welfare needs in the ethnic communities—who will go in to bat for them?
- what happens when families live in two worlds at once, especially teenagers?
- should the Churches speak out more ? On what issues? exploitation of migrant workers? Racism?
- identifying with the Aboriginal people's struggle
- encountering neighbours from other Faiths
- the national policy of multiculturalism—where does the Church figure?
- towards an Australian theology of multiculturalism

To have integrity and humanity the course would also need to include frankly the impact of European settlement on the Aborigines, and their place in Australian society—and in the national psyche—historically and until today. I felt more on home ground here.

The distinctive approach of the course would be its practical as well as its theoretical orientation. Instead of academic essay-writing, each student would gain practical exposure to everyday life within an ethnic community, devising how they could make a useful contribution in a specific situation while becoming acquainted with the realities of migrant life on the ground. I hoped they would take the initiative in locating a suitable setting and making the contact, failing which I would make suggestions for them to follow up. Their report on this field placement would be assessed towards their final credit.

The other vital dimension of the course was the specifically Christian perspective interwoven throughout, with particular attention to:
- understanding and ministering to people of ethnic backgrounds
- relating to ethnic congregations, within or separate from Anglo churches
- educating an Anglo congregation to understand migrant issues
- evangelism and nurture across cultures
- approaches to dialogue with people of other Faiths.

Class time: 2 hours weekly, plus field research and a placement in a minority group setting. Assessment would be through the report on this field placement, and a personal statement of any growth in attitudes and understanding over the period of the course.

Within the above dual framework, the specific focuses of the two-semester course would be upon:

First Semester
- basic concepts: culture, ethnicity, social class, migration as loss, resettlement policies—assimilation vs cultural pluralism
- the social and economic situation of ethnic and racial minorities

- the migrant family, (un)employment, health and housing, children's and welfare services, the law
- language issues: learning English, maintaining home languages, bilingual education, plus the *distinctive personal challenge of trying to learn some Jiwarli (an Aboriginal language from NW Australia) during the first month of the course*
- experiences of racism and discrimination, and the anti-discrimination legislation
- contextual theology and missiology: overseas and ecumenical initiatives

<u>Second Semester</u>
- urban mission, Church welfare agencies, and community development
- Orthodox Churches, inter-Faith contacts: Judaism, Islam
- mission across cultures: parish education, ethnic congregations
- Aboriginal theology

Of course I was not competent to teach such a course—even in academia who could be? It would require both in-depth community experience across a wide range of settings, as well as a profound knowledge of the social sciences. But beyond that, there was need for a 'feel' for ethnic community perspectives: the outsiders' view of our society. Hence a unique feature of the course was the exposure, week by week, to established experts and community members sharing their insights, supplemented by field observations and audio-visual presentations. My task would be to initiate, launch and co-ordinate the course, making the contacts, providing the speakers, and arranging the field observations and, where I had real competence in areas of my personal experience, also by lecturing.

Such was the grand vision for a pioneering course which would be the first tertiary accredited course in its field anywhere in Australia. But who would accredit the course, and which theological college would offer it? Ideally it would need to be held in an ecumenically-oriented institute so that students from more than one Church could take it as part of their studies.

Tackling the theological establishment

But these questions were not my responsibility to resolve. This was where the Melbourne ecumenical community offered its enthusiastic support for the project. The accreditation agency would be the Melbourne College of Divinity (an institution, not a building), jointly linked with the Anglican, Roman Catholic, Uniting, and Baptist Churches, the Churches of Christ and the Salvation Army, which since 1910 has awarded theology degrees obtained by study in its 'Affiliated Teaching Institutions'. There were several of these, some denominational, others inter-denominational or ecumenical. One of the latter was the Evangelical Theological Association, preparing students for ministry in both the Baptist Church and the Churches of Christ. It was a huge step forward when Dr Bill

Tabernee, Principal of the Churches of Christ College (then called the 'College of the Bible' and located at Glen Iris), offered his seminary's hospitality for a trial teaching of the course in the 1985 academic year. It would be open to students doing a degree through any of the other affiliated teaching institutions of the MCD to choose it as one of their subjects. It would be entitled *'The Strangers within our Gates: the Church and Australia's Multicultural Society'*.

I was revelling in the going, exhilarated by the foretaste of success. Not only was there now the outline of a new and innovative course published in a theological college's *Calendar* for the coming year, but new horizons were opening up for me, beckoning me on towards the rest of my life. We had weathered the transition to Melbourne. In a stimulating new metropolis, I had found more worlds to conquer, inheriting a ready-made network of colleagues in a new Christian professional area, while still linked with my old secular network. And exploring the relevance of each to the other: the Christian response to Australian multiculturalism sounded a challenging project.

The icing on the cake

By September 1984, with the most demanding of the five ITEMS tasks bedded down until the theological college's first term opened in March 1985, and with the other tasks yet to be broached, it seemed the time to plan the round-the-world study tour agreed upon by the VCC. In the northern hemisphere it was autumn and the new academic year was just beginning. There would be much to learn and experience in Europe, with its guestworker economies booming and new projects in 'community relations' being implemented in several countries between host and immigrant populations. There were ecumenical Christian and inter-faith initiatives to observe in the UK, Germany and in France. In the USA, immigration over the previous 100 years or more had created the most multicultural society on earth, a model Australia was now pursuing, although our Churches had been slow to relate to it creatively. Some of the better-known theological seminaries, and also projects with Native Americans ('Red Indians') were worth visiting. Elsewhere there were significant Christian cultural sites to experience, particularly the Holy Land, the Vatican, the World Council of Churches in Geneva, Holy Mt Athos, Athens and Thessalonika, the Rumanian Orthodox Church, and on the homeward leg, the Tao Fong Shan inter-faith study centre in Hong Kong.

As agreed by the VCC the study trip was to be articulated with four weeks' recreation leave enabling me also to visit tourist sites and call on friends in Ely and Minden not seen for 21 years. A budget for the study visits was approved, while I would meet the costs of tourist activity from my own pocket. This in order to set aside any scepticism about 'junketing' on Christian monies. Of course the challenge of planning such a dual-purpose exercise was daunting, but from friends in the ethnic scene I had gathered a sheaf of contacts and invitations in Europe, while my ecumenical colleagues recommended many Christian agencies for observations and discussions. I was warned of the hard-headed American academic practice of ignoring overseas approaches unless they could lead to worthwhile discussions for both parties. In all I sent some *60 letters* abroad and planned my itinerary from the responses received.

Among the more significant replies were those from the *'Secretariatus pro Non Christianis'* in the Vatican, the Israel Inter-Faith Association in Jerusalem (with its letterhead in Hebrew, Arabic and English), and the World Council of Churches in Geneva. Melbourne Greek Orthodox Bishop Ezekiel gave me a letter of commendation permitting a non-Orthodox Christian to visit the monastic community at Holy Mt Athos in northern Greece. I also had a letter of invitation from the Patriarchate of the Rumanian Orthodox Church in Bucharest.

'All systems go'. World, here I come.

2
Girdling the Globe ... *Gratis!*

At noon on 1st October 1984 the family farewelled me at Tullamarine Airport with a round-the-world ticket in my pocket with Singapore Airways (for our side of the world) and Trans World Airways (for the other side) at a total cost of $A2,200, and a bundle of documentation which included my itinerary, plus a Eurail Pass and a Britrail Pass together costing $A400, all covered from the ITEMS Project funding. My budget included a total of $A3,200 for accommodation, to be all found by me and virtually all in private venues rather than tourist hotels. My itinerary was wide-ranging, covering the old world and the new—and challenging. It would demand intense concentration, with (foolishly) no built-in rest days.

From my genesis as a romantic, dreaming of what the world offered beyond the Botany Bay heads, I now felt confident and linguistically equipped, with my German and French from university days plus the five years spent in Europe 21 years earlier, supplemented by my Italian (based on Latin studies plus an Italian evening course at the ANU), and my Greek (based on Classical Greek studies at the ANU and backed by an evening course in *Modern Greek* at La Trobe University earlier in 1984). Though versed in the fields of migration and multiculturalism, in matters theological I remained a raw amateur, in any language. But that spring afternoon, as the jumbo-jet lumbered down the runway to leap off into the north-western skies, the lure of the far horizon was again working its magic on me..

Despite constantly flying around Australia as a public servant I had never flown internationally (except for the short–haul flight to New Zealand) nor ever seen the inside of a jumbo jet. What a different world it had become since our six-week ocean voyage to Europe in 1959! A belated entrant to the jetset, I was naïvely glued to the window as the stark emptiness of our continent, seemingly innocent of human habitation, unrolled for hours until we crossed the vast swampy estuaries of the Kimberleys and the day's lustre waned, and beyond the western horizon the blazing orb was quenched by the sea. Though travelling at 900 km/h night was inexorably gaining on us (and ushering in the first of our several gourmet meals).

> "The sun that bids us rest is waking
> our brethren 'neath the western sky,
> and hour by hour fresh lips are making
> Thy wondrous doings heard on high."

These were the days before the advent of in-flight cinema. Later when the cabin lights dimmed I was of course too excited to sleep—and too big to curl up. But not too cramped to write a number of aerogrammes (one-page folding air letters) distributed gratis, with a promise to mail them from the charming hostesses, all of them undoubtedly finalists in the Miss Asia Contest, in national dress.

Landings en route

Singapore Airport, the hub of the airline's international operations (it had recently won the Airline of the Year award), was little less than a palace complex, grandiose in proportions and splendidly appointed. Suddenly I saw Tullamarine as a poky slum. Ah, world standards impinging… While marking time for an hour and a half for the Europe connection at midnight, I paced through lounge after marble lounge lined with luxury shops (staffed, but all devoid of shoppers), some of them in halls bigger than the whole of Sydney or Melbourne Airports.

Under way again, our night was punctuated by dropping in on Colombo—humid, sultry and eminently forgettable—followed by a bleary arrival in the Muslim *jannah* [heaven] of Abu Dhabi airport, a cross between Sydney Opera House and an atomic mushroom cloud, in the form of a simple 'tent' of ferroconcrete boldly draped from a central outbranching column, on two levels, with internal balconies of blue-mosaic walls, into which we were unceremoniously bundled for an hour while the plane was replenished with cheaper Middle Eastern aviation fuel. As though extras in a Hollywood musical, a middle-aged sheikh in white-flowing *burnous* and cotton headdress with twin gold bands, of immense dignity but overfed, stalked past followed at a respectful distance by a file of one, two, three, *four* youthful wives gorgeously robed and discreetly veiled. I wondered whether he felt the scornful barbs aimed at him by the Australian social worker I was chatting with. No one like those early feminists for intercultural sensitivity!

Aloft again in the wee small hours, beset by sleeplessness and colliding time zones, I fall prey to an overwhelming sense of unreality: I am in another world. Who am I? Where am I going? The world below a black ocean studded with winking tankers and rimmed with interminably curving foreshores, defined by four-lane highways brilliantly lit with blue and orange lights but bereft of traffic. Is it all a dream? … When will I wake up? Despite myself I nod off….

> "Across each continent and island
> as dawn leads on another day,
> the voice of prayer is never silent
> nor dies the strain of praise away."

Touchdown in Europe

A fitful dream and a half later we were circling over Athens at the dawning of a European day. Below an undulating city of uniformly off-white masonry, devoid of greenery but crowned by the Acropolis with its glorious ruin. Further afield pale rocky outcrops amid sparse vegetation until we crossed a small gulf to find the airport. Unsurprisingly, my luggage failed to show and I trotted out my best Greek with a baggage handler who promptly steered me to a hangar where I located it. Ominous start—if linguistically gratifying! But I noted that the tiny pocket dictionary kindly given me by a friend had immediately proven inappropriate, being in *katharevousa*, the exalted language of poetry and drama rather than the everyday *demotic*. By 1984 Homer and Thucydides were getting a bit long in the tooth.

To Israel—via Rome!

My two-hour Greek sojourn behind me, we took off for Israel (in the east) via Rome (in the west)! It was not possible to fly from Athens to Tel Aviv with Trans World Airways (TWA), the partner airline in my round-the-world ticket. After Singapore Airlines' state of the art hostesses (and aircraft), this was a bargain basement American airline flying out of its hub of St Louis, with ageing, smaller planes in a garish livery of navy blue and red, crewed by hostesses to match, undoubtedly veterans of the Miss Universe Contests of the 60s. My initial firsthand contact with the USA: 'Good morning, America'. The Captain was ridiculously chatty and wisecracky, enough to put any self-respecting terrorist off his game. Later I learnt that the airline had been the subject of a Court order restraining the dismissal of hostesses on the grounds of age. But given the adulation of youth in US pop culture, it was not to be wondered that in the next decade or so the airline would go bankrupt.

Rome's Leonardo da Vinci Airport near the mouth of 'Father' Tiber, though far larger and more bustling than Athens', also relied on long standing-only buses to ferry passengers to the terminal. While waiting for the flight to Tel Aviv I called the Australian principal of the missionary-oriented Collegio Columbano to alert him of my return a few weeks later, as previously arranged. The first human contact listed on my itinerary had proved heartening: he welcomed me and the forthcoming consultation. At the Collegio Colombano I would meet with a visiting Irish theological educator involved in cross-cultural training.

Joining a flight originating in America, bound for Tel Aviv and full of Jewish returnees, I spied ancient Ostia below, port of ancient Rome (now three miles inland!) near what looked like a drainage canal. The Tiber! How small-scale antiquity was! So the legendary exploits of mighty heroes, slave revolts, gladiatorial contests and world-shaping battles all took place under the flight paths criss-crossing this tired landscape around an unimpressive creek.

3
(Un)holy Land

Our arrival in the Holy Land had all the elements of drama. From the moment the plane breasted the coastline a thrill of emotion quivered around the cabin. Women began to croon ancient Hebrew chants of worship: a Song of Ascents as the plane began its *descent?* A surge of emotion ran through me too. Instantly we were right above Tel Aviv's geometrical city blocks of uniform height, street after street the colour of the desert sands, well camouflaged except for the street trees and the minimal vegetation between them. For minutes on end solid central European apartment houses, tightly packed together, then more contemporary blocks under construction, market gardens flanked by *gumtrees*, Ben Gurion military airfield installations, rows of parked jet fighters, and touchdown to cheers and tears from the homecomers. Since 1948 the home of world Jewry. For me too, journey's end from Melbourne after a day and a night in three planes, and now the first of many appointed lands beneath my feet.

But what a land! the Promised Land, the only place on earth trodden by the long-promised Jewish *Mashiach Yeshua*, Son of God come in the flesh. Suddenly I felt a pilgrim. I prayed that God might speak to me and enrich my insight into what it meant for Jesus to walk this very land.

My musing was rudely terminated by the proddings of a Catholic priest leading an impatient band of American pilgrims. Security brooks no musing. Everywhere stood soldiers, fingering the triggers of guns crooked in their arms: at the passport clearance, the customs checks, the luggage carousels. What luggage? Again I waited in vain. *No luggage!* TWA could only promise to follow it up and deliver it to my accommodation. What accommodation? Tel Aviv was one of the few places on my itinerary where I planned to locate my own cheap lodging on arrival, for one night, before going up to Jerusalem next morning. But Tel Aviv being the only fully Jewish city on earth, I wanted to get some feel for it, or at least establish a nodding acquaintance. Since it was already 5pm I had to agree to ring back next day for my luggage to be delivered to my Jerusalem accommodation at St George's College.

In the baggage hall I had had ample time to note the address of a local guesthouse in the advertising rack. But the Israel Tourist Bureau nearby had never heard of it: *"The taxi-driver will know"*. So out into society beyond the wire barrier where grinning and expectant Jewish faces looked eagerly for Uncle Chaim from New York. No one to meet a wandering Gentile from Melbourne.

Jewish homeland

My first encounter with Israelis was not encouraging. After a number of taxi-drivers declined to take me locally, one agreed but proceeded with the time-honoured trick of driving around in circles to build up the fare, while claiming to be always 'just around the corner' from the destination. When we entered the city freeway, it was clear he was on the make, but he had as much English as I had Yemeni Arabic. Stalemate. Even so I couldn't help but marvel at the array of biblical names on the exit destinations. Didn't seem to be quite right: to Ashdod by freeway?

Whatever had happened to the 'dusty lanes of Palestine' that Jesus trodden with his disciples? Beyond the crowded industrial quarter, open-air markets, jostling with buses and trucks at tight roundabouts (to Joppa by bus!), into the international tourist area. The driver asked me why was I so poor—I was a Westerner? My heart sank. After 21 years out of the tourist game I was naïve and powerless. The Jews might have returned to the Promised Land but what had changed? Certainly not the First Law of Tourism: *the tourist always loses.* Finally he deposited me under the cantilevered awning of the Palace Hotel on the beachside boulevard fronting the Mediterranean. I paid him out in shekels—without a tip (doubtless a spiritual descendant of Zacchaeus, but not yet converted).

From my room on the 9th floor I looked northwards along the straight Mediterranean coastline towards Tyre and Sidon, tourist esplanade in the foreground but immediately behind it in the gathering gloom, down-at-heel factories and a powerhouse. Nothing loth I wandered out into the sultry gloaming, found a small park full of hardy *Australian* flora overlooking the sea from a low clifftop and, with a wary eye for muggers, clambered down and waded into the Great Sea, not far from where Peter had learnt that all flesh was acceptable to God. A gun-toting soldier about Nick's age observed me suspiciously. So this was the reality of the Holy Land in our day?

Wandering south along the façades of luxury hotel towers, past huge outdoor terraces bustling with winers and diners, I turned off into an upmarket residential area, to find myself in Eastern Europe in the desert, in a repetitive pattern of dun-coloured apartment blocks fringed by tiny gardens—an intelligent, artistic place I surmised, but riddled with neuroses, judging from the profusion of professional shingles of doctors, psychiatrists, physiotherapists, advocates, accountants, tax agents *et al.* I happened upon the main shopping area in the city centre, featuring a large 'aerial' square built above a flyover junction, with fountains, garden beds, promenades, and edged with cinemas, taverns, sidewalk restaurants and fast-food outlets. I tried the Yemeni one (probably cheapest) and sat soaking up the atmosphere: signs in Hebrew letters (to be read backwards), price tags in shekels, cinema and TV programs in Hebrew, animated conversations around me in Yiddish and Hebrew. I watched young Oriental Jews trying to pick up skittish Jewish-American girls. It wasn't hard. More established seemed to be the relationships in evidence between young soldiers in uniform, a girlfriend on their arm and a tommy-gun hanging by their side. Would she be the victim of a 'shot-gun marriage'? The sheer vibrancy and energy of the scene brought home to me how tired I felt: I had not really slept for 24 hours, still buoyed up by the excitement of arrival, but it was fading fast.

So this was the longed-for homeland for the Jews? Weren't they the world's original multiculturalists, scattered across the face of the earth but knit together by their common bond of Jewishness? Of Judaism really. So where were the synagogues? Where were the rabbis, the devout men in black hats and long sideburns? The ubiquitous evidence of Jewish religion? I could see none!

Suddenly a wave of lassitude swept over me. I retreated to my hotel by a different route, noting the absence of English-speaking staff in the foyer. Come to think of it, it was uncanny to see only the Jewish alphabet everywhere and practically no Western letters in use on shops or neon signs.

Song of Ascents

Alive again next morning, at 6:30 I was in a taxi heading for the bus station, having been dissuaded from going up to Jerusalem by train, *'too slow and circuitous, narrow gauge, you know. No one ever goes by train'*. The night before I had called the course director at St George's College, adjacent to the Anglican Cathedral, to confirm my lodging there and to join the course on *'Israel—the Land and the Story'* as convenient.

With never a stop, the Jerusalem bus threaded its way under the flyover square through scurrying early-morning crowds of workers, along the beach front, past squalid markets and dingy streets (but I was yet to encounter the appalling filth and decay of the West Bank streets of Jordanian-controlled Palestine). For the hour and a half journey across the Lilliputian country I paid the outrageous fare of 440 shekels (410 to the US dollar)! In the summer haze of the fertile plains, plantations of cotton bushes covered in fleecy bolls (recalling our school project at Hurstville 40 years before) soon gave way to undulating fields and on the hillsides small forestry plantings of gumtrees, as we began the long ascent to the 'hill country' of Judaea. The freeway climbed past ruined farmhouses, in a section where burnt-out tanks from the Yom Kippur war still lay where they died, but with memorial details and battle dates daubed on them. Former fortifications, tanktraps, blockhouses still lie among reclaimed nature, already beginning to 'blossom as the rose' as Jewish settlers took root.

Contrary to my expectations, the ascent to Jerusalem is not so easy, even for modern vehicles: the curves become sharper, the bare ridges steeper as their bones emerge through the surface, some unbelievably rock-strewn. Then without warning, the first tall buildings of the New Jerusalem appear in the middle distance, perched on hilltops, all of white stone and many in bold design. We stop outside the King David Hotel. Daring but devoid of emotional charge. Then along winding boulevards lined by modern apartment blocks we negotiate a series of stony ridges, finally to crest a rise and actually *descend* to Mt Zion, at a height of 2,650 ft. Instantly we are in old Jewish Jerusalem (but not ancient), disembarking at a bus station on an open square from where I take a taxi to St George's College on Damascus Road in the Arab quarter, just outside the ancient walled city. It is part of an enclosed compound focusing on St George's Anglican Cathedral, a sizeable neo-

Gothic church with tower, reminiscent of 19th century England, and surrounded by gardens. The adjacent College is a more recent stone building,

Jerusalem the Golden

I lunched with pilgrims eager to gain exposure to *couleur locale*, drawn from many lands: a Ugandan bishop, clergy from Hong Kong, Canada and the UK, Protestant and Catholic. In addition to training Arab Christians for ministry, the College runs (expensive) residential courses directed by an American scholar, combining lectures on biblical history, archaeology and contemporary Israeli/Palestinian relations, spiced with field trips in and around the Holy City.

Next day I joined a field trip to the Temple Mount, site of the two Jewish Temples (destroyed by the Babylonians in 586 BC and by the Romans in 70 AD) and perhaps the 'holiest' spot on earth, a broad but relatively empty, paved expanse save for two mosques, the monumental Dome of the Rock on the very footprint of the Temple and the smaller al-Aqsa Mosque nearby, all within ancient walled Jerusalem but in the eastern sector controlled in 1984 by Jordanian authorities. Beneath the floor level of the Dome of the Rock we were taken downstairs to view the rocky 'peak' of the original Mt Moriah protruding through the floor—the very spot where Abraham was prepared to demonstrate his obedient trust in God by sacrificing his own son Isaac, the heir of the Covenant promise, until restrained by divine intervention. Over two thousand years later the Koran, in retelling the story, would substitute for Isaac his half-brother Ishmael, son of Hagar, claimed as the ancestor of the Arabs, and also record Mohammad's night journey to Jerusalem and visit to heaven in 621AD, thereby rendering it a city holy for Muslims, as well as for Jews and Christians.

From the mosques we moved to the south-east point of the walled Temple area, traditionally known as *'the pinnacle of the Temple'*, from which Satan tempted Jesus to throw himself down[1]. It is high in the sense that the Kedron Valley falls away sharply below the wall at that point, close to the watershed between the Mediterranean to the west and the Jordan River/Dead Sea to the east and south. Across the Kedron Valley gently rises the Mount of Olives, with the Garden of Gethsemane on its lower slopes and the point of Jesus' Ascension beyond. The classical view of Jerusalem is from the Mount's lower slopes, looking back across to the blue-domed mosque in the foreground and the ancient walled city behind, with the modern city skyline stretching away to the western horizon. *Yerushalayim*, 'Abode of Peace'.

Already it was impacting on my heart and mind, tinged with a vague sense of regret as lifelong imaginings succumbed to the tyranny of the real. But I suspect my imaginings were more about place than people, while now it was the prickly presence of the players in the ongoing drama of the divided city that shaped the sorry reality of Jerusalem. We moved across to the Western Wall of the Temple area,

---

[1] Luke 4: 9-12

the '*Wailing Wall*', where for centuries Jews wept for their loss, beating their breast in symbolic grief, until the 1967 War restored it to their control—but not the Temple area beyond the Wall. So near and yet so far! Conspicuously devout Jewish men in black hats and shawled women still weep there, pushing into crevices between the massive stone blocks tiny rolls of scrawled prayer messages. Already some Jewish hotheads are speaking of seizing the Temple Mount and rebuilding the Temple on the site of the Dome of the Rock—a recipe for the countdown to Armageddon?

Pilgrims' progress

Then there were the pilgrims. Everywhere. Not only Westerners but also Third World Christians—Filipinos, Latin Americans, Koreans, Africans—in droves, often accompanied by bilingual guides explaining points of history or spiritual significance. And older black-clad women (Italian, Spanish?) led by nuns in their various habits, praying, often moved to tears at holy sites like the *Via Dolorosa* (The Way of Pain) along which Jesus carried his cross while some jeered and others wept. I also walked it. Reflectively, trying to repopulate the picture. Did his feet actually touch these ancient paving stones? Had I been there, what might I have made of it all? Whose side would I have been on? After all, '*his own received him not*' and his disciples had fled.

Apart from a couple of field trips with the St George's College people, one to a scaled model of the biblical Jerusalem, I mostly ventured forth alone, borrowed guide book in hand. One warm evening, wandering through alleys of the old city, I discovered a viewing point overlooking the Wailing Wall and found myself in an earnest conversation, reasoning with a young American woman who had come to Israel to find God.

But in the ancient walled city, apart from the Temple Mount, such open vistas are rare indeed. More typical are the congested alleys (*souks*) dark and only wide enough for small knots of pedestrians, in the four 'quarters' traditionally named Christian, Armenian, Jewish and Muslim, lined with ethnically typical businesses and apartments, but in places with elegant new Jewish residences faithfully rebuilt in the ancient pattern, unlike the mouldering Muslim quarter of East Jerusalem—poverty-stricken, overcrowded, clamorous with children, seething with resentments and armed Jordanian police, standing guard at the narrow point of access to the Temple Mount.

The main gathering-points for tourists and observers of the exotic scene were the monumental Gates giving sole access to the old, walled city: the Damascus Gate to the north and west, and the Jaffa Gate to the south-west. Undoubtedly the main site for pilgrims is the Church of the Holy Sepulchre, reputedly built over the tomb from which Jesus rose from the dead. Dating back to 330 AD it is the most ancient church in Jerusalem (entered through a half-sized door, compelling the visitor to bow low—salutary posture). Inside the gloom is profound. I could make out very little nor come to terms with it all, though I can't forget the heart-rending emotion of southern European women on entering such a holy place. But like a good Protestant I didn't attach such significance to places of the dead: "He is not here. He is *risen*." In any case on Sunday morning I joined with my fellow-residents of St George's College in an informal contemporary service of prayer and praise at the Garden Tomb, an alternative location for the Resurrection, just outside the old city walls.

'O little town of Bethlehem'

I also made an afternoon pilgrimage across the Judaean hills to Bethlehem, part of the Palestinian West Bank territory, a mere 8km south of Jerusalem by bus. It is of course universally renowned for the Star of Bethlehem and the shepherds' wonder at the angelic *Hallelujah Chorus* announcing the birth of the Divine Babe in the stable—or was it rather a cave?—since there was no room in the inn. In 1984 it was still almost totally a Palestinian Christian town, with the Church of the Nativity (the most ancient church in the Holy Land, built under Roman Emperor Constantine in the 4th century) as the pilgrim goal. In subsequent decades the town would lose most of its Christian population by emigration.

But Jesus was only resident in Bethlehem as an infant, until Mary and Joseph fled to Egypt to avert the 'slaughter of the innocents', and on their return to Israel after some years the holy family went back to Nazareth near the Sea of Galilee (Lake of Tiberias). With a trip there in mind, I arranged for a Christian Palestinian driver employed by the College to take me, with a British chaplaincy couple visiting from Cyprus, on a personal pilgrimage to the Galilee region. With several ports of call along the way it was still only a shortish day's drive to Nazareth: what a tiny fleck on the world's surface is the Holy Land! As the raven flies, a mere 100 miles long by 45 miles wide.

'Galilee of the Gentiles'

But how God's priorities turn human ones on their head: the Potentate of Time comes to Planet Earth to be born in a stable and reign from a Cross—the whole drama played out in an obscure backwater of the Roman Empire, dominated by great and malign neighbours. But even within that context, Galilee was proverbially scorned for its mongrel race: *'Galilee of the Gentiles',* while Nazareth rates the familiar sneer: *"What good thing can come out of Nazareth?"* The Koran speaks of Christians as *Nazarenes* and to this day, Arabs and Jews use this term. But it is also widely applied to Jesus in the Gospels.

> "Crown him the Lord of years,
> the Potentate of Time,
> Creator of the rolling spheres,
> majestic and sublime.
> All hail, Redeemer, hail!
> for You have died for me;

> Your praise and glory shall not fail
> through all eternity."

In the Judaean hills north of Jerusalem our driver pointed out a bare peak, Mt Gerizim, the site of the Samaritan temple, vaunted by the woman of Samaria in her conversation with Jesus at Jacob's Well near Sychar (Shechem)[2]. We too drank from the well—beautiful cold water (symbol of Jesus' 'living water') that took forever to wind up in the chained bucket. To permit the driver to get home for dinner I agreed we would visit Galilee first and then double back to Nazareth, where I had arranged to stay with the Anglican vicar, Canon Riah Abu al-Assal. We passed through the village of Cana, where Jesus performed the first of his 'signs' by turning water into wine, and soon after catching our first sight of the brilliantly blue Sea of Galilee in its fertile valley, we paused high above it at the Mount of Beatitudes ('Be'-attitudes?) where a modern Franciscan chapel marks the spot Jesus chose to preach his revolutionary Sermon on the Mount—under a large *gumtree!*

We came down to the Lake at Tiberias, now a modern Israeli resort city, and walked on the beach where the Risen Christ prepared the fish breakfast for his disciples before rehabilitating Peter beyond his denial and then commissioning him *("Feed my sheep").* It's my favourite post-resurrection appearance of Jesus by its evocation of sight, sound and smell, and of the fresh beginnings we all need to experience. Next we passed the site of Magdala where Jesus landed once after sailing across the Lake, home of Mary Magdalene, first witness of the Resurrection. In late afternoon we visited the ruins of the synagogue at the site of Capernaum, at the head of the Lake on the Plain of Gennesaret, Peter and Andrew's home town which Jesus made the headquarters for his Galilean ministry of preaching and healing, but which he later denounced for its unbelief. Today it is barely a memory.

In Jesus' home town

The climb from the Lake (it is below sea level) towards Nazareth is considerable but the final pinch is quite steep, since the town is near the cliff edge over which his naysayers from the synagogue tried to throw Jesus but *"he went his way through them",* for his time had not yet come. Known as 'the Arab capital of Israel' (since its population numbers more Christians and Muslims than Jews) it is not part of the Palestinian West Bank territory but under Israeli jurisdiction. Along a higher ridge to the north overlooking the old city is a modern Israeli sector, its upmarket schools and leisure centres harshly out of bounds for the Palestinians.

My host the Canon, minister of the Anglican Christ Church, was a noted spokesman for Christian Palestinians—he had once stood unsuccessfully for the Knesset (Israeli parliament) on a united Palestinian/Jewish list seeking a just settlement. Subsequently he was to become Bishop of Jerusalem. We talked late into the night about the conditions Palestinians lived under in Israel, but also about the possible impact of humanitarians in both communities working creatively together.

---

2   Recorded in John 4:1-26

Sadly, subsequent decades were to see the opposite outcome as Jewish politicians adopted unilateral and increasingly hardline policies towards Palestinians, some of them involving flagrant abuses of human rights, and backed by a formidable—and no doubt nuclear-armed military.

Next day, the eve of the Jewish Sabbath, saw us moving about the Nazareth community, visiting the church's social projects and talking with members of the Canon's flock. I inspected the modern Catholic Basilica of the Annunciation built over the traditional grotto where the Angel Gabriel delivered his pregnant message to Mary. My late afternoon departure launched a race against the impending *Shabbat* that commences at sundown, preceded by the public buses scuttling back to their depots. The Canon drove me to a crossroads high on the spine of the ridge overlooking the Lake of Galilee, where I managed to flag down an inter-urban bus scurrying for its base. The route lay through the West Bank Palestinian territory, traversing the large but down-at-heel city of Nablus and terminating at Ramallah as the sun was setting. From there I had no option but to catch a taxi to Jerusalem, driven by an Arab.

The whole day had represented my close encounter with the tragic peoples of the 'Holy' Land—intransigent antagonists sundered by history, geography, ethnicity, politics, faith—all locked into a devil's brew of mutual resentments and hatreds that tendered no hint of resolution, short of the return of the Jewish Messiah ultimately destined to be recognised as universal Lord.

With stage 1 of my odyssey closing behind me, a wiser but sadder man turning the page to move on, I mused whether I had glimpsed anything relevant to building a vibrant, fair multicultural society in Australia, or to the role of faith in that project? Not there in the world's most volatile and enduring flashpoint.

God help them all!

4
Holy Mountain

Unsurprisingly, there was no direct flight from the Holy Land to the Holy Mountain. If there were, it would have to span centuries, cultures, religions. Or perhaps more authentically, go by Byzantine galley. Holy Mt Athos in the far north of Greece is a mecca for Orthodox clergy, a fabled place of monastic devotion. The very location is exotic because it is out of bounds to common men—and unsullied by women, common or otherwise. Untouched by the Renaissance, the Enlightenment or modernity. Unthinkable for tourists as mutually incomprehensible. Yet making the ultimate appeal to a wandering Christian romantic, albeit neither clergy nor Orthodox.

The Eternal City

In the absence of a convenient galley, I used up my one TWA-sanctioned side trip by flying from Tel Aviv back to Rome again, affording the opportunity for consulting with Catholic mission educators. My earlier letters to the Vatican had elicited courteous replies but no official consultations. As pre-arranged, I made my appearance to stay at the Collegio Colombano, well received by the Australian priest in charge of the cross-cultural training program of the Columban Fathers missionary order. He walked me around the elegant inner core of the city, the while describing the migration process from an Italian perspective. Fortuitously at the College I also met a visiting Irish theological educator, who pointed me to a comprehensive report from the Catholic Diocese of Christchurch on multiculturalism and the Church, which I later acquired, a theologically sophisticated blueprint for practical action among New Zealand's Maori and Pacific Islander communities. Twenty years later, I would edit two books by Fr Tony Paganoni, of the Scalabrinian Missionary Order, on the settlement of Italian Catholics in Australia[3].

As provided in my itinerary, after two days of consultations and tourism I made my way to the Termini (Rome's central railway station) accessible by tram, and entrained for the heel of the boot that is Italy, to take the trans-Adriatic ferry from Bríndisi to Patras, in western Greece. During the afternoon rail journey I fell into the best conversation in Italian of my career, explaining wage levels in Australia to a responsive audience in a 1st class compartment eager to elicit information, until brutally brought to a halt mid-sentence by being summarily ejected by a *Ferrovie dello Stato* (Italian State Railways) attendant. I had deceved myself into imagining I was already using the 1st class Eurail Pass I had in my bag, overlooking the fact that for this short trip I had decided to buy a single-journey 2nd class ticket specifically to avoid starting the Eurail clock ticking away during

---

[3] Anthony Paganoni, *Valiant Struggles and Benign Neglect: Italians, Church and Religious Societies in Diaspora* (2003) and *No Weary Feet: The History and Development of Mission Work among Italian Migrants in Australia* (2005).

my journey through eastern Europe where the Pass was not valid. Fair cop. But for the witnesses: what impression did it leave of Australians: slick—or sleazy?

Greek idyll

Later in the warm night the sea-going ferry eased out of Bríndisi harbour and I watched Italy recede. It was my first sea voyage since our return from Europe 21 years before in 1963. Though most passengers sat up in the saloon all night I had booked a cabin. Out on deck next morning, admiring the Greek tourist island of Corfu (*Kerkyra*) where we called briefly—once a British possession—I fell in with a pleasant chap, a retired Danish public servant travelling to Greece alone. As we docked at Patras in late afternoon we decided to make common cause. We caught a narrow-gauge electric train towards Athens but, intrigued at the Corinth Canal, cut in 1893 through the isthmus where Greece is only six kilometres wide, we decided to break our journey to explore the ancient city, a major centre in ancient and New Testament times, larger than Athens. St Paul spent over a year preaching and teaching in Corinth, and later wrote two of his Epistles to its unruly multicultural church, including the matchless chapter on the sublime gift of love invariably read in wedding services. Overnight we shared a room in a cheap hotel and next morning headed out into history.

The visit was a disappointment: ancient and historic Corinth had been totally destroyed in an earthquake in 1858 and the new town built as a port some miles away. The ruins of the ancient city (Akrokorinthos) formed an enclosure on a baked hillside which you can explore for an entry fee. The weather was too hot for me and I headed back to catch the train onwards to Athens, farewelling my new colleague who had decided to explore the chunky Peloponnese Peninsula.

For a couple of nights I booked into a cheap room in the congested Plaka tourist quarter under the shadow of the Acropolis, and walked miles by day: Omonoia Square, the Hellenic Parliament, the great rock outcrop of the Acropolis with its iconic Parthenon (='*of the girls*'), Mars Hill where St Paul preached his famous message to the Areopagites, idle philosophical dilettantes. In Greek and English the long text from The Acts of the Apostles is engraved at the spot. Nearby I came closest to a real conversation in Greek with a fireman enquiring about immigration opportunities to Australia, but despite my evening course at La Trobe University I failed the oral test.

Despite its unrivalled flavour of antiquity I found Athens lacking the magic of Rome. Four hundred years of Islamic rule under the Ottomans had precluded exposure to western Catholic civilisation and the Renaissance, with its ongoing heritage of elegance and style. By contrast Athens seemed uneasily poised between East and West, its drab streets congested with awful traffic problems like Rome's, yet unrelieved by noble vistas.

To the Thessalonians

For my ongoing journey to the Holy Mountain I found bus travel cheaper than the railways so I booked a seat for Thessalonica (*Thessaloníki*), second city of Greece and capital of its northern province of Macedonia. Along the way I recall the astonishing sight of a bay crammed with redundant shipping—large freighters and tankers anchored cheek by jowl—evidence of the international recession of the early 80s. Still on schedule in my planned itinerary, I was to stay at St Luke's Clinic, a Christian hospital run by the Greek Evangelical Church in the suburb of Panórama, high above the port city, as overnight guest of the medical director who had family links to Melbourne. Next morning we went to their worship service in the city conducted by a visiting British preaching and musical team.

My stroll along the Thessalonica harbour front led me past a Byzantine tower, an ancient church and archaeological remains. In the 9th century it had been from Thessalonica that two Greek brothers, Methodius and Cyril (*Metodi* and *Kyril*), had set forth on their missionary journeys northwards into pagan lands, which led to the Slavs embracing the Christian faith. They also devised the 'Cyrillic Alphabet' of eastern Europe and were the first translators of the Scriptures into Slavonic. Today they are revered by Eastern Orthodoxy as joint saints, 'the Apostles of the Slavs', on a par with the original apostles of the Early Church. In 1980 the Vatican had declared the brothers Patron Saints of Europe, joining St Benedict of Nursia.

There followed an hour or so mini-bus ride to the tiny port of Ouranopolis from where there is a diminutive ferry service to the Holy Mountain. Often in winter because of the heavy seas the monasteries are inaccessible. Along the way, with the rigours of the monastic table looming, I discovered the delights of pistachio nuts with milk chocolate.

Sacred seclusion

After the Islamic conquest of Egypt in the 7th century some of the desert fathers had sought seclusion in this remote location, where since the 5th century a few anchorites had set up their cells. Later, monks from other Orthodox Churches also established monasteries around the coastline, including Serbian, Russian, Georgian and Bulgarian foundations—though the great majority are Greek. From its formal recognition in 972 under a charter from the Byzantine Emperor, the Holy Mountain has been a self-ruled community of 20 monasteries, many with their satellite sketes[4], not part of the Greek state though under the political jurisdiction of the Greek Ministry of Foreign Affairs and the canonical jurisdiction of the Ecumenical Patriarch of Constantinopole, till this day based in Istanbul, Turkey (formerly 'Constantinople'). Down the centuries independence had been guaranteed under diverse international treaties, including by the Ottomans, in return for the allegiance of the community demonstrated by the payment of

---

4   Sketes are communities of Christian hermits following a monastic rule, allowing them to worship in comparative solitude, while also affording them a level of mutual practical support and securityfrom a monastery.

jizya (tribute). During the Nazi occupation, at the request of the monks, the Holy Mountain was put under the personal protection of Adolf Hitler, though Jewish refugee families (including *women and children*) were secretly given sanctuary there, thus cheating the gas chambers.

Visitors are tightly restricted, with precedence given to Orthodox men, and no access at all to women or children. Only members of Eastern Orthodox Churches may reside or work on the Holy Mountain, currently some 2,000 men. Short-term Australian visitors require letters of commendation from our Embassy in Athens, or in my case from the Greek Orthodox bishop (met years earlier during my survey of ethnic organisations) and the Consulate in Melbourne, but in addition must arrive at the Holy Mountain office at Ouranopolis in good time to establish identity and pay the 3000 drachma entry fee.

Savouring Orthodoxy

So how come I was at Mt Athos? During fifteen years of contact on behalf of the Commonwealth Government with the whole range of Orthodox Churches across Australia, I had been struck by their fidelity to their ancient traditions (Orthodox translates as *'proper glory'*), as much ethnic as spiritual—and also by the multi-textured richness of their liturgy (not that the people can understand the archaic forms of language enshrined in it). But, as had often been stressed to me, worship is not only a rational but a holistic experience, more about feeling devotion than analysing it.

But to be frank, I never could understand what Orthodox priests were on about—quite a leap from Christian Endeavour at Punchbowl Methodist! But in my new role as an erstwhile employee of the Victorian Council of Churches, a body comprising more Orthodox than Western Churches, and faced with suggestions from Greek and Rumanian priests in planning my study tour, I sensed the value of experiencing at first hand the Mother Church of their homelands and the quintessential fountainhead of Orthodox spirituality.

Since the 5th century Holy Mt Athos ('the *Virgin's Garden*') had come to embody the inmost substance of Eastern Orthodoxy: the spirituality of the original 'desert fathers' who lived alone in caves devoting their life to prayer and contemplation. Consecrated to the Mother of God, the Holy Mountain is an amazing part of the Mediterranean world, situated closer to Gallipoli than to Athens. It comprises the easternmost of the three fingers protruding from the Chalcidice peninsula into the northernmost reaches of the Aegean Sea, 50km long by some 7–12km wide, a landscape virtually untouched by human hand since antiquity, never having been part of a secular realm. Its primeval forest cover of foliage trees recalls an original Mediterranean flora lost millennia ago. There was even talk of bisons roaming still. At its southernmost tip the peninsula's wooded spine rises to the bare summit of Mt Athos, snow-capped in winter, at a height of 6,670ft (2,033m). To claim that the area is remote from the modern world is a gross understatement. In practical terms it is only accessible by boat—and the imagination!

Today the whole peninsula of Mt Athos is a UNESCO World Heritage site. Not surprisingly, the European Union (to which Greece belongs) is in conflict with the monastic authorities over the breach of human rights obligations explicit in the sexist entry rules, though there seems little likelihood of this aspect of modernity being heeded, any more than appeals from the world ecumenical movement over reconciliation between Western and Eastern Christendom. Moreover there is also a ban on cars, there being virtually no roads on the peninsula. The 20 monasteries comprising the Holy Mountain are all located along the precipitous east and west coasts, serviced mainly from the sea. At the time of my visit a few elderly utility vehicles with trailers were in evidence along the unsealed track linking the two ancient centres, Karyes in the middle of the peninsula (from where the *Protaton* of elected leaders from the monasteries exercises its authority, backed by the State-appointed Governor), and the mini-port of Daphni where visitors arrive.

All the monasteries function as self-sustaining communes, focused on liturgical services throughout the 24-hour day and the spiritual disciplines of prayer, fasting and work, whether in providing food by horticulture, fishing or wine-making, or exercising religious arts of ikon painting, woodcarving, bookbinding and Byzantine music. The Holy Mountain's home page modestly proclaims

> "The Orthodox monk is the guardian and the living proof of a long-standing and holy Tradition. In the monasteries Byzantium lives for ever as an environment of devotion and a special way of worship. All the arts that originated in Byzantium are still performed and flourish in the Monasteries".

'Forever Byzantium?'

However '*Byzantium lives forever*' is to ignore the inconvenient truth that in 1453 the city of Byzantium (= Constantinople, today's Istanbul) was captured by Mehmet the Conqueror, spelling doom for the (Greek, Christian) Byzantine Empire and ushering in Ottoman (Muslim) rule.

> "In Mount Athos, in particular, beyond the performance and flourishing of Byzantine religious arts, there are guarded authentic works and precious artefacts of that era: Mount Athos is today the largest museum of Byzantine art in the world. The buildings, manuscripts, and art treasures kept there constitute an everlasting proof and reassurance of the spiritual and artistic wealth of the Orthodox Church. In other words, Mount Athos is one of the main bearers and guardians of Orthodoxy today. It constitutes a tower of strength, spirituality and morality for Orthodox people everywhere".

The visitor's normative experience:

> "Approaching a monastery, visitors observe that the buildings look like fortified medieval castles with an imposing and very tall wall, with towers now and then, and with loopholes for throwing down hot oil or water, as well as a dominating

tower on the highest point of the monastery. The monks needed these structures to defend themselves against the many enemies who tried to conquer and loot Mount Athos over the centuries: pirates, Franks, Catalans etc. [i.e. Western Catholics from France and Spain.] In the middle of the wall there is a single entrance to the monastery with heavy wooden doors lined on the inside with long iron rods and on the outside covered with big metallic plates. Nearby there is a small cell where visitors meet the gatekeeper, whose job it is to lock the gates after sunset and open them at sunrise. He also checks the permits of the visitors and leads them to the main hall. There the visitors meet the Chief Host who will offer them water, coffee, *tsipouro* (a Greek drink made from pressed grapes), and Turkish delight. Later after they sign the visitors' book, he will lead them to their rooms to rest from their travels. In the late afternoon, the visitors go down to the main courtyard. There stands the church of each monastery, usually in the middle of the courtyard. Around it there are other chapels, various buildings and many trees. Next to the main church hang bells of various shapes and sizes. When the visitors enter the main church to attend the service of vespers, they get the feeling of moving upwards from one chapel to the next, past the wall paintings into the main church and the inner sanctuary: a stair case corresponding to the soul's ultimate journey up to the dome from where Jesus Christ oversees the world *(Christos Pantocrator)*. Immediately after the Vespers the church bells ring for everybody to go to the refectory: time to eat. It is a large, spacious building usually situated opposite the main church. The first to enter is the Superior followed by the monks and the visitors who enter last. The food is generally plain and frugal. Meat is not consumed. Meals consist of beans, vegetables, olives and fruit—and occasionally on feast days fish—and the traditional bread. The wine which is always home-made, is of the highest quality. In the middle of the long table and usually to its left there is a pulpit from which the Reader presents during the meal extracts from the Bible and sermons. After dinner the visitors return to the main church. There they are welcomed by the monk who takes out the Holy Relics from the monastery's safe and places them in the sanctuary so that the people can pay their respects. The rest of the day is free for the visitors to wander around the courtyard, take a rest, or talk to the monks who have the opportunity to offer advice and bestow their blessing. In the early hours of the morning (around 4am) the visitors go to the main church to attend Matins. Then around 8am they have breakfast and leave the monastery to continue their journey".

Monk for a day

And what of my experience? It bore little or no resemblance to the above: clearly the norm is for native Greek-speakers steeped in their own Orthodox traditions. I met only one person, an elderly monk (from Peru!) who knew any English at all, and indeed at that time there could hardly be a way for a monk to have learnt English. Besides, the monks were mostly older men, some indeed quite ancient.

Disembarking at Daphni, the ferry's small complement of men had trooped off to the primitive mini-bus standing by for the rough ride up the mountain to

Karyes for official endorsement. Alone as the only English speaker (as I thought) I was starting to feel uneasy at the experience looming: after all, I was only a tourist, and a shallow one at that. Were all these other men true spiritual seekers, perhaps potential monastics? No way I could read them. Beyond Karyes there seemed to be no transport to any of the 20 monasteries ringing the peninsula. Before long the group of men had melted away in the early afternoon heat, setting off on foot for their goals up to 30km away.

Actually before leaving Melbourne I had done a reasonable amount of research on the monasteries, and had chosen what I thought a spectacularly located one, Grigoriou, precariously clinging to its mountainside not far south of Daphni. Founded in the 14th century, it is considered to be one of the best organized and strictest *coenobitic* monasteries. It is inhabited by 70 monks [1990].

Grigoriou monastery

Negotiating the trail from Karyes steeply cascading down towards the monastery, glimpsed from afar between the wooded folds of the mountain and the dark-blue of the Aegean, I caught up with a short sandy-haired fellow, obviously non-Hellenic. He turned out to be an American journalist, long resident in Greece, writing a feature on the Holy Mountain for the New York Times, of which he had been the Athens correspondent. Kindly he took me under his wing, for which I was grateful, by then feeling quite out of my depth and starting to regret my romantic impulse to flirt with Orthodoxy. At least his purpose in visiting was educative.

The record continues:

> "Aside from the Katholikon [main church], the monastery also features many chapels. Its treasury is very rich in relics from various eras and also houses a fragment of the True Cross and relics of saints. The library is richly stocked and well organized. It contains some 804 manuscript codices, theological, ecclesiastical or liturgical works. One manuscript is an illuminated thirteenth-century Gospel Book."

In the next day or so I seemed to be sleepwalking. I could only sit by as my American protector held interminable discussions in fluent Greek, while making copious notes. Our meals were Spartan indeed: beans, rough bread and olive oil, with some fruits and nuts, washed down with wine (but until that stage of my life I had never tasted alcohol, having signed the pledge of total abstinence as a young Methodist.) My bed was as rudimentary, and the 'bathroom' comprised no more than a series of alcoves with seats jutting over the cliff edge! But it was the intangible life of the place that daunted me most. I found it positively alien: joyously praising God at four o'clock in the morning? And the endless routine, in all its rigour and sparseness, dating back nearly two thousand years, repeated by rote—lifelong? If that was holiness I was lost, a pagan. In the end I felt rather alienated and wanted out. Recognising the opacity of the monastic experience for me, sadly—or was it shamefully?—I settled for the exotic touristic elements. No one could speak to me except my American contact, but of course he was too preoccupied.

Grigoriou monastery

(In retrospect, I am bound to observe that in later years I was to develop a more sympathetic understanding of other modes of Christianity than the activist evangelical one I first knew and which accorded rather well with my temperament: non-reflective, impetuous, romantic.

Though not for me, the contemplative life must be seen as an ancient and authentic dimension of the Faith strongly appealing to other temperaments. Not that my later-acquired eclectic viewpoint—in my observation—is much shared by Christians of any of these persuasions, least of all the Orthodox, locked away as they seem to be in their particularistic national tradition. How pathetically we all cling to the familiar and shrink from the challenge of the unknown—or the universal!

Pristine paradise—lost?

My best memories are of the long walk we took up the mountain on leaving Grigoriou in order to follow the spine of the range southwards to its extremity under the actual Mount Athos. In the latter section the American journalist and I had picked up a ride on an open trailer. Our goal was the oldest, largest and first-ranked of all the 20 monasteries, Megisti Lavra (Great Lavra), founded in 963 at the tip of the peninsula under the shadow of Mt Athos. Its broad central courtyard was full of trees before an impressive church, plus many lesser monastic buildings. The librarian proudly showed us some of the treasures. It was also here that I met a German novice and sought to engage him about the Orthodox faith and world view, and his monastic life, but he wasn't forthcoming.

Finally the journalist and I struck out on our return to the embarkation port of Daphni many miles back up the peninsula, moving along tracks through the primeval forests. In all my earlier years in Europe I had never seen such huge and flourishing trees—oaks, chestnuts, firs, cypresses, laurels—and in such gorgeous profusion. It was a wooded wonderland! And the underbrush also so lush because there are no sheep or goats grazing. It was a veritable Garden of Eden fresh from the Maker's hand. I was spellbound.

Until we rounded a bend to find a section of many hectares utterly laid waste! My companion explained that this was one of the tensions he had been exploring in his conversations, between total preservation of the peninsula and the need to fund necessary works as the ancient buildings deteriorated. Corporate logging interests were pushing for further concessions. And this in an era before the modern green movement had developed much traction with its scientific and ecological imperatives. To me it simply seemed Christian common sense to preserve unspoilt creation. I wondered whether God was really more pleased with the monastic self-denial that was being preserved for posterity. Sadly I have just seen contemporary on-line images of the Holy Mountain which convey unmistakeable signs of further clear-felling.

With a profound sense of ambivalence I bade farewell to my friend, who was making for other monasteries further north. He gave me his card and invited me to visit him in New York City later in my itinerary, and I caught the ferry from Daphni back to Ouranopolis. From Thessalonica my bus journey went north-westwards, through the Iron Curtain to Bitola in the Macedonian republic of federated Yugoslavia.

Three countries, three civilisations behind me, and the rest of the world to come! But first loomed the Iron Curtain.

5
Behind the Iron Curtain

From 1945 until 1989 Europe was divided into two armed camps glowering at each other across a line from the Baltic to the Adriatic, which Winston Churchill famously dubbed the 'Iron Curtain'. Its southernmost point was the frontier between Yugoslavia and Greece, marking the transition not only between Hellenic and Slavic civilisations but also between communist East and capitalist West.

But a more enduring fracture had occurred 1500 years earlier between the Western and Eastern Roman Empires leaving Rome mistress of the Latin West, and New Rome (Constantinople) mistress of the Orthodox Byzantine Empire. In 1054 the Church Universal became formally divided into Latin Catholic and Eastern Orthodox churches, the former totally centralised in Rome under the Popes and the latter a grouping of national Churches under their Patriarchs, loosely linked through the Ecumenical Patriarch in Constantinople (his successor is still located there, now in the Turkish metropolis of Istanbul). Incidentally, the worldwide 'Anglican Communion' also follows this second pattern of allied self-governing Churches.

After the first world war a brave attempt had been made to bridge this ecclesiastical and political faultline running across the Balkans by the creation of a Kingdom of Yugoslavia welding together a number of states: Catholic Croatia and Slovenia, Orthodox Serbia and Macedonia, and Muslim Bosnia and Kosovo. During the Nazi occupation in the second world war, armed 'partisans' from various groups bitterly fought the invaders—but also each other, culminating in the emergence under strong man Marshal Broz Tito, of the unified Socialist Republic of Yugoslavia which became a member of the Eastern Bloc of Communist nations (the 'Warsaw Pact') during the Cold War, albeit in later years a rather maverick one. Through a Migration Agreement it became a major source country for migrants to Australia but also exported some bitter and ongoing tensions between Serbs and Croats forever reliving their wartime hatreds.

In 1984 this stand-off was still the situation, with my trans-Iron Curtain itinerary involving moving from Greece into Yugoslavia and then right across the Eastern Bloc nations to western Europe—Germany, France and Britain—reflecting my dual interests in intercultural theological education and linguistic tourism. My visit to Russia from Minden in 1963 had not touched, apart from Poland, the eastern European satellite states of the then USSR ('Union of Soviet Socialist Republics'). As the leader of the Communist bloc, the USSR was an enormous country comprising today's Russia plus the Ukraine and Byelorussia (now Belarus) and the three adjacent Baltic Republics of Lithuania, Latvia and Estonia as well as the Caucasus between the Caspian Sea and the Black Sea (Azerbaijan and Georgia bordering on Turkey) and all the central Asian '-stans' (as far as the Chinese border) plus the vast reaches of Siberia (sharing a border with North Korea)—an enormous proportion of the world's land mass.

Breaching the Iron Curtain

From Thessalonica in northern Greece a long Saturday in the bus brought me through the tense formalities of the Yugoslav border crossing (forbidden to citizens of the two countries, in either direction) and onto the sunlit agricultural plains of Macedonia, strewn with white-painted villages with peasant women in black working in the fields and high-sided, horse-drawn wooden carts with swaying loads and children perched atop. Under a regime hostile to religion (for understandable reasons, given the wretched history of the Balkans) my goal was a Methodist village! From my membership of the Uniting Church Migration Committee in Victoria I had come to know the leader of a Macedonian-speaking church in Melbourne made up of emigrants from the Kolešino area.

Wooed to sleep at my host's house by a babbling brook tumbling down from the nearby mountains, I was privileged next morning to join in Sunday worship with the community in their modest little church. On the way they had mentioned to me their suspicion about my visit being reported to the local Communist Party by some (unknown) Government informer planted in their church, but they wouldn't hear my objection about exposing them to possible reprisals and insisted that I 'preach' freely and publicly. I contented myself with bringing a greeting from their cousins in Melbourne and from the Victorian Council of Churches—in German because they had no competent English interpreter! Using German I also led a dialogue session with a youth group. After a festive lunch with the hospitable family I enquired about a walk up the mountain, but was deterred by the memorable comment that it would be a one-way trip since the Iron Curtain ran along the top of the range, marked by a death-dealing minefield. When I left I was burdened with a great sack of red peppers grown by the family, for delivery next day to their son in Skopje, minister of the Methodist Church in the Macedonian capital, who had studied in Germany and married a German wife. Subsequently I found them truly hospitable, speaking frankly about living as Christians in a socialist society, so different from West Germany but with a few interesting *pros* offsetting the many undoubted *cons*.

After a day admiring the modern city of Skopje I entrained overnight for the federal capital of Yugoslavia, Belgrade (today capital only of Serbia), situated at the confluence of the Sava and the Danube rivers, a major European metropolis but at that time, in common with the other Eastern bloc capitals, shabby and subdued. During this Cold War period Western tourists were not encouraged and visa controls were strict: for instance, from Australia it was not possible to obtain a visa for entry to Romania, the next Communist satellite country on my itinerary, but only through the Australian Embassy in Belgrade, where I wasted much of the day. Before catching the night train to Bucharest on a warm summer's evening I wandered along the wooded banks of the Danube. My travel plans envisaged travelling by sleeper on night trains between countries and maximising the dwindling daytime hours. Besides, this was cheaper since my hotels were on wheels. In any case, accommodation could only be booked through Communist governments' central tourist agencies, thus minimising contacts by the populace with Westerners—paranoid measures typical of the Cold War period.

Ecclesiastical hospitality in a dark land

During that night's trip to Bucharest summer ended. Until then my entire European journey from Rome to Athens, Jerusalem to Mt Athos, and Skopje to Belgrade, had been undertaken in balmy if not uncomfortably hot autumnal weather. Sweating by the Lake of Galilee, perspiring on the Acropolis, flushed when rolling my suitcase over the Yugoslav border at Bitola—it seemed October's Indian summer would never end. But that morning, peering through the sleeping-car window in the early dawn as the express rolled through the Romanian countryside, I was thrilled to glimpse a lush landscape of pastures and orchards with the snow-capped Carpathians on the horizon. Alighting at the Bucharest terminal in the capital city of Rumania I found it hard to credit how cold the morning air could be. It was never warm again until I reached Honolulu in the tropics on the opposite side of the world.

My itinerary provided for a six-day sojourn in the Communist satellite state as an official guest of the Romanian Orthodox Patriarchate, through the good offices of Fr Dimitru Gaina, priest of the Church's Melbourne parish which had recently purchased an old bluestone church in Carlton. Its inner garb was being progressively transformed from bare, austere Gothic to rich Byzantine by a famous artist painting traditional images on the ceiling. For over a year he had hung upside down on a mobile scaffold outlining, and then richly colouring, saints and apostles and the whole panoply of heaven where *Christos Pantocrator* reigns in glory (Lord of all creation).

I fancy I had been cultivated by the Romanian priest since our first meeting several years earlier during my national survey of ethnic organisations for the Department of Immigration, at the time when the Romanian Orthodox Church was establishing its Melbourne parish. During the Cold War it was a known tactic for subversives (including priests in Orthodox Churches) to engage with strategically placed people who might subsequently prove to be of value. Or was I paranoid?

The first approach by the priest, when I was still a public servant in Immigration, was to offer me confidentially a free trip to Romania, with an airline ticket, accommodation, and the promise of a guided tour of ancient churches and monasteries. The occasion was the celebration of some major ecclesiastical event in Bucharest, to be attended by a party from the Melbourne parish. There was a spare seat available on the charter plane. I was seriously tempted, since I had sufficient recreation leave available to respond to the invitation. But could one just disappear on leave overseas behind the Iron Curtain, as a public servant in a strategic role? When I checked with the Department's personnel section I was told that recently a somewhat similar gesture had been offered to some senior officers, who had in fact travelled gratis to Chile, all expenses paid, on the inaugural flight of LAN Chile Airways. So when my formal application was rejected I felt hardly done by, the reason given (when I pressed the point) was the inappropriateness of a private visit behind the Iron Curtain by a government official. It occurs to me now that this consideration may have been valid: as an alleged Leftie perhaps they had genuine doubts about me! At the time I thought it was simply sour grapes, but perhaps I should have felt gratified to be seen in my true (pale pink) colours!

Certainly suspicions had been widely raised within the Melbourne Romanian community, and which had come to my ears, that their charming young priest was hardly to be trusted, so well disposed was he towards the loathed Communist regime. Leaders in State Churches in Soviet satellites walked a very fine line between fidelity to the universal Gospel and the loyalty demanded by an officially atheistic state. Some clergy, witting or otherwise, had become compromised. But it was difficult for Western Christians to appreciate the tensions, conflicts and alleged betrayals inherent in living with integrity in two mutually antagonistic worlds—although in a spiritual sense that is the challenge to Christians everywhere, even if the choices are not so stark. But then again, perhaps the whole episode reflected no more than an excess of my romantic imagination, in an age of paranoia.

In 1984, a decade after that rankling situation, and now as a free citizen in an overtly Christian role, I thought it not inappropriate to make my own approach to Fr Dimitru (=James). He responded warmly and repeated the earlier offer minus the air travel, since I would already be in Europe. On arrival in Bucharest I would be met at the railway terminal and escorted to the Orthodox Church Patriarchate for a briefing about an arranged program.

Clambering down from the overnight express from Belgrade before the workaday world surfaced, I duly encountered a young and handsome black-garbed priest who introduced himself as Fr Virgil, delegate of the Patriarchate. His English was excellent since he had a doctorate from Princeton (on a study of the Methodist Church!), obviously a bright boy with a future. On the drive to the headquarters he pointed out a small, ancient stone church on a city square which was about to be bodily rolled a few metres aside (without being demolished) to fit in with a broad replanning of the city centre. In fact the whole area seemed to be a huge worksite, adjacent to a grandiose row of newly completed multi-storey accommodation blocks. Everywhere the scale seemed to be over-dimensional, non-human—a visual hallmark of the excesses of Nicolae Çeauşescu's dictatorial regime as czar of the Romanian Communist Party. Fifteen years later he and his wife Elena were to be shot by firing squad after a hearing before a kangaroo court, as his government was overthrown in the mass uprising following the breaching of the Berlin Wall and the sudden end of the Cold War. What came out later was just how ruthless his secret police, the *Securitate*, had been in maintaining his bloody rule in the most Stalinist of the satellite states, backed by a personality cult: 'the genius of the Carpathians'.

Drab austerity

But in my 1984 visit there was no hint of instability. But neither was there much sparkle. In the heart of the city the major thoroughfares were almost devoid of traffic save for a few trucks and taxis, with overcrowded trolley-buses creeping along silently under their overhead power cables (as they did in the Rockdale-Kogarah district in my Sydney boyhood). Occasionally a dark-windowed limousine would glide past conveying some mysterious mandarin to his post. Bicycles were a-plenty, particularly ridden by women but style and fashion seemed to have by-passed Bucharest. In the absence of the capitalistic gloss that we know in the West, it came across as a down-at-heel society, glum and plodding.

Not far from the Church headquarters I had been assigned a large, heavily-draped room in a state-run hotel, seemingly over-staffed in the manner of Communist societies where everyone had a job even if there was little work to be done. By dint of laboriously cobbling together phrases reminiscent of Italian I managed to ask an elderly chambermaid if my washing (now in crisis mode) might be done. She seemed to agree readily. Romanian—as its name would imply—is the easternmost expression of the Romance (Latin-based) group of languages: Portuguese, Spanish, French, Italian—though heavily larded with Slavic words too. Next morning when she presented me with a neat bundle of folded, starched, ironed clothes, not knowing anything of the exchange rate, I shelled out a sizeable wad of *lei*. She seemed genuinely shocked, repeating: "*E molt! Molt!*" which I assumed meant: "Is a lot. A lot!" [cf. Italian *molto*] as she pocketed her windfall. Later I learnt how the populace lived on the smell of an oily rag.

Guarded welcome

At the Patriarchate my briefing was laboured: formalistic welcome, recommendation to do as my shadow-priest indicated, acceptance of my suggestion to speak later with a group of senior clergy, then a lecture by a Church scholar to prove that modern Romania was indeed the lineal descendant of the province of Dacia, part of the Roman Empire. Proof of this was that the modern Romanian language closely reflected its Latin antecedent brought by the military veterans resettled in the province in the 2nd century AD—'soldier settlement', a regular practice of Rome to plant colonies of its citizens in far-flung locations around the Empire to ensure its security and continuity, e.g. Philippi in Macedonia[5]. I was presented with a number of pamphlets and several sizeable books (all in English) to clinch the argument. However the inconvenient truth was that the Romanians looked the same to me as the other Slavs of eastern Europe and in fact their language is a *mélange* of Slavic and Latin-origin words. What was suspicious was the lengths that the country's élite seemed prepared to go to, in obsessively promoting the claim. (*'Argument weak here—speak louder.'?*)

I wondered what was at stake: was there something innately superior about the

---

5   Mentioned as a Roman colony in Acts 16:12: describing St Paul's preaching ministry there.

Romanians? Or inferior about the Slavs? Yet the fact that the Romanian Church was Orthodox linked it decisively with other Eastern Orthodox Churches of the Slavs: Serbs, Bulgarians, Macedonians, Ukrainians, Russians. What was there about that company? Moreover the modern history of Romania revealed a penchant towards authoritarianism: between the world wars a repressive dictatorship, and during the second world war a formal alliance by King Carol II with Hitler and involvement in the Holocaust—but then changing sides in 1944 to embrace Communism brought by the Russian invaders. And since the war the brutally repressive regime imposed in the name of the People. A very different heritage from western Europe. However these misgivings, revealing my ignorance of the historical issues of Romania in 1984—that pre-cyber age without instant access to Wikipedia—had to be set aside as my program focused on the glories of the Romanian Orthodox Church.

Guided but guarded tour

And glories they indeed were. Fr Virgil was a connoisseur of church history and architecture, conducting me around a number of city churches in Bucharest, each with some remarkable feature, while explaining challenges facing Romanian believers. He was neither critical of, nor defensive about the regime. A church diplomat, I thought. But once as we crossed the square before the main railway station in a chauffeur-driven car, he let fly verbally with a stream of abuse against a group of ragged beggars blocking our way. I was shocked: what had happened to his Christian grace? They were gypsies (*Zigeuner*), parasites, scum with no place in a modern state! In Russia I had seen similar reactions against gypsies (*Rum*—from Rumania?). Though they had long association with central and eastern European lands (cf. Franz Liszt's Hungarian *Zigeunermusik* and Johann Strauss's *Gypsy Baron*), in the common people's eyes they were a rabble to be shunned and preferably cast out. Sad as I felt about it, I couldn't help recalling Ceduna.

Next morning we had to leave early for a cross-country drive, initially through the Ploieşti region, a dreary landscape of clunking pumps see-sawing up and down as they spewed crude oil from the wells—as they had when fuelling Hitler's war machine—to the historic monastery and cathedral church at Curtea de Argeş where we were warmly received by the aged Mother Superior and taken on a guided tour. Over a private lunch (with Fr Virgil translating) I asked how long she had lived in her convent. She replied, "Since I was 12." Knowing that hers was a contemplative Order, I was interested in what that lifelong experience had meant. Her answer floored me, "Well, we are still at peace in Europe." On how many such prayers was peace in Europe dependent, as much as on missiles and rockets—the 'balance of terror'? *It is the unseen things that are eternal,* writes St Paul.

Later in the day we moved on to the town of Alba Iulia, capital of the Roman province of Dacia, and the original capital of Transylvania with its 12th century cathedral where kings were crowned before the creation of Rumania in the 19th century and again in the modern monarchy period closing with the abdication of King Michael under the Communists in 1947.

Bucharest interlude

Back in Bucharest Fr Virgil, now on first-name terms, shepherded me to a people's tailor who measured me up for a new three-piece suit (with waistcoat), but there was only plain grey material to be had at the top price range (still dirt cheap), so when I left the country a few days later it was with a dapper if boring new outfit. Exploiting the natives, or just canny shopping? It didn't matter much because back in Australia I rarely wore it, since suits were already out of fashion for people in roles like mine, now garb only for power figures like bankers and politicians—or funerals!. Decades later it would wind up in a Vinny's op shop, its exotic maker's label still intact. I wonder if anyone ever bought it.

My program with the Patriarchate included a reception at the Church's publishing house when books on the country and the Church were presented, and also participating in the national observance of St Dimitru's Day (St James) when, even under atheistic Communism, tens of thousands of the faithful flocked into Bucharest from the countryside to pay homage at the saint's reliquary on display in the Cathedral Square. On the Sunday I had attended liturgies in city churches (including wedding and baptismal services!) and had also worshipped in the principal Reformed Church (of the Hungarian ethnic minority) where I met the minister and brought a greeting from the Victorian Council of Churches.

In 1989 it would be a Hungarian Reformed minister in the city of Timisoara, Laszlo Tokeș, who triggered the people's rebellion against the Ceausescu regime nationwide by initiating a protest in defence of local Christian rights. The spark would ignite a nation-wide inferno that saw the regime swept away in a few days, with the reviled Ceausescus dead. In Bucharest a Father Mehedintu Sandi would become one of the impromptu orators inciting the crowd from a hospital balcony.

The highlight of my Romanian program proved to be the opportunity to address the Faculty of the Theology School of Bucharest University, gathered at the Patriarchate, explaining the religious scene in Australia's pluralist society where Romanians, though few, were devoted to their Church. I got a good hearing but in the ensuing dialogue it was clear that the diversity of our Australian Churches seemed incomprehensible to them, as much as the notion of a multicultural society.

After the formalities and exchange of gifts, we adjourned with one of the professors to the presbytery of a city priest and hospital chaplain, none other than Fr Mehedintu Sandi, for informal discussions over dinner. That last-night socialising took on a quite unimaginable candour: our host turned out to be a delightful character—irreverent, humorous, even then openly disaffected with the regime, and who (in the absence of any English) insisted on communicating directly with me in atrocious French. What a relief to laugh again after the grim earnestness of my Romanian week. Suddenly I was appalled at the terrible gap between our two societies.

That evening I was farewelled on the night express to Budapest by Fr Virgil and his irreverent mate. In parting he mentioned that for him, the week had reopened questions about theological pluralism still unresolved from his study time in the USA. For me it had been a rare privilege to get inside the heads of Christians from a tradition so different to my own, and yet discover real affinity: an object lesson in mind-broadening and suspending judgment. Then—shamelessly at variance with claims about the classless society—I bunked down brazenly in a First Class sleeper.

Routine paranoia—but elegance triumphs

But the night was to become hideous, thanks to a paranoid Communist officialdom. After midnight our sleep was rudely shattered by grinding brakes, jolting wagons, barking of orders, doors wrenched open and slammed shut, demands for papers, passports, visas. Welcome to Hungary, the tourist paradise! And no concessions to non-speakers of Hungarian. A mobile office walked into my sleeping compartment, in the form of a fold-down desk hanging from a uniformed neck, complete with stamp pads and stamps, to which we had to submit our documents for verification: guilty until proven innocent! To me it all seemed outrageous—or a comic opera—but people didn't seem to turn a hair. Just routine.

By next morning it seemed to have morphed into a bad dream, on our arrival in Budapest at an impressive terminal in the grand European manner, curved roof soaring over a multiplicity of platforms, restaurants and offices, and everywhere scurrying workers. At breakfast I enjoyed my first taste of central European cuisine (and coffee) in the terminal's dining room, then discovered nearby an accommodation bureau for home stays. Soon I was allocated to a family in the suburbs, an electric train ride from the city centre, to be warmly welcomed in German—the old Austro-Hungarian Empire lived! They knew nothing about Australia (except kangaroos—I wondered if I should have hopped over the threshold) and had never met an Australian, but it was a pleasant encounter and I stayed for two or three days, exploring the city on foot with the help of my German-speaking guides—actually the twin cities of Buda and Peşt on opposite sides of the Danube.

As befitting one of the two capitals of the Austro-Hungarian Empire (the other one Vienna), and being spared in the world wars, Budapest retains a classic charm, with a cosmopolitan feel about it, laced with multi-car trams, and offering historic monuments and sculptures and grand promenades along the banks of a broad sweep of the Danube, crowned by the famous view across the river from the elevated terraces of St Stephen's Basilica to the imposing Parliament Building. Beyond the city area I was absorbed by the Aquincum Museum (name of the ancient Roman town) with its displays of archaeological relics and artefacts of Pannonia, the Roman province next to Dacia. Multi-layered Europe at its best.

Despite my brush with Communist rigidity on the train, I found Hungary the most relaxed of the five satellite states of eastern Europe that I traversed. Under the rule of Kadar Janos (Hungarian names, like Chinese, put the family name first), in power after the Russian tanks crushed the would-be 'revolution' of 1956, the country gradually came to be known for its liberalised economy, dubbed 'goulash communism' or the 'happiest barrack' during the Cold War. I recall little sign of heavy-handed authoritarianism.

Not so in the early post-war years when the leader of the Catholic Church, Cardinal Josef Mindszenty, was to become a Christian hero of the Cold War for opposing communist oppression and persecution, leading to his arrest, torture and a show trial condemned by the UN. Imprisoned for eight years until liberated in the abortive Hungarian uprising of 1956, he was granted political asylum by the US embassy in Budapest, where he lived for the next fifteen years, finally being allowed to leave the country in 1971.

Communist Czechpoint

My next overnight destination: Czechoslovakia (a union of the Czech and Slovak peoples to be dissolved amicably in 1993 following the fall of Communism). From the moment of my arrival at the railway terminal in Prague, swarming with police and soldiers, I sensed its regime as crazy. After queuing to buy my onwards ticket for travel to Germany, my crime was to use German and I was abused by an official for my trouble (I suppose taken for a hated German capitalist). The saving grace was to have soon found another home-stay accommodation bureau and met a charming couple with experience of travel to the West, who regaled me with frank accounts of the 'idiocy' of life under the Communist regime of Gustav Husák, a hardline Stalinist installed after the abortive 'Prague Spring' of 1977 when demonstrators poked flowers down the barrels of the Russian tanks, only to be ruthlessly attacked. I was impressed by the frankness of my hosts as well as by their hospitality.

But in 1984 it was still a tale of hounding—and sometimes executing—Party officials deemed to be unreliable, of police informers denouncing their neighbours, and with clergy licensed and under constant surveillance. The Catholic Church was particularly repressed as an alien authority. Years earlier, we had heard Czech Lutheran theologian Josef Hromadka in Canberra, a guest speaker from the World Council of Churches, controversially promoting a Christian critique of both capitalism and communism (of course in retrospect he was right—I mean *korrect*).

In the 2000s the Czech President, intellectual Vaclav Havel (imprisoned under the regime) would point out that "oppressed people become so used to living a lie that it infiltrates every aspect of their lives, until they can't deal honestly with each other or with themselves...". He would conclude, "Only if we are willing to speak the truth, to ourselves, to each other and in public, can we hope to extract ourselves from the mire of oppression".

But back in 1984 the Czech situation amounted to a tragic drama set against the charming backdrop of unspoilt mediaeval and classical Prague (now a Unesco World Heritage city), with its stone-arched and statue-lined Apostles' Bridge spanning the Vltava, and with St Vitus' Cathedral and Prague Castle overlooking the city. Here I was mugged by a life-changing experience. Musing on the assassination nearby in 1942 of Reinhard Heydrich, Nazi 'Protector' of

Czechoslovakia and an architect of the Holocaust (the patriots' action avenged by the heinous war crime of exterminating the entire Czech village of Lidice of some 370 souls), I fell to visualising what it might have felt like to be incarcerated for years in that semi-underground cell beside the moat, allowing my imagination free rein. It proved to be all too realistic: as I clutched the bars of the tiny high-set window with the cell door shut behind me, the obsession swept over me that I was never to be released from the living tomb of the five-metre square cage. From that moment of self-induced panic dates my recurrent if passing episodes of claustrophobia.

Alienated *Kamaraden*

The best expedient was a smart get-away westwards by overnight express to the so-called German Democratic Republic, also Communist. While twice during our years in Europe I had prowled around its capital, East Berlin, I had only flown in from the West. Now I was to have the opportunity to traverse the country and view life on the ground in the major provincial centres of Dresden and Leipzig, both art cities of historic Saxony. But how doleful they appeared to be: mere emaciated parodies of themselves, with tawdry rebuilding of once classical streetscapes, occasionally pockmarked by carefully stacked piles of stone on a vacant lot that used to be a historic city church, now reduced to row after numbered and catalogued row of Lego blocks awaiting the day of redemption withheld by the atheistic state with its other spending priorities.

In Dresden and Leipzig I moved about freely enough, chatting in streets and churches. Mostly Australia seemed unknown, sometimes confused with Austria! It was in Leipzig in 1989 that the non-violent 'Monday prayer protests' would be convened on Karl Marx Square before the Nikolaikirche by a courageous Lutheran pastor with the tantalising name of Christian Führer, swelling to 320,000 prayerful demonstrators chanting "*Wir sind das Volk!*" ('We are the People"). Before long the rolling wave of hope and prayer would reach as far as East Berlin where, as in the biblical battle of Jericho, suddenly 'the Wall came tumbling down'.

Hellish transit to freedom

But in 1984 travel to West Germany (for foreigners only) meant piercing the Iron Curtain. In a night train stopped in no man's land I was asked by a border guard whether I was hiding anyone under my seat. Naturally wanting to oblige I got down on hands and knees to help him look. "No. No one there". Then at the border all hell broke loose. It was a known escape route for disaffected citizens of all the East Bloc lands, ranging from political subversives to family groups seeking better economic prospects, or reunion with earlier successful escapees. If the crossing into Hungary had been a comic opera, this was a full-scale Wagnerian epic, with night turned to day by the blaze of high-powered floodlights. Inside the train, the few international travellers crossing into the West sat for an unconscionable time while German travellers were interrogated by security police, papers checked and rechecked, police dogs led through the carriages, and the under-floor areas checked out from below by armed soldiers with searchlights, scouring all the axles and hiding-places because of the ingenuity of past escapees, some of whom had died in their desperate ploys. Finally the train lurched into life again (presumably to dislodge anyone not yet detected underneath) and staggered through the invisible curtain.

The instant sense of relaxation was tangible. In the East the pervasive tensions had frequently come to expression through gratuitous remarks and oblique references in conversations. Moreover there was a lack of anything resembling basic human dignity in shops or exchanges in public: the customer or the enquirer was always wrong, and sometimes ignored. Manners seemed to have become a casualty. What was it about Communism, as experienced in ten different countries with quite a range of ethnicities, that made its public face so harsh, so rude, so paranoid? Why never 'normal', never civil—let alone humane—totally lacking in respect, and the usual courtesy? OK, they'd got rid of business with its self-serving greed and manipulative rapaciousness, and freed the people from the class-warfare it implied. But why couldn't Communism treat people like brothers or even only fellow-citizens with equal rights? The leaders never even took a leaf from the book of their fellow-Communists in China.

So as crazy as it may sound at this remove, in those Cold War years the contest could be a matter of life or death—for many, quite literally. The stakes were high: two incompatible systems of governance vying for the dominance that only one could achieve by bringing about the demise of the other. No expense was spared, even if it meant misery and deprivation for entire populations. Worse, it ensured the ongoing poverty and despair of the Third World by the squandering of resources that might have transformed the existence of their peoples. In short, the costs of the global assault on human wellbeing were incalculable. What greater evidence is required that ours is a fallen world?

6
Picking Theological Brains Worldwide

My escape from the Eastern Bloc made good, I turned to the more prosaic task of calling on the Christian bodies in several European lands kind enough to discuss how they were grappling with the challenges of a multicultural population, mostly brought about by the advent of tens of thousands of 'guestworkers' providing the cheap labour on which the *Wirtschaftswunder* (economic miracle) in Germany and other western European countries had been grounded. By the early 1980s many of them had taken root and established families but the children were often caught between two worlds, yet belonging to neither, the inevitable butt of racism.

Oberammergau Passion Play

This dimension struck me from the moment I walked the streets of the first western city I encountered, *Nürnberg* (Nuremberg) in Bavaria, arriving on my now activated Eurail Pass late on a Saturday evening. After the half-empty and gloomy streets of East Germany with a uniformly Germanic-looking populace, I was arrested by the guestworker presence, from Turkey, Yugoslavia, Greece, Italy, Spain, Portugal interspersed with local revellers noisily overflowing from taverns and night locales. The scene uncannily recalled Pieter Brueghel's painting *The Fight between Carnival and Lent* with the two groups of peasants spilling over the town square between tavern and church, symbolising the social tensions of the Reformation period. In fact this duality was unwittingly played out in my choosing a room for the night in a *Pension* right opposite the cathedral.

Roused by its deafening bells on Sunday morning, I threaded my way across the square through the previous night's detritus to attend early Mass. But to my incredulity (since Bavaria is the heartland of south German Catholicism), it turned out to be a Lutheran cathedral, ancient Gothic though it was, and the service was the Lord's Supper attended by twenty people standing in a group around the communion table, democratically passing the cup one to another. The cup held unfermented grape juice because, as the discreet notice on a stand by the door put it, "*Some of our number were once alcoholics and out of respect for them we do not use wine*".

My first programmed visit was to the ancient Catholic bishopric of Regensburg not far from the Iron Curtain, where Fr Gustav Krämer, familiar to me from Canberra as the German Catholic Chaplain, now had pastoral oversight of a charismatic renewal network. Next day he drove me to the nearby Bavarian city of Landshut for a regional seminar with clergy and religious where I was invited to take part in the dialogue. After the rigours of the atheistic satellite states, to be singing (in German) tunes well loved from O'Connor days proved a balm to my soul—what joy to be worshipping the universal Lord on the other side of the globe with 'family', and in their own language!

Next morning saw me again invoking my Eurail Pass, on southwards to *München* (Munich) for a brief side-trip to the famous Bavarian alpine village of Oberammergau where the 350th anniversary of the Passion Play on the Life of Christ was being celebrated by an out-of-sequence season (normally only performed every ten years). Bearded escapees from the New Testament were to be seen everywhere on the streets pursuing their regular occupations: it was the one 'lay day' of the week without a performance! At least the landscape was charming.

To the Queen of the Adriatic

I took the trans-Alpine 'Venice Express' to traverse the narrow western strip of Austria to Innsbruck, ringed with majestic mountains, and then tackle the Brenner Pass to Bolzano in Italy. The next couple of days were pure tourism. The unfolding spectacle had me glued to the window, marvelling as much at the railway engineering as the mountain grandeur, with the highest point at 1375m. Although since the first world war politically deemed to be Italy, the picturesque Alto Adige province was still largely Germanic in language and sentiment as 'South Tyrol', with capital Bozen (in Italian Bolzano). I stayed in the Italo-Austrian-named Pensione Unterhofer. As late as the 1980s it was not unknown for electricity pylons to be bombed by Austrian patriots.

Come the morning, I joined a cheerily chattering trainload of working girls commuting up a charming valley to the ski resort of Merano, high in the alpine foothills, and ascended the main street beside a mountain torrent rushing down from a melting glacier in the Dolomites above. Blessed freedom conferred by the Eurail Pass … follow up wherever the whim takes you.

In the afternoon to Trento, where in the 16th century the 'Council of Trent' sought to counter the inroads of the Reformation, and then wandering the streets of Verona in search of Shakespeare's 'two gentlemen', and finally crossing over the lagoon to reach Santa Lucia, main station of Venice on the island close to the Grand Canal. Time only permitted my lingering awhile among the pigeons on the elegantly colonnaded *Piazza San Marco*, lost in the romance of it all, then from the shoreline dreamily eying the gondoliers plying their muscly-musical trade out on the lagoon, before wandering unchallenged through the (unattended!) Doge's Palace—in those innocent days before terrorists were invented, I could have made off with priceless works of art gracing every interior. And then across the Piazza, perhaps the most renowned in the world, to the Byzantine opulence of the Basilica di San Marco, dating from the 11th century, originally the Doge's private chapel, with its red brick campanile towering nearby and the ill-famed Bridge of Sighs, and further afield the Rialto Bridge gleaming in its white marble glory.

On that golden evening, myself wracked with sighs because so absurdly captive to my itinerary—I had quite omitted to build in rest days—all too early I dragged myself off to Santa Lucia to take the night express to Milan, 'capital' of northern Italy—though compensated by the excitement of sitting within the very bullet nose of the electric loco, practically at track level anxiously watching the red signals unfailingly turn green an instant before we reached them—at 150km/h!

Under the Alps to Geneva

Next morning the final stage of my brief Italian odyssey might well rate amongst the most scenic rail journeys of the world, threading its way amongst the picturesque alpine foothills, rearing high above Lake Lugano, showcasing the Alps in all their glory before finally plunging beneath them, to emerge from the Simplon Tunnel in French-speaking Switzerland, not far from Geneva, my next port of call. Home to the World Council of Churches, one of the plethora of international agencies based there like the Red Cross and other humanitarian and UN bodies.

Straddling the Swiss/French border at the outflow of Lake Geneva into the river Rhône, the city evokes Jean Calvin, father of the world's Reformed and Presbyterian Churches—his chair is still in the 12th century (Reformed) Cathedral. A tireless preacher and teacher of the new Protestant theology, for a time he was to become virtual ruler of the staunchly independent city-state noted for its earnestness and discipline. Like its Canberra copycat, the iconic jet in the Lake of Geneva hurls water 140 metres into the air, but dwarfed by the splendid backdrop of the Alps, just a little higher than the Brindabellas

I was surprised to discover that the World Council of Churches just outside the city turned out to be merely a tenant of the Lutheran World Federation, than which it had a smaller budget! But I was on home turf, since the WCC was the ultimate parent body of the Victorian Council of Churches and a comprehensive program had been arranged for me. I was to stay in the home of the secretary of the Migration Section and consult with directors of programs on migration, refugees, racism, theological education, and non-Christian faiths—drawn from four different lands.

Now for the first time it became clear to me that actually our social situation in Australia was only slightly parallel to other lands, where one single crucial issue tended to dominate the scene, e.g. in the UK community relations at the street level, in continental Europe guestworker tensions, and in America Blacks and Hispanics. By contrast, our focus on relating to the ethnic communities as equal partners in the building of a new and multicultural society seemed unique, even compared to Canada where a similar approach to ours was overshadowed by concerns about the ongoing tensions between the nation's two charter communities—English speakers and French speakers.

World Council of Churches

A worldwide fellowship of 349 churches seeking unity, a common witness and Christian service

The World Council of Churches is a fellowship of churches which confess the Lord Jesus Christ as God and Saviour according to the scriptures, and therefore seek to fulfil their common calling to the glory of the one God, Father, Son and Holy Spirit together.

It is a community of churches on the way to visible unity in one faith and one worldwide fellowship, expressed in worship and in common life in Christ. It seeks to advance towards this unity, as Jesus prayed for his followers, "so that the world may believe." (John 17:21)

The WCC brings together 349 churches, denominations and church fellowships in more than 110 countries and territories throughout the world, representing over 560 million Christians and including most of the world's Orthodox churches, scores of Anglican, Baptist, Lutheran, Methodist and Reformed churches, as well as many United and Independent churches. While the bulk of the WCC's founding churches were European and North American, today most member churches are in Africa, Asia, the Caribbean, Latin America, the Middle East and the Pacific.

For its member churches, the WCC is a unique space: one in which they can reflect, speak, act, worship and work together, challenge and support each other, share and debate with each other.

As members of this fellowship, WCC member churches are:

called to the goal of visible unity in one faith and one worldwide fellowship;
to promote their common witness in work for mission and evangelism;
to engage in Christian service by serving human need, breaking down barriers between people, seeking justice and peace, and upholding the integrity of creation; and
to foster renewal in unity, worship, mission and service.

Hence the comprehensive (even if superficial) approach of the ITEMS Project was perceived as novel, arousing considerable interest. There were several requests for the supply of documentation, and in return I was loaded with voluminous materials to bring home, then steered off to the WCC bookshop to buy the publications requested by the VCC and the Ecumenical Migration Centre with the funds they had provided.

A Parisian *gamin* strikes!

A day or so later, westward ho! To Paris by the new TGV (*Train à Grande Vitesse*), at that time (and still today) the world's fastest, hurtling in its distinctive orange and grey livery through the lush Burgundian countryside at 300km/h on its dedicated track virtually devoid of curves. After a day's ambling about my beloved Paris (in my take, capital of the world), practising my French with anyone who would listen, I made for the *Gare d'Austerlitz*—terminal for the south-west—and Spain! Why not? I'd paid good money for my Eurail Pass and I'd never been to Spain. Madrid, here I come!

Not so fast, buddy. Moments before the overnight Spanish express pulled out, and while my sleeping compartment companions were still disposing their luggage, a Parisian *gamin* (urchin) struck, like lightning. He raced into the compartment, saw my overnight bag open and deftly relieved me of my large travel wallet. Gone in a flash! He must have leapt out as the train moved off.

I still have a copy of the offical '*Denuncia*' form I submitted to the police in Madrid about the theft, citing what had been stolen: airline tickets to Melbourne, French rail reservations, travellers' cheques for $400, and travel insurance policy document. Particularly galling was the loss of my travel log, recording all costs to date, plus the visiting cards of people interviewed. Really, a body blow. But implausibly, returning to Paris about a week later, my enquiries with the station officials led to my travel wallet being handed back intact. Thank God: it had been retrieved from a refuse bin on the platform: nothing inside to make sense to a *gamin*!

Train in Spain mainly on the plain

But back in the awakening sleeping car of the train to Spain, morning light had revealed a landscape that made me blink. It could have been the central west of NSW, say around Cowra, complete with gumtrees, but with some early snow on a distant range. The central uplands of Spain. And before long, Madrid and the majesty of its city centre, its grand architecture, squares and gardens. My impression was of a relaxed, friendly people ten years after the replacement of the fascist Franco regime by a constitutional monarchy.

Aside from the precious time wasted at the Police HQ, the memory of that day in Madrid rivals my one day in Leningrad 21 years earlier for the sheer pleasure of promenading in beautiful autumnal weather through a city of grace and dignity. Bowing to the tyranny of the itinerary demanded another overnight rail journey, this time by *Ferrocarriles Españoles* (Spanish Railways) to the Mediterranean coast, on the way traversing the Catalan metropolis of Barcelona—but from below so that you got to see nothing but stations and tunnels!—and then northwards skirting the Mediterranean coast to the French border. From there by the *SNCF (Société Nationale des Chemins de Fer Français—French National Railways)*—all these thriving rail networks still owned by the people before the robber barons of neo-liberalism struck!

'Sur le pont d'Avignon'

Journey's end at Avignon, renowned for its 12th century bridge on the Rhône whose arches now end in mid-stream, evoking the folk song that I'd taught Queanbeyan students to sing, and also for the palace of the seven French Popes who in the 14th century ruled the entire Catholic Church from here for 70 years during its 'Babylonian captivity'.

But I was in Avignon to meet Jean-Laurent, the French *vigneron* we had encountered with his partner and their toddler Gypsy hitch-hiking in New Zealand some years before. He drove me to the vineyard that he'd inherited by then on the slopes above Orange, where I spent a relaxing day or two savouring the van Gogh landscapes of Provence, and getting a feel for the leisurely pace of life of *Le Midi*. One day beneath the overarching vines in the courtyard of a rustic *auberge*, we enjoyed a memorable gourmet lunch of roast *lapin* (rabbit). Sadly, by then his partner and their daughter had gone their own way.

Consultations in French

From Orange back to Paris by TGV to stay again, as we three had done in 1963, with my Hughan second cousin David Park at Garches, on the outskirts of Paris towards Versailles, while pursuing the several French missional contacts arranged from Australia.

I was well received by the *Fédération Protestante de France* linking some 20 Churches (denominations) and about a million people, including immigrants. Indeed one of their oldest-established social agencies was CIMADE, conducting anti-racism programs in defence of the rights of foreign immigrants. I was able to attend a meeting convened to consider a joint effort by the Churches for countering anti-migrant racism, where I was warmly received and invited to speak about the Australian experience and our version of multiculturalism. Actually it was the first time I had ever used the language with which I'd had a lifelong flirtation in a real-life formal setting requiring genuine communication about a significant topic.

Later I learnt that CIMADE had followed up by discussing the implementation of a theological education initiative in the Protestant Faculty on the issues we had discussed. I brought home a bundle of pamphlets and publications on the struggle to create a harmonious multicultural society in France, even today a goal far from realisation, given the growing North African community of alienated and largely radicalised Muslims living around the perimeter of Paris (and also by 2014 bidding fair to form the majority of the population of France's second city, Marseilles). On my most recent trip, the Paris Métro by night seems to be almost solely their preserve.

Flashback to 1963. Before being farewelled by the Park family we three had been invited to record our stay in their visitors' book. I had written a detailed note about my Hughan connection with Scotland. This was what led their son Malcolm 28 years later, and beyond the death of his parents, to write to me enclosing a photocopy of that note, and enquiring about our link through William Wright Hughan. He was seeking details of the Australian Hughans and their descendants, like me and Nicholas Hughan and his son Hughan Patrick. We now have a lively electronic correspondence.

Home to Minden

After 22 years' absence I was about to be mugged by the sheer delight of a return to Minden. What joy, as the express from Hanover slid into the station, to spot the entire Greßler clan foregathered to receive me. Twenty years. We fell into each others' arms. Children had grown up, babies had been raised, and older folks were still spry. My German was much less robust than when we had left but all was instantly forgiven. So much to catch up on, so much to re-work.

The next week remains a delightful blur of energy expended on refocusing on previously loved people and places: trips into the country for tavern lunches with extended family members, a Sunday service in the *Methodistenkirche* (now with an English woman minister!) and where several older folks claimed to remember the Houstons, and of course the inevitable *Wasserstrassenkreuz* and the *Schachtschleuse* connecting canal and river, with an excursion up the Weser. On 19th November my 52nd birthday became a grand occasion, crowned by the surprise arrival of dear Lutheran friend, Pastor Dieter Schwerdtfeger by train from Bielefeld, 80km away.

During those four or five days I revisited our house in Karlsbaderweg and called on our elderly war-widow neighbour (her husband never did come home from the Russian front), I returned to the Altsprachliches Gymnasium in the Glacis, and sat in on a lesson in (Protestant) religion. Three teachers were still there from my time, one of them now the Principal. We met for coffee and the presentation of a book on the school's recent 500th anniversary! Next morning an article appeared in the town daily (the *Mindener Tageblatt*) based on an interview arranged for me by the Greßlers. It got a couple of things right.

But duty called imperiously. I had a travel schedule and far to go. Presents bestowed and received, tastefully crafted German Christmas tree decorations purchased at Hagemeyer department store on the Scharn for use back home. Finally hugs and tears at the *Bahnhof* as the Hannover express deigned to hover for a split second, and then the wrenching brutality of departure—for another 20 years, or forever?

Consultations in German

Before leaving Germany I was able to visit and stay with Stephen Castles, an emerging English academic then working at the University of Applied Sciences in Frankfurt, the country's financial capital. He spoke impressive German, having recently studied in Frankfurt, and had arranged for me to have dinner with two noted Lutheran pastors involved in Christian anti-racism campaigning, one of whom was about to take up a post equivalent to Commissioner for Community Relations with the Bundesland (State) of Hessen. A German Grassby! We had a lively discussion, necessarily in the local language, on similarities between Germany and aspects of the Australian scene. Subsequently Professor Castles was to teach at Oxford and later move to Australia, holding posts at Wollongong University and currently at Sydney University. Today he is one of Australia's premier academic multiculturalists.

Back in England—Fenland hospitality

Though the Eurail Pass had served me well, from Frankfurt I reactivated my round-the-world air ticket to land at London Heathrow, the world's busiest international airport. Rolling my two increasingly loaded portmanteaux along its interminable corridors proved a considerable fitness test. Partly in search of R and R, since foolishly I had built in no rest days, I headed off at once to Ely via Cambridge, clutching my new Britrail Pass. What joy to be greeted by John and Eileen Smith in a suitably reserved (but no less genuine) British replay of the Minden railway station extravaganza and be driven to their Fenland farmhouse at Littleport, rakishly angled at the foot of a subsiding levee bank enclosing the New Bedford River ('Hundred Foot Drain' built about 1650 by the Dutch engineer Cornelius Vermuyden) which like all Fenland streams, flows *above* the level of the fields.

I was appalled at the talk of present-day 'globalised' farming methods, whereby soulless insurance companies and other corporations had swallowed up great tracts of once gorgeous English countryside, uprooting all the age-old hedgerows, long the habitat of small wild life, to form Canadian-type prairies for growing wheat crops. Bleak places, created by the neo-liberal mega-planners of the European Union indifferent to the dispossession of the poorly educated farm labourers once celebrated in song as 'the yeomen of England'. John Smith and his sons had gone into trucking the produce to the warehouses.

But as ever, they were the soul of hospitality, still serving roast beef and 'Yorkshire pudd' with two veg., followed up by bread-and-butter pudding. My childhood lives! Next day being Sunday we repaired to the Plymouth Brethren assembly, which in the light of my current Anglican focus seemed quaint indeed. A few brethren claimed to remember me but the charismatic renewal had drained off some of the more adventurous spirits. At dusk John took me off to the Welney 'bird hide' of a conservation trust, where in the failing light you ensconce yourself with night glasses while all around you, in incredible profusion, the waterfowl continue to do their avian thing impervious to your presence. You feel like one of them!

Back to School

My visit to the King's School was a return to another life. I had lunch in the monastic tithe barn, now restyled as the refectory, with five 'masters' from my day (we were never teachers—too 'State') and afterwards was shown around the new developments. Under the leadership of (another!) dynamic Australian the School had made it into the ranks of significant educational institutions in a rather impoverished area of Britain. It had swelled almost to 1000 scholars, had gone co-ed and created new boarding houses, some for girls, including the erstwhile theological college in its fine Victorian redbrick building. The School's visibility in the town (historically still termed 'city'—albeit England's smallest) was now pre-eminent, being said to be the largest single employer. And among its sports facilities, down on the edge of the fens, was a golf course! I celebrated my visit liturgically by attending two beautiful choral evensong services in the cathedral, sung by the choirboys from the junior school. At the cathedral shop I sentimentally bought a school tie and also an audiotape of the choir.

That week I had to ration myself between the two Eileens (Smith and Wade) whom Marjorie had met in 1960, all having their first baby, so after a couple of days moved into town to the Wades—Eileen was an official guide to the cathedral. They were kind enough to drive me to Oxford where their 24 year-old son (confrère of Sara-Jane's) was a doctoral student of minerology. He showed us around some of the Colleges and took us to lunch in a rustic low-beamed inn *(ouch!)* by the river Cherwell (of *Wind in the Willows* fame).

Consultations in England

Finally to work—to London hosted by an expat Richard Hosking, an old Sydney EU friend, and over three days meeting with the leadership of the Community Relations Committee of the Anglican Bishops' Conference of England and Wales, also with its Methodist Church counterpart, and with the Ecumenical Unit for Racial Awareness of the British Council of Churches, set up the year before to develop practical initiatives and strategies for helping churches tackle racial discrimination and build community relations at the local level.

Beyond the Churches I was able to visit an official of the Greater London Council at County Hall just across the Thames from Westminster, and also the Commission for Racial Equality, the anti-discrimination agency set up by the Labour Government under the 1976 Race Relations Act, and empowered and staffed along the lines of the Whitlam Government's proposals doomed to be thwarted by Malcolm Fraser. Both agencies were prolific publishers, evidenced by their commitment to community education as the prime long-term strategy for making society more humane—actively contested though this vision was, in both the political and the social spheres. My luggage was becoming heavier by the day.

And heavier still through my visit to the Runnymede Trust: the Magna Carta signed at Runnymede in 1215 by King John and the barons forms the basis of constitutional law in the English-speaking world. The Trust is an independently-funded think tank seeking since 1968 to overcome racial inequality in Britain and strengthen a common sense of *belonging* by encouraging public debate and policy engagement on the basis of rigorous research and analysis. It made me wonder whether it was precisely such a lack of research and action *at the civil society level in Australia* that had hampered our heroic efforts to outflank racism and racial discrimination, especially in the case of the 'First Nations'. While in the 2000s there have been some encouraging developments in the civil society ('Australians for Native Title', and 'Reconciliation Australia') they do not pack the punch of a well-funded think tank. Sadly, in Australia this type of thrust seems to come mainly from economic rationalist and libertarian quarters (e.g. the Centre for Independent Studies, and the Sydney Institute) largely indifferent to human-relations issues.

My next commitments were in the Midlands, in Birmingham, city of my maternal grandmother Emma Breakwell and her brother Thomas (the devout Congregationalist of my early childhood), but I opted to take a (just slightly!) circuitous route from London via Wales and Scotland. Maxing the value of my Britrail Pass. First to a Sydney EU medical couple in Cardiff, South Wales and then by overnight sleeper to Dumfries in SW Scotland and on by bus to our ancestral home village of Dalbeattie, now bereft of cousins.

In Birmingham is a remarkable consortium of Christian missionary and ministry training institutes related to a number of denominations, called the Selly Oak Colleges. I stayed overnight at St Andrew's Hall and over two days they did me proud, arranging a formal round of consultations for me with Deans and Heads of several of the institutes, many at the cutting edge such as the Cross-Cultural Communications Centre, the Centre for Muslim/Christian Relations, the Centre for New Religious Movements, and the Centre for Black & White Partnership (led by an African). While all were informative and educative, the most strategic contact turned out to be with Sister Mary Hall, director of the Multi-Faith Resource Centre, bringing together leaders from the faith communities of Birmingham: Christian, Jewish, Muslim, Buddhist, Hindu and Sikh, to share their own perceptions and explore those of others. I spent half a day at the centre, and raised the possibility of her coming to Melbourne if we invited her under the ITEMS Project.

A short journey further north, in Sheffield, I looked in on a former colleague from the King's School Ely, Peter Hopper. What fun as we outdid each other recalling some of the more extraordinary foibles of our Common Room fellow-eccentrics. Oddly, a few years later we were to surprise each other by coyly disclosing that we had both just been ordained Anglican priests, at about the same age, in our mid-50s!

The two weeks of the UK chapter of my global odyssey closed with a long train journey from Sheffield to London and on to Canterbury in Kent, well dubbed the 'Garden of England', to permit a passing visit to the historic Cathedral, Mother Church of the Anglican Communion and seat of our world leader, the Archbishop of Canterbury. It was founded in 597 by St Augustine, sent to evangelise the Anglo-Saxons by Pope Gregory the Great, after being captivated by the sight of some beautiful fair children in the slave markets of Rome and memorably quipping: "*Non Angli sed angeli*" (Not Angles but angels). The present cathedral was begun in the year after the Norman Conquest in 1067 and rebuilt in part and extended during the middle ages. It is claimed to be the oldest continuous community in the English-speaking world. A large claim indeed—but Christians have been in Britain since Roman times.

What other organisation could stake such a claim?

7
To the New World and Beyond

Over the Irish Sea and the Emerald Isle, across a cloud-wrapped ocean and the desolate snow-scapes of Labrador, before touching down at New York's La Guardia Airport.Customs cleared, and fairly quivering with excitement, I peered through the cab 'windshield' towards Brooklyn Bridge, as the stunning façade of Manhattan loomed into focus out of the murk—The Big Apple! Hailed as the greatest city on earth, spawning the first skyscrapers, home to the planet's most cosmopolitan population—the world's original melting pot—enshrining the very soul of modernity. Dynamic *Noo Yarrk*. But as we began circling the same city block for the second time, in search of the YMCA Hostel on East 47th Street, not far from the slender UN Building, I twigged to the cabbie's game. Down to earth with a thud. Swindled! But he, black and probably poor, merely chuckled, unembarrassed. Always worth a try!

Digesting the Big Apple

The next three nights, though spent in a not-for-profit 'Christian' hostel, proved to be the most expensive of my worldwide trip. So this was American life, with its high costs and refined tastes, its glitz, its infinite options of food, beverages, creature comforts, attractions, entertainment. The choice of breakfast fare in the (cheaper) YMCA canteen bewildered me—among many others offering Jewish foods I'd never even heard of. Simply to ask for a cup of tea or coffee was to be confronted with a mind-boggling array of subtle variations. Suddenly Australian standards seemed trite and our lack of style embarrassing. Moreover, my inherent parsimony was under constant siege. Of course I do not doubt that, since 1984 the gap in creature comforts between New York, NY and Melbourne, Vic. has greatly narrowed in a world where sophistication prevails and globalisation rules. But in 1984 American power and glory were undimmed while we amounted to a slightly upmarket Birmingham, solid enough but tasteless. If the image of London is of tradition and of Paris elegance, there is no missing the New York image: naked power.

Overawed by the heightened significance of everything, I reacted by setting a manic pace for myself. First a brief tourist visit to the UN Secretariat because it was close at hand on 1st Avenue and East 42nd Street, and because it embodied a vision of internationalism far broader than the mawkish American patriotism vaunted on every hand. Then bussing and walking on southwards towards the tip of Manhattan Island marked by the soaring pre-doomed twin towers of the World Trade Centre, grossly out of proportion to their neighbours (the skyscraper area is several kilometres further north), I came upon Houston Street bisecting the island, spatially and historically. To the south the original site of New Amsterdam dating back to 1614 offered an interesting random pattern of individually named streets, while to the north lay the boring geometric grid imposed in the early decades of the 19th century, of short east/west Streets (numbered 1st to 190th!) and long north/south Avenues (1st to 12th). Hence New York's best-known street, Wall St, south of Houston Street, turned out to be a deceptively harmless-looking narrow, short street of moderate-sized buildings, one of them the NY Stock Exchange, epicentre of world capitalism and worthy target of the 'Occupy' movement of 2011 during the global financial crisis.

But the heart-dropping elevator ride to the 107th floor of one of the twin towers of the newly opened World Trade Centre, among the world's tallest buildings, rewarded you with virtually an aerial view out over the Hudson River and New York Bay with the huge Statue of Liberty and Ellis Island where the immigrants landed in their millions. Next by Subway 'uptown' to the swanky area of Fifth and Sixth Avenues (also called the Avenue of the Americas), the 'skyscraper alley' so familiar from the cinema, including the Empire State Building and the opulent shopping zone. But I was appalled at the graffiti-scrawled Subway, every wall, corridor and train inanely scribbled over—the era of self-expression gone mad. Years afterwards a great clean-up campaign by a NY Mayor would totally redeem the situation. I was surprised to note that throughout the Subway (the world's most extensive) all the notices are bilingual, in English and Spanish. What about all the others?

But what a relief it was, in the heart of this pulsating antheap, to discover Central Park, so huge and natural that you could forget you were in the middle of a world metropolis. Its vast rectangle runs no less than fifty blocks from 59th to 110th Streets, four km long and nearly one km wide, in the epicentre of New York! I saw my first squirrels (so tiny!) scurrying bushy-tailed among the fallen leaves between the wintry trees, planted maybe 150 years before, and admired beautiful toddlers toddling by the lake shores and elegant poodles leading gorgeously furred dames along the curving paths.

Come Sunday, I attended worship in the immensely dignified Fifth Avenue Presbyterian Church and later the Episcopalian (Anglican) Cathedral of St John the Divine, both full of well-heeled parishioners, with robed choirs, great organists and fine preaching. True, everything in America is on such a massive scale, and so rich: how can you not be impressed? As the patriotic hymn put it, *'God bless America'*. It was easy to believe He had.

But I was soon to learn that this was not the full story. Firstly, late that evening I gave myself quite a fright, recklessly wandering alone in the cold dark of the deserted financial district south of the Houston line. I had emerged from a Subway entrance to find myself the only survivor of the end of the world, not counting some huddled figures on a wintry night bedding down to sleep on flattened-out cardboard boxes, wreathed in clouds of warm steam rising from the Subway gratings beneath. Not a soul stirred. Pretty soon I sensed my vulnerability to a mugging (reported all too often in the media). To avoid two rugged-up men approaching I crossed over and scuttled down another re-entry point to the Subway.

Consultations across the USA

Then next morning I met with my mentor from Holy Mt Athos, the urban affairs correspondent of the *New York Times*, who drove me across the East River to Brooklyn. I was incredulous: it reminded me of an East Berlin post-war bombsite, with burnt-out tenement houses, shattered glass, boarded up shops, all graffiti-scarred, deserted—and in sight of the opulence of Manhattan just across the river. They had been like that for many years since large-scale urban rioting and, in his view, they might never be rehabilitated, since there is no money in restoring cheap rental housing in a Black ghetto. And there's not much scope in America for losers. Years later a book I read on the industrial 'rust belt' of Detroit and Ohio would make the claim that it was only under Democrat President Franklin D Roosevelt in the Great Depression of the 1930s that the novel political idea was first mooted that administrations should govern for *all* Americans. Recent Republican administrations seem to have repudiated that doctrine, preferring to 'blame the victim' and preaching economic recovery by cutting taxes on the rich and repealing health and welfare provision for the poor. Could that become symptomatic of a future Australia?

It offered a salutary backgrounding for my consultations across the country with seminary lecturers grappling with a theology that can find a place for poor Blacks and struggling Hispanics besides well-groomed Republicans. But since most of the responses from Americans to my introductory letter had come from other cities, my only visit in New York was to the headquarters of the 'National Council of Churches of Christ in the USA'[6] on Riverside Drive by the Hudson River near Columbia University. It was the massively funded ecumenical counterpart of our Australian Council of Churches (now similarly renamed the National Council of Churches in Australia) but it linked no less than 37 Member Churches, 15 of them 'ethnic', and employed 28 staff members co-ordinating seven program areas. Unusual for that period: in the lobby I was confronted by a high-security screening not even imposed then at airport departure gates.

My host, the director of the Program on Racism (Americans are nothing if not kind), received me warmly and outlined for me a plan for visits in cities across the country with noted specialists in the theology of race and inter-group relations. Generously he allowed me to telephone all over the country. As it was Human Rights Day we attended a special service in the chapel, after which we adjourned to lunch with the other program directors, several of whom had visited Australia. Finally, laden with a bundle of relevant documentation, I was ready to fly on but the weather took an unexpected hand, with a shocking drop in temperature and a prodigious snowstorm.

Shivering in a temperature of -21°C (the coldest I had ever endured, despite

---

[6] The member bodies of the National Council of Churches encompass a wide spectrum of American Christianity, representing traditions as varied as Protestant, Orthodox, Evangelical, Anglican, and African-American, historic peace churches and ethnic-language immigrant churches.These include more than 100,000 local congregations with 45 million members.

our record German winter of 1962/63), without an overcoat and with ears fairly burning, I arrived at the airport in the evening for my TWA flight to Philadelphia in Pennsylvania, only to find all flights cancelled. But overhearing a frustrated passenger loudly negotiating with a Philadelphia minibus operator, I horned in and soon we were on our way. That city turned out to be less than two hours' drive down the New Jersey Turnpike from New York. My only travelling companion brashly identified himself as a professor from Rutgers University, one of the most prestigious research schools of the USA. It is in neighbouring New Jersey, just across the Hudson River, and was founded earlier than Sydney Town. After enduring an earful of rabid right-wing, racial prejudice all the way it was only in the last few kilometres of the journey that I threw caution to the winds, as a polite overseas visitor, and spoke out with passion. He seemed shocked at my identifying with the underdog, delivered with such conviction, and after he alighted and disappeared into the night the Black driver turned around to me and said, beaming, *"Good for you, brother. That blowhard sure needed to get an earful of that!"*

My day in snowy Philadelphia was spent at the Westminster Theological Seminary and with the Jubilee Fellowship, an ecumenical house church. At the seminary the great pioneer of urban mission and missiology, Harvie Conn, was gracious enough to spend a morning with me. He had recently published his major work *Evangelism: Doing Justice and Preaching Grace* (the dual vision that later we would modestly seek to earth in Broadmeadows.) He explained that in its old decaying centre Philadelphia had become an amalgam of clearly demarcated ethnic neighbourhoods: Blacks, Hispanics, Asians, with the middle-class whites escaping to the leafy outskirts—a familiar pattern across the older American cities. All of the groups had their own segregated churches.

Responses by Westminster Seminary included initiating reconciliation courses straddling two or more communities, seminars on racial awareness for middle-class whites, and training initiatives to help Christians from many backgrounds make contact with the real life of the streets. The central mission of the church was to incarnate the Gospel in the streets and tenement blocks. All these initiatives grew out of a theologically rigorous commitment to biblical justice for minorities, a field no longer the preserve of theological liberals.

A leader of the Jubilee Fellowship opened up for me some fascinating semantic issues: campaigners habitually close their ears at the mention of a 'cult word' from the 'opposition', e.g. *'dialogue'* can become a dirty word for evangelicals and *'evangelism'* for liberals, so the answer is to stick to the great scriptural words of the Faith. By the early 1980s new material was appearing that bridged the divide between the *'spiritual'* Gospel and the *'social'* Gospel. [Of course there is only one Gospel, good news for both dimensions]. The issues are too crucial to be owned by any one party. The challenge is to focus on the actual needs of real people encountered in the life of the streets. I was starting to see how very genteel are urban Christians (like me) in Australia: we need liberating.

Next morning I was off by an early TWA flight to Washington, DC where

I was hosted by Quaker House, a peace-and-disarmament lobby group targeting Congress as well as the local 'apartheid': a majority of Washington residents are now Blacks! After New York there was a tangibly different feel about Washington, essentially because of its mission but also for its monumental scale (its town plan dwarfing Canberra's, another American creation) with a large lake and river, the Potomac, and the long vista up Constitution Avenue towards the majestic Capitol (Congress). Equally impressive was the White House glimpsed through the trees in its dignified garden setting. In those relaxed days before 9/11 changed the world forever, you were free to nose about, just outside these focal points of power, though time failed me to join the tourist parties inside the Capitol. Around Washington travel was by the newly opened Metro (subway), after New York's now the second most patronised in the USA.

A black angel

Inappropriately, I landed in Chicago quite late on a weeknight. Noting that the Divinity School of the University of Chicago where I was to stay was remote from the airport and city centre, in order to save on taxi fares I opted to travel by the mass transit system (in Chicago an elevated railway twisting and turning above the main city streets and across the suburbs). It took forever to reach the appropriate station but on descending to street level I noted the neighbourhood was dark and deserted. So how to find the university late at night? Fortuitously at that moment a taxi drew up and the Black driver hailed me, "Hey, whitey, whaddya doin' here?" When I explained my purpose, confirmed by my large suitcase, he nodded, adding that anyone arriving so late in the Black quarter was just asking for trouble. Providential protection! Perhaps modern angels drive taxis....

Next day I made contact with SCUPE (Seminary Consortium on Urban Pastoral Education), based in the area where the young Barak Obama would later cut his teeth as a community worker. I found the new insights gained to be of inestimable value to my project and my future ministry. SCUPE bridged 12 seminaries from several denominations (Protestant and Catholic) in a number of States 'seeking the *shalom* of the city' by training leadership 'to view the inner city prophetically, in all its struggle and pain' and become change agents for justice for all, including the minority groups. More vital than 'correct' doctrine and church order (middle class stuff) is it to listen to ordinary people's story, all of whom have some insights of truth and hope. Nevertheless *'the pearl of great price'* is not itself divisible but needs renewed oyster shells around it: Asian family loyalties, Hispanic worship styles, black preaching all have aspects of truth to unfold, especially in the dimension of community sadly overlooked in our rationalistic and individualistic middle class church. By contrast the Early Church was an urban church, set in the Graeco-Roman world, and pioneered in multicultural Corinth by Paul, the first urban missioner. Theology is people's work, to be done interactively in the neighbourhood, emphasising the dimension of human dignity common to us all created in the image of God: "You should bring people with you, not keep them under you." *Mutatis mutandis* (of course) I wondered whether the ITEMS Project was not groping towards a similar vision in Melbourne.

Later I was taken on an inner city tour: The Loop, the centre of downtown Chicago named from the early pattern of elevated rail lines, with the Sears Tower of 108 storeys, at that time the world's tallest building. I was also driven along a skyscraper-backed esplanade around the shores of Lake Michigan, one of America's Great Lakes, stretching off to the horizon like an ocean. Traditionally Chicago had been America's second city, until in recent years overtaken by Los Angeles. In size it compares with Melbourne.

My next leg across the United States with Trans-World Airways, to Los Angeles on the Pacific coast, required making a detour via St Louis, Missouri, 'Gateway to the West', for me to change planes, because that was TWA's 'hub' from which all its flight destinations branched off like spokes. St Louis is famous for its Gateway Arch, a wide but seemingly pointless stainless steel structure half as high as the Sears Tower, and perhaps the inspiration for the McDonald's inane Golden Arches. From the air it stands out like a great nose-ring with which to pick up St Louis.

Agonising encounter

On my arrival mid-afternoon at Los Angeles (LAX Airport) an unguarded moment crept up on me. Met at the terminal by my hostess, I walked out into the street where her small Corolla was parked and went to lift my heavy suitcase into the boot. At that instant a lady driving a large 'Yank tank' came up to park at the kerb behind us but waved to someone waiting for her. Momentarily she forgot that her automatic car was still in 'Drive' and it continued to creep forward, squashing my left leg between the two car bumpers. I let out a yell, and my hostess leapt into the small car and took off the handbrake. As my leg expanded again it pushed the Corolla forward! A sharp pain shot up my leg though somehow I sensed it wasn't broken. But neither was it OK.

I was driven to a hospital where reams of paper work had to be done before any attention could be given, despite the pain and my assurances that it would be fully covered by my travel insurance! Finally it was accepted that I did not need to pay before being admitted to the Outpatients, where a number of examinations and X-rays revealed that the posterior cruciate ligament in my left knee was snapped. Since I was travelling, no time was available for bed rest, ice packs or relaxation. But crutches would keep the weight off the leg, and in time there might be a measure of restoration, failing which an operation back home would be necessary, with a tendon-graft from elsewhere in the body. Meanwhile pain killers would assist. Expecting difficult days ahead on my itinerary (with more than a week to go before returning to Melbourne, still half a world away) I bought the best crutches available, a de luxe pair in aluminium and white leather.

Overnight I stayed at Whittier, a suburb 25km east from 'downtown' Los Angeles, at the home of Brian Coulter's parents, my offsider in the Ceduna racism investigation seven years earlier. Next morning I had an appointment at Fuller Theological Seminary in Pasadena, a regional city 30km to the north, accessed by a terrifying six-lane freeway. LA seemed to be more a web of widely-spaced suburban hubs within a vast built-up area held together by freeways, than a true, focused metropolis. Urban spaghetti. Doubtless the most car-dependent city in the world.

Because of its strategic role in educating specialists in world mission, Fuller is famed well beyond the borders of the USA. A solid proportion of its students come from overseas countries and former mission fields. Among these, many evangelical Australian clergy have done higher and doctoral studies there. My contacts, particularly Charles Kraft, a writer of international repute (*Christianity in Culture*, a people's theology) offered some fresh ideas for encouraging clergy to move out of their comfort zone in learning to relate across cultures. Rather than offering all the answers, a creative course would encourage participants to research the questions for themselves. In the West we have been accustomed to ministering to the powerful but now we are struggling to accept the reverse situation: allowing the powerless to minister to us their insights into the Gospel. But for that we need to encounter them. Hence the pulpit must come to terms with the life of the streets—a liberating perspective. And of course in modern metropolises the streets are multicultural.

I had also been invited to present a seminar about the ITEMS project to a group of Fuller staff. But I was in pain. Screwing up my courage to the sticking place I hobbled into the seminar room on crutches and more or less battled through. At the end Charles Kraft came up to me and said, "Thanks for that, but I couldn't bear to look you in the face because of the pain you must be in. Would you let me pray for you?" It was still the heyday of the charismatic renewal in the churches, but many in evangelical circles seemed to feel threatened by the implication that, maybe after all, they did not have the last word on understanding the Bible and on Christian doctrines. Be that as it may, Charles Kraft prayed fervently and lovingly for me, a total stranger. With him, I also held that God could bring good out of evil and that I was surrounded by his love, whether I felt it or not. Afterwards he confided that he had never before prayed for anyone with an injury to be healed. I thanked him warmly for his new venture into healing and hobbled off to keep my next appointment—a visit to an Indian reservation in the Arizona desert.

Consultations with Native Americans and Blacks

This implied an hour's flight back over the High Sierras and the Sonoran Desert to Phoenix, capital of Arizona *['arid zone']*. Arriving overhead, a weird phenomenon greeted me: a modern air-conditioned city of a million people[7] set on an arid, mountain-rimmed plain punctuated by great randomised columns of solid rock—

---

7   By 2012 grown to four million by intensive immigration from the colder northern States.

even rearing out of suburban backyards!—a city where summer temperatures can touch 49°C. Mercifully it was now mid-winter.

Without asking, I had been driven out to the plane in a buggy and loaded on first, to be met at Phoenix by Rev Mike Smith, a Native American ('Red Indian') of part-Black ancestry teaching people's theology at the Cook Theological School in the city, which since 1890 had been training Native American clergy for ministry throughout the USA within many denominations. He was very knowledgeable about the national race relations scene as well as very compassionate. During an hour's drive into the desert to Fort McGregor Reservation (the fort originally set up to protect the white army of occupation) he gave me a broad backgrounding on the social and political, as well as the spiritual situation of his people. Along the trail we passed many of the tall, two-armed cactus 'trees' so familiar from Hollywood cartoons.

Arizona has always been—and even today no less—the heartland of American redneck culture, now fuelled by 'Tea Party' xenophobia towards Mexican border-hoppers. Attitudes towards the 'First Nations' evoked some distressing parallels with the Aboriginal scene on the frontier regions of Australia, but also evinced some heartening progress being made in independent Reserve communities through well-functioning Indian organisations. The amenities they had created were far superior to anything in Aboriginal Australia and the spirit of the people correspondingly buoyant. They were Christians who had long since made their accommodation between the Gospel and the Red Indian world view: their theology grew out of this dual experience of life. The elder statesman whose home we visited was a man of immense dignity.

This brought home to me again the terrible human toll that racism has exacted in Australia by beggaring the spirit of the indigenous people, more so than in the USA where today they seem if anything only to be *resented* rather than *despised* and *rejected*. Of course in the USA it is the Blacks rather than the Indians who tend to be the racial scapegoats. Perhaps the greater secularity of Australia since our dubious beginnings and the very marginality of early settler life had militated against the advent of such fundamental Christian attitudes as goodwill and respect for all as equals in God's creation. And it is only in recent decades that an authentic Christian leadership seems to be emerging in many Aboriginal communities.[8]

Back in Phoenix we visited the Indian leadership training school where Mike taught, and spent some hours discussing the history and social situation of the Native Americans and theological education models with the principal, a senior man of great discernment. On his bookshelves were several books on the Aborigines. Indeed some Aboriginal Christian leaders were planning a study period there. Later we visited a retired director of Native Indian ministry, who had visited Elcho Island off Arnhem Land studying the people and their needs. He was delighted to hear of the emergence of an Aboriginal people's theologian from Elcho Island,

---

8   Since 2010 a national gathering.of emerging Aboriginal Christian leaders has been convened each year in Melbourne

Rev Dr Djiniyini Gondara, then teaching at Nungalinya College in Darwin. I was given a bundle of documents about Native American ministry training, including a document resulting from a lengthy consultation process sponsored by the National Council of Churches called *Goals for the Indian Ministry*.

Returning to Los Angeles I had a brief discussion with the pastor of a Hispanic church about appropriate ministry training. In his view only moderate educational qualifications were called for, lest there be too wide a gap between pastor and people: a high-powered pastor would not be content to stay long. Besides, the theology of people's churches was often charismatic, expressing the conviction that the Gifts of the Spirit were more significant than education. Certainly that recalled the experience of the first apostles.

A healing miracle emerging?

By the time I touched down next morning higher up the Pacific coastline in San Francisco a miracle of healing was becoming manifest: the pain of my knee was abating remarkably and I was beginning to wonder whether I even needed the crutches. The San Francisco Theological Seminary is also a mecca for post-graduate Australian clergy. In fact in my last year with the Community Relations Office in Canberra I had conducted a workshop on racism against Aborigines for a group of local clergy doing an external doctorate there. Dr Gene Farlough, an Afro-American, had come over to supervise the students. His visit had led to the launch of an Aboriginal pastorate in Canberra under the AEF (Aboriginal Evangelical Fellowship) through the fund-raising efforts of his doctoral students and their congregations, at which Gene was so touched that he produced an audio-visual on Aborigines, for use in his Church in Oakland, across the Bay from San Francisco.

With my arrival at the Seminary the wheel had turned full circle: he was now my genial host for a productive two-day program. At a meeting with missiology faculty members in the charmingly gabled and turreted Seminary high above the city, I was indulged and blessed with a great deal of documentary material to take home. In the afternoon he drove me around the tourists' hillside city of antique cable-car trams with the Fishermen's Wharf, and then across San Francisco Bay to his *Sojourner Truth Church* in Oakland to observe its holistic ministry in a depressed Afro community. Its strange name recalls a famous Black slave woman, born in upstate New York in 1797, who in her childhood spoke only Dutch until she escaped into freedom, becoming famous as the first Black woman to win a legal case against a white man, for the recovery of her stolen and enslaved children. In 1843, in her forties, she changed her name to Sojourner Truth, saying, "The Spirit calls me, and I must go." She became a Methodist, and left to make her way travelling and preaching on the abolition of slavery. She joined an emancipist organisation that also campaigned for women's rights and religious tolerance as well as pacifism, travelling widely for the next 20 years, helping recruit Black soldiers for the northern forces in the Civil War, and later she met Abraham Lincoln and President Ulysses S. Grant and addressed the Michigan State Legislature. But her campaign for Blacks to be given land grants after the war was unsuccessful. To this day she is the only Black woman to be honoured with a bust in the Capitol in Washington.

We also visited the TAFE College nearby for lunch with the Principal, discussing possibilities of an exchange arrangement with the Canberra TAFE where I had been a Council member. It emerged that Dr Farlough laboured under several misconceptions about Aborigines based on false analogies with the US Blacks, but was glad to revise these. It reminded me how easily we can jump to conclusions when travelling, by fitting new ideas into our existing frame of reference: we see essentially what we want to see, and probably pontificate about it on our return!

One of the finest human beings I met anywhere was Harold Hunt, professor of Urban Ministry at the Seminary, who related the spine-chilling tale of how his father would have been lynched by a Ku Klux Klan mob in the Deep South in the 1930s except that he caught the wrong train from the one to be ambushed by a posse thirsting for his blood as an 'uppity nigger'. But many times in the USA I was told that by the 1980s, things were worse than before the Civil Rights movement began, because it had proven a failed dream that now engendered cynicism.

However the afternoon with Gene Farlough would afford my last and abiding image of the United States, land of racial and ethnic diversity struggling against its past, viewed from the Pacific coast with its Latino tensions—providing the other book-end to the dismal Black ghetto of Brooklyn on the Atlantic seabord.

Amazing grace

At that time, landing in Hong Kong was a stimulating experience: looking *up* at the skyscrapers all around you in the congested downtown area of Kowloon, as you sidled past them seeking out the canyon below that was Kai Tak airport. It had been the longest ocean flight on earth, losing a day of my life in the process, and broken by a refuelling stop at Honolulu in the Hawaiian Islands where I had distinguished myself by needing to be paged to avoid missing the plane. At least I was exploring on foot—without crutches!

Arriving at the 'Holy Carpenter Guesthouse' run by an Anglican Mission in Hung Hom, not far from the airport and the terminus of the China railway, I thankfully presented my now superfluous crutches to their disability unit, and took the lift to the top floors of the inner-city building which offers spartan accommodation for tourists—bare concrete floors and hard beds (Chinese style). Mobile again on two legs. Healing miracle complete. *Thank you, Lord, for the prayer of faith*[9]. I never would need that operation.

The aftermath was interesting in two ways. Judging by his later writings, Charles Kraft's theological emphasis shifted to embrace more of the charismatic gift of healing. Yet when I met him decades later in Melbourne, at a meeting I

---

9   "Is any one of you sick? Let him call the elders of the church to pray over him ...in the name of the Lord.. And the prayer of faith will make the sick person well." (James 5: 14-15)

attended specifically to thank him for his prayer for healing, he had no memory of the occasion. *Gulp...*

Three-month round-the-world study tour—at a *painful* profit!

Equally providential, though in a hard-headed way: the kerbside encounter at LAX airport opened the door to legal action against the negligent driver of the Yank tank. Not that I would have thought of launching it. But my brother Max on one of his trans-Pacific flights 'happened' to be sitting next to a lawyer from LA who specialised in damages claims: *'lose the case, no charge; win the case, keep a quarter of the proceeds'*. On the day of the case the other party opted to settle out of court and I wound up receiving $US7,500. The total costs of my three-month round-the-world study safari had amounted to $US6,600. So the pain and discomfort endured had produced an *overall profit* of about $A1,000 on the round-the-world study tour!

Thank you, Father, truly *'Your ways are past finding out'!*[10]

The icing on the cake was that the projected loss of use of my left knee in later years, as anticipated in the Melbourne orthopaedic surgeon's report—which as evidence presented had clinched the legal case—has never transpired! Ironically the following year it was my *right* knee that required an arthroscopy, caused by the exciting event of jumping down a 40cm gutter on an unmade Eltham street!

Consultations in Hong Kong

After the high stimulation of the American program, the last few days of my trip proved to be something of an anti-climax. Three months was doubtless too long, I was approaching exhaustion from the intensity of meeting so many high-powered people, plus the constant alertness of mind and body demanded by the process of travelling alone.

The final professional encounter was with Rev John England, a New Zealander leading the Tao Fong Shan Ecumenical Institute and Study Centre at Sha Tin, in the New Territories on the China mainland leased by the British in 1898 as an adjunct to Hong Kong Island. The New Territories are quite mountainous and rugged (*shan* means 'mountain'). On a mountain top a remarkable Christian/interfaith centre had been built by a Norwegian missionary in 1930 in order to address Buddhism, faith of the higher classes. It is reminiscent of Buddhist architecture but embraces a Christian chapel, conference hall, library, porcelain workshop, and a publishing centre producing books and a glossy periodical on inter-faith issues and contextualisation initiatives (authentically rooting the Gospel in the local context). It sees itself as a bridge between the traditional, unadventurous churches of Hong Kong, still faithfully reflecting the missionary era, and the robust church emerging in the People's Republic of China, authentically Chinese and committed to living simultaneously in two worlds, with all the tensions involved. I gathered an amount

---

10   Job 9:10

of material concerned with inter-faith dialogue, common people's ('*minjung*' theology), and the bridging of faith-cultures.

In retrospect, this turned out to be a momentous occasion: my first contact with China, destined 20 years later to usher in one of the most fulfilling chapters of our lives, inter-twining strands of theological study, language teaching, cross-cultural awareness and international friendship, all bound together by a deep and growing love for China and its people.

Christmas homecoming

The last port of call was necessarily Singapore, in order to effect the change-over from Trans-World Airways back to Singapore Airlines, which flies into Australia. I had one day left and could only wander about rather aimlessly in the heat and humidity (it is on the equator), after the northern wintry skies to which I had become accustomed. The transformation from the tawdry colonial *entrepôt* that we had encountered on our voyage to England in 1959 was by now complete. But the earlier cosmopolitan population seemed to have become more monoculturally Chinese. However with its clusters of contemporary air-conditioned skyscrapers, shopping malls and massive apartment buildings it had lost almost all appeal: I ambled about the botanical gardens admiring their riot of tropical blooms, whiling away the hours and then buying gifts of electronic gadgetry for the family until the late-night departure. This precipitated a final calamity of imagining the exchange rate with the Australian dollar to be as in Hong Kong (about seven to one), so that I could afford to lash out and buy each of the three boys an expensive 'Sony Walkman' for playing audiotapes through headphones. To the family's general amusement and delight, the accounts later revealed a paternal generosity bordering on recklessness!

But Christmas was three days away, so the timing was right. Of course I was so spaced out as to have retained virtually no memory of that first Melbourne Christmas, except of being received back at the mudbrick villa with love and gratitude to God for his sustaining care. Even Angus, celebrating his newly acquired paternity status, slobbered over me affectionately.

8
Reporting In

Whereas the previous, first year in Melbourne had been largely exploratory, familiarising myself with several new domains and drafting the theological course, now 1985 brought the challenge of actually delivering the goods. But first came my report to the Victorian Council of Churches.

Evaluating the outcomes

What had the three months overseas achieved? And what had they meant to me? My encounter with 'global Christianity' had been heartening. Apart from experiencing goodwill and hospitality, everywhere I discovered a seriousness about the task of relating the faith to the culture in which it was embedded, and in the old Christian heartlands also to addressing the growing challenge of secularism. Beyond that I came across the phenomenon of exploring positive relationships with the great world faiths. But on the other hand I had had no encounter with the dynamic spread of the Gospel reported in many Third World countries (beyond my brief), though perhaps destined to reposition Christianity in the entire world.

The more obviously beneficial outcomes of the study tour were:

- Meeting interesting and creative people: indispensable to Australians because of our remoteness and the insularity of our outlook, and especially when attempting cross-cultural links. It is salutary to see people of a 'migrant' culture in their own homelands, e.g. Greeks *in Greece*–relaxed and 'normal'.
- Gathering documentation in several lands about Christian initiatives on projects bridging cultures and sub-cultures.
- Perceiving the reality of world *Oikumene* (the Household of Faith): Anglican, Catholic, Orthodox, evangelicals, charismatics—liberating to the mind and spirit.
- Reflecting on our own praxis, and seeking to discover why we do things the way we do, when there are so many other viable options to be observed overseas.
- Within this framework, discerning the possibility that in its orientation and method, ITEMS is on the right track—an Australian counterpart to some overseas initiatives likewise responding to the prompting of the Holy Spirit.
- From time to time being heartened by the impression that overseas hosts might even glean some value from the Australian experience of immigration and multiculturalism—and maybe even from the approach of ITEMS.
- The inevitable realisation on a number of occasions that a long, lone

journey can produce moments of threatening disempowerment: variations on the similar challenges presented by ignorance, misinformation, perplexity, real or imagined antipathy, even danger—producing a degree of frustration, anxiety or downright panic—but also experiencing the mercy and protection of God. Perhaps the eclipse of the familiar mental landscape opens up a sharper perspective on the actual human scene. Of course episodes of vulnerability expose you—albeit in a minor way—to the classical experience of migration: wholly threatening but ultimately salutary. And worth a lot of simulation games—but just stay away from public telephones in non-English-speaking countries, oppressing of the spirit!

Over and beyond all this, the trip brought many moments of sheer delight, whether in historic sites, ancient buildings, places of art and culture, loving family circles, natural beauty or inspiring worship. Even if it was a rush from start to finish, and ultimately exhausting. Certainly no companion would have tolerated it!

In my report to the VCC I tried to capture something of my new perspective, not only on the countries visited but also on Australia itself. It was as if scales had fallen from my eyes (after all, why else does one travel?). I began to ponder some profound divergences such as:

- The extreme secularity of contemporary Australian society, in contrast to the evidence on every hand in the northern pre-Christmas season. In our society commerce seems to have quite sapped the lifeblood out of Christmas. But compare for instance the wide public representation- of the Crib (even in town marketplaces) in England—faith-related, tasteful, traditional—with Myers' Bourke Street shopwindows peopled by garish hobgoblins, or again compare the *Christkindlmarkt* ('Christ-child market') in every German city with the tawdry Santa's sleigh banners disfiguring our shopping malls. So it came as a pleasant surprise to discover that even in Santa's American adopted homeland, in 1984 the Christ-child still held pride of place!
- With our weaker sense of identity or 'settled-ness' we seem to live in a state of constant agitation, playthings of the media. On the other hand the countries that I visited, shaped by centuries of being at home in their land, seemed to have retained a strong sense of national consciousness—peoples comfortable with and proud of their traditions, able to withstand the power of the exogenous media—which in any case represents a broader spectrum of viewpoints than here. Overseas, particularly on the Continent, I was struck by the small evidence of disaffected youth on the one hand, and on the other by the diligence and decency of ordinary people. And this particularly among the Germans, who identify themselves nationally by their *Fleiß* (diligence and earnestness). Perhaps in Australia, not having an uplifting foundation

myth as in America, the heightened degree of alienation reflects our ambivalence about our raffish origins and the manner in which we took over and occupy our land. But at times we seem to fall prey to a sense of panic at the widespread evidence of alienation: our veritable addiction to sport, excessive gambling, binge drinking and drug-taking, the AIDS epidemic, widespread racism, outrages against the environment, and now the appalling rate of domestic violence and family breakdown—matched at times by a sense of societal guilt.

[Today (2012) for instance, comes the distressing news item of a Sudanese pedestrian knocked down by a Mercedes, whose driver sped off. The five following cars all swerved to avoid the man lying in the roadway but none stopped to assist.]

- Are we living in some sort of bland all-embracing present, as though coming from nowhere and going nowhere? Does our white 'Dreamtime' palely evoke an idealised society of pioneers and bushmen and later, heroic Diggers? But which we know to be counter-balanced by our near-extermination of the original Australians and the sacrifices of our young men in overseas wars at the behest of politicians and captains of industry? Is it then the brevity of our history that constrains our search for heroes or archetypes from which to frame our national identity: outlaws, Anzacs, sporting stars, celebrities? Why not also scientists, writers, inventors, social reformers, philanthropists, entrepreneurs ... Christian leaders? Aborigines?
- At their best, some of the Churches I encountered overseas seemed boldly prepared to transcend narrow self-interest: for example in Europe and America, by going in to bat for unpopular causes like migrant workers and the exploited minorities rather than tamely settling for the sanctity and inviolability of the private realm. Nowhere did religion seem so unimportant as in Australia, where the Churches mostly appear uncritically to undergird the status quo rather than overturning the tables of the money-changers. But in a democracy where only powerful interest groups gain access to political power, there are also indications that some of the declining Churches are becoming united in their advocacy for the Aborigines, the disadvantaged, asylum seekers and newly arriving ethnic groups, and this in the face of the brewing backlash from the 'poor whites' [later to be courted by Pauline Hanson's One Nation Party] and encapsulated in the 'unfunny' material circulating on-line.

Of course, apart from (far more briefly) grappling with such melancholy musings, my report covered significant contacts and learnings made with socially engaged theologians and the innovative programs encountered in urban mission. It was duly acknowledged by the Commission on Community and Race Relations, with compliments, and filed away in the VCC Archives, now at Deakin University in Geelong. Much of the documentation that I brought back found its way into the VCC library or the Clearing House on Migration Issues at the Ecumenical Migration Centre.

Financial rigour

On the financial side, conscious as I was of the potential sneer about junketing at public expense or wasting Christian money (in this case arguably both!) I had covered myself, like a pettifogging public servant, by keeping track of every cent laid out from the Tullamarine departure early in October to re-arrival there just before Christmas. Only a third of the total costs were met from the ITEMS budget, all costs of touristic activity being rigorously segregated from professional engagements and met from my pocket, with everything calculated in each of the 16 countries' currency at the exchange rate of the day against the US dollar. Rarely did I eat in restaurants nor use commercial accommodation, though I did have a budget for gifts and a supply of low-kitsch Australiana. Overkill? Just slightly!

Life outcomes

Up to that point of my experience I judged the round-the-world journey as the highlight of my life. At one level it convinced me of my competence in managing an intense and demanding program for three months unaided, in relating as a layman to experts and gleaning knowledge and inspiration, in building self-reliance and assurance—at times in the face of vulnerability. But also, through enabling visits to many significant sites it also afforded rich cultural experiences, at times as the recipient of formal hospitality programs. Again, linguistically it was gratifying to relate to many people in their own language: in some lands the limited familiarity with English was quite surprising. Probably most monolingual English travellers merely gloss over the surface in attempting genuine cross-cultural contacts, so that their judgments may turn out to be facile and superficial, mediated by better-educated bilinguals. At times I sensed the privilege of being taken beyond this comfortable familiarity by the demands that my program imposed. On the other hand, in the goodness of God, I never had a day off sick.

Inevitably there were also negative aspects. Given my determination to encircle the globe (which is very big!) it was inevitable that the process had to be extensive rather than intensive—and therefore essentially superficial. It must also be acknowledged that, by not visiting the Third World, I missed the encounter with the *'people's theology'* movement (apart from contact with the Native Americans) but also with the grinding poverty. Finally, it was all a rush from start to finish and ultimately exhausting. Only after recovering my equanimity could I become productive again, but certainly at a new and enhanced level of awareness.

9
Charting New Waters

By the start of 1985 I had passed the mid-point of the 21-month ITEMS project with its five focuses: stimulating theological responsiveness to our multicultural society; trialling an innovative course incorporating what was missing; publishing a textbook for such a course; exploring relationships with other world faiths now in our community; and preparing materials for small groups to use in exploring all these issues.

The Melbourne theological scene

The overall challenge was to engender a heightened awareness across the theological community that, as Melbourne's population grew ever more culturally diverse, the Churches ran the risk of appealing to a shrinking component of our society: the Anglo-Australians. Unless the theological leadership could refocus on the wider cultural scene, in time the major denominations could find themselves left behind in the evolving society. Actually this prophetic insight was to prove true, as new and often charismatic churches were already beginning to spring up bridging a wider cross-section of the community, while many traditional Anglo parishes went into reverse. Of course Jesus' Great Commission to go to all nations could now be applied in our own backyard, since 'the nations' had come to us!

But the church leaders seemed oddly unaware of this significant cultural shift happening around them, compared for instance with marketers, advertisers and educators. At very least it seemed to highlight the cultural captivity of the Protestant Churches in associating the Gospel with the status quo, rather than unchaining it to critique and transform every culture. Where were the prophetic voices? And the innovators in urban mission such as I had encountered overseas? In the theological seminaries? In the local churches? Rather, it seemed that in the mainstream denominations the cultural overhang from the old Anglo-oriented Australia was stifling new expressions of church.

Taking stock

To make progress across such a broad front in the next ten months was a big ask, especially as the whole range of activities needed to be developed simultaneously, rather than in series. But it wasn't meant to be a one-man band (scarcely a Christian concept), so I had established reference groups for the new theological course, and for the preparation of a text book. Before long would come the launch of a committee spanning the other world Faiths now in Melbourne.

With the approval of the VCC Commission that I reported to, I now wrote to Sister Mary Hall at the Birmingham Multi-Faith Resource Centre, inviting her to be keynote speaker at a seminar to be jointly convened in October by a representative group from the Melbourne faith communities, funded from the ITEMS budget. So it was time to locate appropriate enthusiasts. Some were known to me from as far back as the days of the national groups survey (a Reform Jewish rabbi, John Levi, who had presented me with his book *Australian Genesis* on the history of Jews in Australia since the First Fleet) and a Muslim imam, Sheikh Fehmi Imam from the Preston mosque, while others were sought through formal letters addressed to their faith associations: Buddhist, Hindu, Sikh, Baha'i. I also wondered where Aboriginal spirituality fitted in with this company.

Producing the theological textbook

It was time to take up the challenge of producing the textbook of readings in cross-cultural theology mentioned in the funding application to the Victorian 150th Committee. Now I could turn to account the contacts made over the years with theologians throughout the land interested in multiculturalism, mainly within the Uniting and Catholic Churches. Of course I was not qualified to do more than convene an advisory group to assist me in determining the topics to be explored, and then choose appropriate academics to be invited to write the chapters of a book of readings on the interface between the Gospel and our increasingly pluralist community. It would be the first book in Australia to explore religion in the multicultural society.

We sketched out a schema for a book of readings with a dual focus—on theory and praxis—covering ministry issues posed by the presence of the minorities, both ethnic and Aboriginal, and sent this around, suggesting for each author a possible topic to be addressed. The response was immediate and enthusiastic, and the papers were forthwith commissioned. The schema fell naturally into two halves: 'Theology and the Multicultural Vision' (nine papers) and 'Theology and Multicultural Praxis' (twenty papers).

Archbishop David Penman contributed a Preface to the book and I wrote a practical Introduction to using it. I also prepared a 16-page bibliography, 'Guide to Further Reading: the Churches in a Multicultural Society', covering both Christian and secular writings, and divided into functional areas such as concepts of multiculturalism, pastoral care of migrants, combat of racism, and Aboriginal issues. Our son Christopher, then a student of sociology at La Trobe University, suggested the felicitous image of the oyster shell and the pearl. Hence the book became *The Cultured Pearl: Australian Readings in Cross-Cultural Theology and Mission* with his father as editor. We commissioned a book design featuring a stylised oyster shell with Jesus as the Pearl of Great Price overlooking a sea of faces.

The 294pp. book was produced by a Brunswick printery and published by the Victorian Council of Churches in 1986, with a second edition published in 1988 by the Joint Board of Christian Education of Australia and New Zealand. As they came off the presses I gave particular attention to checking the 'galley proofs' to identify misprints and mistakes. My generous offer to pay a dollar to anybody subsequently finding a misprint has never been paid out. We held a book launch at the VCC headquarters in Melbourne and another one in Canberra at the Woden Churches Centre. The volume sold at the competitive price of $14-49.

It served as a textbook for the ongoing lectures of the ITEMS course at Whitley College. Among the subsequent reviews was one by Douglas Hynd in *Zadok Perspectives*[11] entitled "Towards an Australian Missiology":

> "The editor is to be commended for his initiative in conceiving and bringing this volume to publication, the first-ever collection of readings focused on the Australian context for issues in cross- cultural theology and mission. Theological educators in Australia are in Jim Houston's debt for putting together a comprehensive agenda on a range of critical issues for both leaders and theological students. The theology of this volume is certainly public in its orientation. His activist stance seeks social transformation towards a more just and consciously multicultural society: a commitment to the Christian faith as world-transformative."

'Christian Book of the Year' for 1987

In 1987 *The Cultured Pearl* gained the award of 'The Christian Book of the Year' by the Australian Christian Literature Society. As I write, the framed Award looks down benignly on my desk. I treasure it as tangible acknowledgement of sustained activity in a pioneering field of Australian Christian history. But at the time I had no inkling even of the book's nomination for the Award and certainly would not have attended the ceremony had not the organisers warned me by a pointed phone call that "I would regret my absence for the rest of my life!"

Introducing the pioneering course

Of course the strategic centrepiece of the ITEMS project was the experimental course to be taught in the Churches of Christ Theological College in 1985 entitled The Strangers within our Gates: The Church and Australia's Multicultural Society. It was vital that it succeed in order to demonstrate that an innovative pedagogy was possible in Melbourne's rigid academic climate. It had now been accredited by the Melbourne College of Divinity as a course on offer through the Evangelical Theological Association towards a Bachelor of Theology degree. Its outline was included in the ETA. Handbook and it was arousing some interest within theological circles.

To my immense relief enough students chose to enrol to ensure the course's viability. They paid significant fees for each degree subject but in this case the lecturer-in-charge was not remunerated (since it was part of my work responsibilities). On the other hand, quite frankly I was not professionally equipped to teach it, having no theological qualifications myself—a quite irregular situation. But given the course content and novel approach to teaching it, equally unthinkable

---

11   No. 17, March 1987

was it that any conventionally accredited theological teacher could cover the range of topics it covered. The two worlds were poles apart: biblical scholarship, systematic theology, church history and training for ministry on the one hand, and on the other studies in migration, inter-cultural sensitivity, the resettlement process (employment, language, community services), urban mission, inter-faith relations *et al.*—but all in the perspective of training for Christian ministry. It amounted to a quite specialised type of course in applied theology, and I was determined that what it may have lacked in academic rigour would be more than offset by its social reality and its community authenticity. Certainly it was no soft option.

Historic launch

Its launch was something of a gala event, with the Theological College Principal present and a veritable spate of messages of goodwill received from the State Governor, the Premier of Victoria (who had also written letters commending the course to the heads of the main denominations), from the Minister for Immigratiion, the Director of his Department in Victoria, the Victorian Ethnic Affairs Commision, the Victorian Ethnic Communities Council, Archbishop Penman and the heads of other Churches, together with a handwritten letter from Rabbi John Levi of the Temple Beth Israel and (the crowning glory!) from the new Commissioner for Community Relations in Canberra addressed abstractly without mention of my name.

In Australian educational history there had never been a tertiary cours on the interface of church and the multicultural society. I outlined the approach of the course, particularly the field visits and the challenge of relating to minority group people (incorporated as an authentic component of the 'teaching faculty', as it were). The enthusiasm of the 15 students from three denominations was palpable, though perhaps somewhat tempered by the segment in the early weeks on learning Jiwarli, language of the Port Hedland Aboriginal people in which a visiting retired missionary was fluent. It was of course a deliberately disempowering experience meant to convey something of the 'lostness' experienced by many incoming migrants from non-English-speaking countries—even though Jiwarli grammar and pronunciation were expertly explained! We all felt appropriately lost.

Tertiary lecturer

Beyond my input in formal lecturing and holding it all together, in virtually every week's two-hour session we would have a visiting lecturer/speaker opening up grassroots experience of minority group life, or analysing authentic Christian responses to the challenges presented. We also undertook a number of 'field exposure' visits. I remember a scary class visit to the General Motors engine-block factory at Fisherman's Bend on the lower Yarra, with chips of molten metal flying around amid a deafening racket, and later relating to migrant shift-bosses. And at the other end of the spectrum evening lectures on Judaism at the Reform Synagogue and one on Islam at the Preston Mosque, besides a lecture on Orthodoxy at the Greek Orthodox church in North Carlton.

I found the lecturing task congenial, since I had personal experience of what I was teaching rather than it being simply 'head stuff.' I believed in it! And it was so important for the young Christian workers doing the course also to experience something of its life-changing potential. But equally important was it, through exercising rigour in preparation and presentation, to ensure it was no 'Mickey Mouse' course. Seeing themselves as pioneers, the students were committed to proving the value of what they were studying and its relevance to their future ministry in a multicultural community. At the end of the first semester their field reports on the face-to-face research projects undertaken within an ethnic or Aboriginal community, plus an account of their own cross-cultural journey, in addition to confirming the value of the course's innovative approach, reflected a genuine commitment to personal growth.

In the second semester, besides the formal program of lectures, the students undertook a field placement, preferably of their own devising, in either a secular setting (e.g. a large public hospital, a Centrelink office) or a church location (e.g. a parish refugee resettlement scheme, a chaplaincy, a Baptist Church with multiple ethnic-language congregations), while others assisted in the further development of the ITEMS Project such as the forthcoming inter-faith seminar. The last of the 26 course evenings focused on 'theologising across cultures' with components on a 'people's theology' emerging in the Third World and an Aboriginal theology developing at Elcho Island in Arnhem Land. The completion of the course was marked by the students joining in an 'At Home' at our Eltham family base on a Sunday afternoon, and a little later by the screening of a segment about the course in the SBS television program *Magazine* prior to the evening news.

An established future for the course

Beyond this initial successful trialling of the course in 1985, Trinity College Theological School (Anglican) agreed to offer it in the following years. In the event I was to teach it—in collaboration with outside experts—for several years there and at Whitley (Baptist) Theological College. More significantly, in time this breakthrough course in 'multicultural church' would pioneer a broadening of the cultural focus of theological courses on offer in seminaries in Melbourne and Sydney and around the country. To this time (2012) a version of the original course is still offered in Melbourne by Whitley College (Baptist) and a not dissimilar one at Ridley (Anglican) Theological College. But probably the uniquely innovative focus, with input from outsiders and minority group people and experiential learning techniques, has given way to more orthodox lecturing styles. That is to say, beyond the day of the inspired amateur, this area of theological training has now become 'professionalised'.

'Faith in the Future' Seminar at Monash University

On Sunday afternoon and throughout Monday, 27th October 1985, a unique gathering of 100 Melbourne religious leaders and their nominated delegations took place at the Centre for Religions at Monash University. The Christian Chaplain to the University, Rev. Phillip Huggins (later to become a Bishop in the Melbourne Diocese) was extremely supportive of the initiative.

The *Faith in the Future* Seminar was the outcome of long and careful planning by a committee of nominated representatives of the Christian, Jewish, Muslim, Buddhist, Hindu, and Sikh faiths, and it also figured as an official initiative for UN International Youth Year.

For me it was not altogether unfamiliar territory: throughout our time in Melbourne I had belonged to the Jewish-Christian Working Group and the Council for Christians and Jews, as well as the Muslim/Christian Dialogue. Once I had spoken by invitation at the Victorian Inter-Faith Council. I had also led a multi-faith day at the national conference of the Australian Teachers' Christian Fellowship (featuring visits to an Orthodox church and a mosque) and had given the keynote address at the national association of private school chaplains, calling for enhanced respect for cultural diversity and attention to the specific needs of students from other faith backgrounds.

The Monash seminar represented the fulfilment of the ITEMS Project's commitment to foster relations between the faith communities as an aspect of the Victorian 150th Anniversary celebrations, and it was certainly the most ambitious initiative yet taken in that field. In Melbourne the Christian faith was the only one involved in the training of religious professionals. Hence the challenge of initiating a project that no other faith might have been expected to mount. But its aim was not theological (still less 'imperialistic') but *practical*: to strengthen community solidarity by increasing all the participants' awareness of other people's faith-commitments, and in particular to acquaint Christians with a sound understanding of the other faiths practised in Melbourne and counter some historically incorrect stereotypes. It was significant that it was the representatives of non-Christian faiths who proposed that Christians should provide the largest contingent of participants, since they were the 'host faith'—and their divisions all too well recognised from outside!

The Seminar program ultimately provided for three major sessions. In the first two of these, papers were presented by and on behalf of all six faiths, sharing concerns about the prospects of their children practising the faiths when they grew up in the Australian secular climate. Could we learn anything from each other that might help us identify aspects of each other's practice fruitful for our own endeavours?

In the mutually-owned Seminar project, all the faiths were responsible for presenting their position paper, providing a chairman for a segment of the program, and supplying appropriate food for the closing dinner (respecting the food taboos of all the other faiths!).

The Christian position paper on transmitting faith values to the next generation was presented by Rev. Dr Denham Grierson, leader of the Victorian Council for Christian Education.

Significantly, an evening session was devoted to Aboriginal spirituality and experience, led by the Aboriginal Research Centre at Monash University. All the faith groups joined in honouring the land's first peoples, implying that there can be no respect for religious values in a society where any cultural group is devalued or oppressed.

In a world of lethal, flawed technology the modest aim was to build mutual understanding leading to greater respect. Thus by mutual agreement, agendas about proselytising (even if sub-conscious) were to be excluded. Neither was there any real dialogue between faiths: that is, inviting representatives to explain what they believed and interpret it in terms meaningful to other faiths. That would need to be for another time and place, beyond the focus of this seminar on practical problems in transmitting faith traditions to a new generation shaped by Western materialism and sceptical about the 'big story'.

At the third session our keynote speaker was the Catholic sister, Dr Mary Hall, director of the Birmingham Multi-Faith Resource Centre whom I had met in England. The ITEMS Project was sponsoring her program in Australia, which included public and media engagements in Melbourne, Sydney and Perth. She recounted her UK experience of exploring common cause among people of the faiths in the face of racial & religious intolerance, and striving to build citizenship across the divisions—for the Seminar then to evaluate within the Melbourne scene. She stressed the wider range of common ground than might be imagined when the objectives were not competitive but collaborative, leading to shared action in seeking the common good in real-life community situations in Birmingham. Following her presentation the session was opened to general comment.

An enthusiastic outcome

Immediately I was struck by the positive responses and the enthusiasm engendered and evinced. Beyond the plenary sessions, structured cross-faith groups then discussed their understanding of the essential issues in transmitting faith to the new generation and sought common ground for future interaction. Even in this restricted sense the seminar proved a great success. Moreover it was hailed by all participants as an enriching experience. It was polite and civil all round because it didn't attempt too much. Who among Christians had ever participated in a formal public discussion of differences between Catholics and Protestants in regard to theology and practice, let alone between Christians and Muslims, or Jews and Buddhists? Indeed, it was likely that most of the participants would never have encountered practitioners of other faiths in a non-threatening civil setting, nor had an opportunity of sharing their personal insights into their own faith with outsiders. Hence its chief accomplishment was simply to have brought people face-to-face across so many differences.

Such was the interest generated that ABC Radio's Division of Religious Programmes attended and recorded the whole proceedings, which led to a later programme broadcast nationally. Letters subsequently received about the value of the seminar included from the Anglican and Catholic Archbishops, the Jewish and Hindu communities and the Religious Studies Division of La Trobe University.

In the closing session the first recommendation put forward by the consultative process was that the momentum from such a stimulating encounter should not be lost, to become just a pleasant dream or a passing whim. An interim committee was set up to explore ways of stimulating further contacts between the faith communities. I was asked to be the co-ordinator of the process.

But a familiar ambivalence

Immediately I found myself in a quandary. Over the past twelve years or more my whole public activity had been focused on concepts of culture, not religion. Whereas culture was in the public realm, open to debate and discussion, religion had been held to be a private matter. Yet in the real world religion and culture are inseparable. As a Melbourne Archbishop once observed, "All values claim either a religious foundation or are held with religious zeal."[12] Indeed many Christians (and doubtless people of other faiths too) would define their identity more by reference to their faith than their citizenship or their ethnicity. This because the nub of their existence is bound up with their relationship with divinity, however conceived. Who would make so bold as to separate out the religious from the cultural elements: what is the pearl and what the oyster shell? For instance, what are the cultural and what are the religious elements of Aboriginal spirituality?

On the other hand there were understandable reasons why public policy had stood aloof from the issue of religious pluralism. Across much of the world religion is perceived as rather a curse than a blessing: religion, politics and race is a volatile cocktail. Yet if the religious dimension were to be publicly ignored in Australia, we would restrict the freedom (at the heart of multiculturalism) to enjoy one's heritage and identity in a new land while resisting the dehumanising pressures of Western secular conformity. Surely at its deepest, multiculturalism must be a free movement of the spirit.

So without great enthusiasm I accepted the invitation to explore future possibilities of developing an inter-faith network. And this with a limited focus, falling far short of promoting ongoing dialogue between the faiths. Frankly I wasn't much interested in such a grandiose vision. But there were elements within the VCC Commission on Community and Race Relations (sponsor of the ITEMS Project for the Victorian 150th) that were pushing hard for this new initiative. Indeed before

---

12   *The Age*, Melbourne, 28.11.1988

long the name of the Commission was to be changed to Commission on Living Faiths & Community Relations which appeared to make its *raison d'être* a brief for developing inter-faith dialogue. But that is to jump ahead by several years.

Study-group materials

The final commitment under the ITEMS Project was to produce a set of small-group study materials for use in spreading the multicultural word around the parishes and across the Anglo Christian community. Given the demanding pressures of the more publicly-oriented activity I had had to leave this until fairly late in the 20-month period. Finally I decided to engage an agent to undertake the task and pay for his services from the ITEMS budget. A friend from the Ecumenical Migration Centre with whom I had spent a good deal of time since we both came to Melbourne, and who possessed admirable competence in the wide lore required, agreed to do the task. Together we sketched out the ground to be covered and the approach to be taken. But alas! It was not to be. Despite our investing a deal of finance in the task and working closely together in defining it, my friend was not able to deliver the goods and at the close of the ITEMS period we had to acknowledge defeat. It left a nasty taste in my mouth.

On the other hand the project as a whole had attained signal success, making a historic impact on strategic quarters within the Melbourne theological scene through the multicultural course—and even beyond through *The Cultured Pearl*. It also led to the coalescing and emergence of a 'multicultural coterie' spanning the Melbourne denominations (and wider than the formal ecumenical movement) which in the next few years would become established as the 'Churches Cross-Cultural Network' convening many training seminars and inspirational encounters. Beyond that it would spawn the Melbourne Multi-Faith Resource Centre.

Near the end of 1985 when I handed in my remit to the Victorian Council of Churches, with my final report on the ITEMS Project and an account of it all to the Victorian Government's 150th Anniversary Committee, it was with a warm glow of 'mission accomplished'—and a deep gratitude to the Lord who had inspired, energised and consummated the whole initiative. Certainly our own lives would be forever recast.

10
Surveying the Broad Meadows

Scarcely had I ever set foot in AIMA's charming heritage building on upper Queen Street, a three-storey Georgian mansion faithfully restored and tastefully refurbished for its use, since as part of the 1983 Enquiry team I had been deemed a foe. Now become an insider through the outworking of poetic justice I had a desk and access to stenographers, (invariably) women skilled in typing and shorthand and by 1986 moving into the new field of computing. From there I drafted my introductory letter to be sent widely around the Broadmeadows community, introducing our study and soliciting support for my forthcoming visits. It went to the ethnic community leaders, social workers in community-based agencies, secondary school leaders and counsellors, clergy and imams, field staff of the local City Council and elected Councillors, and to the area's State and federal politicians.

Field HQ for the study would be the Migrant Resource Centre at Glenroy, operating under the charter outlined in the Galbally Report on *Migrant Services and Programs* and facilitating interaction between migrants from myriad backgrounds and locals, while serving community needs. The staff were my closest allies. Coincidentally, during the three months of the study the MRC relocated from Glenroy to Olsen Place, in archetypal Broadmeadows—failed shops locked and barred, overweight women and work-injured men hanging around the central concourse of cracked concrete where the garden-boxes grew cans and cigarette packets. Broadmeadows held the lowest socio-economic rating in all of Australia. In 2014 that unenviable distinction was still held by Dallas, the next suburb, three kilometres north of Olsen Place, and destined to be our focus of ministry.

Melbourne's northern fringe

Since the 1840s a sparsely populated rural area 16km north of Melbourne, the Broadmeadows district had been closely settled in the early 1950s, originally through slum clearances from the inner-city and then in the late '50s when cheap, low-quality workers' housing had been built for the mostly-migrant workforce of the new Ford motor works at nearby Upfield and Campbellfield. Many were British, though later intakes reflected the complete range of unskilled migrants. These included many from Turkey, though contrary to the terms of the Migration Agreement signed with that country guaranteeing skilled workers, they proved to be all unskilled and almost all from remote rural parts of Turkey—and often Kurds. It was the first (and last) Migration Agreement signed with a Muslim-majority nation. We were taken in.

My field research was to prove an unrivalled means of getting to know Broadmeadows closely, in its physical character, its economic structure and its social composition. Its location is unprepossessing, built on featureless basaltic plains (apart from the deep twisting trench of Moonee Ponds Creek), rock-hard in summer and a quagmire in winter. Its natural vegetation had been lank grassland with sparse and stunted eucalypts, occasionally interspersed with small waterholes. So attempts to develop 'normal' suburban gardens had mostly proven thankless. Hence the bleak character of the streets of small monocrete boxes, almost invariably unrelieved by greenery. Street plantings had either languished or been put out of their misery through vandalism. This depressing aspect seemed somehow to be reflected in the marginal status of the bulk of the population, either 'oldcomers' relocated from the slums of Collingwood and Abbotsford or else newcomers from many lands with little education, often illiterate women, and with minimal aspirations

An ethnic focus

Of particular interest for the AIMA study was the ethnic component, some 33% of the 10,000 population being born in non-English-speaking countries (i.e. not counting their children) and drawn from a wide range of backgrounds—but primarily Turkish/Kurdish and Arabic. It was (and still is) the largest Turkish community in Australia, with three mosques serving these and some other Muslims. By 2012 Dallas had a 45% Muslim population, with the newer area of Meadow Heights at 42%, and the suburb of Broadmeadows approaching one third[13].

Many of the migrants had originally intended to return home (like their 'guestworker' confrères in Germany) after capitalising on the opportunities of unskilled factory work, unknown in eastern Turkey or other pre-industrial societies. But few made the break, staying on dreaming. Sadly, there was a high rate of industrial accident victims, many injured through their inexperience of industrial machinery but trapped here through the inaccessibility of social services back in their homelands. Other significant ethnic groups were Lebanese, Iraqis and Syrians (some of them Christian: there is a Syrian Orthodox Church in Westmeadows), Vietnamese, Latin Americans and Pacific Islanders. Almost a quarter of the people in Broadmeadows professed a non-Christian faith, by far the largest group Muslims. The nominally Christian had almost no affiliation with the churches.

The study required a constant balancing of the data gathered from within the ethnic communities (consumers of services) on the one hand and from the providers of the services—social workers, community developers, interpreters, liaison people, teachers, religious leaders—on the other, in seeking to establish realistic and credible findings. While the bilingual welfare workers proved to be the most authentic respondents they too had to be viewed within their own ethnic context: of course they could not be value-free and were sometimes controversial. Hence the challenge was to draw sound and objective conclusions from all the evidence available through necessarily applying one's professional judgment.

13   *Herald Sun*, Melbourne, 27.6.2012

Portending the future

For me one of the most significant interviews turned out to be with a future colleague, the long-term Anglican vicar of Dallas, Rev Harry Kerr, publicly involved with community welfare agencies and from his Ulster background also a peace activist. St Mary Magdalene's church was an unprepossessing building of unpainted besser blocks set starkly on a bare corner paddock on a main industrial route out of Melbourne.

As we sat in his lounge room, discussing his views on the many unmet needs in Broadmeadows—interrupted every ten minutes by a jet airliner passing a few hundred feet overhead on its final landing approach to Melbourne Airport—I had no inkling that it was destined ere long to become our own home, and that for seven years!

Broadmeadows—a researcher's paradise!

What did the study bring forth? Firstly, the wry discovery that Broadmeadows was arguably the most-researched area of Melbourne. Such was its long-term reputation, that a large number of social agencies, government departments, and individual academic researchers had examined the context and identified the mismatch between the unique blend of socio-cultural groups in the area and the services provided to meet their needs—and even then mostly after many years of open neglect. But despite all this penetrating study, little seemed to have changed on the ground. Perhaps it was all too hard. Or too late: it had gone on for too long and problem issues had become too entrenched. Of course there was one feasible solution: actually make funds available more generously to address the hard core intractable problems. But this had never been tried, for obvious political reasons: conservative governments would have obtained no political traction since so few locals would ever be so grateful as to vote for them, while Labor governments did not need to improve services out of fear of losing votes. Politically, the people had nowhere to go. They were not even pawns in other people's political games, but classically disempowered, reminiscent of the Third World poor.

The high proportion of people with intractable problems was a depressing feature of all the field studies: basically, poor outcomes of schooling were projected into adult life in a poor sense of self-esteem or confidence, resulting in a lack of employable skills. Of course ignoring the life-changing power of education is a sure way of perpetuating disadvantage. Moreover all too seldom were stable homes encountered based on stable marriages between two coping people. Child neglect was not uncommon, and the aspirations of youth low, with truancy a factor in dropping out of school often before the minimum leaving age.

Paid work for such young people was scarcely available, especially in times of economic downturn, so that in the years immediately before my survey, youth gangs had become a feature, widely reported in the Melbourne media, adding to the sense of siege and truculence. The 'Broady Boys' were known to slug it out on the streets at night with gangs like the 'Anzacs' and 'Young Turks'. On the other hand at that time drugs hardly seemed an issue, doubtless because cost put them out of range. But a sense of malaise seemed to pervade the community—a self-perception of inferiority, lack of worth and powerlessness, a sort of loser mentality sapping initiative and confidence.

Even the physical features of the district were soul-destroying: graffiti everywhere, litter uncollected, the few parks practically bereft of trees and shrubs (often vandalised). I came to envisage the Broadmeadows 'coat of arms' as featuring a stylised barbed wire fence draped with plastic bags blowing in the winds which unimpeded, swept across the dreary plains, searing in summer and bitter in winter.

A cloying cynicism

Report after report, the same old issues were addressed by enthusiastic analysts (like me), naïvely offering thoughtful, practical and even innovative proposals, but all destined to wind up in the archives, gathering dust. Cynicism was the main local product of the process. Such were the explanations offered me by a range of professionals attached to the community agencies.

With the AIMA study, the saving grace was that it did not portend to offer any new solutions to specifically local problem issues, but in a wider sense to take the temperature of inter-group relations in an intensely multicultural area, in the hope of gaining creative insights for application throughout the country. Beyond that, it was concerned with examining how the civil society could address the specific issues raised by ethnicity, since by 1986 it was clear that Australia could never again be a basically monocultural or monolingual country. And as I had experienced myself on my overseas study tour, no other country provided a blueprint for Australia, so different were the historical, social and political factors in the Great Southland.

Actually it was becoming clear that the civil society barely functioned in Broadmeadows, since community volunteering was thin indeed and virtually the whole welfare workforce drove in from outside—and hence would not often be available for evening consultative meetings. Besides, turnover rates were high. Mostly not having grown up in the outer northern suburbs, community workers had little real 'feel' for the place and before long the temptation of more genteel jobs in the south and east took its toll. An ABC radio journalist well known for creating probing social documentaries would later confide to me that she had *"never set foot west of Sydney Road"*! Who then was willing to identify with these people?

Sadly the locals were all too aware of the scant respect that their suburb commanded in the eyes of Melbournians. The stigma of Broadmeadows seemed to triumph every time. The local Uniting Church minister told me that when his daughter gave a city department store her address, her credit card was declined. In one of the community houses a local activist, Linda Blundell, was employed fulltime seeking to rescue people from the outcomes of a scam shamelessly perpetrated on gullible local residents years earlier by the mail-order house Waltons (linked with

Walmart, the giant American superstore chain). Later she was to be elected Mayor of Broadmeadows, and is now commemorated by a park in Dallas.

The City of Broadmeadows was the poor relation of Melbourne local government councils. With its featureless plains its area was as industrial as residential, with the vast Ford works, Dunlop Tyres, Erickson's Australian headquarters, Nabisco biscuits, Yakka overalls, Hoadley's chocolates, Visyboard, Rocla pipes, Commonwealth Serum Laboratories and dozens of well- and lesser-known factories and warehouses. The Army Camp dated back to training the original diggers for Gallipoli and Flanders, and later for the second world war, and even till now functioned as Maygar Barracks.

In the 1960s sections of the camp had been designated as the Broadmeadows Migrant Hostel, where a generation of British migrants would find their original shelter. Early post-war residential suburbs like Glenroy, Oak Park and central Broadmeadows had been matched in the 70s and 80s by new mass-produced Housing Commission areas of Meadowfair North, Dallas, Coolaroo and Coolaroo West, and Westmeadows. Inexplicably, the physical characteristic of Broadmeadows City centre was a donut with great tracts of undeveloped land at its heart, except for the stark brick Council headquarters and town hall beside a new single-storey shopping plaza. The terminus of the electric railway was insignificant, though at night featuring stabled trains defended by barbed-wire entanglements (complete with flapping plastic bags caught on the barbs). Railway tracks, freeways, trunk roads and high tension power lines fractured the landscape and divided communities. From my outsider's perspective the whole district was aesthetically a nightmare, soul-destroying. My experience of growing up on the wrong side of the tracks in Sydney, then of living in country NSW, followed by exposure to life in devastated but rehabilitated urban centres west and east of the Iron Curtain had ill prepared me for such a preposterous human experiment.

Training ground for ministry

However at the level of human relations, one of my most frank and fruitful interviews was held at the Council offices with a community liaison officer, Alan Aylward, with a heart of gold who proved a veritable mine of information. While an astute observer through the many vicissitudes, including the Council's inept policies, he had remained deeply identified with the people, living locally. Later he and his wife Gwenda would rank among our closest associates and mentors.

But of course my report to AIMA on the civic relations in Broadmeadows contained no hint that I would ever set foot in the area again once my three-month employment contract was fulfilled. Such a thought never entered my head: how could it? So the report was duly lodged and acknowledged, and with that I completed my 20 years in the Commonwealth Public Service. The terms of my pay-out were a lump sum of $59,000 and accessing a Superannuation Pension at the rate of approximately one third of my final salary of 1983, then some $40,000. (But around that time I would encounter reports of lump-sum payments made to senior administrators in the State service of up to $200,000.)

That evening as I reported in to the family at Rosanna, not only did I feel no qualms about severing myself from a safe if dull future but rather a sense of euphoria at the high adventure looming beyond the opening portals.

"I have set before you an open door which no man may close" (Revelation 3:8).

11
Family Fortunes

And what of the home front? About mid-1984 the family had welcomed Nicholas home from Tiffin, Ohio with his final school year in America behind him. His rejoining the family, in his absence transplanted to Eltham, was marked symbolically by his leaping bodily (like an AFL player) through a paper curtain pasted up all around our front doorway, boldly proclaiming *'Welcome home Flying Kangaroo'*.

But it seemed his experience of the international student exchange had proven rather ambivalent because his host family had declined my request that he be enrolled at a public high school, insisting that he should attend the small Catholic college with its restricted curriculum and social life. Generous (since they paid) but manipulative—how we regretted our acquiescence later, though at the time it was made clear that Nick would have to find another family. Some positive highlights of his year had included flying over Tiffin in the light plane owned and piloted by the father, who owned a furniture store; a clandestine nocturnal escapade to the Canadian border by a car-ful of youths; and heroic deeds in his first inter-school gridiron game when his soccer skills led to the winning goal and subsequent presentation of the full kit of protective gear as a souvenir to bring home. His photo in it with an article entitled 'Gridiron Nick' appeared on the front page of our local paper, the *Diamond Valley Leader*.

Pending entry into tertiary studies he located a job in the city selling opals to wealthy Japanese tourists, and later as a labourer in a steel fabrication plant in Greensborough, while I took up the cudgels with the tertiary education authorities to seek recognition of his American results for entry into Melbourne University. A laborious process: it would prove too late for the 1985 intake.

A holy moment with three sons

Come Sunday morning the family would all troop down to St Margaret's for the Sung Eucharist, so utterly divergent from the O'Connor worship service. We all came to appreciate the stately measure of the liturgy and appreciated its predictability. The people had taken us to heart and vicar Ron Dowling exercised a caring pastoral ministry. But once when we mentioned that the boys had not been baptised (since we had never considered infant baptism to be demonstrably scriptural, unlike the baptism of adult converts), in puzzlement he queried why then did they receive the elements in Holy Communion? That's for church members! The upshot was that all three agreed to do a short course for church membership, and at the midnight Easter Vigil at St Margaret's Eltham in 1985, in the presence of Archbishop David

Penman, all three were baptised by the Vicar and then confirmed by the Archbishop. For us parents, one of the highest and holiest moments of our 29 year marriage.

Nick's European ramblings

After Easter we farewelled Nick, still smarting from the disappointments of his American year and smitten by the urge for independent travel, as he headed off alone to Europe. Initially to Germany, where I had arranged for him to work as a volunteer in a German Methodist youth home at Timmendorfer Strand on the shores of the Baltic Sea 20km from the historic Hanseatic city of Lübeck not far from the northern end of the Iron Curtain. This was facilitated by Karin Recknagel, niece of the Gresslers in Minden, who worked in the Methodist Church HQ in Hamburg. Nick joined young German volunteers opting for civil service instead of military training in maintaining the property and the garden, but with generous free time to explore the region: cycling to organ recitals in Lübeck's mediaeval brick cathedral, to Berlin by train, hitch-hiking—in his father's tradition—to Hamburg and southern parts of Sweden and Norway. He recounts one bright summer morning waiting for a ride for two hours near the Norwegian/Swedish border on a highway quite devoid of traffic. Only after some time did he realise it was still only five o'clock. Deluded by the near-midnight sun he had been hitch-hiking vainly since 3am!

After summer he went on to the UK and stayed for five months in Nottingham with a former team mate from the Canberra Arrows national youth soccer squad, a returned British migrant now become a political activist organising against the Thatcher Government's attacks on civil society. Nick was happy to join the cause and together they were involved in major street demonstrations in Nottingham, Blackpool and London. It was his blooding for a life-commitment to the struggle of ordinary people against corporate greed and self-serving vested interests backed by powerful party machines drawing on wealth and status. His place in the national economy was delivering Indian take-aways and again he hitch-hiked widely around the north of England, severely constrained by lack of funds though acquiring a nodding acquaintance with grassroots economics.

Household of study

Early in 1986 he would rejoin the family at Eltham. My representations with Melbourne University were ultimately to prove successful, enabling his acceptance into the Faculty of Arts for the 1986 academic year, transferring to Law in 1989. Proudly, we would all attend his Arts/Law graduation ceremony in the Wilson Hall in 1992. About that time he brought off the epic feat of riding his bike from Sydney to Melbourne with a university friend from the Student Christian Movement, almost entirely using back-country trails through national parks and along the Great Divide, through the Monaro to the Victorian coast and even across French Island in the middle of Westernport Bay to the Mornington Peninsula and then by ferry across the mouth of Port Phillip Bay to the Surf Coast and the Otways. An intrepid if circuitous route home. (Over twenty years later our sons Chris and David would participate in the gruelling Great Victorian Bike Ride through the NE high country in summer heat with our first grandchild Raphael, 15).

Living with us at Eltham in 1985 were David, doing Year 10 at Donvale Christian School, and Christopher and his student friend Darren, both engrossed in their Arts courses at La Trobe. as well as making their contribution to the Student Christian Movement. International students (mostly ethnic Chinese) were now appearing in larger numbers at Australian universities, some of them Christians who launched an international fellowship. By his excellent results Chris was fortunate in attracting the interest and academic mentoring of some key staff, later moving into advanced anthropology. At one point he stood for the university's Student Council.

Darren was completing his Honours thesis in sociology. He had bought an elderly and bronchitic Toyota Crown, which he lovingly fiddled with at weekends. On one memorable occasion, with it facing downhill, its brakes relaxed and it took off for the street running behind our block, with a drop of two metres awaiting. With a dextrous leap Darren managed to dive on the handbrake and thwart nature, on the very brink.

At this period Sara-Jane, using her UK passport as a born citizen, was on a working holiday in England and requested parental funding support to undertake a short, intensive course in Teaching English as a Second Language, under the auspices of Cambridge University. It was to prove a strategic moment for her, marking the transition from a rather 'rolling stone' existence over several years to the launch of the professional career in adult migrant education that she has pursued ever since. The following year she would commence tertiary studies under a provisional entry arrangement for mature-age students at Macquarie University in Sydney—on passing all first-year subjects you could qualify for retrospective matriculation. Gallantly I offered to help her with her first tertiary-level essay, on the Aztecs, and made a sizeable contribution to it. Never again would she get such a mediocre grade for an assignment!

Meantime for me every day brought its stretching challenge. But God was in his heaven and it was good to be alive.

12
The Year of Living Dubiously

Pivotal year 1986, opening up prospects of a definitive move towards my third profession, beyond language-teaching and community education: the Christian ministry. But not without misgivings. In early 1986, with my two years' leave without pay from the Public Service in Canberra almost spent, the ITEMS project moving towards completion, and the lease of our Eltham house running out, an uncertain future was looming. Adventure past, was it time to slink back to Canberra—though all three boys were now rooted in Melbourne? Of course I still had a position in the Public Service, but what of my earlier sense of a purpose unfolding? (Hadn't I responded to our Canberra friends farewelling us for two years with a "Yes... maybe"?) But what if I'd only imagined an ultimate purpose? Or if it had become derailed? In times of perplexity...

> "E'en though I walk through death's dark vale,
> yet will I fear none ill, for Thou art with me,
> and Thy rod and staff me comfort still".[14]

Life-changing conversation

Before having time to nurture such gnawing doubts, I experienced the subtle nudge of the Shepherd's staff, perhaps in an unlikely setting. One afternoon standing on the kerbside in Flinders Street before the building where the VCC then had its offices, and chatting with Helen Hunter, the benefactor who had brought me to Melbourne, I was to receive the message from Archbishop David Penman that if I wished to stay on he would like me to work with him. Heart ablaze, it took all of five seconds to ponder the prospect before comfortably settling into a berth on Cloud Nine. No other way would I have been able to contemplate staying on in Melbourne. Once again I discerned the pattern of surprising grace familiar from previous life-shaping moments: knowing how temperamentally averse I was to defining what I wanted and then vigorously pursuing it, the loving Father had again confronted me with unsought prospects of joy: *'This is the way; walk in it'*[15]. How then could I turn away?

With my loving family in agreement on the prospect of the new adventure, I called again at 'Bishopscourt' and the Archbishop outlined his concern for the wellbeing of minority groups and his enthusiasm for the Federal Government's policy of multiculturalism. Since publicly taking this stand he was being regularly approached by the media for comment on specific issues cropping up, but of

---

| 14 | From the universal favourite, the 23rd Psalm commencing *"The Lord is my shepherd"* in the metrical version for congregational singing from the Scottish Psalter |
| 15 | Isaiah 30:21 |

course this had to be kept in balance with his over-riding vocation of leadership of the Melbourne Diocese. So he needed a readily available advisor and asked whether I would be willing to 'become his minder' in this field? For ready access, we would be able to live in the apartment attached to his 'Bishopscourt' palace at East Melbourne when it became available.

Meanwhile he indicated that he was contactable daily until midnight (implying the prospects of my being approached for comment during such hours). Indeed, in the next few weeks I did receive such late calls, resulting in my preparing briefing notes for his engagements and writing a keynote paper for him to present at a significant public conference. His public profile was becoming such that when the new Hawke Labor Government decided not to abolish the Australian Institute of Multicultural Affairs (in the review of which I had participated significantly two years earlier) but to restructure it more democratically, David Penman was appointed as its Chairman. Earlier Helen Hunter and I had visited him at 'Bishopscourt' to suggest he nominate for the publicly advertised post.

(Phone) call to ministry

Quite late one night I received a call from the Archbishop, explaining that he was under pressure from his adversaries in the Diocese (his election had swung the balance for a time in the direction of the 'liberal evangelicals', as he identified himself). One objection was to his recruiting people into significant positions who were 'not even Anglicans'. I suspect I was not the only one in their sights. His reaction to the criticism was typically feisty: would I mind if he ordained me? (Then I would be a 'proper Anglican'.) Would I *mind*? Had I heard aright? *Ordained*? I had never heard of anybody being ordained by invitation of the church hierarchy—though later in my Church History studies I was to learn that in earlier times it was not at all unusual, e.g. St Ambrose had been so invited and in one week had segued from Chief Magistrate of Rome to deacon, to priest, and to Bishop! Would I come to 'Bishopscourt' to see him next day?

Before the meeting I contacted a leading Uniting Church theological educator well known to me[16] to ask him, in the light of the Archbishop's invitation, whether ordination in the Uniting Church was a possibility. Sadly he replied, "I wish it were, but you would be over the maximum age for entry". Door slammed, closed.

Next morning to my objection that it would be odd for a Methodist layman to become an Anglican minister, the Archbishop not unreasonably reminded me that John and Charles Wesley, viewed as founders of the Methodist Church, had lived and died as good Anglican clergy. Disarmed. He went on to discuss where and how much theological training I should undertake, suggesting that it need not necessarily amount to a complete degree but would at least need to cover Christology, Old and New Testament, and Anglican Liturgy. I could sit in on

---

16   During the past two years in Melbourne I had been a member of the Uniting Church Synod's Committee on Immigration Matters, comprising clergy and laity, several from ethnic congregations of the Church.

lectures in these (and other) subjects without necessarily doing the full year's study and examinations. My (polite) response was that, if I were to become an Anglican priest, I would want to be a proper one. The Archbishop observed that the Diocese was 'littered with' half-baked clergy who had never fulfilled glib promises to complete studies after being ordained. I replied that he didn't know me: there was no way I wouldn't revel in the privilege of returning to study late in life, and would complete the task with delight.

Since by then I knew the Melbourne theological world well enough I suggested studying not at Ridley College (the evangelical seminary) but at Trinity College with its 'broad church' emphasis and liturgical tradition. In my (ignorant and vainglorious) estimation I claimed I had a good grip on evangelical theology from my Evangelical Union days at Sydney University and lifelong membership of the Methodist (later Uniting) Church. The Archbishop was gracious enough to allow me the choice, adding that as a newcomer to Anglicanism in later life, I would certainly get a better feel for liturgy at Trinity College and develop greater confidence in conducting worship services.

Acquiring a new home base

But as time passed and there was no further mention of moving into the 'Bishopscourt' apartment, the question was, where would we live? We had a house in Canberra—our underlying financial security—and for the past two years it had served as base for a residential Christian community connected with O'Connor Uniting Church. To sell it would seem a rather wanton act, ahead of its time, since our future was only just beginning to evolve. Then I suffered a rush of blood to the head: because paying rent for a house lease seemed a futile exercise, we'd *buy* another house! The thought was father to the deed. Brandishing the deeds of Moss St, Cook as security, we raised a sizeable bank loan and bought from a big Catholic family their large, tasteless timber home in Berrima Road, Rosanna, long languishing on the flat property market—no wonder, since it was the era of extreme interest rates reflecting the 1983 recession, of which we were hardly aware, so preoccupied had we been with our challenging new life in Melbourne. Heedlessly, unaware of property loans in general, we signed a contract to pay 16% interest—*16%!*—a bonanza for the bank! Instalments were met from the rental paid by the Moss St Christian community plus Marjorie's social worker's salary at the Preston office of the Social Security Department. It was a viable arrangement and the house proved a great base—but only for the next 18 months.

Early on there Christopher, beginning the third year of his Arts degree at La Trobe University, announced his intention of marrying Yvonne Kelley whom he had met three years earlier as fellow-resident of a Uniting Church community house in Adelaide where he had spent a gap year, also doing an introductory theology course. The wedding was a great milestone in our family life. With Fr Ron's agreement, the text of the wedding service at St Margaret's Eltham (where we were still parishioners) was partly written by the couple themselves and afterwards the occasion was celebrated in the mudbrick parish hall. We took our first daughter-in-law very much to heart. They set up home in Pascoe Vale, leaving Nicholas, soon to begin his Arts degree at Melbourne University and David transferring from Donvale Christian School to East Rosanna High, holding the fort with us, ably supported by black Angus. One painful memory from this time was of slipping on wet grass one evening when putting out the milk bottles and falling heavily, bottle in hand, on a bluestone garden rock. With my right hand running in blood I was driven off to the nearby Austin Hospital for needlework which failed to address the damaged nerves. It would take all of the next 25 years for the nerves along three fingers of my right hand to gradually redevelop alternative paths conferring normal feeling out of the numbness.

'You're a bloody idiot!'

After receiving my final stipend under the ITEMS Project I called the Department of Immigration in Canberra and boldly told the pay clerk to work out my entitlements. I was resigning. He cavilled at the suggestion but I stood my ground. (*'The gifts and calling of God are without repentance'*)[17] Even more boldly he expostulated, *"You're a bloody idiot!"* Including the last two years of leave without pay, I had served for nineteen and three-quarter years. With 20 years I would be able to claim the full pay-out of my superannuation contributions plus the employer's component, payable either as a lump sum or as a (modest) pension for life—or even as a combination of the two. A long silence, before I stammered, *"OK, I'll think about it"*.

How gracious of God, not only to make accessing these entitlements possible but to provide robust advice at the crucial moment. I needed to be shocked out of my manic hyperactivity. Even if I felt (maybe for 10 seconds?) that it might detract from the heroism of my new commitment, common sense dictated that, with a considerable period likely to elapse before being on a parish payroll and while still responsible for maintaining a family through expensive years to come, proper attention needed to be given to the financial considerations. Once again the practical God had provided, and to this day the major source of our income is my superannuation pension. Even more remarkable that I also qualified for a small lump sum (tiny by contemporary standards) but which, under the sound advice given by a Christian financial counsellor, has grown over the years into a legacy for the next generation, despite losses sustained during the Global Financial Crisis of 2008.

Advent of globalisation and neo-liberalism

Back in 1986 the immediate hurdle remained of how to bring up the crucial 20 years of service in order to qualify for early retirement. It wasn't the best time to be seeking a new Public Service placement because we were on the cusp of the era when the 'economic rationalist' policies inspired by Margaret Thatcher in the

---

17   Romans 11:29

UK were starting to be aped by governments around the English-speaking world cutting staff and 'rationalising'.

In Victoria before long the redoubtable Jeff Kennett would go further than any other Australian head of government, laying waste the Public Service and public utilities, closing hundreds of schools and sacking 10,000 professional teachers alone! There would follow bargain basement sales of railways, tramways, bus services, electricity and gas supplies, banks, insurance companies, even prisons, and at the national level whole areas of the Public Service such as telephone services, airports, the Public Works Department, the Commonwealth Employment Service, the Commonwealth Serum Laboratories, the largest Health Insurance provider in the country, and even the worldwide migrant selection arm of the Immigration Department—in short, the most essential service instrumentalities owned from the outset by the people of Australia would be sold off by temporary political leaders (as though they were theirs to profit from, like the *apparatchiks* would do in Russia after the fall of Communism)—sold off to the highest bidders among the clamouring financiers and overseas interests such as the Singapore *Government*. The expertise and continuity of service long acquired by the Australian public agencies was being hollowed out to suit the shallow fad of the moment. Moreover the naïve assurances that heightened competitiveness would now bring prices down proved to be 100% false: the opposite has been the outcome. Later experience would demonstrate that the inevitable outcome of privatisation is avaricious monopolies that make us all pay more to ensure their soaring profits, for instance the airports.

To the modish catchcry of *"What right has the state to be running businesses?"* the equally vacuous response should have been, *"And why not?"* The claims that private enterprise could do everything better were soon experienced as simply untrue: invariably costs to the users went up while quality of service and accountability went down—how else could a public utility be made into a profit-making business? The grim answer turned out to be, 'By getting rid of large numbers of staff and making the rest work harder', perhaps by multi-skilling the workforce and introducing electronic devices—the computer age had arrived!

Moreover, in many cases after a public asset had been privatised, it would then be on-sold to an overseas company that had even less concept of social responsibility, cf. the rail freight services. Alternatively, two or three giant corporations would collude to create a cartel holding the public to ransom, for example in the supply of electricity, whereby the whole nation would end up paying inflated prices to offset the number of customers deserting in favour of alternative sources of energy: solar, wind, etc. All round, it has been the ordinary people of Australia who have lost out from the boardroom antics that have debased the sense of community. The people have been the losers: non-human corporatism swallowing up the civil society.

So before long our greatest export would turn out to be *jobs*, as whole industries (for instance the clothing and footwear industries in the inner north of Melbourne) closed under the flood of imports produced by sweated labour reflecting the advent of globalisation, and in the more distant future our entire car-building capacity was destined to be destroyed without trace. It would also turn out that a further new factor had come into play: some of the new private suppliers of employment services were corruptly lining their own pockets from public funds. Enter the profit motive into an area of public service... A sorry new casualty: the loss of integrity. The world had turned!

In the Public Services in the States and in Canberra a common stratagem now was 'downsizing' the staff, mostly by offering 'redundancy packages', especially to older workers, to induce departures on the grounds that if declined, the alternative might turn out to be simply dismissal, since the concept of permanency was being reworked. Indeed a large proportion of the lesser-paid workforce now became casualised, losing access to the hard-won benefits gained through union struggles since the second world war. In particular, thousands of people in their fifties and beyond were thrown onto the labour market with scant hope of finding alternative jobs, and of course wage levels were much depressed by the process. Had we not come to Melbourne in 1984, it is quite conceivable that two years later, at the age of 54 and rendered redundant by the demise of Al Grassby's Community Relations Office and not gaining a position in the fledgling Human Rights Commission—and perhaps also being *persona non grata* to the Immigration Department—I might have found myself relegated to 'growing tomatoes down the South Coast' for the rest of my days (doubtless shortened by lack of motivation). But who knows: maybe this is just evoking the dismal 'glass half-empty' syndrome?

Be that as it may, in this developing climate where time-honoured practices were being overturned willy-nilly, my prospects of locating a position for three months in an area where I had something to offer would have been slim indeed. Impaled on the horns of the dilemma, I would have been obliged either to go back to Canberra and throw myself on the mercies of the mandarins, or stay with the family in Melbourne (where I was hardly known to the Immigration Department, let alone elsewhere in the Public Service), and try to pick up something. Bleak prospects, both of them.

A timely provision

Again the all-wise Shepherd came to the rescue of the bemused sheep: Helen Hunter, head of Anglican cross-cultural ministry based in the Cathedral buildings, mentioned my situation to Archbishop Penman, whose role as Chairman of AIMA brought him into contact with the Institute's current work projects. The timing was critical: AIMA had just decided to undertake a study of a Melbourne suburban area known for its concentration of immigrants from non-English-speaking backgrounds. After a preliminary survey the City of Broadmeadows had been selected over Dandenong, and the project involved examining the role of the civil society in creating social wellbeing within a culturally diverse setting.

I was interviewed by the Acting Director of AIMA, who offered me a temporary post as senior research officer responsible for completing the project within three months. By the end of that period the 1986 academic year in the theological seminaries would be under way. While the timing of the project worked perfectly, it is certainly arguable that I was quite the best-qualified researcher available by virtue of my study of ethnic organisations in Melbourne, recently supplemented by becoming conversant with the non-Christian faiths and beyond that, my familiarity with field research techniques, data analysis and report writing. Of course the irony was not lost on me that, having been responsible for the nationwide field research consultations during the damning Parliamentary Enquiry into AIMA, I would now be contributing to its new incarnation as a community-responsive agency under a Labor government.

The moving finger writes, and having writ, moves on.

13
Grappling with Theology

*"Study to win God's full approval, as a worker not ashamed of
his work, correctly teaching the way of truth." (2 Timothy 2:15).*

In the second week of first term 1986 when I belatedly joined the classes in the United Faculty of Theology within Melbourne University it was to rediscover a half-forgotten world. Established in 1853, barely three years later than my Alma Mater of Sydney, Melbourne University rates higher in contemporary world rankings[18], in student numbers and in financial endowment. Its Latin motto translated '*I shall grow in the esteem of posterity*' was to prove strikingly prophetic.

Melbourne's most dignified quarter

Sharing the late-Victorian dignity of Parkville on the northern edge of the city, the university is flanked by grand boulevards lined with over-arching elms, gloriously green and gold in season. Although the campus is now a farrago[19] of architectural styles, the original sandstone Gothic survives in the cloistered Old Arts building but more particularly throughout the ecclesiastical sector beyond Tin Alley, the line of demarcation. While humanistic learning went unchallenged on the secular campus to one side, in the larger religious sector the Churches built monumental residential/theological colleges of architectural note, spaced in generous grounds. A serene ambiance reigns: Trinity College (Anglican) the oldest and largest, Queen's College (Presbyterian) perhaps grandest with lecture rooms in its broad tower, the solid granite pile of Ormond College (originally Methodist) graced by its charming springtime garden yet also boasting a contemporary circular residential tower. All of them offset by the shockingly avant-garde creation of Walter Burley Griffin's (Catholic) Newman College, *circa* 1918. Discreetly tucked away around the periphery are the redbrick women's colleges: St Mary's, St Hilda's, Janet Clarke Hall and University College, in recent years all of them gone co-ed.

The theological classes were physically strewn among the men's Colleges, taught by scholars from the three contracting Churches of the United Faculty of Theology: Anglican, Uniting and Catholic (Jesuits), all of them teaching the common faith, albeit tinged with their historic perspectives—in itself a paradigm of mind-broadening tolerance in the name of charity. The prevailing spirit was exploratory rather than dogmatic, evocative rather than didactic. But by no means tentative: like Jesus these men (and one or two women) 'spoke with authority and not as the scribes'[20]. In a time when many retirees, of both genders, were taking up

---

18   In the Times Higher Education world university ranking for 2011-2012, Melbourne was placed 37th and Sydney 58th among the top 400 universities

19   Also the name of the university's student newspaper.

20   Matthew 7:29

theological study I rated as one of the older students, though not all were seeking ordination.

Rediscovering the joy of learning

After half a lifetime, some 36 years, I marvelled at the privilege of this second chance of university study so unexpectedly placed before me. As a training for a new calling it also posed the challenge of reworking my sense of identity. Of course I had just been teaching a theological course myself and continued to teach it during each year of my studies, in later years within the same United Faculty. But now I was focused on the mainstream disciplines, and to me the lectures were simply a delight, bringing together and systematising the random strands of knowledge gleaned through a lifetime of hanging around churches.

Beyond plumbing the ancient near-eastern historic and cultural contexts, the subject[21] of all our learning was of course the *triune, self-revealing God* and the mystery of his *being*, his *purposes*, and his *ways. His three-rôled being:* as almighty Creator, loving Redeemer and transforming Companion. *His purposes*: as redeeming and restoring the human race—and all creation—through Jesus his son; *his ways* as revealing himself through transforming lives from within by his spirit. And of course beyond all this, the study of the written record that tells a story of love divine otherwise unknowable. Far above the privilege of returning to study loomed the opportunity of winning God's approval in *'correctly teaching the way of truth'* and encouraging people to experience its reality for themselves. But of course "who is sufficient for these things?"[22]

But before long the notion of being a spectator in the classes, not obligated to write the prescribed essays nor sit the examinations, began to pall: what sort of a minister did I intend to become? A cardboard cut-out? Next term I paid the full fee and saddled up for the long haul of a full Bachelor of Theology degree.

No longer did I merely revel in the *atmosphere* of scholarship. Now there were serious choices to be made from the 'UFT Handbook': what to study and in what order? Committed to internalising the rigorous knowledge on offer, my life took on a new dimension of pleasure in exposure to learning for its own sake. Beyond the lectures I would spend days on end among the treasures of the Joint Theological Library in the circular building, absorbing both atmosphere and knowledge. I was determined to play the serious, responsible student, atoning for the largely squandered years of my original tertiary studies (when—unwittingly—my agenda was all other) and hopefully in time gaining commensurate recognition as well as the acquisition of learning. During the years of my study—a fulltime student only in the first year—I was to gain 'Distinctions' for every essay and in each exam. But to my frustration never did I crack a 'High Distinction' though in my final essay, on

---

21 'Subject', not 'object' – as though the ineffable Creator of eternity and infinity could be put under a human microscope: "Can you fathom the mysteries of God? Can you probe the limits of the Almighty? Such knowledge is higher than the heavens, but who are you?" (Job 11:7–8)

22 2 Corinthians 2: 16

the significance of Mary Magdalene for gender understanding, in my arrogance I appealed for a re-mark by another examiner, only to be advised that, while well and professionally written, my work lacked creative incisiveness. (Actually, a fair commentary on my lifelong œuvre, I must concede.)

My degree covered the core disciplines of New and Old Testaments, Systematic Theology, Christology [who is Christ?], Christian Ethics, Church History and Pastoral Ministry. Because of my Classical Greek studies at the ANU I was granted an exemption from New Testament Greek. Hebrew was not commonly taught. To this day I retain warm memories of several of my teachers, some of them world-level scholars and authors. Brendan Byrne, Jesuit academic, whose fresh analysis of John's Gospel had recently been acclaimed, Norman Young, Professor of Systematic Theology whose lectures analysing the person and nature of Christ went to the core of the faith, and Professor Dorothy Lee (both Uniting Church) on gender studies and the New Testament. From a class prayer of Professor Norman Young's:

> "Grant us to manifest our oneness even in our diversity
> that we may become light to the world,
> dispelling rather than reflecting the darkness of its strife." *Amen*

In particular I found Church History absorbing (in childhood I had had to drop history in order to take up German—a frustrating transaction!), covering the interface of church and world from the apostolic age till the present. Soon I discovered how thin is our Protestant understanding of the history of our faith, as though it leapt over the centuries between the apostolic age and the Reformation! Were there no significant figures between the Apostles and Martin Luther? In fact a whole theological discipline of Patristics studies the role of early figures such as Augustine, Origen, Jerome, Polycarp, Athanasius, Ambrose, the two Gregories, and St John Chrysostom (the *'golden-mouthed'*). Not to speak of saints like Anselm in England, Francis of Assisi and Vincent de Paul, and scholars like Thomas Aquinas and Erasmus—or for that matter modern martyrs like Dietrich Bonhoeffer and Archbishop Romero.

Nurturing relationships

Sometimes during the lecture breaks over morning tea I would take the opportunity of gauging students' sense of call and their feelings towards their various Churches (Anglican, Catholic, Uniting) in an era of thoroughgoing reappraisal. It led to some budding friendships with Uniting Church and Jesuit students. Fridays were given over to segregated denominational studies and training. At Trinity College, under voluble Irishman Dr Dick McKinney, we learnt Anglican ecclesiology and liturgy, plus practical approaches to meeting the challenges of parish ministry.

At the personal level my relationships with the Anglican students were initially rather tentative: all came from the Anglo-Catholic tradition (the evangelical Anglicans having opted to study at Ridley College). Far older than them all, and with no common cultural (let alone ecclesial) background, I felt an uneasy outsider. For their part perhaps they sensed my diffidence about their approach to the ministry task: in an agonised world they seemed preoccupied with fripperies about seasonal liturgical colours and observing the 'precious' high church frills. Besides, following the weekly Eucharist in the serene Trinity College Chapel that we all assisted in conducting on Friday afternoons, I didn't drink with them at Norton's pub over the road. However during the Trinity years I thawed out until, with the announcement in 1987 of my 'Christian Book of the Year' award for *The Cultured Pearl*, my stocks rose and we all ended up in mutual respect and have enjoyed a deal of ongoing cordiality since. One of the older men was to become an assistant bishop in Bathurst, while a quiet but confident achiever, Rev Dr Phillip Aspinall currently Archbishop of Brisbane, would become in 2005 the Primate (Head) of the Anglican Church of Australia.

Chaplaincy focus

One long vacation I undertook the compulsory intensive course on Clinical Pastoral Education taught by hospital and prison chaplains. All but two of us did field placements in hospitals but unfortunately my placement was at Turana Youth Justice facility in Royal Park. One of my early contacts was with a young murderer, while another turned out to be the first member I met from my future parish, gaoled for raping a girl on the way home from the Youth Fellowship. The task was to acquire the pastoral skills to identify with the alienated youth and inspire their confidence to respond to your caring concern, but this was too big an ask—for both parties. A pity really, because the *outré* experience of a junior gaol, unlike that of hospital visiting, offered very little of value to training for future pastoral care in a parish. (Though later at Dallas we were to cordially visit a parishioner held in a special prison at Ararat for sexual offenders.)

Near the end of my degree, already an ordained clergyman, I opted out of Trinity College to do two or three final subjects at Whitley College (Baptist) and the Churches of Christ College, both also affiliated with the Melbourne College of Divinity (the degree-awarding body). I found the teaching refreshingly down to earth but no less rigorous. One wide-ranging course at Whitley on American Church History was an eye opener on the historical development of non-conformist church life in Australia, and also for the intentional creation in the 1920s of the dubious principles of advertising, a bane that has degraded the dignity of God's world to a market. It was in that era of woolly theological liberalism that the term *'fundamentalist'* was coined defensively, simply to mean 'orthodox'.

Of course ministry training is about far more than garnering knowledge: the heart too must be involved, perhaps more crucially than the head. At the centre of what I was learning (and the ground of all Christian belief) was the amazing fact of God's love for his whole creation, especially the human race—and even for me!— calling all and me to a heart-response. But as the doctrines and biblical teachings loomed larger, this emphasis faded somewhat. Probably a theological college is not the venue for heart-encounters with God yet without this inner reality the rest turns out to be simply packaging, as intriguing as it may look. Coming to Melbourne from the head-and-heart experience at O'Connor, and impelled by the energy it generated, initially we found this dimension somewhat lacking. But before long I discovered that all my fellow-students had experienced some direct encounter with God, whatever their theological orientation or churchmanship, implanting the desire to minister to others. This shared inner bond 'rendered all distinctions void' and opened us up, not only to perceiving God's dealings with us in love, but also to conveying it to each other. Apart from this inner understanding, a ministry role would have little to offer.

Academic ambiance

Aside from the academic, professional and personal impact of my theology studies, over the years I never ceased to take pleasure in the august atmosphere of Trinity College with its many striking buildings grouped around the vast quadrangle, the 'Bullpaddock', closed on one side by the College Chapel, the whole ensemble faithfully reflecting its Oxbridge antecedents. But although we few Anglican theologs were fully-fledged members of Trinity College with the right to dine at the long tables of the Refectory under the portraits of illustrious past leaders and alumni, in reality we were poor relations of the scions of the great Victorian families who comprised the student body of the University's premier residential college. Was it by chance that, for our studies, we theologs were relegated to the shabby seminar room in the back corner of the grounds? Or did it reflect the relative social status of secular and Christian learning? In either case the contrast with my concomitant Broadmeadows existence was total!

The long years of part-time study ended in 1994 with the scary discovery that I had reached the maximum time for completing a degree while still four subjects short of the requisite fourteen. In a blaze of commitment amidst the tumult of parish life I managed to do all four that year, only to find afterwards that I had miscalculated and completed fifteen—always better with words than with numbers! My graduation as Bachelor of Theology (in borrowed robes) in Melbourne University's Wilson Hall in 1995 would prove a memorable occasion, with the Melbourne family foregathered to witness the public fulfilment of my vow to the late Archbishop Penman.

But that was merely the formal recognition of having finally acquired the academic qualifications undergirding the practice of Christian ministry, some years after my actual ordination as a servant of the people of God, a task more oriented to the heart than the head, and well nurtured in those Friday afternoons of Anglican formation at Trinity Theological School.

14
Journey to Parish Ministry

Back in 1987, family life was focused on the big white weatherboard home at Rosanna, with Marjorie driving the Corolla back and forth from Preston Social Security, Nicholas doing Arts at Melbourne University and David taking his first drama course at Preston TAFE. In a safe backyard Angus was revelling in his newfound freedom. But now in the stylish Toyota Corona bought from the Eltham church organist I was driving daily to my new parish appointment.

According to the informal arrangement made with Archbishop Penman whereby I was to undertake theological studies and he would ordain me to the ministry (while also remaining available to him as a specialist advisor), my ordination to the diaconate had been scheduled for early in 1987. As a Methodist I had never understood that ordination to the Anglican ministry was a two-stage process. The first was to become a *deacon*, a 'servant'[23] like the original ones set aside in Acts 6 to focus on the material needs of the bilingual/bicultural church in Jerusalem (Hebrew-speaking and Greek-speaking). Doubtless the essential challenge to the deacons was to resolve the mutual discrimination between the two cultural groups, in what from the outset should have been a diverse but unified community in Christ. Then a year or more later would come the ordination as *priest*, beyond which the full powers conferred by ordination could be exercised—often trivialised as the A, B and C of liturgical power: the Absolution of sins after the Confession, the Blessing at the close of the service, and the Consecration of the elements of bread and wine for the Communion.

Ordained in the Church of God

On Saturday afternoon 29th March, 1987 with about 12 other men and half a dozen women, I was ordained deacon in a packed St Paul's Cathedral, only the second year that women in Melbourne had been ordained to the diaconate, and still nine controversial years before they could also be ordained priest—and to this day never yet in Sydney, the most populous diocese in Australia.

During the previous year at Trinity College I had learnt of 'Church Order' and its historical background since New Testament days, reflecting the apostolic pattern of the 'threefold ministry' of bishop (*episcopos*), priest (*presbyteros*) and deacon (*diakonos*), appointed by the laying on of the hands of bishops. This was observed across the original Church Universal (before Orthodox, Catholic and Protestant awareness emerged) and it is still maintained in all three divisions. But non-conformist (i.e. non-*episcopal*) Churches without bishops, like the Presbyterian, Methodist, Baptist, Church of Christ, Pentecostal, etc. all have a leadership that is chosen (elected). I doubt that either approach can be consistently established by

---

23 As Jesus taught, "If anyone among you would be great, let him be the servant of all" (Matthew 20:27).

reference to the New Testament epistles on the life of the Early Church. Hence the ongoing debate about church order.

But like a good Anglican, at ordination I had to swear 'canonical obedience' to the Archbishop and allegiance to the Queen as titular head of the Church—no one had told me about this bit! But it was just a little too late to have a debate with myself on the monarchy while kneeling before the Archbishop and other Bishops and a phalanx of clergy. Indeed my strongest memory is of the immense weight of their hands on my head and shoulders, practically forcing me onto the floor tiles before the altar—a salutary pose (and prescribed as a requirement in Roman Catholic ordination).

Of course the profound personal significance of the occasion remains forever etched into my consciousness as I willingly took the vow to be set apart for the ministry of the Gospel, though also awed at the significance of the step I was taking, no longer to be merely a church attender but responsible for leading the worship of a congregation (in its Latin origin *a gathered flock*) and for the wellbeing of all the parishioners at every stage of life and unto death. It was a public role: henceforth every aspect of one's behaviour and family life had to be blameless as under the microscope of public scrutiny. And above all the holiness of the calling to 'work and speak and think' for God as his minister, *'correctly teaching the way of truth'*. Who indeed is sufficient for these things[24]? I thank God through our Lord Jesus Christ.

> Jesus, confirm my heart's desire
> to work, and speak, and think for Thee;
> still let me guard the holy fire,
> and still stir up Thy gift in me.

I suppose that early autumnal afternoon became one of life's grand moments, marking a total disjuncture from all my previous activity and ushering in the rest of my life. In a profound sense my Employer was now the Lord, and the structure of my life became more focused than ever on a narrowly defined task, 'the cure of souls[25]'. My Duty Statement became to teach the Faith and to love people into God's Kingdom; my Work Hours became indeterminate: to be available and on call at all times; my Remuneration became the joy and privilege of being involved in so many people's lives, together with the appreciation they returned; and the Professional Development program became the Regional Bishop's supervisory group, plus the caring support of my far younger contemporaries in ministry.

It had also been a very public occasion with Anglicans from all over Melbourne present to celebrate its significance for the Church as well as for the new clergy. I was touched that several friends from my 'old' life had travelled from far afield for the occasion, including from Canberra and Sydney. Some of them reported that, as we newly ordained deacons processed regally down the long aisle of St Paul's to the peals of the organ and led by the uplifted gilt cross,

---

24 1 Corinthians 2:16
25 From the Latin cura, 'care', cf 'curate'

behind the Cathedral staff, choir, future ordinands and clergy from many parishes, and following us the Bishops and the Archbishop in all their pomp and dignity bringing the stately parade to its climax, my unseemly grin would have rivalled that of Alice's Cheshire cat. The final act saw all the new deacons gathered around the Archbishop on the cathedral steps for official photographs, plus family, friends and parishioners popping off flash bulbs.

In all a profound, life-renewing experience. Not merely a change of role—I'd been there before. But in a sense I was returning to the teacher's role, but now of crucial truths of ultimate significance to our human existence. But more profoundly, I was embracing servanthood and my core identity was to be a servant of the poor, following hard after Jesus.

The immediate irony was that, by a misunderstanding of transport arrangements to my new place of ministry, Marjorie and I lost contact and turned up separately for a celebratory supper—not the greatest start to modelling the solidarity required in parish ministry!

Curate of West Coburg

Archbishop Penman had appointed me deacon for two years in the parish of St Alban's West Coburg with St George's Pascoe Vale South, a lower middle-class area in the north of Melbourne, under the tutelage of Rev. Ron Browning, some 15 years my junior but an experienced vicar with much to teach of Anglican lore and practice. Because the parish lacked the financial resources I was to serve half-time: Sundays and two weekdays. My first appointed task was to visit patients identifying as Anglicans in the Sacred Heart private hospital nearby. More familiar with visiting gaols than hospitals I went in trepidation, only to find my first patient was a charming member of the congregation! At once she put me at ease. Really she ministered to me. The hazard was overcome once and for all, and soon I came to find pastoral care congenial, so positive were the people, as I got in touch with my own unplumbed wells within.

More daunting initially was the challenge of conducting a worship service under the watchful eye of the Vicar, meticulous in his attention to the High Church proprieties. Though familiar enough with the newish *Prayer Book for Australia* from our two years in the Eltham parish, I had really never stood in front of a congregation other than to preach on one occasion at Eltham on Aboriginal issues. You couldn't literally read the whole service out of the Prayer Book, but neither could you trust your knowledge of it. Obviously it needed to become very familiar, but how long would that process take? Wisely Ron Browning took the line of throwing me in at the deep end: on my tentative first Sunday I concluded the service with the misbegotten exhortation: "Go in peace to love and serve *the world*" ['the Lord']. No one turned a hair—perhaps they thought I meant to establish my credentials as a Christian socialist.

Gradually a work pattern started to emerge. The day would begin with our saying Morning Prayer together in the vestry, then my list of parishioners to be visited in their homes would be handed over, perhaps with a hospital call or two thrown in. Before every second Sunday, time out would be granted for sermon preparation, and the following Monday for evaluation of my halting efforts. Occasionally there would be a fraternal meeting with other clergy in the area. Of course with the Uniting Church minister I could feel really at home, unlike at the austere Roman Catholic presbytery.

For me the saving grace was the natural growth of friendship with particular parishioners with whom I discovered common bonds—being of comparable age. Often I would be invited for lunch and we would talk into the afternoon about the parish: its history, recent vicissitudes and current dreams. Also about their district. I surprised myself just how natural it all came to me, without the stiffness or awkwardness that I might have imagined. I found a good deal of common ground with the people, in background and status not unlike the Punchbowl Methodist members, though I was often surprised at the exaggerated esteem accorded my Anglican clergy status. (Non-conformist churches are noticeably more egalitarian and democratic.) With one dear couple we have remained close friends to this day. Early on I was to discover that Christian ministry, more than mere preaching, was mainly about loving people for Jesus' sake. And that began with exploring our common humanity and sharing our hearts' desires as well as our beliefs. In return you encountered respect and kindness that triggered more joy in self-giving. Unlike relationships in the office or workplace, there was an underlying sense that we belonged to each other because we all belonged to Christ.

As I identified more and more with the parishioners and with the parish, focused along the western end of Bell Street—that vital east-west artery running right across the inner north of Melbourne—it became clear to me that I had no right to be living beyond its bounds. A parish needed its clergy to share the same community life as its people. Traditionally the vicarage was beside the church. Marjorie agreed at once to my suggestion that we sell our Rosanna home and rent a house in Coburg. The thought was father to the deed, and by mid-year we had sold the house to the first enquirer (for a goodly outcome) and moved into an older weatherboard rented house just off Bell Street. There we would live until moving into our own parish vicarage eighteen months later.

But because of my unusual story—changing professions in later life, being decades older than my vicar, new to Anglicanism but anticipating a special role as advisor to the Archbishop, I had to serve two full years as Curate. The parishioners seemed to welcome the unusual arrangement of an older man learning what they had known since childhood, while modelling being humble and teachable (because so tentative!).

Perhaps the most memorable episode from this period was when black Angus, having been taken for a walk by one of David's TAFE student mates who lived with us, on condition that he keep him on the lead—but subsequently let him run loose—turned up in the dark some hours later, after being mourned for lost, none the worse despite having crossed both Sydney Road (main road from

Melbourne to Sydney, trams and all) and the Bell Street rat-race, in *peak-hour* traffic in mid-winter darkness! We had never taken him to Coburg Lake Park before—how could he have known his way home? Certainly he received a loving reception.

Surprised by joy—and daunted by parish culture

Towards the end of 1987 a letter had turned up from the Archbishop about the impending ordination service to the priesthood. My heart missed a beat—never had I anticipated being other than a deacon for the rest of my working life, a specialist but satisfying role with little responsibility for managing a parish. Later I was to discover that the normal expectation was for priestly ordination to follow on swiftly unless requested otherwise. And this further ordination was normally to be priest in charge of a parish!. I had never considered such a prospect. Clearly I was by no means ready for it. But always being one to let life unfold as it came, it seemed right to go with the flow.

The ordination service in the Cathedral was in early December, and followed the same lines as the deaconing, except that now I understood it more. I shall never forget the choir singing Stainer's beautiful anthem *For God so loved the world* as we took our priestly vows and experienced again the oppressive laying on of hands of Archbishop, Bishops and clergy friends.

My first duty, of conducting the main Parish Eucharist next morning (traditionally a signal occasion) passed off safely. I had finally 'arrived'. With newly conferred authority as a priest, and by then with a good knowledge of the two-church parish, I was in a better position to appreciate the typical tensions generated by the two groups of parishioners of St Alban's and St George's, each claiming 'ownership' of the parish but coming at it from different angles. A generation earlier the two churches had been planted by two separate parishes of differing churchmanship, leading to the uneasy co-existence of two traditions. It was a useful introduction to Melbourne Anglicanism and also to the reality of the concept of the 'Traditional Owners' of a parish (evocative of indigenous communities) who brooked no infringement of their right of determining what happened in the parish and what changes would be acceptable (typically, none!). It is an arena of power in which the vicar, though accorded genuine respect (or even affection), may not necessarily have the last say. Hence the challenge of 'managing' a static Christian community where God seems to have been domesticated. Ludicrous concept.

In 1988 towards the end of my second year when my long-suffering mentor Ron Browning announced his move to a historic, more traditional (one-church) parish across town, I took on added responsibilities, though Noel Delbridge was appointed *locum tenens* [stand-in] and acting vicar. This was a mercy because I hadn't learnt nearly enough about managing a parish to exercise such leadership and the new man, recently retired and older than I, was a good teacher.

As my term at West Coburg was drawing to a close I was invited to Bishopscourt to discuss my future area of service with the Archbishop, in addition to being available for advising on multicultural matters. In view of my age and experience, he said, he wanted me to go to 'the worst parish in the Diocese' and teasingly asked me where I thought that might be. After a couple of false responses he announced, "No, Dallas". Of course—as former Chairman of the Council of the Australian Institute of Multicultural Affairs, he knew of my 1986 study of Broadmeadows and maybe even that I had interviewed the vicar in his house beside the church. Ironically, once during my time at West Coburg I had attended—but out of solidarity—a small gathering of local clergy convened by the vicar of that parish, on *'What can be done about Dallas?'*—a parish bereft of people!

I would commence ministry at St Mary Magdalene's early in 1989, after taking the holidays due at the end of my two-year stint at West Coburg. We had arranged for the use of the vacant manager's cottage at the Wandiligong Uniting Church camp near Bright, in the Victorian 'Alps', and headed for the hills. Both 56, in rude health, and rarin' to go, our new life beckoned.

What's in a name?

The six-kilometre drive from Coburg to Dallas was remarkable for bringing about a profound change of identity from the curate to the embryonic vicar: I was farewelled as *Father Hughan* and arrived as *Reverend Jim!* Upon ordination I had conceived the bold idea of marking my radical new life in ministry by a name-change: swapping my first for my second Christian name. I recalled my namesake in Scripture (Jacob = James) who after his nightlong wrestle with the man of God (was it an angel, or even Jesus?) was renamed Israel (= *'who struggles with God'*). So during the two years' curacy at St Alban's no one knew me as Jim. But ultimately it was to prove too late in life for such a radical change. Beyond the parish no one had ever known me as Hughan. I had never thought of myself as Hughan so the hope of doing so at the age of 56 was just a tad unrealistic! Too hard to internalise. It was the dismal end to the bold experiment, so I was stuck with Jim ... or was it James?

15
Up like a bird...Down like a Stone!

During 1986, the year after the historic inter-faith seminar convened under the ITEMS Project at Monash University, considerable progress had been made on the proposal to create in Melbourne a multi-faith resource centre along the lines of the Birmingham model. As the 'honest broker' I had been convening meetings of the representatives nominated by the six faith communities. By late 1986 we had elaborated a firm proposal to be laid before a public meeting to be held at Trinity College on Sunday afternoon, 7th December[26].

A leaflet prepared for the occasion explained, "The very success of the seminar and the joy experienced by the participants encouraged them to believe that the time had come."

Through the generosity of the Uniting Church a property would be made available rent-free at Hawthorn. The theme envisaged for the exploratory meeting would be 'Love thy neighbour', with each faith community presenting an iconic statement from their sacred texts to be printed on the program leaflet. The Christians brought verses from the first epistle of John, "God is love...and he who loves God should love his brother also"[27]. Likewise there were statements from the Talmud, the Qu'ran, from Sikh and Hindu writings, and by the Dalai Lama. Following discussions in cross-faith small groups on the role of a resource centre, a draft constitution would be put forward for adoption and a balanced committee would be appointed, with guidelines for future programming. Invitations were sent to all participants in the seminar, to the leaders of Melbourne's faith communities, plus a number of public and community bodies: Immigration Department, AIMA, Victorian Departments of Education, Ethnic Affairs, Health, Police, plus academic and theological groups—and the media.

Birth of the Multi-Faith Resource Centre

Come the great day, our high hopes for the venture were more than vindicated. A representative crowd of some 130 appeared at Trinity College, their enthusiasm matched by a sober recognition of the ticklish character of the enterprise. But goodwill won out. Discussions were frank and fearless but love, in its six faith-manifestations, held sway. By the end of the day, amidst high hopes, the Melbourne Multi-Faith Resource Centre was born, initially chaired by Dr Abdul Kazi from Melbourne University Islamic Studies Centre. As the initiator of the long process leading to this outcome I was appointed Convenor (a sort of executive officer answerable to the Interim Committee—but unpaid). To be brutally frank, I was

---

26   A date also expressed in five other forms – including 5th Kislev 5747 for Judaism, the year 1407 for Islam, and the year 2113 for Buddhism.

27   1 John 4: 16 and 21

the only one who had done the practical work on the ground to lend the new MFRC any reality. The others were more or less decorative figureheads from several faith communities. At the close of the formal meeting our reward was payable in delicacies and sweetmeats from a swirl of cultures. Who wouldn't believe in *multiculinaryism?*

I recorded and later published a consensus of the day's dreams: the Multi-Faith Resource Centre should 'belong' jointly to all the contracting faiths, to which the Baha'i Faith (*'Religion Renewed and the World United'*) was soon added. While each faith was invited to contribute in its own idiom, other faiths' values would be respected through mutual friendship and interaction, with a special respect due to the Aboriginal people. The Centre would facilitate grassroots dialogue among people of all faiths, and collect and publish resources geared to educating the general public about their beliefs and values. A vision splendid!

Its programs would be developed consensually, focusing on the needs and challenges for the next generation. It would function like a Migrant Resource Centre but with an intentional emphasis on faith and belief (within Australian society awkwardly but habitually downplayed). There would be a library, a multi-media unit, kitchens for preparing food from different traditions, and meeting rooms. In tackling the twin problems of ignorance and apathy, it could contribute to public observances of national days and community festivals, offer its resources to schools and youth, and encourage community services to take greater account of religious sensibilities, particularly among newer migrant groups. *The Sun* (highest circulation morning daily) assessed its advent as of greater significance for Melbourne than the Pope's recent visit to St Paul's Cathedral!

Inter-faith journey

Early in 1987 the MFRC's initial public function, convened in a hall kindly made available by the West Hawthorn Uniting Church, offered the opportunity to hear the visiting leader of the World Conference on Religion and Peace (whose Fifth Assembly was being planned for Melbourne in 1989) encouraging all the faith communities to actively back the International Year of Peace. Also present was the visiting Director of the 'Unit on Dialogue with Living Faiths' from the World Council of Churches, which three years earlier I had visited in Geneva.

Our first year was given over to developing an appropriate structure for a unique body reflecting ownership by people from a number of faiths—some of them with centuries of mutual distrust behind them—but answerable to none. Hence the constitution being laboriously drafted sought to balance the involvement both of individuals (to provide human energy and initiative) and of the contracting faith communities (to lend it integrity). However a promising sign was the degree of cordiality and even pleasure discovered in each other's company: what Sikh had ever related to a Jew, or Muslim to Christian, in a shared building task? At that point there were about 50 paid-up members.

In his presidential report to the first Annual General Meeting Dr Kazi wrote: "In a world where tensions and hatreds all too often explode with crazed destructiveness, we the people of faith dare to believe that, ultimately, the only safeguards that we can rely on for the preservation of peace and sanity are those embodied in the lives of people—themselves imbued with inner peace and a harmony of life—from whom will flow the desire to be active in the service of humanity and in the never-ending search for justice in this world. We cherish the hope that the MFRC will become the living embodiment of such a vision, which we first glimpsed at Monash University." Grand sentiments indeed.

A mixed blessing

But enter a *deus ex machina*, a surprising new player, which upped the stakes enormously: the Australian Government! It appeared in two manifestations, one fortuitous (the looming Australian Bicentenary of 1988) and the other statutory (the new Office of Multicultural Affairs—OMA, based in Melbourne).

But as a former public servant I was blissfully unaware of the potential for Government involvement to subvert a civil society project like the MFRC. Like its Birmingham model it was seeking to build an alliance across the faiths for their mutual benefit—not a channel for government involvement. But at the time it seemed to me to be an opportunity too good to be missed for achieving public recognition and financial stability for the new initiative.

The timing too seemed expedient: as far back as our last year in Canberra official planning for the Australian Bicentenary 1788-1988 had been under way. When working with the Australian Council of Churches in 1982 I had responded to a public invitation to proffer suggestions towards a wide-ranging community program embracing all Australians.

My submission had claimed that the religious dimension characterising Australia ever since the evangelical Anglican chaplain to the First Fleet, Rev. Richard Johnson, had stepped ashore at Sydney Cove on 26th January 1788, needed to be appropriately acknowledged and traced out. In subsequent planning the Bicentennial Authority appointed a National Advisory Committee on Religion which agreed *inter alia* that "the program should encourage dialogue between people of faith and foster recognition, in touch with the needs of the minority-faith communities struggling for recognition, respect and understanding among Australia's future generations"[28].

The eventual Bicentennial Inter-Faith Program agreed for 1988 would include a weekend of prayer within the various faith groups, publication of *A Guide to the Major Faiths and Denominations in Australia*, 20 radio programs featuring sacred music and dance from cantatas to corroborees, and an inter-faith education program *Learning about People of Other Faiths*. This latter would enable Australians to learn about, meet with and discover how people of faith can all contribute to the Australian way of life. It would also feature a resource book of text and photographs

---

28   Official brochure of the Bicentennial Interfaith Program

"evoking the richness that faith groups provide through differing values, lifestyles and worship". The Bicentenary Committee on Religion would conclude that "the spreading of unbiased information about each faith is an important basis for inter-faith dialogue".

Now, early in this Bicentenary planning process, enter the newly-born Multi-Faith Resource Centre in Melbourne, well timed to become a showpiece of the Federal Government's inter-faith aspirations within a largely disinterested community climate. But maybe this 'nanny state syndrome' should have rung warning bells?

Hosting a national consultation

At about the same time, the Government's interest in the MFRC was expressed by the newly constituted Office of Multicultural Affairs which had replaced the late unlamented AIMA and was doubtless looking for new worlds to conquer. As part of its brief to formulate a National Agenda for a Multicultural Australia, to be produced for the Hawke Government in 1988, it was considering the religious dimension. Since there was no other such body in the country, it approached the MFRC seeking agreement to conduct on its premises an Australia-wide consultation and workshop on 'The Religious Dimensions of Multiculturalism'.

The historic one-day event in September 1987 brought together in Hawthorn some 40 enthusiasts from all States, fourteen of them MFRC members and one third of the group from non-Christian faiths, to determine a possible project 'of national significance' about enhancing tolerance between faiths. During the morning, background papers were presented on the world perspective, and on the Australian scene. I had been invited by OMA to present the latter, in which I made the following points, as recorded in the published record:

- "The most recent Census figures indicated that 75% of Australians identified as Christians and 1.4% as of other faiths. One third of Australians had attended church within the past month but overall numbers were in decline;
- Both historically and in the present the Churches played a significant role in shaping Australian society: schools, hospitals, welfare agencies, media and publishing; and also in migrant resettlement, sponsoring of refugees, fostering non-English-speaking Churches and through the Ecumenical Migration Centre's research & documentation;
- Racism was endemic since the beginning; racial discrimination still particularly targeted Aborigines despite anti-discrimination legislation; frankly, at the pew level many churchgoers were not necessarily more liberal;
- Australians were notoriously diffident about talking religion and politics, strongly reflected in the media's disinterest in religion, but a multicultural society cannot be coy about religion;

- The origins of the MFRC and its objectives were presented, including its brief for building a new consensus across the faith communities, in seeking wider public recognition of their cultural differences, and the promotion of tolerance".

In the afternoon, the workshop canvassed ways of ensuring a religious input to the National Agenda for a Multicultural Australia and mention was made *inter alia* of enlisting the faith communities in combating intolerance and of promoting possible media and community projects. But soon it became apparent that actually, OMA was intentionally focusing the discussion on the potential of the MFRC for advancing the aims it wished to further: it offered a historic opportunity, and the MFRC was unique in Australia. Already the amount of $25,000 had been earmarked for an 'inter-faith project of national significance' as a one-off grant, but the workshop would have to reach a consensus on the recipient. Working in two groups the workshop discussed the MFRC's capacity for meeting the requirements. While some interstate participants considered it unwise to put all the eggs into one Victorian basket, the absence of other baskets was crucial. The OMA representatives explained that the greatest value would accrue from the grant being applied to the salary and support costs of one person to be based at the MFRC, involved in developing its programs while also acting as a facilitator for other states.

In the next few weeks the Committee, meeting at West Hawthorn, drew up a submission to OMA laying out the MFRC's objectives and specifically recommending my engagement under the grant as Project Officer & Consultant to work half time in 1988, assisted by a support group and managed by a sub-committee of members drawn from all the faiths, with the project ultimately to be evaluated by the MFRC in concert with OMA. In explaining these developments to the first Annual General Meeting in December 1987, Dr Kazi said,

> "We are delighted at the confidence that the Office of Multicultural Affairs is placing in our plans for the future and in our general credibility. I wish to express thanks to all who have contributed their time and energies to bring us to this point where we stand on the threshold of a new period of growth. They have enabled the viewpoints of the various faith communities to be heard. We owe a special debt to Manjit Singh Sekhon and our legal officer, Wafa Payman, for their work on the Constitution, and to Jim Houston as Convenor of both the Monash seminar and subsequent planning work. Jim has accepted to be the Project Officer and Co-ordinator of the MFRC, a position that the Executive Committee unanimously invited him to take pending the availability of the government grant for that purpose. With his dedication to the cause we should make considerable progress next year. Incidentally I understand that he was ordained as an Anglican priest last Sunday."

An episcopal warning

But now as an Anglican priest I was no longer free to commit myself to employment elsewhere without reference to my Archbishop. When I spoke to him about my aspiring role in the project I was taken aback at his wariness. He expressed misgivings about its universalist implications ('*We all worship the same God under different names*'—a classical Hindu formula), thus detracting from the uniqueness of Christ as the world's Redeemer. But since it was a half-time position and I was employed by the West Coburg parish half-time, he reluctantly agreed, though not without a stern warning to take no part in joint prayers with people of other faiths, as compromising my Christian vocation. I was happy to assent to this and in fact the situation never cropped up.

Co-ordinator of the MFRC

I took up the half-time role in February 1988. Apart from Dr Kazi the new Committee comprised a range of people eminent in their own communities, including Seth Phillips, American Rabbi of the Liberal Reform Jewish Synagogue at Kew, Sheikh Abdullah Nu'man from Bosnia, Dr Eve Fesl director of Monash University Aboriginal & Islander Studies Centre[29], Hindu priest Chintaman Datar, Rev. Hugh McGinlay, a writer with the Joint Board of Christian Education and later with the Australian Bicentennial Authority, and Martin Chatfield who had lived and worked in Iran as an advisory air traffic controller. He insisted that with the government funding the MFRC should buy a new-fangled computer system, and even persuaded me to buy a second one for our use at home! This proved a disaster all round since I couldn't make head or tail of the byzantine guidebook nor fathom its user-unfriendly and primitive operating system. In the end ours at home was only used by children of the parish to play on, while the MFRC one stood in silent witness to my defiant Luddism.

But we did publish and circulate an explanatory brochure on the MFRC on glossy paper with six 'sides':

- Why a Multi-Faith Resource Centre?
- Who and what is the MFRC?
- Who may participate?
- An invitation to get involved in various ways
- Details of location and contacts, including reference to the OMA funding for the provision of consultancy services.

Its cover panel featured our new logo—a green globe with the names Kooris, Sikhs, Jews, Baha'is, Christians, Hindus, Buddhists and Muslims occurring repeatedly in random order, and the sub-text *Humanity through Understanding*. Across the top front corner we proclaimed *The only place in Australia where the Faith communities meet each other as equals and friends*. Overblown? No, true!

---

[29] Sadly, the Aborigines played no part in the ongoing project, doubtless because of the chasm between their concerns and those of the other MFRC faiths.

Public activities

A subsequent public meeting considered a set of eight questions we had drafted for discussion by members of the various faiths present, in order to explore and share their beliefs and practices in regard to specific issues such as special times and seasons, festival observances, personal worship practices, faith-specific diets or taboos, significant aspects commonly misunderstood by outsiders, and difficulties often encountered by young people of the faiths.

Later in the year, in conjunction with the Lincoln Institute of Health Sciences (now part of La Trobe University) and the National Association for Loss & Grief (where Marjorie was working as the project officer), the MFRC convened a historic seminar at the Royal Melbourne Hospital on *'Dying with Dignity'*, examining the diverse cultural and religious factors across the various faith traditions. Hopefully its published report became a useful resource in training programs for health workers.

In order to create a range of larger and smaller rooms in the barn-like church hall we had bought some second-hand partitioning material, but a year later we got a better offer from the Auburn Uniting Church in the next suburb, a remarkable Victorian-era brick 'cathedral of Methodism' now under-utilised. In 1988 we moved into its larger and much superior amenities. Room now for future expansion and a wider diversity of activity. Things were coming together well.

Inter-Faith input to the '*National Agenda for a Multicultural Australia*'

Then by way of following up on our public discussion session about beliefs and practices, we responded to the first approach from OMA, seeking a comprehensive inter-faith input to their policy-making for the 'Agenda for a Multicultural Australia', and reflecting the consultancy role they envisaged us carrying out. In response we devised a more detailed questionnaire for completion by individuals and organisations across the Melbourne faith communities. Guaranteeing privacy, we explained that the 37-item questionnaire would take some two hours to complete, hopefully in company with other members of the faith, and perhaps in a formal meeting. Though it amounted to an imposition, and at fairly short notice, it would provide the only inter-faith input across the country to the 'National Agenda for a Multicultural Australia' project.

The questions covered such issues as:
- the likelihood of respondents having contact with and knowledge of faiths other than their own;
- awareness of any common ground, concern about their next generation and possible 'out-marriage';
- how they read Australian society's interest, apathy, discrimination or hostility, and suggestions for improving the situation;
- their reading of the current scene and the future, both for their faith and the Australian multicultural society;

- the particular contribution that their faith might make to the general society and barriers to this, including factors in public attitudes, and practices arousing particular concern;
- how their faith understands conflict, injustice and suffering in the world;
- how it views Christian ideas and values.

Then the questionnaire broached the MFRC's potential for addressing crucial issues, for promoting the interests of the minority faiths in general (a range of possible options were canvassed) and of their faith in particular. It concluded by asking what initiatives the government might take to encourage each faith to feel more 'at home' here.

This questionnaire garnered some 25 profound, beautiful and even moving responses, immensely valuable for the preparation of an MFRC input to the National Agenda. These are still among my treasured papers, recalling the high optimism engendered by the advent of the MFRC as a mutually owned instrument for contributing to the emergence of a more humane society, even beyond Melbourne. We received a number of replies from well beyond Victoria, presumably reflecting the interstate connections of the faith networks. The material was also drawn on in preparing an input to the 5th Assembly of the World Conference on Religions and Peace to meet in Melbourne in January 1989, for use as discussion questions in a workshop on inter-faith dialogue and co-operation .

Storm clouds gathering

But at the height of our achievement, and all unbeknown to the Committee, an ominous storm cloud was building up on the horizon. Unwittingly I had contributed to its looming deluge of accusations and misunderstandings. As so often it was an issue over money. Until the OMA consultancy became operative, for want of funds we really had no budget nor any financial planning. Such membership fees and sundry donations as we had received were handled by the treasurer, Manjit, a be-turbaned and bearded Sikh. Presumably for bureaucratic reasons, several months elapsed until August 1988 before any money was actually received from OMA as final evidence that the consultancy was operational. The treasurer then reimbursed me for several hundred dollars that I had been spending out of my own pocket while working as a volunteer. For the next twelve months I would be a paid employee.

Apart from the projects described above, which I had more or less carried out as desk jobs single-handedly, as an organisation we now seemed to be groping. In the absence of any real leadership, inertia seemed to be setting in. Before long I came to the realisation that the Committee was proving non-functional, with poor attendance at meetings (no doubt the members were heavily committed to their responsibilities within their own faith communities) and little continuity from one meeting to the next. I was only at the premises three days each week, alone. And I was not CEO but a project officer. Of course after the three years of the ITEMS

Project I was used to working as a lone ranger, but that Project had enjoyed clearly set guidelines and timelines, and I reported monthly to a Commission of the Victorian Council of Churches. At the MFRC it had become more like shadow boxing, with no one taking any responsibility for proposing programs, so that by contrast any initiative I might take could have been construed as headstrong or ego-involved or, still more problematical, as Christian: it was not *my* MFRC. In fact the Committee and I had quite different perceptions of my new role as an employee: I considered my task was to carry out what the Committee resolved but there was not enough resolve for anything programmatic to emerge. For their part, if they imagined I should be acting on my own initiative, this could have been quite unacceptable for a conglomerate of such disparate elements—and actually none of them on my wave-length. It amounted to a power vacuum, since I was not creative or confident enough to generate activity *ex nihilo*. But on the other hand, since there had never been a moment of dissent or tension at Committee meetings (ineffectual as they were), I sensed I enjoyed the full confidence of the President and Secretary and those who did attend more regularly. I tried to encourage them to agree upon a modest program for implementation.

But as the situation deteriorated, in September 1988 I felt constrained to write to Dr Kazi to throw down the gauntlet. I expressed my regret that, despite having acted with due diligence in the past months, including consulting with members, proposing projects to develop, organising the health seminar and presenting a paper at a national library conference, I had not managed to retain the confidence of all the faith communities comprising the MFRC. One of them (not identified in my letter) was deeply antagonistic towards me personally, and the Committee had neither attempted to resolve the difficulty nor laid down firm policy guidelines for the future. Some resignations seemed imminent and the collapse of the organisation could not be excluded. Yet under the terms of our grant we needed to produce advice to OMA. Nor had I yet received any pay, but only reimbursement of my own money spent. Under the circumstances it seemed best for me to suspend my activity until the Committee resolved the crisis. It was not the job of an employee to resolve difficulties among the Committee members.

An ill-judged move

Then finally, early in 1989, a cheque for $15,000[30] arrived from OMA in the Friday afternoon mail (in those times of real public service there were always two suburban deliveries on weekdays). I was bemused about what to do with it. I had no access to the MFRC bank account (rightly the preserve of the treasurer), I had no secure place for it at the Centre, and I shrank from taking such a large sum home in my pocket, so I made the unfortunate decision to park it, only over the weekend, in our own family bank account. Actually more than $3,500 of it represented my unpaid salary and reimbursements for the past three months. But this ill-judged action

---

30   In today's terms likely to be worth in the vicinity of some $25,000.

turned out to be high explosive that would blow the Multi-Faith Resource Centre apart.

The following week I duly transferred the cheque (intact) to the MFRC account and Marjorie and I went off happily on holiday to Bright in the Victorian alpine region, prior to taking up my vicar's ministry at St Mary Magdalene's Dallas. But an ATM I accessed there informed me that there were no funds available in our joint account. The statement of our account subsequently obtained from the bank indicated that the OMA cheque had been dishonoured! My immediate call to the MFRC's bank elicited the fact that, on the instructions of the treasurer, the account had been frozen and that in situations of dispute, bank policy with organisational accounts was to give credence to a treasurer. Not only did I have no access to my salary and the reimbursements due, but other cheques for recent payments to suppliers would now also bounce.

A malevolent indictment

Unilaterally the treasurer had declared open season on me! It turned out that he had long harboured a towering animosity towards me, maliciously misinterpreting much of what I said and did, and weaving his own creative theories to justify his hostile actions. I still have a copy of his extraordinary 13-page A4 document entitled

> FACTS ABOUT THE MULTI-FAITH RESOURCE CENTRE
> HITHERTO UNKNOWN,
> *Prepared by the Sikh Community Melbourne'*

But I suspect he did not circulate it beyond the Sikh community, for which it amounted to a call to arms. Their honour had been impugned! Well laid out, with a Table of Contents and nine annotated sections rising to a powerful climax, it charged me *inter alia* with enriching myself from the outset with MFRC funds—and particularly with the large government cheque—and seeking to dominate the Committee.

> "Doubts have arisen concerning his motives and credibility... He treats the MFRC as a private concern dedicated to his personal glorification and a source of extra pocket money. His attempts at manipulation of the minutes of meetings have not gone entirely unnoticed by members of the Committee... In particular he no longer enjoys the confidence of the Sikh community".

In fact Manjit was the only Sikh I—or the other Committee members, I supect—had ever met through the MFRC, and ironically I quite liked him and had naïvely assumed the sentiment was reciprocated!

Further, he charged me with initiating the approach to OMA in order to seek funds for the Interim Committee's work, later stacking it with my trusted friends, since the President was unable or unwilling to make any decisions, but was content to let me run the meetings. To be frank, he was accurate in identifying the inertia of the Committee as the key problem. He charged the members with being "well-meaning volunteers ... interested in basking in the glory of being the faith representatives without shouldering their due share of work. If every member was willing to help there would be no need for a hired hand around the place. After meeting for over nine months, the management committee has achieved very little in practical terms." *Touché.* But he could not refrain from including me in the condemnation:

> "His pragmatic approach towards management of the MFRC inhibits members of the Committee from being fully effective... They are so confused by his fast talk that they consider leaving everything to him to be a relief".

One of the specific challenges (and rightly so) was the Committee's failure—because of the turbulence—to commit to a 2nd Annual General Meeting, already long overdue. I don't know whether the Committee ever considered Manjit's *magnum opus.* Finally the AGM was set for a Sunday afternoon in March 1989, beyond the close of the Bicentenary Year. Its outcome was to prove cataclysmic.

Coup d'état

By now perturbed about the indications of possible trouble looming, I had brought the potential for civil disturbance to the attention of the local Police, who stationed a car outside the Auburn church hall. Well before the starting time a scary phalanx of Sikhs in turbans appeared out of the blue and marched into the Centre, where Manjit sat at a table by the door enrolling them as new members. By the time the meeting got under way (though well attended) a solid majority of those present were Sikhs—all men.

Under Dr Kazi's eirenic chairmanship the agenda was worked through in an orderly fashion but when the election of the new committee was broached, mayhem broke out. Manjit was instantly nominated as President and on a show of hands declared duly elected. Likewise for the other executive positions, all of them filled by Sikhs unknown to the members of the other faiths. Howls of protest broke out, soon degenerating into a shouting match of Sikhs vs the Rest which ended any possibility of a decent outcome. Horrified I held my peace. The objections and pleas of the beneficent President Kazi for a return to order went unheeded because unheard. Finally the resignations by the faith communities began, led by the Baha'is and followed, at first hesitantly, by the Buddhists and then by the Jews, and finally by all the other faiths amidst a clamour of protests drowning out the speakers. After chaotic scenes that seemed to go on forever angry people started filing out of the building and clustering in traumatised knots outside or driving off. The last non-Sikhs to leave the premises were Dr Kazi and Rabbi Phillips, each with one arm around my shoulders, in a defiant but touching display of inter-faith solidarity and respect among the People of the Book—Jews, Christians and Muslims. Behind us we left the Multi-Faith Resource Centre inexplicably become a *Mono-*Faith Resource Centre.

Though deeply agitated from the beginning of the afternoon I could never have apprehended such a weird outcome. I felt shocked, stunned, totally traumatised. How could it have come to this? And with such rapidity? Could it have been averted? If so, how? In one hour a veritable *coup d'état* had laid a brave dream of mutual understanding and respect in the dust. Though we had all begun our project with the uplifting expressions of *'Love thy neighbour'*, an earthy resentment, rivalry, and hatred never earlier manifest had suddenly triumphed over the creeds of all the faiths. Worst of all, I seemed to have unwittingly triggered the avalanche that swept us all away.

It was the worst day of my working life. My degree of disgust, anger and shame was demonstrated by my utter and unconscionable irresponsibility. Gutted, I literally walked away from the Centre without a backward glance, and never set foot there again. I have no idea what happened subsequently with the office equipment, the resources gathered, the grant from OMA, or the relationships nurtured with the members of the Committee that I had sought to serve. I have never seen any of them since.

What did the Sikhs do with their prize? But was it really the Sikh *community* that planned to betray the other five faiths and destroy the MFRC? Or was it only Manjit in his paranoia of hate against me, blind to the cost of his madness? Did he write an explanatory letter to OMA and return the funds? Did the church withdraw use of the premises? Or did the whole enterprise simply sink without trace? Was that Manjit's plan? But how could he have conceived that engineering a *coup* by one faith against an agency jointly owned by seven faiths could make any sense? Mercifully, there was no public report of the demise that I ever saw. Doubtless shame took over and silenced us all.

My final memory is of Marjorie and me, numbed, driving off into the sunset towards our new home in the Dallas vicarage, stopping off for dinner (appropriately of goat's meat!) in a restaurant on Richmond Hill.

A tardy vindication

It was not until some six years later that the next word was spoken, and then by two Sikhs calling one evening at the Dallas vicarage door to explain that they had come to make an apology to me for the misdeeds of Manjit. He was currently in gaol, they explained, for tax evasion offences relating to a long-term marriage racket that brought brides from India for young men in the Woolgoolga Sikh community on the mid-north coast of NSW. Maybe some of his wild allegations against me had been projections of his own mishandling of the Sikh community funds. Indeed I was told that the completion of the Sikh Temple near Craigieburn had been delayed for years because of his embezzlement of the funds. So he had been a wild card, reckless in his determination to replace me, cost what may.

But this confirmation came all too late. Needless to say, in my disillusionment, never again have I felt the slightest interest in inter-faith encounter. Archbishop Penman's misgivings had been vindicated. Besides that, the cause in Melbourne would be set back a quarter of a century until another generation would come on the scene. Back in 1989 the soaring eagle of hope had petrified into a stone effigy of itself.

Epilogue

Full twenty-six years later, by the grace of God I have had occasion to revisit Manjit's actions towards me and review my bland unawareness of his growing animus. Doubtless I was not merely the injured innocent. Unwittingly I must have contributed towards shaping his attitude, doubtless by my insensitivity to him and his faith, conceivably even betraying a mute sense of Christian superiority. If so I was the last person to merit appointment to a role honoured by the Government with its resources. I might have been a multiculturalist but my philosophy (theology?) cavilled at the notion of a plurality of equally valid faith-commitments. I was not humble enough to learn from other traditions, perhaps revealing deep ambivalence about my own. Ah, the lifelong theme remained unconquered.

But at this remove the trigger for revisiting such a painful episode has been to truly forgive Manjit's actions. And from the heart. Twenty-six years later is not too late: *"Forgive us our debts, as we forgive our debtors."* As the Sikhs themselves express it in their sacred writings, *"Treat others as you would be treated yourself"*.

16
P-Plate Vicar

It had been a long journey, and by a circuitous route. But the timing was perfect, since *'Our times are in His hands'*.[31] Each of the many stages was essential. Each had made its mark, left its legacy. Forty years after the local preachers' class at Punchbowl Methodist Church I had the honour of entering my own 'pulpit'—amounting to a wooden lectern on an open platform raised all of 25cm 'above contradiction' in a poky little flat-roofed, concrete-block church, unpainted inside and out. They don't come less decorative than that! In fact the type of building was known as a 'Dann box' from Archbishop Dann's policy of establishing new parishes with cheap little churches in unlikely new suburbs.

From the outset St Mary Magdalene's, Dallas had been beaten by its demography: established in 1966 by a handful of UK migrants from the nearby Broadmeadows migrant hostel, who were subsequently allocated government housing in the earliest days of the area, the suburb had all too soon been overtaken by Continental migrants who were not Anglican and before long by many from the Middle East who were not Christian. Besides, after generations of ignoring the church back home, why would working-class Brits transplanted 'to the colonies' suddenly change their life style? The Census confirmed that Broadmeadows had one of the lowest proportions of Anglicans in Melbourne, but even that was a meaningless figure. Fortunately I wasn't aware of such statistical stumbling-blocks, despite my study of the area for AIMA, because the religious dimension had not been given prominence. So it was clear that we would certainly need to take a less conventional approach to ministry. What it should be we had no idea, but 'more of the same' as attempted by previous Vicars would clearly be no answer.

In the face of this considerable challenge we felt humbled but excited and full of hope, grateful for the opportunity to minister in such a needy area. We brought all our previous life experience: professional training, parenting of our children, 40 years' involvement in parish life elsewhere, our working class backgrounds transcended through education, our commitment to social justice, my multicultural and multi-faith experience—together with our failures, our woundedness and our desire to be totally reliant on the Spirit of God. The parish had been without a vicar for the past twelve months, and numbers at worship had fallen to a low ebb.

Conferring a new identity

But like all inductions of clergy into a new parish, mine at Dallas—shortly before the MFRC fiasco—was remarkably well attended. The building was virtually full. Of course many present were my future colleagues in ministry from other parishes in the northern deanery, garbed in cassock and surplice, while others were local

---

31   Psalm 31:15

clergy of various denominations. To my joy a goodly company of West Coburg parishioners also turned up. In a moving ceremony I was installed by the Bishop of the Northern Region, John Stewart, the best comedian in the Diocese and oozing with bonhomous goodwill. He preached an encouraging sermon and commended Marjorie and me to the people of the parish—all sixteen of them, though two of them were never seen again (clearly they didn't like the cut of my jib).

After the service quite a company repaired to the vicarage to celebrate on teacake and coffee. While somewhat absent-mindedly listening to the conversation, I counted thirteen jet aircraft coming in literally over the house on the eastern approach path to Melbourne Airport, two miles away as the Boeing flies. By contrast with Sydney, Melbourne had always prided itself on having no curfew on passenger or freight operations by night. Despite my cheery countenance my heart was in my boots. Going to bed that night I prayed in desperation, "Lord, if you want us to stay here and function, please do something". From my predecessor I had inherited a bulging file on representations to the Civil Aviation authorities on the terrible effect on local residents. But instead of imposing a curfew, after a few nights the Lord granted us the miracle of sleeping undisturbed, hardly hearing the jets passing a few hundred feet overhead—though the daytime remained awful. Or maybe they never flew over again at night! Perhaps more than anything else in those first days, I knew God had brought us and was shepherding us, so that we need fear no evil—though hardly yet led "beside the still waters".

Indeed the musical counterpoint was rendered more complex by the incessant flow of semi-trailers night and day along Barry Road (fortunately before the advent of B-doubles), while the *obligato* of the *trio con brio* came in those sublime moments when the railway 200 metres behind the vicarage joined the cacophonous symphony with a rhythmical *bass continuo* from a double-headed Sydney-bound freight train half a kilometre long. For my sins I had always loved the romance of transport—but this was ridiculous!

A dismal parish history

As we met and talked with our mini-flock we could detect no hint of celebration nor sense that they had anything of value to offer towards Christian service. There was no history of community involvement, from either the Catholic or the evangelical tradition: no evangelism, no service to the disadvantaged, no ecumenical links with other churches, no awareness of a prophetic role for a church set in one of Australia's most marginalised districts.

The one exception was the parish's day kindergarten, originally established with the aim of serving community needs, but which by our time retained no link with the church other than paying to use our hall and outside play facilities. But the vicar's duties still included chairing the annual general meeting. The first Eastertime I expressed surprise at the lack of any decorative reflection of the triumphant season, to be told by the teacher that in a multicultural society like Broadmeadows you couldn't have any public religious references. In a church kindergarten! Outraged

I pointed out that rather, multiculturalism was about letting *all the flowers bloom*: making references to the *Eid* festival at the end of Ramadan, Buddha's birthday, as well as Christmas and Easter, or any other occasion significant for the children. But to deprive Christians of the resurrection joy of Easter for fear of giving offence amounted to a total misunderstanding of multiculturalism, as well as a slur on the kindergarten's church connection. The outcome was the resignation of the teacher, soon replaced by a nominal Catholic of Italian background—though still no meaningful link to the church resulted.

From its inception the parish had struggled. We wondered in what sense it might be called a church at all. True, the Eucharist (Holy Communion) had been celebrated every Sunday, a few babies baptised and older children confirmed. So the faithful few wanted a church to be there, ministering the sacraments, providing comfort and security in a changing world, reinforcing their respectable conservative values. After all, the members came from a restricted range of backgrounds reflecting colonialism: UK migrants, Anglo-Indians and Anglo-Sri Lankans, sharing the cultural identity of citizens of the British Empire, and a few local Anglo-Australian residents. In vain we looked for evidence that the church had ever challenged their values, disturbed their life style, opened them up to the winds of change, let alone sounded *Jesus' call* to his followers to be self-giving, adventurous, risk-taking. They were into *'maintenance'*—with a vengeance! In attempting to preserve their Anglican soul they ran the risk of losing it. Did it all reflect a lack of teaching by our predecessors? Or simply a dogged resistance to what might have opened them up? In our first year in Dallas the parish remained something of an enigma.

Unsurprisingly, I never mentioned to the folk of St Mary Magdalene's that, as the *leitmotiv* of our past decade in Melbourne and of my ordination to ministry had been my ongoing passion for fostering multicultural ministry and mission among the Churches. In fact we disclosed very little about our past life and work either in Melbourne or in Canberra. Nobody asked and we didn't volunteer. It seemed irrelevant, since we had embarked on a totally new phase of our lives and wanted to demonstrate by life rather than by lip that we were there for them and for the long haul. Of course where relevant we acknowledged that we were in our first parish (so they might pardon our false starts and inexperience, and not judge us too harshly). But the crucial challenge was to identify with them rather than projecting ourselves. There's got to be some advantage in starting a professional career in one's mid-fifties, beyond the posturings of young manhood! Likewise Marjorie never disclosed her professional background. In a way it was a sort of mild charade that we were playing, lest by validating and projecting our past experience we might be misled into imposing middle-class expedients with little relevance to Dallas. So we had to feel our way, tentatively yet not without enthusiasm. On the other hand I made no secret of my working-class origins—a highly unlikely background among Melbourne Anglican clergy—which might enable us to be seen as non-threatening and non-directive.

Where to from here?

In reality, at the outset I had had little idea of what to aim for in such a demoralised parish that seemed never to have flourished: there was virtually no oral history on anyone's lips, no story to relate with gratitude or joy. It might even have been more practical to plant a new church from the outset rather than to inherit a dysfunctional and somewhat cynical handful of parishioners who seemed to have little understanding of what the Faith was all about and whose experience of church was mostly negative. In the absence of any grand designs for ecclesiastical development we could only go through the motions on Sundays while praying and waiting for God to turn up.

My first home visit was to the Vicar's Warden, Anne, to whom I confided my desire to join her weekly to pray for God's guidance as I sought to become familiar with the parish—its history, contemporary life and future hopes—and to seek God's blessing on the people. She seemed bemused at such a strange approach, but after a time also began to join in praying. Throughout our ministry in Dallas we exchanged prayer visits with the Vicar's warden every week, alternating between their home and ours. Anne and her son, Noel, the parish treasurer, lived outside the parish, as did Olwyn, the organist. It was the skills of these three 'imports' that had kept the place functioning. So our actual ministry to the locals was initially focused on eleven good people and true (an evocative number), mainly women and none of them young—though not all of them were regular worshippers. The lack of a critical mass meant that the worship services were pathetic and embarrassing rather than joyful and life-giving. It is in such a context as Broadmeadows that the widespread alienation of working-class people from the institutional church comes home to you, endemic as it now is in Western industrialised societies.

But unlike probably all other parishes, St Mary Magdalene's had only ever survived through sizeable grants from the Diocese. Its own giving was minimal. Very generous this arrangement, except that it reflected the unrealistic Establishment ethos of maintaining an Anglican church in every suburb, which people would automatically attend because it was the right thing to do. No allowance needed to be made for the particular needs of ministry among the urban poor or the underclass, let alone migrants from non-English-speaking backgrounds. One size should fit all. Even for the native English-speakers the social realities of educational deprivation or structural poverty were ignored—a manifestly impractical policy stance over many years by the Diocese, quite out of touch with the social and cultural conditions on the ground. No wonder the plaintive question raised by the recent seminar for district Anglican clergy: *"What are we going to do about Dallas?"*

By contrast the Broadmeadows Uniting Church was structured as a 'mission' with appropriately skilled professionals coming in from outside, undergirded by wide publicity around the Melbourne parishes to elicit financial and prayer support. With us, the funds for my stipend simply appeared from the Diocese each month and everything then devolved upon the clergyman to provide an Anglican ministry in Dallas single-handed. Admittedly Dallas and Houston went together, but that was where the matching of needs and resources ended.

Moreover the parish area was enormous. Dallas where the church was located (but literally on the suburb's northern boundary, Barry Road), was one of the district's smaller suburbs. Coolaroo on the other side of the road was far larger, and to the east Upfield stretched as far as Campbellfield on the Hume Highway, main route to Sydney past the mammoth Ford works. But on the western side of the railway lines, Meadowfair North and Coolaroo West were as large as all these put together, and in our time there the further new suburb of Meadow Heights was being added and Roxburgh Park also beginning to emerge. So our parish's population of 80,000 souls was almost double the population of Mildura and its surrounding fruit-growing districts. I wonder whether a single Anglican clergyman ever ministered to Sunraysia single-handedly.

Laying foundations

But 'single-handedly' is quite wide of the mark. From Day 1 Marjorie functioned as a second clergy person (and better than many a professional). Her range of skills was prodigious, more than I had ever imagined despite knowing her for 35 years. She bubbled with creative ideas, there was nothing she wouldn't attempt, and her social work training and experience fitted her admirably for the task of pastoral care and, before long, particularly for community development. Not that she ever let on that she was qualified. People just saw her as a kind and caring person—which was of course truly her essence.

She was also a great home-maker. The vicarage was a sizeable and fairly modern four-bedroomed brick-veneer, with a lounge/dining area suitable for small meetings and a study by the front door. Further back beyond the kitchen was a large family room, with bedrooms and a second bathroom. In the semi-enclosed courtyard on the church side Angus presided from his pitched-roof kennel. A connecting gate led to a side entrance to the church beside a small enclosed memorial garden with the ashes of departed parishioners. After many years of cumulative neglect the Vestry had spent a good deal of money, under the Bishop's orders, restoring the vicarage to its pristine condition to welcome us. The rooms were modishly painted in shades of pale mauve, light blue and lemon, and appropriately carpeted. Everything worked. We were touched by their thoroughness.

In response we dedicated our home to the service of the people, so that they felt free to drop in—and did so constantly, with the Vestry and other meetings being held in the lounge room, and older kids using our neglected computer. We could always offer a bed to friends visiting from interstate, and at different periods we had Nigel living with us and helping in the ministry after years of development work in Nepal, and Mary-Rose, a robust Cook Islander girl eating us out of house and home. Once we heard her answer the phone with a cheery *"St Mary Magdalene's here …Mary speaking."*

The church and vicarage were located on a large corner block on Barry Road, then a linking section of the main truck route from the industrial zone west of Melbourne to Sydney. The grassy corner section of the block was unused (except when we would later offer pony rides for children to mark St Francis' Day) and boasted an angled church sign on the actual corner, with space for a key Bible verse visible to the incessant traffic along the road. Bearing in mind the number of Muslim workers regularly passing we put up in large computerised and painted letters 'All who call on the name of the Lord will be saved'[32] (from the first Christian sermon ever preached—by Peter on the Day of Pentecost addressing the multicultural throng drawn by the manifestation of the Holy Spirit's power). I saw it as expressing a most basic truth about God (however named) in his relationship with the world. The viewer could make what he would of being 'saved'—whether in the physical or theological sense. After all, it is better to be saved than lost.

Transforming the wilderness

Arriving in late summer I thought it might be nice to cover the nondescript corner block with trees and shrubs to beautify the property and help safeguard the air quality from the diesel fumes. So I made so bold (so foolhardy, actually) as to borrow a rotary hoe from a British migrant whose adult son I had buried as my very first duty in the parish, even before our first Sunday (not that he was a parishioner—it was arranged through a funeral director). The young man had died from impaling himself on a wrought-iron spike on top of a fence at St Kilda while running from police after a drug bust. At the first turn of the rotary hoe, a tyne snapped clean off, unable to penetrate the rock-hard baked black clay. Welcome to Broadmeadows. Was there a parable here about the human heart?

Though the forestry dream died at that moment, we ultimately managed to soften the hard lines of the ugly, unloved church building by planting across its featureless street frontage a dense row of purple-flowering *hebes* (NZ veronicas), on either side of two bougainvilleas that later flowered scarlet as they climbed up V-frames installed on the blank wall. To cope with the dry summers we installed a timed watering system which I could turn on as required. Two specimen alder trees became featured in what became the lawn, flanking a heavy-duty sign in solid wooden planking, varnished and angled both ways to address passers-by, with deeply engraved and buff-coloured letters.

Though it seemed rather a radical thing to do I had unilaterally revised the geography of the parish to incorporate the more significant and growing area of Coolaroo, especially Coolaroo West across the railway tracks.

> St Mary Magdalene's Anglican Church
> Dallas-Coolaroo

---

[32] Acts 2:21

A love-gift to the parish

All these works came about after a year or more, triggered by the fraternal link established from the outset with our neighbouring parish of St Michael & All Angels Broadmeadows (the old notorious 'Broady' around the station and the Army Camp, centred on Olsen Place). This emerged from a pledge by the two Vicars to pray together every week, alternating vicarage lounge rooms, as we interceded for God to bless the people and grow the parishes. The close bond developing with Rev Geoff Glass, a pronounced charismatic, later embraced some of his key laymen. One upshot was an offer on their part to come and paint our church one Saturday, inside and out, the team led by Ken Harman, a master painter. This free love-gift transformed the 'feel' of the church and its public presentation. In its new and crisp cream tonings, as people drove or walked along Barry Rd it burst out from the shadows it had skulked in, as though ashamed, since 1966. It also got rid of its particular shame: a large graffito daubed across its bare front wall proclaiming *'Timor Gap—Australia's shame'*. I never did discover why this unusual political comment was put there and why the vicar didn't remove it (unless he tacitly favoured the sentiment!). It offended me aesthetically rather than politically.

But the new clean look was then out of kilter with the rubbish and traffic droppings incessantly lying or blowing around the open unpaved church carpark: a sorry image of Broadmeadows. Over the years our vicarage cutlery, glassware, and tools were to be considerably supplemented by what I picked up—and even some of my clothing! It became a bit of a fetish, particularly keeping the unfenced land around the church door and the carpark free of rubbish, doing a regular emu-bob to pick up every can, bottle and scrap of paper. Years afterwards a friendly Turkish neighbour told me that the Turkish family opposite the church had marvelled at the love the *hodja* seemed to lavish on the surrounds of the unlovely building: "*He must be a good man*". It seemed a sensible approach because the locality suffered manifestly from want of civic pride, so that to make the church as attractive as possible (given the dismal example of architecture that it was) might give a lift to the spirits of the miniature congregation.

To this point the handful of parishioners, none of them involved in the beautification activity, continued to eye us without much interest or involvement: clergy came and went, but nothing ever changed. I suppose the jury was still out on us. After all, they knew we were not from Melbourne but Sydney, a semi-unpardonable sin. In any case we were not there to rehabilitate a building or tend its surrounds but to minister to the spiritual needs of the current few parishioners and seek to build up a viable Christian community. The process could only begin with getting to know the gallant few in their home settings.

Tending the 'flock'

A very early home visit had been to Alan and Gwenda Aylward. Alan was the leading figure of the church, a denizen of Broadmeadows with a background in community work that had led to his appointment by the Broadmeadows City Council in such a role. During my AIMA study of the district he had proven an invaluable informant, a veritable fount of knowledge about the district, its history and its mentality, and also a key link between church and community, a long-term Vestry member and parish representative at the annual Diocesan Synod meetings. We spent a long evening around his kitchen table, by the end of which we were mates for life. A signal initiation to the parish and the area, and an auspicious opening to our ministry. I had gone home jubilant and grateful. Not only were the Aylwards to become good friends (even until today) but warm supporters of the many initiatives we were to launch in the coming years. But it was also clear that, "unless God builds the house, the work of the builders is in vain." Hence our dependence on prayer.

Before long I had visited every parishioner in their home, and some turned out to be interesting indeed: among the British migrants one dear man was chief propagator of the Melbourne Botanical Gardens and formerly head gardener on a great English estate. He was a walking encyclopaedia on plants, especially under the austere Broadmeadows conditions and his own garden was a showpiece. Then there were two Anglo-Indian ladies whose husbands never came (a common situation), and a recently widowed Ceylonese Burgher. So we had the nucleus of a multicultural church, and actually Anglo-Australians were in a minority—and none of these were '*Broady types*'. So in its actual composition the parish proved to be a tad upmarket to the area. Later this would become something of a stumbling block: they were all of them '*good Anglicans*' used to a weekly Eucharist as the only form of worship they knew (Anglican equivalent of the Catholic Mass) and initially unsympathetic to the parish welcoming 'outsiders': "*Really we don't need them, Vicar, the Diocese keeps us going*".

However in those early years we were the soul of discretion, taking to heart advice for clergy moving into a new parish by an old schoolfriend long experienced in Anglican ministry: "In your first year, change one thing; in your second, you can change two". Contrary tales of tear-away clergy bent on changing long-established traditions in their first five minutes provided a salutary warning. So we continued with the Parish Eucharist, sticking to the letter of the new Australian Prayer Book, and offending no one—though we had no illusions that newcomers could ever find that indigestible diet very meaningful. On the positive side, we stressed the importance of after-church fellowship over tea or coffee in the hall (beyond the folding doors at the back of the worship space).

Signs of hope

Gradually the people were thawing out and ... miracle! one or two newcomers were appearing, from a variety of cultural backgrounds. It marked the beginning of transformation in the parish. What brought them?

Initially, the desire of some young parents from a church background (maybe elsewhere, such as Army wives from the Maygar Barracks in Broadmeadows) for their children to be baptised, though having no association with St Mary Magdalene's. Using recommended preparatory material, which included an audio-visual, I made it my business to pay a home visit as soon as I received such a request in order to ensure that parents understood the implications of baptism, which included providing a spiritual home in a church for raising the child. To my joy, upping the ante like this worked: several families responded positively to the challenge of coming to our worship services for a month as a prerequisite. Several of them stayed on, leading to young families becoming involved in the life of the parish. This called for a new openness and welcoming spirit to be displayed on the part of the 'chosen few'. To break down the 'club mentality' seemed essential if the church were to grow as a public institution truly serving its local community. Over the years baptisms were to bring many quality people into the parish. Surprise! With baptisms, enter children into the parish, a phenomenon apparently not seen for years past. The timing was favourable. We had concluded an arrangement with St Andrew's Hall, training college for the Church Missionary Society, where for years I had been actively promoting multicultural mission among ethnic groups in Melbourne as well as overseas. At different times several of the married missionary candidates with children were attached to our parish on Sundays to gain practical downmarket experience, and so we were able to launch a Sunday School with skilled teachers.

Praise be, that was to become the joyful story of the following years.

Devastated!

But in October 1989 a body blow floored me with the all-too-early death of Archbishop David Penman, in only his fifth year of leadership. He had indicated that, in the pattern of his family, he did not expect to live a long life, so crammed an amazing amount of activity and achievement into his 53 years, blazing brightly as Archbishop for a few short years before being burnt out. He and his wife Jean had been missionaries in Lebanon and Pakistan, training students for leadership, and building friendship and understanding with leaders of the other faith communities. He had a doctorate in Islamic Studies from the university in Karachi, largest city of Pakistan.

It was in Manila, at the 2nd World Conference on Evangelism convened by the Lausanne Movement where he was presenting the Bible Studies, that he suffered a major heart attack and never regained consciousness, though lovingly tended in St Vincent's Hospital over several weeks, with clergy and friends constantly praying for him in an adjacent room.

His biographer, Alan Nichols, writes:

"David Penman [previously Bishop of the Western Region] had been elected Archbishop of Melbourne in 1984 after a nine months' deadlock. He was an evangelical, an outsider, uncontrollable, with little experience of the Diocese and relatively unknown. He was faced with coolness and a lack of acceptance from many among lay and clergy who saw his election as unfortunate. Penman capitalised on the mood of change, making appointments to ensure a blend of evangelicals and Anglo-Catholics. His vision was that a true understanding of the nature of the Gospel would lead to a unifying commitment to Christian mission in Melbourne that would make all the differences between the factions seem trivial and unimportant. He was a strong supporter of multicultural ministry and in 1985 chair of the Federal government's Australian Institute of Multicultural Affairs which worked with ethnic and Aboriginal communities. His leadership was crucial in marshalling support for the ordination of women in Melbourne. In 1986 women were ordained deacon. He restructured the diocesan administration to reflect mission and not maintenance. He continued his commitment to the wider church, in 1988 becoming President of the Australian Council of Churches. He was an acknowledged world expert in Middle Eastern and Islamic matters. In five years as Archbishop of Melbourne, David Penman changed the definition of church leader, making positive statements on government policies and community attitudes. He was a forthright commentator with a unique capacity to dialogue with multicultural groups in Australia while holding faithfully to his own religious convictions. He offered Jesus Christ to the Australian community in a way that was non-offensive even to people of other religious convictions. His faith was unshakeable and his essential commitment to ecumenical bridge-building, peacemaking and social justice marked him out most distinctively. His selflessness and tireless dedication and commitment led to his premature death at only fifty-three."

My longer-term dreams lay in ruins. After gaining the necessary parish experience at Dallas I had expected to be appointed to his office as advisor in multicultural and Aboriginal affairs, thus completing my transition from the Public Service to the Church, and offering my knowledge and experience for the Kingdom of God. But God must have other plans: was I to remain in parish ministry? And at Dallas for the long term? In time, inspired by David Penman's example, I felt I was genuinely able to say, "So be it, Lord."

I felt the least I could do to honour the man who had been God's minister of love to me, recasting my life in a way unimaginable, was to plant an evergreen alder in the hard Broadmeadows soil outside the church door with a small bronze plaque worded *In loving memory of David Penman, Archbishop of Melbourne 1984-89.*

After church one Sunday morning we consecrated the memorial, the costs being met from my own pocket.

Strengthening local ecumenism

With both Marjorie and me coming from a non-conformist background and only worshipping with Anglicans rather late in life, we never saw Anglicanism as of particular virtue (though 'a good boat to fish from'). Hence from the outset at Dallas we made fraternal links with the area's other churches: Uniting, Baptist and Catholic—though our original parishioners seemed unexcited at this development.

But in an unchurched community set within an indifferent if not hostile society, we clergy were all in the same game together. In particular we became close friends with Peter Clark, newly appointed pastor of Dallas Life Centre (the Baptist Church) just a few metres beyond the Dallas Shops gathered around their central courtyard. Though established at about the same time, what a dramatically different history it had had from St Mary Magdalene's! From the beginning it had responded to local needs, sponsoring the first medical clinic in the new suburb, then moving into child care, an Opportunity Shop, and a hardware store selling home maintenance materials at cost price. It also had a brave history of essaying Christian residential community (shades of our stillborn Maranatha Community in Canberra) in the large custom-built house opposite the church. Peter Clark initiated the Broadmeadows Inter-Church Council (BICC) which, as well as linking clergy in prayer and mutual support, would later organise some creative worship and outreach projects. The Easter Festivals became a feature of the Dallas scene, bringing Christians together to serve free Easter eggs and sizzled halal sausages (free from pork, a love-gift for the Muslims) with a sunrise (Sonrise) service in Broadmeadows Town Park on Easter morn. Some of our newcomers joined in heartily.

We also related warmly with the Holy Child Catholic parish and Fathers Barry and Joe. In one combined service there to mark the Week of Prayer for Christian Unity I actually served the elements of the Holy Communion to Catholics as well as Protestants! We also borrowed their parish hall for our Bush Dances. In the same spirit, on St Mary Magdalene's Day in July during one of my lone safaris overseas, Fr Barry preached the sermon. Like other enthusiasts for women's ordination Marjorie was keen on rehabilitating Mary Magdalene from the bad press she gets in the Catholic tradition. In fact Scripture does not endorse her reputation as patron saint of prostitutes (cf. the Old English word 'maudlin'), pronouncing simply that she was one of a number of women whose mental health had been miraculously restored by Jesus, and who out of their own means helped support his itinerant ministry with the Twelve.

One of Marjorie's latent interests was in liturgical dance. Now with a number of junior and pre-teenage girls in the parish she trained a group (by personal demonstration) to present on St Mary Magdalene's Day or other great occasions graceful and simple movements evoked by some modern worship song, such as we had been gradually introducing into the services to complement the hymnbook. The colourful dresses were generously lent by the Craigieburn Catholic parish.

The beginnings of outreach

As the parish now grew in numbers and in its breadth of socio-cultural diversity it became more appealing to other newcomers, including some recent arrivals in the area like Army families. We tried to get them involved in new ways. This opened up prospects of diversifying our ministry beyond simply running worship services. For example, Friday lunchtime would see a queue forming outside the Hall door waiting for the Food Bank distribution. One of our new men would drive his van over to the warehouse west of Broadmeadows to collect the free produce and groceries gathered from supermarkets because of damaged packaging or approaching 'use-by' date. We had our regular customers, though I doubt that any of them ever came to church. But that wasn't the point: didn't Jesus say that whatever we did for the least of his brothers & sisters we did for him? Besides, in a stressed community where there were many casualties truly in need of caring support, it roused the local Christians to see some of these literally on their own doorstep and, in responding to human need, grow into more than 'Sunday Christians'. Soon it became quite an operation with a team doing the unpacking and reparcelling, chatting with the customers, trying to make the supply go round as fairly as possible. Of course there were often a few dubious characters prone to abuse the system but we weren't into playing favourites.

Christian and Islamic education in schools

After a few years we offered to teach Christian Religious Education at our local primary school, Dallas North, where Marjorie had been one of a team teaching an annual course on sex education. But the staff were not very sympathetic to Christian teaching, since so few of the pupils (or teachers!) had had any connection whatsoever with any church—far more children had connections with the large Turkish mosque nearby. When the Pincipal checked it out with the Education Department, he was told to conduct a survey with Muslim parents before a decision on Christian teaching could be made. When this produced strong support for Islamic teaching to be introduced, through volunteers, it was agreed we could all make a start—but in each child's case, only after parents had given their consent.

So each Tuesday afternoon the classrooms would ring with the loud choruses of rote learning, with the Koran being chanted back and forth in a language foreign to the Turks (ancient Arabic that no one can speak today), while two small knots of pupils participated in a contemporary approach to Christian education, according to the Agreed Syllabus of all the Churches, using glossy learner's books and teacher's materials prepared by the Council for Christian Education in Schools. One day, after I had occasion to rebuke an oversized Pacific Islander boy for disruptive behaviour in my class, I found the tyres of my Corona slashed. The

Bishop agreed with my claim that it was suffered in the course of my duties and the Diocese paid. One Easter time a Turkish boy (oddly enough in Marjorie's class), on hearing about the Crucifixion, cried out in alarm at the enormity of the claim: "God can't die!". What a pity that we Anglo Christians mostly find the stupendous claim so ho-hum.

Besides this community-oriented activity, there was already a small group of women loosely linked with the church meeting in homes for morning coffee, as nurtured by the previous vicar. Encouraging this group, Marjorie found some newcomers joining in before long, so that it too became a point of growth. It also attracted a desperately needy family consisting of a non-coping mother of several children from different fathers, whose Housing Ministry home was truly disgusting inside. There was a strong case to be made for maternal neglect leading to the children being fostered out. Over the years, despite the prodigious amount of love and care invested in this family by Marjorie and others, there was little to see for their labours, though the little girls often came to Sunday School and the mother to church. But the process did help many of our parishioners for the first time confront some of the unmet social needs of the area, and maybe foster the parish growth towards becoming more of a community of love.

Blessing dinkum Aussies

From time to time people in crisis would call at the vicarage door begging for money to tide them over an emergency. The Bishop provided a small fund to draw on for this purpose, so on principle we never turned anyone away. Of course the word would get around and inevitably some go-getters would try their luck. From time to time there would be Aborigines seeking petrol money to drive to grandmother's funeral in Numurkah (always Numurkah, as though some fictional town)—and some must have had multiple grandmothers! But was this their way of expressing their extended-family obligations to an ignorant white man? Maybe or maybe not, at least not on one occasion when I drove behind one guy to the local service station and, to his chagrin, filled his tank for him. Petrol wasn't the fluid he was craving.

One evening a tall, well built Aboriginal man and white wife knocked at the vicarage door, not to beg, but to seek pastoral assistance in joining the church community! Touched, we ministered to the need they confessed as they opened their life to Christ, and next Sunday they duly showed up with their three girls, twins of about 13 and a little one.

We were awed: was the Lord sovereignly building his church from the truest locals?

17
Encountering the Chinese Dragon

Rooted and grounded in the baked/boggy clay of Broadmeadows, towards the end of our first year I was toying with the idea of a short holiday trip to China to get away from it all. 1989 had been a strenuous year struggling with new beginnings in a sea of inertia, and unrewarding to say the least. But China had worked its magic on me at the tired end of my round-the-world study tour of 1984, when I had spent a few days in Hong Kong and in the mainland New Territories. I knew then that return I must, and now because of a serious hiccup in relations between the People's Republic and America following the massacre of student democracy activists in Tiananmen Square, there were travel bargains to be had. With Marjorie declining to be dislodged I hit upon the brainwave of taking Sarah, now 29 and a graduate of Macquarie University. It turned out to be a powerful gift that would help to refocus her life.

Manila stopover

Cracking a bargain-basement fare with Philippine Airways we sallied forth late in November by a night flight memorable for a worrying explosion towards the back of the plane at midnight over the South China Sea, followed by a long gliding descent. What a relief to make out the ill-lit environs of Manila below and emerge into a bath of humidity in the terminal, running the gauntlet of the knot of poverty-stricken humanity hanging on the wire mesh that kept the world at bay. Our booked hotel was mercifully air-conditioned, not that this deterred the cockroaches so generously in evidence, particularly in the bathroom. But unfortunately I couldn't deter Sarah from making use of a bedside telephone to call a friend in Sydney which was to cost an arm and a leg—a sound learning experience for her but which I felt obliged to fund.

With a day's stopover planned in Manila we had a brief look around the modern downtown area by the gardened foreshore before taking the bus to Quezon City, the governmental and political hub some 15km across the Metro sprawl, to the national HQ of the Wycliffe Bible Translators. Our route led past some appalling slums, the like of which I had never imagined: shanty towns built from junk with rocks holding down makeshift 'roofs', unsewered drains, filthy alleyways between, all swarming with ragged children, dogs, chooks—and fairly reeking of despair. Unsurprisingly, Manila turned out to be the world's most densely populated capital. The contrast to the American walled oasis that was our goal proved shocking (the Philippines had been an American colonial possession before the 2nd world war). I deplored the brutal juxtaposition but understood that the multi-national Bible translators scattered among tribal minorities across the country's 7,000 islands needed a safe haven and convenient focus for their conferences and time out. One of them, a valiant middle-aged lady from NZ living for decades with an indigenous tribe in the mountains of Mindanao, had been a friend of ours at Sydney University EU. We were courteously shown around the base by the American staff and stayed on for lunch. But on the elevated train ride back to town I had to endure the hostile stares of passengers deploring the sick spectacle of an ageing man accompanied by a beautiful young blonde (all too sleazily common in the Philippines) but felt it inappropriate to shout in their teeth, *"She's my daughter!"*

The only other memory I retain is of our visit to the birthplace museum that honours José Rizal, the national hero of Filipino independence from the Spanish, a remarkable figure and non-violent revolutionary executed in 1896 at the age of 35—a physician, artist, poet, novelist who had studied in Paris and Heidelberg, a polyglot speaking over 20 languages. Today a public holiday commemorates his martyrdom.

Savouring Hong Kong

Across the South China Sea next morning, surviving the foolhardy landing along the canyon of Hong Kong's Kai Tak airport flanked by skyscrapers, we made for the nearby quarter of Hung Hom with its 'Holy Carpenter Guesthouse' where I had stayed five years earlier. Its bare concrete floors and community bathrooms as forbidding as ever, like the intrepid tourists that we were, we tackled its spartan delights. For breakfast we walked all of 50m downhill to one of the teeming eateries, threading our way past a streetside Taoist shrine, exotic with its joss sticks and goddess statues. There followed our introduction to *yum cha* ['drink tea']—the daytime festive meal with its wide selection of savoury snacks pedalled by diminutive waitresses pushing their own barrows while 'singing' their wares in the nine tones for which Cantonese is notorious. We found the styles of food familiar enough from our family celebrations of academic successes in Canberra's Chinese restaurants but the range of dishes on offer daunted us. In fact 'Chinese' restaurants in Australia (as throughout SE Asia) turn out to be really Cantonese restaurants serving only one of the four famous cuisines of China (the others, all notably different, from Shanghai, Beijing and Szechuan).

We wandered happily around the foreshore past the huge 'ocean liner', forever moored in concrete and offering upmarket tourist accommodation and dining. We caught the Kowloon ferries threading their way across Victoria Harbour (really an arm of the sea between the mainland and Hong Kong island), we took the funicular tramway to The Peak to survey the teeming Colony at our feet traced out in its daring skyscraper terraces, with Victoria Harbour, Kowloon and the green hills of China beyond. (Not until 1997 would the term of British administration come to its end.) We rode the ancient, lumbering double-decker trams along Hennessy Road and ambled through tumultuous shopping streets festooned in red and gold banners bearing the traditional Chinese characters (though now updated in mainland China), marvelling at the give-away prices of the goods, tempted to buy everything but bemused at the *embarras du choix*.

One of my lone safaris into the New Territories beyond Kowloon had taken me to Tuen Mun, a large satellite area of commuters where a light rail network had just been inaugurated using Melbourne's articulated trams. At one point a flock of schoolgirls descended on my tram, performing an impromptu operatic chorus of avian communication in nine tones. In a Taoist temple I watched worshippers presenting offerings of fruit and flowers, bowing before images of gods and heroes, lighting joss sticks, and drawing rolled-up notes from a vase containing messages about their future fortune. The return trip on the top front seat of an outsized double-decker bus offered one of the Great Bus Journeys of the World, whirling at speed around giddy bends high on the cliff face overlooking the wide estuary of the Pearl River crammed with shipping at anchor. *Phew!*

More leisurely was our route-bus trip over the spine and down the far flank of Hong Kong Island to Aberdeen Harbour where we indulged ourselves in a cruise by junk among exotic oriental craft before adjourning to a surf beach with no surf.

Portuguese safari

But with Sarah exhaustion or lassitude seemed to set in. Maybe overwhelmed by China (and at first encounter who isn't?), while I champed at the bit she took to gradually rallying her energy for a midday emergence. After a couple of days when I spent the morning adventuring alone, I thought of a new option—a day trip to Macau necessitating an early start by sea-going ferry across the gaping mouth of the Pearl River and down the South China Sea. It proved an immediate success and we spent a fascinating day in the Portuguese enclave dating back to the 16th century, offering a rich historic blend of European and Chinese cuisine, motifs and architecture.

We found the territory to consist of a former island long locked to the mainland by a sand spit, plus two low islands interlinked by bridges and causeways, the whole utterly urbanized. Though the people seemed to be almost universally Chinese, it was intriguing to see evidences of Portuguese culture on every hand: shop signs, street names, plazas and gardens—and Police and Customs uniforms. However I was dismayed to find that the icon of Macau, St Paul's Gothic cathedral dating from 1602, is but a free-standing façade minus a church! Doubtless amidst the customary blend of Taoist, Buddhist and Confucian themes there must also be vestigial remains of Christian religion dating from 400 years of Catholic missionary effort, such as Easter processions and saints' days. But the only festive occasion looming was the Macau Grand Prix, with deafening practice runs by high-powered cars around boarded-up streets in the city centre, a madness that I could not foresee would also overtake my home city a few years later.

We settled for lunch in an authentic Portuguese restaurant, of roast rabbit and baked vegetables spiced with southern European flavours but memory fails me whether we accompanied it with the traditional dessert of egg tart. Our nautical journey back passed Lantau Island, part of Hong Kong, where four years later the world's largest statue of Buddha would be erected.

Foray into Red China

Then it was time for our finale: in the wake of Tiananmen Square a foray deep into Red China, undergoing the stirrings of transition to a more liberalized administration under Chairman Deng Xiaoping. Prior to this I had only peered into Red China from the border fence at the last outpost of Hong Kong's New Territories. But now, offsetting the boycott by American tourists we had scored a package deal: an hour's flight south-west to the premier tourist destination of Guilin [*gwaylin*] in Guangxi Autonomous Region, plus a few days in a resort hotel. We qualified for the royal treatment accorded American tycoons: met at the airport by black limousine, deposited in an upmarket tourist compound featuring a five-star hotel on the banks of the Li River, offered a program of excursions with English-speaking tour guide in and around Guilin, a traditional goal for Chinese honeymooners. Marvellously exotic sights like Reed Flute Cave with its stalactites and limestone shawls and Elephant Trunk Hill, climaxing in a leisurely afternoon cruise down the Li River meandering between the astonishing rock outcrops rearing sheer out of the hazy plains, as enshrined in traditional Chinese landscape painting, where obedient cormorants fish for their master, and in the meagre late-autumn flow women push our frequently grounding vessel off into the stream again by slender bamboo poles while we sip green tea and savour the delicacies, finally to disembark at a riverside town where we run the gauntlet of stalls peddling local crafts before settling into our comfortable seats for the coach trip home.

'Clash' with the People's Liberation Army

Next day, back in the real world, rubbing shoulders with a navy-blue-coated army of workers, minus our guide, we wander across the Li River Bridge into town to poke about the shops and markets, conscious of our intrepid venture behind the Bamboo Curtain where Communist overlords rule the compliant masses—and strolling Westerners offer a rare spectacle indeed. So rare that one day, riding hotel bicycles into town, we cause a military incident. As we pause at a city intersection to concede right of way to a People's Liberation Army convoy, the motor-cycle outrider notices the blonde bombshell beside me and instantly brakes to a halt to offer an exaggerated mock-deferential salute. He is collected by the staff car behind and knocked off his bike. The first two cars then collide. *"Wow! Sarah, all your own work! Let's get out of here—fast! Down this alley. Come on!"* We skedaddle, instantly absorbed into the surging throng of bike-riders and pedestrians. In China, there's always safety in numbers.

Peasant life

On our last day we finally prevailed upon our guide to take us out into the countryside to gain some impression of life in a peasant community—the classic situation of China's millions then still living in Chairman Mao's communes. Eschewing sealed roads, we nosed our way down rural lanes till the black car pulled up beside well-stocked duck and fish ponds. As the three of us threaded our way along a causeway between the ponds we were greeted by a hail of stones thrown by village urchins. Resentful of a Party official's visit, or of prying outsiders, or foreign devils—or just rich Westerners?

Oblivious to the intrusiveness of our visit we ploughed on relentlessly down a village 'street' (dirt-track) of ramshackle houses (huts really), peering rudely inside as we passed. In one we saw a pig in the family's living quarters. Of course now in far retrospect and with months of living in China to draw on, it occurs to me that Guanxi is not a Province but an Autonomous Region mainly of the Zhuang minority (of several millions) maintaining their life style and practices quite alien to the national majority of Han Chinese. But at the time we were goggle-eyed.

The last word

The tail-piece of our holiday came as we drifted in towards Sydney airport, when Sara-Jane turned to me with a satisfied sigh and said, *"You know, Dad, you're quite a fun person to be around"*.

For her a door now stood open to a beckoning world. In the next few years she would travel alone to the land of her birth, visit Ely and meet her fellow-babies from the Ely Maternity Home, then undertake studies for the Cambridge ESL Diploma opening the way to English teaching posts in Prague, Oviedo (Asturias region on Spain's northern coast), South Korea, and North Carolina. Since then she has worked with AMES (Adult Migrant English Service) in Sydney and also later with Navitas, its competitor, a multinational which, by under-bidding the government system won the Sydney tender for teaching migrants and international students (undoubtedly because it pays lower salaries for lesser qualified staff).

The wonderful Age of Privatisation was dawning.

18
A Ripening Harvest

In 1992 St Mary Magdalene's parish celebrated its first glorious quarter-century. We had a number of special events but also saw steady growth around that period. Since my advent in 1989 I had been 'Priest-in-Charge under the supervision of the Regional Bishop', a formal status pending qualification to become vicar, granted in 1992. Bishop John Stewart exercised his supervision through regular sessions at his home in Flemington with the obligatory attendance of a number of newcomers in charge of a parish. Because he was such a character, they were great fun. But they also offered unique opportunities among non-threatening peers for the getting of wisdom.

I recall one session when we P-Platers were giving situational reports on our parishes. When I mentioned that the previous Sunday we had 60 people at worship (and not just because it was a baptism with lots of doting relatives) the Bishop cried, "Sixty at Dallas, I can't believe it!" But true it was, unlikely as it may have sounded to someone who had known the parish over so many years. People were simply turning up, some from baptismal obligations, some moving into the area (the new suburb of Meadow Heights was growing apace) others through servicemen's families on transfer, still others from contacts with the multicultural community as I moved around the Broadmeadows suburbs, always backed up by continuing home visitation.

A parish broadening in cultural diversity

To me, of particular delight was the widening cultural diversity of the growing congregation, reflecting the recently re-worked identity of Broadmeadows from a place for 'little Aussie battlers' into a multicultural hub. Among our regular parishioners at times we had (naturally) some Anglo-Australians, but also English, Scots, Indians and Anglo-Indians, Sri Lankan Burghers and Sinhalese, Germans, El Salvadorans, Cook Islanders, an Italian, a Maltese, a Vietnamese, a mainland Chinese, a Lebanese, a Maori, a Mauritian, an Iranian, a Turk and an Aborigine. Not all were Anglicans by any means, coming also from Catholic, Eastern Orthodox and non-conformist backgrounds but in a new land happy to worship together. A hint of the Kingdom of God, and a heartening one. In God's good plan I was feeling in my element.

But the Bishop also struck a sobering note in pointing out to us beginners that we should not be tempted to over-weening pride if the Lord should bless our ministries. A sad but not uncommon experience is the contrary, he said: following the departure of a popular minister there can be a mass exodus of parishioners, so that "the place thereof knows them no more". Hence his warning not to think of ourselves more highly than we ought to think. It is God who builds his Kingdom.

But who wouldn't be touched by the personal stories of such special people as the El Salvadoran family and the lone Iranian? Mario had been a young teacher in El Salvador when, with US support it was hellbent on staving off a budding people's revolution against the five families who owned the country. One day some Government-paid assassins came to his school and shot the teacher dead in front of his class in the next room, mistaking him for Mario, the union rep. A gentle, peaceable man, he freaked out and fled into the jungle and was able to emigrate to Australia through a special humanitarian program initiated by a Labor Government, subsequently sponsoring his wife and four little girls to join him under family reunion arrangements. Nominal Catholics, they made no bones about joining St Mary Magdalene's and became among the most faithful worshippers, celebrating by having a fifth girl baby. One day I met another El Salvadoran and invited him to come to our church too, but when I reported this to Mario I was shocked at his vehemence: "Father, if that guy comes, we're out of here! He was our village headman, strutting around with a revolver in his belt, and he wasn't shooting scrub turkeys!"

Phillip was an Iranian Christian who had fled his country after the Ayatollah Khomeini came to power in the Islamic revolution of 1979 that overthrew the Shah of Persia. A lecturer in the Naval Academy on the Caspian Sea, he had always had a Cross on his desk until the day a colleague said to him, "You'd better get rid of that now, or they'll kill you." Not doubting it he fled into the mountains on the Iran-Turkey border and for some years linked up with the Kurdish rebels. Once standing on the skyline, checking the valley below for signs of military operations, his companions on either side of him suddenly slumped to the ground with bullets in them. He fled across Turkey and for some years lived in Istanbul from where he ultimately made his way to Australia with a Turkish wife. He too was traumatised by his experiences, suffering from recurrent nightmares and at times exhibiting really quirky behaviour.

Local Ockers too!

Some of the Anglo-Australians were also social casualties. Jane, loud-mouthed mother of three boys by Ian, her disabled partner, was quite devoid of social graces, let alone attitudes appropriate in church. Arriving at the service with her herd she was prone to shatter the contemplative peace and quiet by giving voice to quite unprintable comments at maximum volume. To put it mildly, the older boy was 'behaviourally challenged'. We ministered quite intensively to this family, often visiting in their home. I baptised the baby, Timmy, in their chaotic living-room from a wahing-up basin balanced on top of a space heater flanked by two candles. Later her aunt who was a keen (but equally voluble) Christian from another church threw her lot in with us, joining a home fellowship group. Ian worked in a sheltered workshop nearby, from which he supplied the church and vicarage garden with new plants. Sadly, some years afterwards he was to drown in the Murray, perhaps while having a fit.

Another Ian was incredibly challenging, though we had no illusions about him. A notorious identity around the Dallas shops, he had been banned from the Catholic parish for interfering with children in the toilet, and had done time in youth reformatories. He was an epileptic, with a mental age of perhaps ten, though well built, strong—and loud-mouthed. We had to supervise him constantly around the church building to protect the children. Invariably he called me 'Jimmy', including on the only occasion in our seven years when the Archbishop paid a formal Sunday visit to the parish, when he interposed himself between us as we politely chatted over a cup of tea after the service, to loudly announce to Archbishop Rayner, *"Jimmy's my offsider"*.

Another Sunday, also in the after-church fellowship, as I was talking with him (hard to avoid), without warning he suddenly crashed insensible to the ground at my feet with a heart-rending crack of a skull against the parquetry floor!

I also built quite a close relationship with his father, grateful for a new focus in Ian's life. In our last years I would take him once a week to the Turkish men's *kahvehane* (coffee house) at Olsen Place, way out of bounds to non-Turks, but they were aware of his needs and kindly accommodated us. But when one of the original Fourteen objected, *"Jim, you're filling the church with broken-down people!"* the only response had to be, *"Wouldn't Jesus?"*

Advent of team ministry

On the other hand, after the Aboriginal guy Phil had come to church for two or three Sundays, with his wife Lynne and her twin girls, plus their four-year-old daughter affectionately dubbed *'Shithead'*, he confided to me that, with little formal education, they couldn't make much sense of the service. But we had another option up our sleeve. Some time earlier, a bright-looking young couple had turned up at the morning service, joining in heartily and singing the songs with zest. Afterwards, preoccupied with passing the time of day with those leaving the church, I missed having a word with them. When I realised this I tore out of the building, to see them walking off 100 metres away. White clerical garb streaming out behind me I managed to catch up with them, breathless.

The conversation marked the launch of a ministry relationship with Ian and Ruth Fuhrmeister which continued while ever we all lived in the area. Ian's father had been an Anglican vicar in Craigieburn and he himself was a former high-school teacher. The couple had a passion for Christian witness and ministry with ordinary working people. Later when we shared with them the background of our struggles and prayers for the parish, they agreed to throw their lot in with us. Certainly they were to prove a godsend to the ministry *of* (though not necessarily *at*) St Mary Mag's.

We agreed to launch a small house-church, meeting fortnightly over dinner and rotating between the vicarage, Phil & Lynne's place, and the Fuhrmeisters' home in Coolaroo West, backing onto the deep gash of Moonee Ponds Creek.

How we came to revel in these occasions, all of us! Featuring typically knockabout, ockerish humour disguising ever deepening relationships of honesty and intimacy, good plain Aussie fare (and mountains of it!), a simple, practical Bible-teaching segment followed by frank questions and discussions, and then praying for all our concerns, often very practical ones about employment, making ends meet, and raising the kids (the five of them always present). In time another needy family or two joined in. As offbeat as these encounters undoubtedly were, there was also something beautiful and even holy about them. As we honoured each other in his name, Jesus deigned to join us.

But over several years, with many moves to new rental houses along the way, Phil's old life resurfaced. Once he was summonsed to appear in court for having committed the heinous crime of relieving a supermarket of a glue stick. I found it hard to believe that the justice system worked like that, or was it only in the case of Aborigines? Or the poor? Or both? In high dudgeon I went to the hearing in the Broadmeadows Court of Petty Sessions and put in a passionate plea for leniency, observing that Phil had needed the glue to hold together a model of St Mary Magdalene's Church that he was giving me, made out of matchsticks. The magistrate promptly threw the case out of court with costs awarded against the police. The model church still has pride of place here in my study.

But Phil's next court appearance was for real: it had come to light that for some time past he had been molesting his twin step-daughters, now young teenagers. Possibly this had been the reason for his initial call at the vicarage that first night seeking absolution for his sins. I had taken it very seriously but without knowing the full details. Believing he was genuinely repentant, we sought to build him into the support network of the church, a potent factor in his desire and attempts to go straight. But the power of his damaged past was too insistent, and this time there could be no leniency. He was sent to a newly opened prison for sexual offenders at Ararat, segregated from other prisoners for their own safety, where we visited him in the name of Christ.

Canvassing the need for new approaches

Such experiences brought home to us just how inappropriate the Anglican model of parish ministry was for such an area, implying a sole ubiquitous and multi-talented vicar to be available for all, parishioners and the community, twelve hours a day, visiting, counselling, caring, preaching, planning and administering while maintaining his equilibrium, kindly, unflappable, a veritable icon of Christ, while also being a loving husband, a wise and steady father, helping around the house, washing the dishes, doing the gardening, cleaning the toilet, and taking the dog for a walk—until he suffers the inevitable burnout and breakdown. (There are said to be 10,000 ex-clergy in Australia.) Whereupon the parish simply advertises in the diocesan newspaper for a super-human successor.

Clearly a structured team ministry was called for (in those charismatic times acknowledged as the 'ministry of the Body of Christ') interweaving varied ages and talents and gifts, working to individuals' strengths, supporting and backing each other, and with permission to experiment, change and adapt, even to reject some of the traditional practices. The nearest we could approach to this was to draw on the energy and wisdom of the Fuhrmeisters, supplemented by the St Andrew's Hall missionary trainees, and inviting lay witness teams and clergy from other parishes to visit us for special Sundays. Twice teams from St Mark's Niddrie conducted 'missions' in our parish, and once the St Andrew's Hall trainees, led by their Principal, conducted a total letterbox-drop of Coolaroo West outlining St Mary Magdalene's range of activities and inviting people to join in our down-to-earth services. Significantly, not one person responded to this scattergun approach!

About this time I wrote a candid article on ministry in Broadmeadows, published in the Christian magazine, *On Being*. It raised more questions than answers, broaching the issue of how the Protestant church in Australian cities had become locked into the middle-class, having little or no contact with people of lower socio-economic status—except as recipients of their 'charity'. In view of Jesus' ministry among the poor and the needy, this was a disturbing situation. Further, there was little if any awareness in 'successful' middle-class parishes of the unequal struggle of under-resourced ministry just across town in industrial or poor neighbourhoods, with a high proportion of newcomers of other cultures and faiths beside the customary social casualties. Subsequently my specific appeal for resources to the Diocese's most successful and wealthy parish of St Hilary's Kew landed a high-quality second-hand piano—but what I had in mind was some ongoing financial or personnel support, such as would actually be provided in later years by St Jude's Carlton to an inner-northern parish. It seemed I was ahead of my time.

Marjorie also wrote an article published in the Christian periodical *National Outlook*, entitled "Hard Labour in the Vineyard", and there was a report in the national Anglican newspaper *Church Scene*, as the feature article of their section The Inside Magazine, "Why is my church not flourishing?" illustrated by four wretched photos of the underbelly of Dallas and Upfield. Another outcome of these articles and a number of speaking engagements that followed was for groups of ministry students from various seminaries to visit Dallas for a colloquium in the vicarage and a conducted tour of the district, in its residential, industrial and Islamic dimensions. Mostly the middle-class students appeared suitably shocked. Sadly, it demonstrated the wealth-segmented character of contemporary urban life, reinforced by the insidious media coverage geared to making wealth the norm and ignoring the existence of the poor. Sadly, there were more forces working to maintain the chasm than to bridge it. All our cherished rhetoric about the Australian way of life and the fair go remained just that. The 'have nots' languished while the 'haves' enjoyed their fortune. As Al Grassby was fond of saying, Australia's greatest ghetto was Sydney's North Shore [or Melbourne's inner east?]

But what of the reality at Dallas?

What then were the needs of a challenged area like Dallas, and how might a small, under-resourced church go about confronting them? Of course like all human communities, the basic need is for meaning, security and hope—including beyond this life. The antithesis of this is represented by the massive refugee camps in parts of the world, with hundreds of thousands—mainly women and children—living just for to-day while despairing of a future, with no dream left. So the central task of any church is to present and model God's dream of a Kingdom of forgiveness, love and justice, earthed in Christ, to be both personally experienced and collectively shared. From this should flow action, both through repentance leading to personal renewal and restored relationships, but also practical outcomes geared to blessing and benefiting others—a creative focus based on Jesus' dual commandment to love God and to love one another.

Today such a model of God's radical good news is in fact being incarnated in poor communities around the world. Some of this I had witnessed in the north American urban mission initiatives. But Dallas too needed to see it and experience its power and opportunities. And the key resource required, even more than what money can buy, is people. Local people to be sought out, welcomed, loved, hopefully touched by the Gospel, integrated into an accepting community, nurtured and built up, and encouraged to serve the Lord within their own situation. A grand vision, demanding both time and workers.

After our first few stumbling years, once God began sending us people, a community development prospect seemed to become feasible. But moulding people as middle class, or weaning them away from their old frameworks didn't figure among our aims. The longer-term objectives and outcomes remained in God's safe hands—as assuredly did the power to attempt them. Sensing that I had little aptitude for leadership after the classical model, I sought to major on love: acceptance of people just as they were, respect for their humanity and their personhood, 'love covering a multitude of sins'. I used to think of it as 'leadership from the back' though of course that is a nonsense. At the time we didn't have all this thought through and tabulated in quintuplicate: we simply sought to be available and respond to those God sent us, with general guidelines in the back of our minds. The theorising about it was to come only in retrospect.

Our last few years at Dallas saw a harvest ripening. By then we had a good feel for the area and the parish, with its strengths and limitations. Likewise the people were comfortable with us. I had adopted a more ockerish conversational style—a sort of working class throwback (yet not so hard to resurrect). The well-spoken English public schoolmaster was a distant memory. I used to wonder whether Jesus, in his ministry amongst Galilean ignoramuses, would not have communicated through a robust vernacular. I didn't imagine him as *'a cut above the others'*, a factor not lost on the scribes and Pharisees enraged by the quality of what he said in his homespun Galilean accent.

In their communication the common people everywhere affect few airs or graces. Nor tolerate humbug.

Preaching the Good News

On the other hand in my preaching I sought to maintain an open and straightforward style, as befitting the exposition of the Scripture readings laid down for the day in the Common Lectionary used by all the mainstream Churches. As a late beginner this was a discipline I gladly accepted, though I have since wondered whether it wasn't creative enough, geared towards a dull conformity with conventional religion, prone to empty churches. At Dallas of all places we didn't need such conformity.

My answer was to use imaginative images from everyday life to open up understanding of an ancient text reflecting an age and culture lost on most people today. This approach was *topical preaching* on themes grounded in Scripture but applicable and vital to life in Australia today. Trying to scratch where it itched, and in the process attempting to convey what Christian faith has to say. For instance my first sermon at the church was 'The God of the Second Go', on God's patience.

A different (and traditional evangelical option) for preaching would have been to expound one book of the Bible in a series of sermons over several weeks in the expectation that the text, properly interpreted (or '*exageted*'), would speak for itself. But my judgment was that the people were not formally educated enough to profit from that approach.

Naturally over the 20 years spent in ministry my ideas about slipshod preaching were to develop considerably. Looking back on Dallas I think I was careless and lazy. The people deserved better. I now agree I was also indulgent in the length of many sermons, often going on interminably in the hope that something might lodge somewhere. But it took me a while to tune in to their wavelength, taking factors into account like their educational level, the limits on their capacity for abstract thought, the restricted range of their life experiences to relate to through the pictures I was trying to draw—and of course their attention span. Also I didn't rate preaching highly enough.

But as a creative initiative, in the rather elaborate '*pew bulletin*' that I prepared for each Sunday outlining the week's activities, I would write a brief reflection in simple, punchy English about the subject of the sermon. Reviewing some of these years later I was struck by their topical relevance and even their homespun eloquence. But I fear I was selling the people short. Frankly, I have to acknowledge that the growth in the parish came not through my 'brilliant' preaching but more from a wide raft of activities we devised, and the personal relationships built up, reflecting the time that we unstintingly invested in the people. Of course really it all came from the goodness of God.

But on leaving Dallas, I would totally forsake that slapdash approach to preaching, and ever since have invariably devoted seven hours in one sitting to the crafting of a worthy sermon, completed word for word by computer and presented next day with confidence and conviction. In retrospect these still seem to read well, but clearly my writing skills outranked my preaching.

Green shoots from the baked black clay

The range of new and group-focused activities and structures that arose at St Mary Magdalene's in those years were all *ad hoc* responses to particular situations rather than being part of some comprehensive plan. For example after Ken Harman, who had organised and led the painting of the church in our early days, moved into our parish territory he threw his lot in with us, to became a tower of strength: hearty, diligent, supportive, godly. I appointed him Vicar's Warden, my right-hand man: prayer companion, advisor, helpful critic. Before long I nominated both him and Alan Aylward, Chairman of the Vestry, to the Diocese to be licensed as Lay Readers with authority to lead worship services and preach, a role which they both took very seriously. Now we could go on holiday for a week or two and confidently leave them in charge, thus avoiding paying for outside help to be supplied by the Diocese.

But often the innovations seemed to arise spontaneously, as if their time had come. Of course they amounted to gracious answers to the regular, ongoing prayer that undergirded the parish and its people. For instance creative assistance was lent gratis by Nigel, an overseas aid worker who lived with us for some months, and also by the Rev'd Rick Cheung and his wife Jessica, originally from Hong Kong, but temporarily between parish placements. So for some months I had a reliable Associate Priest sharing the Sunday duties of leadership and preaching, and being a sounding board for our dreams and aspirations. It would lead to a lasting friendship, to my becoming godfather and now mentor to their two sons, both full-time tertiary students, and finally to that exquisite chapter of our lives represented by our love affair with China.

Focus on group life

With new personnel resources and a critical mass of parishioners, it was now time to create small groups focused on age, gender and interests. The Sunday School was functioning, the Food Bank was blessing some of the hungry in the general community, the house church was nurturing hitherto rank outsiders, the women's morning coffee group of about twelve was offering friendship to some who never came to church, while through the Christian Religious Education program Marjorie and I had contacts among non-Muslim families from North Dallas School such as the El Salvadorans with their five daughters (and later at Coolaroo South School also). Of course Marjorie had now come into her own, with multiple talents and aptitudes, full of ideas and as game as Ned Kelly, blessed with a king-size heart for building and sustaining loving relationships across the parish. She also launched a parish magazine entitled *Mary Mag's Mag* appearing monthly with newsy and inspirational articles, to build up the sense of parish identity. By ourselves we were a team ministry!

But what of the men?

We discovered a real gem in Ronny, an energetic young man of Italian background who had married into a Ceylonese Burgher family in the parish, a professional restaurant chef, amateur drummer in a band, and a weight-lifting enthusiast. With the help of some other younger men in the church he agreed to help launch a youth club, and later a monthly men's dinner, both of which took off like rockets. At its height, the kids' club was drawing 40 (mostly quite unchurched) teenagers to the church hall on Fridays for an early evening program! The word had quickly got around the kids in the local community, starved of a forum for meeting outside school. Borrowing the minibus from Broadmeadows Family Services, an Anglican welfare agency at Glenroy, I would weave my way around the suburbs, picking up and delivering the precious cargo.

The men's dinner became something of a legend, bringing a good number of newcomers into the parish life. In Tony I had another loyal offsider, a knockabout bloke who had done time for affray but later became a Christian. I appointed him the 'verger' (how Anglican! But at Dallas of course, honorary) to look after the property and its facilities, a rouseabout always on hand and willing to try anything. While Ronny officiated in the hall kitchen (quite well equipped), heating massive trays of luscious dishes he had cooked at home or brought from work, Tony and I would turn on the heating, set up the dinner tables, and lay them festively with tablecloths, chinaware, cutlery and place-cards, even the odd vase of flowers. It would look positively elegant—and certainly welcoming. And how it was appreciated: no way any of us would have got such a great meal at home! No wonder numbers climbed into the 20s, each man paying only a token contribution but revelling in the raucous humour of the night and becoming bonded through the experience. We had hit upon a winner. Thank God. There was always a speaker, sometimes from outside, sometimes one of us with something to share of our background or experience. Our twin objectives: sharing faith & and building community.

Youth ministry

Meanwhile to further the Christian nurturing of the secondary-age children of parishioners Marjorie began a junior youth group, partly drawing on contacts from Dallas North School. The small group enjoyed a balanced program of Christian and 'fun' activities, with the girls being trained up for liturgical dance. Twenty years later one of these, Simone, would invite us to her wedding! Despite the yawning age gap, a real love relationship grew between Marjorie and the group members. Particularly did we resonate with a German family with two boys, Alexander and Daniel, who often used our redundant computer. In my frequent visits to their home I was delighted to have the opportunity to speak about the Gospel with their mother and grandmother in German. From their dormant Lutheran background, soon they all became regular worshippers. For another boy, Mathew from an Army family, we facilitated a transfer to a new school after being bullied at Upfield high school with its majority of Turkish students, and later collaborated in his entry by scholarship into Ivanhoe Grammar School, which would change his life forever. He was to become the only university graduate from either of the Broadmeadows parishes, and that through accessing a New Zealand university (Otago, in Dunedin) under more favourable HECS arrangements. In his Arts degree he would study theology!

Spiritual growth group

Strangely enough, until this point the parish had never had any small groups specifically focusing on stimulating growth in faith through Bible study, prayer or fellowship. Sensing the sluggish spiritual pulse of the place (one token Eucharist on Sundays), I had hesitated to launch a white elephant. But now we judged the time ripe and Shirley, Ronny's Sri Lankan mother-in-law, was glad to open her home to a group of earnest believers. The simple Bible study materials used were geared to the needs of new Christians from a nominal Catholic background, prepared in Chile by the (Anglican) South American Missionary Society. They seemed to be appropriate to the group which grew in spiritual confidence and trust in God. And got to know and relate to each other as Christians, a new experience. For us sheer delight.

There had always been a problem of transport to the church, poorly located as it was on a main connecting road, isolated from any shopping centre and surrounded by small Housing Ministry and private homes. The original Fourteen drove their own cars, but now that the church—by the grace of God—had gone down-market we needed to ensure some means of transport for many of the less well-off newcomers living in the far-flung reaches of the parish. Initially Marjorie and/or I (with our two cars) would pick them up for church and drive them home but later we managed to persuade other parishioners to divert from their route to do the same. We were always at pains to ensure that young people were taken home safely from the youth group.

Celebrating the Parish's 25 years

But how spectacularly did the system fail on the evening of our grand festive day, the parish's 25th anniversary! Out of the blue a group of nubile nymphs from a girls' shelter appeared at our barbecue dinner on the vacant block beside the vicarage, (unbeknown to us) to be groomed and courted by one of our disabled guys, many years their elder. Later, after it got dark, he spirited one of the girls off, disappearing down to the oval, initially all beyond our ken, and we had to call the police. As Bishop Stewart, ever the humourist, put it to us later, "You know, it could have made the front page of *The Truth* (a ghastly Sunday scandal rag, mercifully now defunct): "Girl raped at church party". No matter how busy, you could never relax at such semi-public functions, reflecting as they did that proper Anglican tradition of being a public church, the antithesis of a closed sect.

On the other hand we did enjoy three or four swinging 'fun nights': twice we danced the night away at bush dances in the borrowed Catholic parish hall, attended by virtually our whole congregation plus inter-church visitors. We also ran a parish dinner & concert in our own hall, with musical items and ludicrous skits, and our son David and his dramatic mates staging his own play *Going my Way?* which he had toured to the Edinburgh Fringe Festival. What a great hit these fun nights: we were in our element.

Glory days

Undoubtedly in St Mary Magdalene's 26-year history these were the glory days. The struggles were now memories, the present was vibrant and the future assured. The proof was in the financial record. I had made it a matter of spiritual principle never to harry parishioners over money for the church. I never once preached a sermon on giving. We never ran a stewardship campaign. I doubt that the Early Church did either. It just seemed unacceptable for me to be burdening people almost invariably with incomes lower than ours—indeed a high proportion of them (to use the local *patois*) Social Security 'bennos' (beneficiaries). Instead, with our prayer companions we looked to God to supply our needs, bearing in mind the dictum of Dr Hudson Taylor, founder of the China Inland Mission: "The work of God, done in God's way, will never lack for God's resources".

The only point I ever made about money was made, not to the congregation but to the Vestry, which in the later years agreed to my suggestion (at first tentatively) to distribute a tithe (10%) of the church's regular income to Christian work *beyond* the parish: the Anglican Board of Mission, the Bush Church Aid Society, the Brotherhood of St Laurence, the Bible Society, etc. To the quite rational objection, "Vicar, this is crazy, we're a poor parish, we need the funds here", I would reply with conviction, "Look, God can do more with nine-tenths of our income than we can do with ten-tenths!" And precisely that was what we experienced: we gave it away, God gave it back—with interest. So much so, that in our last year we were contemplating telling the Diocese to forget their subsidy. We had come of age. It bears out a phenomenon discovered during charity door-knocks in Canberra when our kids were little: the poor are more generous than the rich. It's no wonder God has a heart for them.

At St Mary Magdalene's we now had a virtual team ministry serving the needs of a growing congregation, with the Fuhrmeisters, lay readers Ken and Alan, and Marjorie and myself all planning, praying, and working heartily together. One Sunday I published in the 'pew bulletin' a complete list of all the activities of the parish, with the names of all those responsible for them. To my surprise it turned out to be almost a complete list of the parishioners, demonstrating the holistic ministry of the Body of Christ at Dallas.

An external challenge

Alas! The glory days were not to last. A quite external factor arose which would ultimately change the whole equilibrium of the parish. At the neighbouring parish of St Michael & All Angels Broadmeadows, the world had turned. My praying colleague Geoff was invited to minister in a church in his old stamping ground and departed honoured and sung, after long years of successful ministry in an equally challenging parish to ours. The Bishop appointed a young man, Rev. John Power, from a small country parish in the Bendigo Diocese, decreeing that henceforth the two Broadmeadows parishes should collaborate closely in a joint ministry. Initially this worked well: we led services and preached in each other's church and would sometimes hold a joint service, in which the Dallas people were a clear majority.

Then the newcomer suggested a bold expedient: rotate the church layout clockwise! Instead of a long, narrow arrangement of the pews facing the front, it became a wide but shallow seating plan, crosswise—more contemporary, more intimate, more congenial. It seemed to work well. By then the diehards had either *died* (i.e. gone), or come to terms with the new stage of parish history which actually filled the church, mostly with people unaware of and unconcerned about its traditions. For a while we even tried two morning services, the traditional Eucharist early and contemporary worship later. But in the absence of a band it languished.

Preaching at St Michael's Broadmeadows one morning I well remember issuing a solemn warning (a prophetic word?) when the congregation objected peevishly to the antics of half a dozen rough country youths whom Rev. John had brought to Melbourne and set up as a Christian community in a rented house nearby. They had the charming habit of standing on the pews during a service to belt out the modern songs loudly and raucously. The Gospel reading for the day included the ominous verse, *"Every branch in me that does not bear fruit my father prunes ... and they are cast into the fire"*. Citing this, I warned the congregation that in God's Kingdom people rate more highly than furniture or proprieties. But the congregation was heedless and soon the youths, frozen out, had vanished and the community house fell through. At St Michael's it would indeed mark the beginning of a steep decline in spirit—and in numbers. So much so that, about this time the Bishop closed St Michael's altogether and the remnant of its congregation joined our parish, with Rev John appointed my associate priest.

Grandiose dreams

But ironically this was also the period when our discussions with Bishop Andrew Curnow, Bishop Stewart's successor in the Northern Region, looked promising about reconfiguring Anglican ministry across the whole expanding Broadmeadows area, including Coolaroo West, the new upmarket Meadow Heights, and the

Canberra-like satellite city of Roxburgh Park taking shape to the north. With the Bishop on board, our dreams encompassed a strategic approach by him to the billionaire tycoon who owned and was planning to extend the large Meadowfair shopping complex near Broadmeadows Station, hoping that he might allocate a corner section of his land for the building of an Anglican Centre for worship *and community service*. We had even roughed out a plan for a modern building with an internal courtyard garden setting. Convinced as we were of the unsuitable location of St Mary Magdalene's on its down-at-heel Dallas site and on the wrong side of the railway tracks, we could not envisage it ever being likely to attract upwardly mobile people from the new, higher quality and swiftly growing suburbs to the north-west, bereft of a church of any description, though blessed with a mosque and an Islamic Centre. As a regional hub now after decades reworking its social identity and experiencing increasing numbers of Muslim residents, Broadmeadows city centre was a strategic point for multicultural Christian witness.

One day I picked up the telephone in my study to hear the billionaire tycoon himself, the late Richard Pratt, on the other end of the line enquiring about our project, and in quite positive terms. What did we need? How would the project be realised? My heart leapt within me. I passed the call on to the Bishop, but later discussions were to prove fruitless, I suspect because the Diocese simply could not come up with its share of the funds required. Certainly our unsophisticated parish had nothing to offer, even if the land was gifted by the philanthropic owner of the shopping centre and the huge Visyboard manufacturing plant nearby.

Of course the dream was never going to succeed, but during our later optimistic years in the parish our fantasy had begun to spawn grandiose visions of a Christian advance in the newer areas. Having by then set aside my earlier aesthetic prejudices about the district by becoming increasingly identified with the people, I actually began to savour my evolving '*feel*' for Greater Broadmeadows and its future. For her part Marjorie loved Broadmeadows and its people so much that she declared her desire to retire there.

The sequel was that a large office for Centrelink was built on that choice corner block, opposite the Courthouse, the Leisure Centre and a medical complex. The dream had been a mirage, shimmering away in an uncertain future. With the city becoming increasingly Muslim, there were simply too few Anglicans—and in many cases those associated with our parish were non-viable. What *was* needed was not bricks and mortar on strategic sites, but human and spiritual resources to staff a Mission. Reality bites!

Incarnating urban mission?

The essential issues posed by the episode were the mismatch between Church insights and community realities. Doubtless there were 'little Broadmeadows' happening all around the growing edges of a metropolis of over three million, with a population drawn from around the globe with allegiances to a number of faiths. As members of the prim and proper Church of the Founding Fathers, Anglicans were (unwittingly) becoming increasingly concentrated in a band of affluent suburbs to the city's east and south while the population diversified elsewhere, unmatched by the slender resources of a Church unwilling (or unable) to transform its strategies from *'maintenance'* to *'mission'*.

Yet our experience had offered another dream: it *was* possible for the Gospel to win its way into the lives of people of all cultural backgrounds through incarnating the approach to urban mission glimpsed in the depressed inner-city communities of America. Though to us at the time testing yet tumultuous, our seven years at Dallas had seen our community of Christian worship grow exponentially. *Welcomed by **fourteen diffident Anglicans** we would be farewelled by **130 Christians**!*

Yet would it prove to be more than a momentary glint of light on the dappled sea of eternity? Ultimately only God can make that judgment. Our task was *'to be found faithful'*. Certainly for us those years in our early sixties would prove the most satisfying and joyful of our professional lives.

> "To God be the glory, to God be the glory,
> to God be the glory *for the things He has done.*"

19
Seeds Blowing in the Wind

Such was the backdrop against which Archbishop Keith Rayner invited me in 1993 to take on a not unfamiliar challenge: over the next six months: to examine the progress made in the Diocese in developing multicultural ministry and mission. Since at the time I was still teaching the ITEMS course on Multicultural Church each year at Trinity College or at Whitley, the Baptist College, I had a continuing awareness of the evolving Melbourne scene. He suggested that I work half-time on this project, over a period of six months (at my request later extended to eight). This came as a surprise to the Vestry and the people. A couple of senior leaders wondered aloud whether I knew anything about that esoteric field. I smiled indulgently. My involvement in the project was only feasible because Rev John was now available to work fulltime among the people of the merged parish, and I considered him well able to hold the fort for the next six months.

Multicultural research across the Diocese

But it wasn't the first such Enquiry in Melbourne Diocese. In 1984 Archbishop Penman had set up a Commission of Enquiry into Multicultural Ministry & Mission to grapple with the reality that *'the Anglican Church is a monocultural Church in the midst of a multicultural nation, and this implies the need for very considerable change'*. After six intensive months and with the involvement of some 100 people, the Archbishop's Commission had issued a splendidly comprehensive report entitled *A Garden of Many Colours*, unique for its time anywhere in Australia, a brilliant charter for a very different Anglican future for Melbourne, closely according with David Penman's inspired leadership. The following year, when I completed my assignment with the Victorian Council of Churches, that was the vision that he had recruited me to help him realise.

But in those years he had generated among Anglican diehards a reaction which distracted him from the task, so that at the time of his death in 1989 few of the 99 recommendations had been implemented. With his passing the vision had altogether languished, although the under-resourced diocesan Department of Multicultural Ministry continued its co-ordinative role since 1979 among the few ethnic congregations and its educative work with parishes. Now ten years later, Archbishop Rayner wanted a fresh examination of the situation to be made (raising hopes that reinvigorated action matched by adequate resourcing might be the outcome). I can only surmise that proposals had been put to him by some of the authors of the 1984 report, since I had had no contact with him and he would not have known of me. Neither had he evinced any personal interest in this focus of ministry.

Gathering data far and wide

Readily accepting the challenge of moving back into an operational space far wider than the parish I set to work with a will. An office for my Enquiry was set up in St Andrew's Hall, the CMS missionary training college at Parkville, within chattering distance of the monkeys in the Zoo nearby. To my surprise, my request to the Diocese for clerical assistance was granted and Rosemary Box, fresh from missionary experience in Tanzania, was appointed. At once we became a functional team, launching a spate of activity.

The first phase was to investigate and assess what was actually happening across the Melbourne Diocese in the realm of ministry to and among people of non-English-speaking backgrounds (NESB). In an effort to engage the whole Diocese, we sent an explanatory statement inviting a response to every member of the clergy and to all Anglican bodies: parishes, ,missionary societies, schools, theological colleges welfare agencies and chaplaincies. Also I actively sought interviews with whoever I considered might have some experience to share or an insight to impart (particularly clergy leading the NESB congregations such as the Tamils, the Chinese and the Persians) and over the next couple of months produced reams of handwritten notes on these encounters for transcription by Rosemary. In all I interviewed 75 knowledgeable people and in response to our invitation we received 36 submissions, plus 19 papers specifically commissioned to examine relevant issues. We also gathered 73 documents about multicultural ministry and mission, including some from the Sydney Anglican Diocese and from other denominations in Melbourne. It was clear that beyond the confines of our Diocese a great deal of thought and action was being devoted to the issues by the Churches.

In its range and depth I found this response heartening. Indeed such an outcome would dwarf the response to some government-sponsored enquiries Australia-wide! It proved conclusively that in certain quarters of our Diocese there was no lack of interest in addressing the issues posed by the increasingly multicultural character of Melbourne. The challenge was how the Anglican Diocese as a whole might relate to the scene with a practical and loving concern. But first we had to decide how to handle the masses of data that we had gathered and make it widely accessible.

Reporting findings and framing recommendations

Recognising how much my approach to the Enquiry had been informed by my earlier experience with government enquiries, it seemed appropriate to produce a sort of comprehensive 'governmental-type' report based on an interpretation of all the data gathered, but with a bias towards practical action. Our report would cover very broadly:

- The historical background to the Diocese's work with migrants
- The demographics of Melbourne
- Multiculturalism in Australia

- Relating to the ethnic minorities
- Towards a theology of cross-cultural ministry
- Mission—a call to engagement
- The Way Ahead: recommendations for action.

In October 1993 our Report was published as a book of 135pp. entitled *Seeds Blowing in the Wind: Review of Multicultural Ministry & Mission*, with the imprint of the Anglican Diocese of Melbourne, and myself as author. I met the costs of its publication from my own pocket, since funds available to me only ran to producing an in-house typed document, and I submitted it to the National Library of Australia for cataloguing in the national collection. Its title wryly but deliberately evoked the previous report of 1984, *A Garden of Many Colours*, implying that the garden had never truly taken root within the Diocese. But why was this so? As I noted in the first few pages:

> "The seeds of a strong future growth in the multi-coloured garden lie dormant upon the fallow land of our present uncertainties. Whether they are to germinate and take root, or are to be blown away by the harsh winds of this present socio-economic climate will emerge in the decisions that now lie before us as a Diocese".

As true as this undoubtedly was, it begs the question whether laying down the gauntlet from the outset amounted to wise psychology. To some readers the book may conceivably have appeared as a blockbuster, from the pen of a single individual at that time not widely known in the Diocese, though expressing strong yet idiosyncratic views. *"Who is this upstart, too clever by half?"* My answer to such an objection was by producing a thoroughly professional document, comprehensively based on current data and so cogently argued that by the end it might make a compelling case, scarcely deniable. Hence the wide-ranging chapters grounded in socio-economic imperatives as well as ecclesiastical perspectives. I sought to disarm objectors by an introductory paragraph:

> "I take responsibility for what is put forward on the basis of my own judgment, honed from over 25 years' involvement in the formulation of public policy and practice in the multicultural field in Australia, and observation of Christian ministry in a number of denominations and overseas multicultural societies, together with my role as incumbent of one of Melbourne's most multicultural parishes. I cannot vouch for having adequately represented every shade of diocesan opinion, nor to have been able to transcend my own social and theological stance. Nevertheless I have sought to take account of significant bodies of opinion within the Diocese, and to present a balanced set of findings".

Naming the reality of class

From the earliest pages the shock tactics are evident, aiming to bring home to the Anglican Church leadership how much they were out of step with the surrounding society—and this in two dimensions: ethnicity and class. As a particular instance, in my Dallas-Coolaroo parish resided more than one third of all the Turks in Australia! They were almost exclusively workers in industry. But the fact was that throughout the Diocese Anglicans were overwhelmingly identified with the Anglo-Celtic middle class (though now also embracing newly arriving Chinese and Indian *professionals*, indicative of the overriding affinity with class rather than ethnicity)—but not with workers of any background, old or new. Yet migration to Australia had essentially been by workers. So much so that in the older inner suburbs some Anglican property had been sold off, attesting to the traditional non-involvement with the urban working class.

Though scarcely commending itself to the church Establishment, this ethnic and class critique was a background to the thrust of the Report. The National Church Life Survey revealed that, against the overall Melbourne figure of 36%, only 8% of our parishioners were from NESBs[33]. In effect but unwittingly we were an 'ethnic Church', akin to the Greek Orthodox Church, but focused on our British Empire constituency[34], as archaic as that might sound near the end of the 20th century. This section of the Report concluded that, given the uneven distribution of Anglicans across the suburbs—now becoming ever more cosmopolitan—a circuit-breaker could be the growth of a 'missionary' concern across the parishes, implying *caring for* outsiders as well as proclamation. After all, that was the essence of Jesus' Great Commission in Matthew's Gospel: in his name to *go 'beyond'*, balanced by John's Gospel's challenge to Peter to *feed the sheep*. That is, the dual call to mission and ministry. This involvement opened up two vital sections of the Report: on the nature of mission and towards an understanding of Australia's multicultural policy.

The justice challenges of an increasing multiculturalism

As a very public body, the Anglican Church needed to base its policies on the most objective statement about multiculturalism, especially in the face of conflicting and sometimes emotional claims and counter-claims. The most recent policy statement on multiculturalism had been published in the 1989 Government document *National Agenda for a Multicultural Australia* and the philosophical underpinnings reflected Christian values of respect, equality, justice, and social responsibility. Multicultural policies were based on the premise that all Australians of whatever background should have an overriding commitment to Australia, and accept the basic structures and principles: the Constitution and rule of law, tolerance and equality, parliamentary democracy, freedom of speech and religion, equality of the sexes, and English as the national language. Multicultural policies conferred rights and imposed obligations, including the equal right of all to express their views, to

---

33   non-English-speaking backgrounds

34   That is, Anglo-Celtic Australians, plus migrants from former Empire lands such as India, Sri Lanka, Pakistan and Mauritius.

be protected from discrimination, to share their cultural heritage, to acquire and develop proficiency in the English language, and to enjoy equal life chances[35].

But there was still a vast unfinished task ahead, before all Australians (including the First Peoples) could enjoy anything like equality. The policy statement represented an aspiration and a charter, rather than a description of what had actually been attained. But for Christians, migrants were 'our neighbour' and 'the strangers within our gates', hence the scriptural injunctions were plain, in both the Old and New Testaments. Thus multiculturalism was not some optional statement about culture but a justice issue. Moreover, Australia was pledged to safeguard the human rights of all residents, of whatever background. Actually, it was largely the prudence and sanity of the evolving multicultural policies of governments of both stripes that had enabled our integration of more than four million migrants since 1950 to be so harmonious—world's best practice.

The Report then drew attention to the pale Anglican response beyond the Penman years, boldly claiming that a stumbling block in the Diocese appeared to be a lack of motivation, in that the main body of opinion at the decision-making level was not sympathetic to the underlying rationale of multiculturalism (though not from theological misgivings). "Basically not enough of us are interested in migrants and have limited personal knowledge of them—merely as part of the backdrop of our lives."

The chapter concludes with my impassioned confession:

> "I have to testify with real conviction that my cross-cultural contacts over the years, both in public life and in the ministry, have immeasurably enriched and delighted me. Some of us are no longer interested in a ministry closeted within a monocultural 'ghetto'. We desire to be modern Australians, oriented towards the future and not so much the past! And we have discovered that the vast richness of human cultures presage for us the wonder of belonging to the Kingdom of Heaven, of which our staging camp in this world is but a pale foretaste".

Comparisons odious?

On the basis of my ten years as consultant to the Victorian Council of Churches, two of them as a full-time worker, as well as from the fieldwork undertaken for the Review, I went on to outline our findings about the cross-cultural activity of other Victorian Churches, as well as the Anglican Diocese of Sydney. By comparison, though our Melbourne Diocese had the best formulated policy statement of any Church for adapting the life of a Church to the multicultural social reality—

---

[35] Viewed in retrospect from 2013, the only migrant group ever to breach this definition would become some radical Muslims, calling for instance for adjustments to be made across our whole community life in order to *accommodate their desires*: for 'halal' certification in major supermarket chains and elsewhere, and for the celebration of Christmas to be removed from the public sphere as offensive to them. One result of this extra-ordinary demand has been an understandable hardening of attitudes towards multiculturalism among certain quarters of the 'Aussie' community.

thanks to the holistic blueprint in *A Garden of Many Colours*—in practice we had relatively little to show. Doubtless this was related to factors such as our inward-looking preoccupation, the chronic unavailability of (financial, rather than human) resources, competing priorities and theological emphases, excessive social segmentation, lack of vision and confidence, the leadership issue, and even a degree of cynicism. On the other hand, several denominations were currently drawing up blueprints for reform and action at the national level, particularly the Uniting Church and the Salvation Army.

One of the indicators was the number and range of 'ethnic' congregations worshipping in their own language: in Melbourne the Jehovah's Witnesses had 30, including Japanese, Turkish and Aboriginal. In the Melbourne Catholic Archdiocese 52 ethnic priests were conducting masses for congregations speaking their languages. Our Diocese had five congregations: Tamils and Persians, two Chinese and one Japanese.

Further, in contrast to the Catholic schools, Anglican schools seemed to be bastions resisting change, in terms of their social composition and focus. Ironically, in the currently constrained economic climate some actually appeared dependent on recruiting students from Asia while (ironically) their orientation towards the local multicultural society remained quite nominal. Their replies to our questionnaire produced little grounds for hope.

On the other hand two of the Anglican welfare agencies focused on the needs of poorer NESB people, while Anglican Homes for the Elderly and several of the day kindergartens offered special programs geared to the needs of people from many backgrounds. Many parishes reported having NESB people among their worshippers, mostly from a variety of backgrounds.

Yet all too often it was in the parishes that conservatism and stuffiness ruled while the Church declined. Nor were we always seen as a particularly outgoing or friendly denomination, with our firm ideas of doing things decently and in order, rather than making concessions to today's community and our evolving lifestyles. Yet the Sydney Anglican Diocese offered evidence that parishes could introduce successful programs of making contact with new NESB residents, especially through organising programs of teaching English, often led by former schoolteachers. Of course it necessitated a clear rationale and a good measure of unity in a congregation desirous of launching out into the deep. The old watchword of 'assimilation' needed to be publicly repudiated, as indeed it had been by Australian governments fully 20 years earlier! Significantly, in the Sydney Diocese no less than half the growth was now coming from initiatives in multicultural ministry.

Responding to a unique community

Lest all this seemed to be high theory, the Report brought a case study of a parish where interesting things were happening. Of course (with all due modesty!), I chose the one I was most familiar with. After noting the harmony in diversity of the parishioners—a sign of Christ's unifying presence—but which precluded any *ethno-specific* programming, we cited a range of activities such as the weekly distribution of food to the poor, running a series of learning sessions in the vicarage about Islam, the priest learning Turkish through an evening adult-education course, renting our parish hall for Turkish women's pre-wedding parties, explaining Australian multiculturalism (through an interpreter) to the newly arrived local Turkish *hodja*, and tutoring him in English in the mosque house (by reading the psalms together—which count as part of Islamic sacred writings, the *Zabur*)—involvement in the local Migrant Resource Centre and the local Migrant Settlement Network of professionals, and offering support to a non-Anglican missionary couple working among the Middle Eastern communities of the area. The unifying motivation was to build up parishioners' confidence, by modelling the patient seeking of openings for friendship and Christian witness beyond our own Anglo-Celtic comfort zone.

Motivating change

In a chapter exploring the nature of mission, the Report then tackled 'the elephant in the room': the Melbourne reality of the two theological understandings of the Faith (the Anglo-Catholic and the evangelical), both of them shaping their expression in worship and service. But my experience from the extensive fieldwork over several months was that as a Diocese we seemed to be *'polarised and paralysed'*, so that we virtually ignored the presence of about a million NESB people in Melbourne—one third of the population, and with a younger age-profile than the Anglo-Celtic community. For the sake of our mission in the world we needed the power of the Holy Spirit to rebuke, renew and reform our Church, making us willing to forgo our mutual suspicion and antipathy. Where else to start but with repentance and prayer for healing? And praying too for the Holy Spirit to lead us into a new collegiality that might bridge the chasms of our theologies and traditions.

After a long chapter on concepts of Mission and the Kingdom of God, exploring dimensions such as the relationship of Gospel and culture—mission as *evangelism*, mission as *social action*, mission as *presence*, and mission as *dialogue with other faiths*—the Report proffered suggestions for the way ahead. The ultimate challenge was to encourage and empower more Christians to get involved, and this at their local parish level. At Dallas twice we had held a Multicultural Night, where all the parish cultures, including the Anglo-Australians and the Brits, shared their traditional foods, music, song and dance. But how would parishes widely find the will to engage?

We needed to recognise that the people of God had two roles to play in relating to the world around them, including in its multicultural dimension: those of the prophet and the servant. The former grappled with communicating God's message in meaningful terms (and language), shaping it to the hearers, reading their culture(s), moving with the times. The latter called for sensitivity and compassion in engaging with human needs at the local level, not with condescension but through identification. In general the Anglican Church had not been known for this, focusing rather on maintaining its traditions than following Jesus' model of *'emptying himself of all but love'*. Given the high status accorded to its clergy, and even more to its Bishops, who else could initiate profound change? But this implied a multicultural focus during their seminary years—and not only in academic terms but existentially, through practical exposure to culture and cultures. Hence the main thrust of the ITEMS Project, and the need for further follow-up. But sadly, and significantly, the questionnaire that I distributed around diocesan agencies had elicited *no response* from the theological colleges and subsequent discussions were to prove fruitless!

Fortunately Victoria had long been in the forefront of educational initiatives in this field: not only through the Victorian Council of Churches but across the Catholic Archdiocese and at the State level of the Uniting Church. Further, through the Ecumenical Migration Centre, Australia's premier documentation unit on migration, multiculturalism and community relations, programs had been devised for parish education. The best coverage of possibilities in this field was the fine chapter by Rev John Evans in *The Cultured Pearl* on 'Educating the People of God: Multicultural Awareness for Parishes and Clergy', a veritable treasure trove of practicable ideas. But unless opportunities for acquiring cross-cultural awareness were taken up, the Diocese's monocultural character and focus would be likely to endure into each new cohort of leadership.

In order to address these challenges through providing inspiration, taking soundings, and gauging the level of awareness across the Diocese, towards the end of the eight months' project we convened a one-day Consultation at Glen Iris parish, with some 60 key parish and agency representatives present. Speakers included representatives from Sydney Diocese, the Uniting Church, AIMA, and leading multiculturalists and ethnic clergy of Melbourne Diocese. The program featured a simulation game, plenary and group discussions and reports. The recommendations that emerged included ways of making contact with newcomers while avoiding paternalism, developing English-teaching programs, launching ethnic congregations, ministering to the ethnic second generation, and proposing a diocesan Director of Multicultural Ministries under a specific Bishop. This consultation was covered in an Appendix to the Report.

Blueprint for a different future

Seeds Blowing in the Wind closed with outlining a way forward, with proposals for action in the parishes and the wider Church (noting the reality that Anglican institutions do not take kindly to being externally influenced). On the other hand the urgency of the need was pressing, and no doubt whenever action was proposed there would be financial constraints in our less than affluent Diocese (compared to the resources available in Sydney). Though $10,000 had been earmarked for my Review and a mere $15,000 for the next year when the action recommended would be implemented (amounting to funding one half-time person!), every effort would need to be made to locate further sources of finance. Experience in Sydney had demonstrated that cross-cultural ministry, energetically embraced, brought life and growth, reviving a sense of mission and releasing the requisite resources.

Specific recommendations covered:

- A public commitment to a great leap forward to be made by the diocesan leadership;
- Clergy education and in-service training;
- Parish education;
- Welcoming NESB parishioners and adapting parish life to incorporate them;
- Facilitating ethnic congregations;
- Creation of a Cross-Cultural Ministry Unit;
- Committing to co-ordinated ESL teaching programs;
- Compiling a directory of cross-cultural resource people;
- Exploring public sources of funding;
- Monitoring the public arena and offering policy advice to leadership;
- and finally (tongue firmly in cheek): "For detailed proposals, see the 99 recommendations of *The Garden of Many Colours*." [wide-ranging and comprehensive—though after nine years still awaiting implementation!]

The qualifications desirable for a Director of Cross-Cultural Ministry were laid out in Appendix A of the seven Appendixes with which the report closed.

In order to expedite the Report's appearance on time the manuscript, deftly typed by Rosemary Box, was formatted and computerised by an external consultant and printed by a city agency for submission to the Archbishop with my covering letter, printed on page 1 of the 136 pages—production costs all out of my own pocket (though of course there was no mention of this!) *Seeds Blowing in the Wind* was well produced and quite handsome, the cover featuring original artwork of a hand scattering seeds, brown on yellow. The blurb on the back cover detailed the purpose of the publication and the imperatives it addressed to the leadership of the Diocese in Australia's most multicultural city. I was well pleased with it. Later, with the Archbishop's agreement it was sent (gratis) to all parishes and diocesan agencies. Subsequently I would receive many requests for copies by booksellers and enthusiastic multiculturalists around Australia. Above all, *locally* I awaited outcomes.

A deafening silence

I might as well have saved myself the trouble. The silence of the Diocese was deafening. To this day still irresolute about it, I muse about the reasons. Certainly the report pulled no punches, but surely a public body like a major metropolitan Church can handle truth-claims?. It was well reasoned and amply backed by evidence. Anything less forthright would have been mealy-mouthed, especially after having worked on it for eight months and gained such a comprehensive exposure to the actual situation in the Diocese, with its glaring lack of commitment.

Moreover I was reassured by the fact that *A Garden of Many Colours*, produced by a committee, was in many ways just as polemical—and was likewise ignored! But even more remarkable had been the forthright tone of the Report by the Archbishop's Theological Commission on Mission set up by David Penman and tabled at the 1989 Synod after his death—but *not endorsed!* It observed (truly):

> "We have not developed the important organisational skill of being able to read and interpret the Church's real condition
>
> ...Why is it that the Church is not adequately involved in mission? The world out of which Anglicanism emerged is quickly fading. There is no indication that we are attracting people from the diverse ethnic communities, or from youth, young adults or men."

Had the prophetic tradition of speaking truth to power no more validity in the Church?

Perhaps the very stones might cry out. Admittedly a stricture addressed to the Archbishop and Bishops such as *"Perhaps the primary challenge of multicultural mission is to repentance, faith and obedience"*, coming from a relatively new arrival in the Diocese (who *extolled Sydney* in the Report to boot), would smart. Still, silence is not an honourable, let alone a gallant response. I cannot recall receiving any letter or message of acknowledgement, let alone of appreciation or thanks for my eight-months' intensive work!

But at the Diocesan Synod a few weeks later a resolution I had sponsored was passed "calling on all parishes in the Diocese to study *Seeds Blowing in the Wind.*" Our group of multicultural Synod members had produced a leaflet to publicise the book, with some quotable quotes and some key recommendations.

But what diocesan action arose from "all parishes studying the report"? I had completed my task and I had no ongoing mandate to organise its acceptance and its implementation. The Report was out there in the public domain and had to stand or fall on its own merits. But it required someone in authority to take up its vision: pre-eminently it targeted the leadership. Doubtless it would have been perused and subsequently discussed at Bishops' meetings, but presumably the decision must have been made to ignore or dismiss its pleas—but by whom?—the Archbishop himself? (His antipathy alone would have ensured its demise.) And on what grounds? Maybe in the secular sphere its critical judgments might be cogent enough, but was the sub-text in fact threatening a Church's long-established sense of identity and practice? Or had I exceeded my mandate, in arguing theologically to the official theological experts? And were its judgments too harsh, or too reflective of evangelical theological perspectives? (In fact the overwhelming majority of the 'multicultural fraternity' in the Diocese were from the evangelical wing, the ones with a heart for mission and with a message.)

Finally, and most fundamentally, were the financial resources commanded by the Diocese so limited, compared to the Catholic and Uniting Churches, that we simply could not afford any further outlays? That would amount to an unanswerable case. In the end, shrugging it all off as a lost cause, I re-immersed myself in the ministry at St Mary Magdalene's.

A surprising—if belated—outcome

The best part of a year later in 1994 a letter arrived from Archbishop Rayner offering me the role of Director in a new Department of Multicultural Ministry—half time! So much for my sombre musings! Had my concern about the lack of reaction merely reflected a Public Service mentality anticipating prompt action rather than the Byzantine process of Church decision-making? If in fact they had accepted the Report, I was the one designated to carry it all out—single-handedly. Did that amount to a cynical decision: "He's proposed it all, now let's see what *he* can do"? How will we ever know? All I do know is that, when I re-read the desirable qualifications for the Director put forward in the Report, I was amazed to find myself looking into a mirror.

20
The Heartache of Parting

While on the one hand I now belonged to the Anglican Diocese's head office staff, which grouped together specific ministries (evangelism, chaplaincies, youth, community development, etc). I continued my role at St Mary Magdalene's leading a *de facto* ministry team consisting of Rev. John Power, with Marjorie as pastoral carer and director of Op Shops, assisted by Ian & Ruth Fuhrmeister in the home fellowship group. It was an exciting period of parish development: the place was abuzz.

Vainly trying to do the diocesan half-time job from my study in the vicarage, it soon became clear that I needed to physically separate out the two strands of my existence so that each would not obtrude upon the other. St Matthew's Glenroy came to my aid by offering space in their large late-Victorian mansion, largely under-utilised, for me to set up office. There I spent a few months devising policies for fostering the cross-cultural vision in Anglican parishes, within a theoretical framework of the 'manager-speak' laid down by the Director of Diocesan Services. It distracted me from real human-oriented ministry. So much so that in the end it became obvious that the double-barrelled—or rather, schizophrenic existence—would never be productive, in either direction.

The agony of choosing

I wrote to Archbishop Rayner, outlining the dilemma. Kindly, he offered me free choice between the two options. If I chose parish ministry I should continue to exercise it full-time at St Mary Magdalene's. But if I chose cross-cultural ministry with the Diocese the resources would only permit half-time employment. Torn between two loves, I appealed for guidance to Fr John Stewart, leader and chaplain of Retreat House in Cheltenham where many clergy had spent times of prayerful refreshment and guidance over the years. Staying there for a day or two, reflecting upon the pattern of God's good guidance throughout my life, the gradual emergence of a life purpose, and then envisaging which future path might release the most creative energies, I was referred by Fr John to the famous maxim of Ignatian spirituality: *'Go deeply within thine innermost being, and profoundly and prayerfully examine both options until one begins to speak of desolation and one of consolation, one of death and one of life'*. The concentrative process was facilitated by the presence of a silent retreat group with whom I had my meals. The shadows began to edge back as the light on the path grew stronger.

On the one hand at St Mary Magdalene's I had poured my very being into a ministry among poor but choice people whom I had come to love. Inevitably the issues of multicultural ministry had receded, though in time the parish came to reflect the diverse character of the local community and point the way to a more creative future. Moreover by their respect, warmth and love the people of the church had powerfully changed us (particularly me!). So how could I turn away to pursue a private agenda? And where would that leave Marjorie, the beating heart of our joint ministry?

On the other hand the passion running like a golden thread through my whole life was about managing difference: different languages, different lands, different cultures.. In search of what that all meant I had travelled the world—observing, contemplating, feeling, dreaming. My whole work life, in three professions and three lands, had focused on facilitating connections for people whereby they retained their identity and their humanity while coping with a different environment: kids growing up, migrants learning new ways of surviving, governments broadening their concerns, parishes seeking to draw in outsiders.

But more specifically, didn't I have a background of unique experience and cultural/political savvy to draw upon which could now be turned to good account for the Church in Melbourne? Wasn't that why God had led us here and guided us along the paths leading to this moment? Joseph in Egypt? With this new prospect on offer, would it be right to leave all this hard-won experience on the back burner by continuing to focus only on the small-scale project in Dallas? Besides, deep within, wasn't there a passion stirring? It seemed good to...

I informed the Archbishop of my choice to pursue the cross-cultural ministry role, on the half-stipend. I withheld from him that I would in fact be working full-time, since half-time would be unthinkably ineffectual. And over the next four years that was to be the story, incomprehensible (if known at all) to the bean-counters but to me deeply satisfying. If you believe in your work that's already half the battle won. Let the other half be remunerated!

Drastic domestic implications

The decision to take up the cross-cultural ministry task full-time was to put us out of our home at Dallas, and face the gut-wrenching prospect of saying goodbye to the people who for the past seven years had been the focus of our life and our love. On entering the ministry no one had ever forewarned us about the pain of such a dismal scenario. This seeming betrayal of friendship was made worse by the parishioners' incomprehension of why we were leaving or of what cross-cultural ministry meant, since I had never mentioned it as a concept (but simply practised it without fanfare as the membership diversified). Even my vicar's warden was unconvinced at the wisdom of my decision. What did St Ignatius have to say about *desolation*?

So where would we live? There was no house that went with the job and, unlike many of my Melbourne-born colleagues, we had no home of our own here. Providentially (funny thing that) a vicarage became vacant beside one of the oldest churches in Melbourne, St Stephen's on Richmond Hill, in the first historic suburb east of the city, built in 1851 on extensive land marked today by a massive oak. The original vicarage having been sold off, we could occupy the more modern brick building (c. 1970s), forsaken by the vicar for an expensive purpose-built residence next door. Though on Church Street, a tram line and a major north-south route crossing the Yarra, behind the bulky Gothic church and beside the overlooking massive bluestone Catholic parish church of St Ignatius (now also become my patron saint because of the guidance maxim?), we were to find a haven of peace.

Gut-wrenching farewells

With their expressions of sadness and affection our final days at St Mary Magdalene's were rather poignant. Actually we were quite burnt-out, and probably should have been thinking of the long-service leave soon becoming available. But shortly before, when we had copped from a leading member the first (fairly mild, though honest) words of criticism ever addressed to us we had fallen in a heap, saying to each other this confirmed it was time to move on. Our farewell Holy Communion service in October 1995 was memorable for the large congregation and the emotional charge. Referring to our own servanthood in the parish, I preached on the text from Luke 17:10 when Jesus told his disciples: "Likewise with you, when you have done everything you were told to do, you should say, *'We are unprofitable servants, we have only done our duty'*".

Later circulating among our friends over a copious morning tea in the church hall, we were bidden by the Vicar's Warden, Ken Harman, to close our eyes and when we re-opened them, there sat our Regional Bishop, Andrew Curnow, ensconced in all his episcopal finery.

We were touched: there was no expectation, let alone obligation, for the Bishop to favour us. The ensuing speeches were a wonderful mix of maudlin emotion and ockerish sincerity—a well-educated Indian proclaimed that if I'd entered the priesthood earlier in life I would have been a Bishop—culminating in the whole congregation trooping out to stand in broad array in front of the building while Alan Aylward, photographer *extraordinaire*, recorded the moment for posterity (now framed and hanging on our walls). If we had begun our ministry at St Mary Mag's with 14 or so diffident locals, after seven wonderful years we were privileged to be farewelled by some 130 affectionate friends. *To God be the glory for the things he has done...*

Time out

Now in pensive retrospect we view the Dallas years as the most gratifying and fruitful time of both our working lives. To be sure, the parishioners made large demands on us—we were learners in their school—but on the whole we managed to meet the challenges. We worked hard and long. For instance, once feeling utterly drained, on checking back in our diaries we found we had worked 21 consecutive days without a break. Then I would freak out and, while Marjorie would sometimes plug on indomitably, I would go bush alone into the Dandenongs (always a mountain man), and after an indulgent lunch in a tourist venue, spend a lush afternoon reclining in the laid-back driver's seat of the Camry station waggon: lost in the healing tones of ABC Classical FM, transported by the splendour of a baroque oratorio or moved by the beauty of a Dvořak symphony: the blended glories of music and nature applying soothing balm to the soul.

Over the years in our recuperative times out, we had explored the heart-rending desolation of the clear-felling of Mt Disappointment on the Great Divide north of the city (and also on Mt St Vincent), had stayed for short breaks at Pallotti College near Warburton, sometimes camped in an on-site van at the Wycliffe Bible Translators HQ at Kangaroo Ground, and once had got lost in the bush after sundown on a rainy midwinter evening at Blackwood in the central highlands.

"The night is dark, and I am far from home, Lead thou me on".

Daunted by the prospect of a winter night huddled in a burnt-out car body by the track, but then glimpsing shimmering reflections on a waterhole (or was it a will o' the wisp?), we stumbled upon the only occupied house in the whole Wombat State Forest! Soaked to the skin, we were taken in and dried out by a kind lady who ran a wildlife resucue centre in her home. She rescued us!!

"Lead, kindly light, amidst the encircling gloom.
Lead thou me on".

With son David I had stood long and silently in the snow on Mt Baw Baw before lunching in a remote bush pub at Noojee, and another day we lay head to head yarning on a long thin seat on Flinders Peak, summit of the You Yangs near Geelong. Other times I would take my mountain bike in the Camry station wagon and amble along disused rail trails, and once around the heritage gold-mining town of Maldon with its evocative railway museum. Choice memories of a rare tranquillity equally part of our tumultuous Broadmeadows years.

The heartache of parting

At Dallas we had reconnected with working-class and unemployed people and were recognised as being on their side. But we also brought them the precious gift of the Gospel of hope that we had encountered and internalised many years earlier, and at times had the joy of seeing a growth in grace and maturity. Mostly we were spared the heartache and tragedy—often the inescapable cost—of ministry, and as we made our final farewell we rejoiced in the goodness of God and the loving warmth of a special band of his faithful people.

But actually, Marjorie harboured an unspoken resolve to continue her work in the two Op Shops that she had set up during the later years: in the Dallas shopping court and in Olsen Place, Broadmeadows, now no longer manager but a helper driving across from Richmond. They had been her love-child, and they had thrived in both dimensions of raising finance and building parish community. Several of the voluntary workers with no links to the church enjoyed the fellowship of the busy 'workplace' which enhanced the shape and meaning of their lives. But this link was brusquely terminated by the Archdeacon's intervention that, as etiquette and custom demanded, clergy having once completed their ministry in a parish must not maintain ongoing contact, beneficial as it might have proven. *Just go!* Albeit with the pain and loss of parting.

21
Challenging the Church Establishment

At Richmond our two-storey vicarage was well-appointed, with family facilities upstairs and a public area downstairs looking onto a pocket-handkerchief-sized garden where I replanted bushes from Dallas which, unlike the church, had only ever languished in the baked black clay. We soon came to love the convenience, style and verve of inner-city living, finding the three east-west shopping strips of Richmond with their worldwide cuisines a collective mecca. On establishing ourselves there we both took up new posts in the Anglican Centre in the cathedral complex overlooking the City Square across Flinders Lane, in the minuscule 'Department' of Cross-Cultural Ministry and Marjorie in the 'Department of Community Development' researching the provisions for disability around the parishes and supervising a social work student's field placement.

Networking and campaigning

It was late in 1995 that I took up my fulltime calling to encourage the development of cross-cultural ministry in Melbourne Diocese. Having forsaken parish ministry in order to grapple with the challenge, and before that having written the handbook for the task, I was rarin' to go. To fail would be to set back the cause by years. Already from my temporary Glenroy base I had organised a meeting of all the ethnic clergy, since they didn't really know each other—what else would bring a Chinese and a Japanese minister face-to-face? Now at Richmond we began with a celebratory multicultural lunch in the vicarage, sharing hopes and visions and prayers. This was to become a regular gathering, Richmond being so central, and over the years the number of clergy and the range of their ethnic backgrounds expanded. Later, Rev Robert Vun from east Malaysia, newly appointed to the Mandarin and Hakka-speaking congregation at St Matthias North Richmond, would become a leading figure in the cross-cultural movement, offering his parish facilities as venue for our regular cross-cultural working lunches.

It was also important from time to time to join with the ethnic clergy in their own worship services and community life: at the Chinese Chapel in Little Bourke St, with the Sri Lankan Tamils at East Malvern, the Mar Toma (Indian) congregation at Mitcham, and at a Persian house party on Phillip Island. In reality, the earliest ethnic congregations were mostly from the far-flung reaches of the former British Empire, often reflecting a colonial cringe and perhaps worse, a stuffy Anglicanism out of touch with contemporary Australia.

But ten years later it would be the advent of the Sudanese fleeing oppression by the Arab Muslims in their tortured country that would shock the Diocese into practical action. They were the product of colonial English and American missions (and teaching of English) among the animistic tribes of south Sudan. Their arrival in considerable numbers, including several ordained Anglican ministers, would shift the emphasis of my successors: no longer salespeople promoting parish recognition of the multicultural environment, as much as mentors of resettlement ministries happening among new language groups.

Indeed, by 2013 no less than 31 congregations across the Diocese would reflect 15 ethnic groups, mostly formed well after my time: Dinka (with eight congregations alone!), Nuer, Moro, Chollo/Shilluk, Bari, African Arabic, Karen, Malayalam, Hakka, Indonesian, Pakistani, Maori, Samoan, and Tongan, joining the original Chinese, Tamil and Persian congregations. By way of reference, by 2013 there were people of 199 overseas ethnic backgrounds resident within the total Australian community.

But back in the 1990s the key thrust of my program had been to persuade the traditional Anglican parishes of Melbourne to perceive and relate to the migrants living around them from all parts of the world—a transplanted mission field—but this was an uphill slog. Comfortably tucked away in their islets of refuge from the swirling currents of cultural diversity lapping at their doors, almost invariably they were into *ministry* rather than *mission*, that is, self-focused rather than other-oriented. I preached in many parishes, spoke to parish vestries and at one stage pleaded with the Council of Bishops, organised regional workshops, convened and attended seminars and consultations, wrote articles for the Church papers.

Above all, each year at the Diocesan Synod the small but potent 'ginger group' of multicultural enthusiasts used to scheme with me about how best to make an impact on the decision-making and resource-allocating annual assembly. Most of the group were Anglo-Australian clergy but spiced up by some feisty ethnic colleagues—Chinese, a Japanese and a Tamil. Over the years we made some creative presentations and voiced plaintive pleas, often backed up by the ethnic leaders themselves. But to little avail. Unfortunately it was the time when the Church was hitting its nadir, with declining numbers, dwindling finances and ponderous leadership. To seek extra funding, or even to maintain the shaky *status quo*, was made to appear visionary—or just plain out of touch!

A bridge too far?

Sometimes I have wondered whether my final make-or-break appearance by invitation at Bishopscourt before the Bishops' Council didn't actually entrench their disinclination. Having presented a compelling case based on immigration statistics and social indicators from the Census, backed by Scriptural imperatives about 'making disciples of all nations', and reaching out beyond Jerusalem 'to all Judaea and Samaria and to the ends of the earth'[36], I made so bold as to issue a final challenge: "Gentlemen [they were all men], unless the will to respond is present in

---

36   Jesus' final words to his disciples in Matthew 28:19 and at his Ascension, Acts 1:8.

this room, we will see no change in the parishes" or some such impertinence. I was icily thanked and departed in disarray. *Just slightly injudicious...*

What did eventuate however, on the retirement of the Director of Diocesan Services, Rev. Howard Dillon, was a mini-palace revolution leading to a rationalisation of the agencies grouped in the Anglican Centre, whereby the mission-oriented 'departments' were sidelined or abolished. I continued as a one-man band, typing my own correspondence and documents on my own new-fangled 'Brother' word-processor (forerunner to desktop PCs), though very friendly with the Personal Assistant to the new Director who used to alert me to looming crises in the shrinking church bureaucracy. A pale reflection of the old Canberra intrigues, but challenging withal.

Supplementary projects

More positive was my role in facilitating the Melbourne Diocese in following Sydney's lead by mutually recognising the Mar Toma Church in South India, traditionally held to have been planted by the Apostle Thomas (at the outset a doubter of Christ's resurrection)—and more than a thousand years older than the worldwide Anglican Communion. Once I had preached and helped lead a Holy Communion service in the Church's well-heeled Melbourne congregation, meeting in an Anglican parish church at Mitcham, and had subsequently been approached about arranging for their Singapore-based Archbishop to meet with Archbishop Rayner in his capacity as Primate of the Anglican Church of Australia. I prepared briefing notes for the occasion, and hovered at the back of the formal photograph recording the moment when the two leaders consummated the act of mutual recognition. Shades of St Paul meeting with the Apostle Peter to resolve tensions between Gentile and Jewish Christians—though in this case it wasn't clear to me which one was which!

Once I preached in St Paul's Cathedral at a Sunday evening service (never well attended) but for me a memorable milestone, marked during the solemn liturgy by the sacristan's dignified shepherding me up to and down from the exalted pulpit.

Promoting the teaching of English to migrants

But undoubtedly the most enduring outcome of these years spent in the diocesan HQ was the emphasis on promoting the teaching of 'English as a second language' (ESL) to migrants. Clearly it could be an effective means of a local parish community making contact with newcomers to Australia, as well as a strategic gift of loving service. The key figure was Jan Shattock, former missionary turned ESL teacher and later teacher-educator, who called at my office one day and took all of five minutes to open up a new dimension in the Diocese's cross-cultural mission—and in my life. It triggered distant memories of teaching English in Germany (for which I really had no formal training) and later, in the Commonwealth Office of Education, of preparing the practice exercises for migrant English textbooks. To my shame as a linguist, I now realised I had never actually taught English to any migrant. In retrospect Marjorie and I regretted that at Dallas we did not have the courage to close the unproductive Day Kindergarten and offer daytime English classes in the parish hall for newcomers. In particular Middle Eastern women in the area were cut off from any participation in the local community through their lack of English.

So the new challenge was how to promote ESL teaching around the parishes. A quick check indicated that there were a few active spots (Clayton, North Richmond, South Melbourne, North Melbourne come to mind), but no wider policy commitment because of the exclusionary British Empire syndrome: 'our only overseas parishioners already speak English—and no Vietnamese or Turk is going to turn up at our worship services'. I couldn't recall Jesus mentioning anything about languages in urging the disciples to go to the uttermost ends of the earth to proclaim the Gospel. But I doubted that Aramaic or Hebrew would have met the challenge. Maybe the Holy Spirit gave the gift of tongues to make such contacts possible? Or did cross-cultural mission by its very nature demand that the central role of language be addressed?

Well aware of the sophisticated network of parish English classes in the Sydney Diocese, using locally prepared materials which included biblical material in simple English and a centralised advisory system, we organised a two-day seminar featuring the Northern Gurus which led to a number of our parishes taking the plunge. Later it would include St Michael's Bennettswood, along the way ushering Marjorie and me into a brand new day—of adventures in China!

Going national

In 1997 the Anglican General Synod (national parliament of the Church meeting triennially) set up a Multicultural Committee with the short-term brief of advising the Australian Church on how it might more sensitively relate to the full ethnic range of the Australian population. (My erstwhile Melbourne challenge now finally gone nationwide!) The immediate task was to draft a background paper for discussion by the next General Synod, to meet in Adelaide. In view of the analytical and prescriptive documentation previously prepared for the Community Relations Office in Canberra and later for the Victorian Council of Churches (obviously both with a far broader scope than Anglicanism), it was unsurprising to find myself nominated for membership.

At the first meeting, held in the General Synod's offices in St Andrew's House beside the Cathedral in Sydney, I became secretary, as one of a handful of Anglicans in Australia working fulltime (if on half-pay) in the field, all the others being in Sydney—but oddly enough co-ordinated by a reactionary cleric bent on safeguarding the Anglo hegemony, the while paternally presiding over a major English-teaching thrust!

I enjoyed working closely with the committee chairman, Roger Herft, Bishop of Newcastle. A Sri Lankan Burgher (reflecting earlier colonisation of Ceylon by

Portuguese, Dutch and English) and the most senior NESB figure in the Australian church, in 2000 he would come close to being elected Archbishop of Melbourne (including on my vote) when Dr Rayner's successor would become Peter Watson, from Sydney Diocese, a fellow-Cantabrian of John Howard's vintage.

While the Multicultural Committee brought together the full range of outlooks, the convinced multiculturalists held sway. Ironically, the charming troglodyte of Sydney turned out to be another fellow-Cantabrian of my era who lived near me. Still fighting a rearguard action, he was yet to come to terms with the cultural diversification of Punchbowl, let alone of Australia!

The new Committee, comprising two bishops, an archdeacon and two 'hands-on' cross-cultural workers (from Sydney and Melbourne), duly produced a strong case for profound change in attitudes and practices, to be tabled for discussion at the 1998 General Synod in Adelaide, together with a punchy brochure for mass distribution around the Australian churches[37]—*mission accomplie*.

Scarcely. Understaffed and overworked, the General Synod Office (national co-ordinator) seemed unable to cope with the task of getting the material down the line and into the hands of the rank-and-file. Worse, come the five-day Adelaide session of General Synod, in which I was proud to be an elected Melbourne representative (the apex of my Anglican career), the agenda was so full and the factions so stroppy that it was only on the last afternoon that a motion on Multicultural Ministry was slated for discussion. Though empowered with the right of addressing the Synod and fingering my prepared speech, I had sat through the days of stultifying debate over what I considered enormous trifles, the playground for canon lawyers remote from the everyday scene. I was dumbfounded when a slick final motion was passed that the bundle of remaining agenda items be remitted for future consideration by the Standing Committee. That is, relegated to limbo!

Later I would be assured by the wiseheads that it was par for the course with General Synod, chaired by our own Archbishop Rayner as Primate. Unlike with the Uniting Church (whose National Assembly I had attended a decade earlier in Adelaide as an observer from Al Grassby's Community Relations Office) societal issues related to mission were of secondary importance. Issues of church structure and administration held pride of place. Naïve me for imagining otherwise!

Pity the pioneer

In the light of the escalating commitment to multicultural ministry and mission that would become manifest in Melbourne Diocese over the next 20 years, pre-eminently triggered by the advent of more exotic newcomers, it seems clear in retrospect that my role was destined to be that of a prophet ahead of his time, a voice crying in the wilderness, but whose vision no matter how clearly perceived (and I trust, articulated) had to await its time. Of course this was also true of the

---

[37] *Disciples of All Nations*, pleading that the Church be no longer seen as merely the church 'of the English migrants' but rather, mirror the ethnic mix of the local population while initiating practical action at parish level in worship, outreach, and recruitment/training of clergy.

advent of the Federal Government's policy of multiculturalism. It goes without saying that the pioneer's is often a lonely, controversial—and maybe thankless role. But gratifying withal!

22
Battling for Two Asylum Seekers

One day during my early years at the Anglican Centre an epic saga was heralded by a polite tap on the Penman Room door while our Divisional staff were in conclave. It was reported that two Indian-looking men were seeking help, and the Director nodded to me, *"They're yours. Just see what they want, briefly."* I ducked out and spoke to the two. They had arrived from Pakistan a few days earlier and were seeking help from the Church in resettling in Melbourne. I asked them to wait a short time until the lunch break, when we could go across to an Indian take-away nearby to talk. I recruited my colleague Murray Seiffert, leader of the Community Development section, to join us.

Enter two asylum seekers

What we heard rocked us. They were Pakistani Anglicans who had fled their country after being threatened and bashed by Muslim fundamentalists, and had arrived legally by air on a short-term visa to attend a training course at the Alan Walker Institute of Evangelism in Sydney, but had left the party en route to seek help in Melbourne for their real agenda of being allowed to stay in Australia. We were touched by their story but also wary: in the Immigration Department's unofficial ranking of ethnic groups' credibility Pakistanis came second lowest. Sternly I warned them: if their story was true we would go to hell and back to help them, but if not "we would drop them like a hot potato". A harsh opening stanza to a seven-year human drama.

An hour later, convinced of their *bona fides*, Murray and I swung into action. His phone call to a Uniting Church refugee support group at Ivanhoe immediately struck gold: as it happened the house acquired by the parish for emergency refugee accommodation stood empty. They could move in that evening. There was food in the refrigerator and the beds were made. The parish would take them under its wing and assist with initial familiarisation and care. Like stunned mullets they were driven off by Murray, who lived nearby.

Though both from Lahore and both named Saleem it turned out that they were no relation and had only recently met. The older man, Walter, was well educated and well spoken, with documentation purporting to confirm his claims that he worked as editor of publications for the Bishop of Lahore in the United Church of Pakistan and belonged to the Association for the Protection of the Human Rights of Christians. He had been comfortably off but had had to leave his wife and four children behind after suffering back injuries in a beating by thugs threatening to kill him as an activist when they broke up a Christian march. (The rights of all religions are guaranteed under the Pakistani Constitution.) It was the

Bishop who had suggested linking him up with the party travelling to Sydney for the course.

The younger man, Saleem Artur, likewise fleeing from fundamentalist-inflicted injuries—bashed and left for dead under a bridge, but taken in by a group of Christian 'Untouchables'—had been tucked into the party as an afterthought. In his late 20s and far less sure of himself, he was something of a shadowy figure with an aptitude for massaging the truth, as we were soon to discover from his variable stories and claims—a tendency reflecting the majority Islamic culture of expediency in regard to truth when the interests of Allah are at stake. Pakistan [= *Land of the Pure*] had been created as a homeland for Indian Muslims on partition of the sub-continent in 1947, loosing a savage welter of mutual bloodletting by both Muslims and Hindus.

Though from a large and dysfunctional family of Christian slum-dwellers[38], Saleem had been given the opportunity by a Hindu benefactor for whom he worked as a child gardener, of studying at a Catholic school that was later Islamised under the military president, General Zia ul-Haq. He notably strengthened the Islamic institutions and in 1986 enacted the infamous Blasphemy Law with its mandatory death penalty. Saleem had even completed some tertiary study, though it had exposed him to overt hostility culminating in the attack that caused him to flee to Karachi and later to Melbourne. Both spoke excellent English with strong accents.

After only a few days of living together, they were already finding it a challenge to get along. But our commitment to both of them meant that their lot was irrevocably cast with each other. For instance, early on we drove them out of town up into the Kinglake ranges for lunch in a country pub, and walked them through the bush to get a feel for the land, as well as demonstrating our caring support for them both. And later we were to take them to Wodonga for the AGM of the Victorian Council of Churches, where they were billeted with Christian families over a weekend.

But in our ignorance of the new asylum seeker scenario then starting to emerge—compared to Malcolm Fraser's orderly refugee resettlement program well understood and widely supported from the post-Vietnam War days, and even decades earlier with the Jews and Displaced Persons from Europe—here we were now thrown in at the deep end. We had to shoulder the full responsibility for their longer-term prospects, as well as for their immediate wellbeing. But never had it occurred to us that the story could become so protracted or so anguished.

Initial Immigration Department hearing

Having consulted with my contacts in the Melbourne Office of the Immigration Department, the opening gambit was to arrange for them to be interviewed

---

38 The Christians are found largely among the poor; before Partition many would have been from lower castes or even Untouchables (Dalits). Often they were characterised by higher status Muslims as 'the dirty Christians', illiterate or poorly educated, working in the most unpleasant jobs as street sweepers or in the sewers, etc. Not all were churchgoers, though they were well aware that their faith sundered them from the 96% Muslim majority

separately to have their stories assessed. As a favour I could sit in on the interviews but without permission to speak. A few weeks later came Walter's appointment and I went along to give him heart. To my amazement he took the floor at once by announcing (uninvited) *"First let us pray for the Lord to bring about a just outcome"* and led off with a prayer! Probably he thought that, Australia being a 'Christian' country, this would be a normal way to begin, like a church meeting. But I suspect it failed to impress the hard-bitten Immigration officer who, after conducting a cursory interview in a rather offhand manner, dismissed us. Saleem's interview was even sketchier, but in my *naïveté* at the time it didn't dawn on me that they were both 'being given the run-around' by officials. Imagine my shock a month later when they were both sent bald letters of rejection. They were shattered.

Follow-up enquiries elicited the fact that there was an independent body called the Refugee Review Tribunal, unrelated to the Immigration Department and pursuing its own legalistic procedures, before which it was highly advisable to have legal representation. But how to arrange this and how to find the money? And how to strengthen the credibility of their cases? Now Murray and I began to re-examine the considerable material which Walter had brought with him in support of his claims, quizzing him closely and deliberately acting sceptical and hard to convince. We concluded that it hung together plausibly enough (to us) but that we would need to find a barrister specialising in such cases. As for Saleem, his prospects seemed far dimmer, given that he had limited documentation and often changed tack in claiming what it represented (much of it was in Urdu, for which I needed to arrange expensive certified translations).

Engaging a legal advisor

About the same time, taking my turn to conduct an after-work Holy Communion in a side chapel of St Paul's Cathedral, I was approached by a lady from Colombia about seeking asylum. Next day we met and, on hearing her story of fleeing from a death threat by FARC guerillas because she was working with an American university research team, I outlined the procedures and conducted a tough mock interview to dispel any illusions. But when the real interview took place some weeks later, Cecilia was granted immediate asylum, despite the lack of compelling evidence other than her word. Later I was shocked to learn that the interviewing officer was leaving the Department that week and had simply followed her heart, irrespective of procedures.

In the men's case, we were directed to Erskine Roden, an older lawyer well experienced in asylum cases and a considerable humanitarian. He was kind enough to charge far less than the going rate for a barrister, and by then we were so deeply identified with the case that we footed the bill from our own pockets. As a result of their failed Immigration interviews, the two asylum seekers had forfeited the right to work to support themselves. Their case was to become my blooding in the contemporary immigration scene which had moved on well beyond my earlier experience. It seemed more about keeping people out: Al Grassby used to term it 'the Department of *Emigration*'. Also it fell within my line of work as the Anglican Church 'expert' in such matters—though this didn't count for anything in impressing the authorities.

Outside our office life the case came to preoccupy many of our waking hours, aggravated by the glacial pace at which the review system moved. Always there were months of waiting for the next review, during which time we had to empathise with two men being drained of hope and with virtually no contact back home. With their lives on hold, the agonising years of a meaningless existence ground them down. They were surviving on a small regular payment from St James' Anglican parish Ivanhoe for doing church gardening, cleaning and maintenance. During this period the Uniting Church parish wanted them out, since the refuge was for short-term use only and (ironically) they wanted to install a Muslim family. By then coming to terms with the local scene, both men managed to find alternative accommodation, Walter quite close by in a furnished garage, and Saleem across town. He had developed links with a Catholic parish.

Years into the drama, for Walter the saga was to climax one evening when I was visiting him and he was sharing news from home—all bad. His tormentors were now threatening the family he had left behind in Lahore. I took him down to an Indian restaurant in Burgundy Street, Heidelberg where over Chicken Tikka he slumped into utter despair. Maybe my instinctive reaction was the appropriate one. I could only lean my head on his shoulder while we sobbed together—in a crowded restaurant.

The firstfruits of a Pakistani martyrdom

But finally rescue was to come from the most unexpected quarter—Pakistan! And through a public tragedy. The Catholic Bishop of Faisalabad, John Joseph, having sat through the trumped up blasphemy trial of one of his flock and on hearing the death sentence pronounced, moved out onto the courthouse steps where, voicing an impassioned plea for justice, he drew a revolver from his robe and shot himself dead. The Christian movie subsequently produced about this act of desperate self-sacrifice underlined Jesus' words, "Greater love has no man than this, that a man lay down his life for his friends. You are my friends if you do what I command you: love one another as I have loved you" and "The Good Shepherd lays down his life for the sheep"[39].

In Melbourne the repercussion was immediate. Walter could produce documents conclusively demonstrating his collaboration with the Bishop in the Christian human rights association. So his case never came before the Refugee Review Tribunal. It was resolved 'on the papers' and he was forthwith granted asylum. The firstfruits of the Bishop's self-sacrifice.

To this day (2012), armed religious extremists in Pakistan are playing havoc in the society, especially targeting the minorities. The Bishop's heroism seems to

---

39   John 15:13 and John 10:12–13

have gone unheeded. Despite worldwide pressure from governments and human rights bodies, the Blasphemy Law still stands. But what Christian in his right mind would risk his livelihood, his home and his very life by indulging in one breath of public criticism of Mohammad or the Koran? Yet a number of Christians are still in the court process: a teenage boy who is an illiterate charged with writing insults against the Prophet on the wall of a mosque, and Christians often unjustly accused by neighbours eager to get their hands on disputed property. At law, the testimony of one Muslim man is worth that of two Christian men or four Christian women!

In Melbourne, almost delirious with relief, Walter immediately set about bringing his wife and children to this country under the Family Reunion program. Now officialdom co-operated: no longer was he a pariah. But on the day the family left Lahore they had to run the gauntlet of an anti-government demonstration on the way to the airport, during which his wife Shirley was recognised by some of the Islamist fundamentalists. Despite the *mêlée* they were able to make it into the terminal. Next evening Murray and I welcomed the party arriving at Tullamarine and drove them to a motel at Brunswick where we had booked them in for the first night: the mother and four children, two boys and two girls ranging from about eight to eighteen, all arrayed in gorgeous Pakistani garb, and all stunned mullets.

As we shepherded the family into their quarters, together again for the first time for years, we literally stood on sacred ground. I could hardly forbear from weeping when the father and oldest son carried mattresses from the different booked rooms and assembled them on the floor of the main room into one huge family bed. When we crept out they were already in each others' arms. Does heaven come any sweeter?

Agony prolonged

But Saleem Artur , now all alone, went into a tailspin of despair: his story with its variable and partially incoherent elements impressed no one. Again and again we had sessions with Erskine Roden in his chambers in North Melbourne, sifting through the papers with their new translations, clutching at straws. We sought to make contact with the Catholic sisters in Lahore who might vouch for him and enlisted a returned Anglican missionary academic—but to slight avail. There seemed to be a diffidence about confirming his story. However we met with greater success in having a social housing agency accept his credentials as needing homeless accommodation, and over the next few years he was to live in several of their group houses in inner-city suburbs, though at times threatened by racist yobbos. Unfortunately for him he seemed to attract trouble 'as the sparks fly upwards'. Once he was robbed, and also lost my bicycle lent to him. He was always calling on 'Brother Jim' to bail him out of scrapes and dilemmas. Ultimately he became the 'lead tenant' in a pleasant modern and well-equipped house at Kensington, where his flair for home-making now came to the fore. He was adept at scrounging indoor plants, furnishings and decorations.

Finally came the day of his hearing before the Refugee Review Tribunal and we sat anxiously in the gallery while his claims were dissected. Without experience of such a body we couldn't anticipate the outcome, but after more months of anguished waiting he was informed his case had been rejected. The moment of truth. How to handle it? Tell Saleem, "Sorry, we did our best. If you don't leave you'll be deported"?

Erskine Roden urged us to take the fight up to the Federal Court of Australia but this would amount to 'going for broke'. If he won, court costs would be payable by the Commonweath Government, but if he lost...? We allowed ourselves to be persuaded by Erskine's judgment and expertise: a win was conceivable. He would brief a barrister colleague to represent Saleem at the hearing. With his case once registered with the Court, he would no longer face the deportation he dreaded. Further months ticked by, as we accompanied Saleem on a number of visits to Erskine, laboriously verifying fact by fact, claim by claim, from his memory and from whatever documentation he had. Though his claims still sounded slim, essentially we wanted to believe that there was enough veracity about them to qualify him as a refugee seeking asylum. Certainly his injuries had been real enough.

When his case came up for hearing before the Federal Court of Australia, Saleem and I sat in the front rows, assured this time at least of a resolution by the end of the day instead of six agonising months later. I was fascinated at the legal panoply and aura of power, at the rigour and aloofness of the judge, and the demeanour of the competing barristers. Whereas 'our man' was earnest, meticulous and confident (as befits one working for a humanitarian cause), the Government's champion sounded uninvolved and bored: nothing at stake for him, he'd get his reward willy-nilly. Saleem of course didn't get to speak. Finally with both cases presented and the Court adjourned, we went off for a nervous lunch. The financial implications of the outcome loomed ominously over us.

When the Court reconvened the judgment was handed down: neither case was definitively proven but the balance tilted slightly towards Saleem's plea. An honourable draw! As a result costs would be awarded *against* the Government. Phew!

A laborious campaign

So where did this leave Saleem? In such cases an appeal direct to the Minister for Immigration, Phillip Ruddock, now became possible. We had three months to prepare it, but it had to be on the basis of new evidence and documentation supplied. So now the veto on Saleem's working became more stringent: but without money how could he survive? On Walter's success Murray had virtually left Saleem's struggle to me, so I thought of appealing to many Christian friends around the country. Putting my own credibility on the line, in a detailed statement I told his story and requested prayer on his behalf, and also appealed for small but regular financial help. How gratifying that virtually all our friends responded with generous compassion, and a commitment to pray.

We kept the supporters *au fait* with the legal process, to focus their intercessions and also to fuel their representations to the Minister for Immigration, Phillip Ruddock, sometimes via their local MPs. I never let up on sending him any shred of new evidence about the dire situation of Christians in Pakistan. The Minister's Office would later report Ruddock as saying, "This appeal has had the greatest amount of documentation of any case to come before me" (during his seven years as Minister).

We formed a steering committee of Melbourne Christians to strategise and pray, which included Keith Riley, an Urdu-speaking former missionary from a hospital in Pakistan, well versed in the local mentality. A spectacular demonstration of this mentality was the receipt of a letter from the Pakistani Embassy in Canberra in reply to a question I had raised with them—the envelope graced with a *New Zealand* stamp—and a *used* one at that! Triumphantly I sent off the envelope to the Minister's Office in Parliament House where I had a sympathetic contact: "Look at this. It's Exhibit A! What credence can be attached to the Pakistani Government's claims about Christians being respected?" Of course I received no reply.

In a sense I now had to become Saleem's guardian. Readily he accepted that I should be the trustee of an account in his name into which friends' donations would be paid, and I trickled them out to him while he lived literally on the smell of an oily rag. He was a frequent visitor in our home, where our adult children befriended him. Particularly at Christmas dinners and birthday celebrations was he a de facto member of our family, and also at '*Summer under the Son*', the annual summer school of the Church Missionary Society at a Phillip Island resort. When speaking at seminars and conferences, or even at church services, I missed no opportunity of canvassing Saleem's story, including at a seminar on human rights convened by the Catholic group Pax Christi. His case was becoming something of a *cause célèbre*.

With a deadline hanging over our heads I set about compiling the personal appeal to the Minister. In the end it ran to some 50 pages including the supporting documentation, sent off through the new fax machine bestowed on us by St Michael's Bennettswood in lieu of paying me a proper stipend. We had been assured that a definitive response would not be long in coming.

Christian minorities the target

Probably for all of us the episode served as an introduction to today's crucial issue of protection for Christian minorities in Muslim-majority lands. With the increasingly public anti-religious stance of Western nations, who will go in to bat for the Christians? Besides, foreign policy considerations (not to mention the reality of our dependence on Middle Eastern oil) combine to leave our governments unmoved: unlike the Middle East, we are officially secular, sundered from our Christian heritage and values. Our vaunted concern for the underdog doesn't extend to Aborigines, let alone to *Christian wogs*! By now the Immigration Department had become an impregnable bastion, closed to public contact, inaccessible by telephone enquiries. I used to call the direct line of a departmental social worker I once met on a Richmond tram, who had agreed to put me through to the appropriate officer-in-hiding.

A political ploy

Re-enter an old friend: Peter Kidd, who at Wagga Wagga High School in 1955 had shared accommodation with me, now principal of Katoomba High School. As part of the network of praying friends contributing to Saleem's support, he had requested his local Liberal MP, Kerry Bartlett, a Christian friend, to make representations to the Minister. The MP reported that he was hopeful of a positive response. Peter also enlisted his well-attended Baptist Church in generously backing his personal '*Walk-for-Saleem*' fund-raising appeal, along the ridges from Glenbrook to Springwood, covering some 20km—in his mid-seventies!

Then suddenly the logjam of ministerial appeals began to edge forward—ironically the outcome of Ruddock finding himself cited in Parliament for allegedly according favours in exchange for donations to the Liberal Party! In 2003 his seemingly interminable stint as the implacable Minister for Immigration suddenly ended. Overnight he was replaced by the affable Senator Amanda Vanstone, one of whose first actions in clearing the decks must have been to rid herself of troublesome cases like this one.

Muted victory

The decision came in a phone call to Saleem one sunny afternoon during the Church Missionary Society's Summer School at Phillip Island: asylum *granted!* Dare we believe it? *Asylum?* Or could it be some sick joke? While angelic choirs filled the sky, the world ablaze with glory, we fell into each others' arms, hugging, laughing, crying, praising God. Somehow the moment seemed too sacred to squander on strangers: with Saleem we leapt into our car and took off, as far as the western tip of the island, where the wild seas meet at the entrance to Westernport Bay, swirling around the offshore islet rookery of Seal Rocks. The miracle we had long prayed (but hardly dared hope for) had delivered Saleem's future!

But not unqualified. Stringent conditions applied: the Minister's decision on my appeal was made under an employer nomination scheme for skilled workers to fill current labour shortages. Subsequent contact with the Immigration Department made it clear that the Melbourne Anglican Diocese would need to become the employer guaranteeing that the conditions were met. I threw myself on the mercy of my Bishop, Andrew Curnow, well versed in the background of the case. Without hesitation he announced that Saleem would be employed by the Diocese, under my supervision—but at no cost to the Church! The Immigration official had declined to stipulate a term for the employment, nor that any verification procedures would be required. We got the message: it was a sort of legal charade meant to look good on paper. What employer could ever give a guarantee that an employee from overseas would continue in a position? So it was certainly a game we could play too.

Saleem signed up for a year (or at least until my trustee bank account of donations dried up) with a work plan as an assistant within the Division of Diocesan Services. I launched him by introducing him around the office and outlined his role, but at no point could he fulfil expectations, appearing much more damaged than we had reckoned on. He would wake up late, turn up when it suited him, find the terms of his job uncongenial and the language of church bureaucracy incomprehensible. He showed no initiative at all, nor even any desire to please. My credibility took a beating, but I didn't know whether to vent anger or pity. After six months or so we declared the game over, and he found a part-time job as a wardsman in a Melbourne hospital where he could work at his own pace—until being found asleep on duty one Christmas Day!.

Subsequently we have kept in touch with him but despaired of being able to encourage him towards a more conventional lifestyle. He is simply not a systems man. But to our surprise, in later years he has turned out to be a minor property entrepreneur, buying and twice extending a small house in Coburg to take in boarders and overseas students. In an increasingly Muslim area, every Christmas the roof of his house presents an ingenious display of spectacular lighting, with a prominent Cross as centrepiece. He claims to be sending back a good proportion of his income to his brother's family in Lahore, unable to work after a vicious attack years ago by Islamist fundamentalists.

And twice he has undertaken overseas trips, to the Middle East and Turkey and (I suspect) to Pakistan! He remains a mystery man, although (like Walter and some of his family) an adherent of the Pakistani Christian Fellowship, meeting monthly. Perhaps most incredible of all, having already taken Australian citizenship, in 2010 he actually stood for the Victorian Parliament on behalf of the Australian Christians party, garnering a handful of votes!

A sober warning

From time to time Saleem has reported on his ongoing contacts with radical young Pakistanis in Melbourne, many of them permanent residents, who openly despise Anglo-Australian society and advocate *jihad* towards the introduction of *sharia*, boasting of the time when they will have the numbers to prevail by their single-minded zeal—and propensity for begetting large families!

In a world of sectarian violence and with the ongoing expulsion of Christian minorities from Muslim-majority countries, we may ask if such a future clash of civilisations is thinkable—or merely alarmist? At the time we had never heard of ISIL (Islamic State), by 2014 its hands steeped in blood, slaughtering and even crucifying Christians in northern Iraq and Syria, proclaiming the bloody overthrow of all opponents of its restoration of a worldwide Calpihate under *sharia* law.

Already the likelihood of a Muslim-majority Holland and some other European countries seems inevitable, given the electoral (and bedroom!) mathematics[40].

Then what of the longer-term future of our (and the West's) ethically flabby society so largely indifferent to Christian faith and values, but committed to an effete humanism which often connotes libertarianism? Already the draft national secondary-school history curriculum appears to have written Christian influences right out of the national memory. Karl Marx claimed that to conquer a nation you just need to block the transmission of values, morals and beliefs between generations.

---

40   Daniel Pipes, "Eurabia–Europe's Future" in *Islam, Human Rights and Public Policy*, ed. David Claydon, Acorn, Melbourne 2009, reports future conflict as undeniable, given not only the soaring Muslim birthrate in all west European countries, but also the sad reality that "Never in history has a major civilisation peacably dissolved, nor has a people ever risen to reclaim its patrimony". Unfortunately contemporary 'political correctness' ensures that these issues are ignored or blandly denied, while in the western world anti-religious secularism advances unchallenged on a broad front, making this thesis ever more thinkable.

23
'In Journeyings Oft'[41]

This was the season of my life to heed the inner promptings to punctuate the rigours of parish and diocesan ministry by undertaking further ventures in travel. Over several years I would venture forth, both by myself and once with sons David and Nicholas, climaxing in several working visits to China with Marjorie adding up to the best part of a year.

What is it about travel that transfixes me? Lures me ever onward, outward, seeking ... what? The American poet (and priest) Gerard Manley Hopkins put it: *'The world is charged with the grandeur of God'*. Someone else said, *'I became a detective of divinity'*. Something akin with me. Nothing so shallow as mere curiosity about exotic people and places, cuisines and experiences—leave that to the Hollywood travelogues. Rather it is the wonder of walking out into a *'God-enchanted world saturated with grace-giving, wonder-evoking moments, collecting evidences of God's genius'*[42].

For the nine-year-old during wartime gazing out the Hurstville classroom windows at the twin capes of Botany Bay framing the great beyond: not only the urge to discover what was out there but the yearning to heed a heart-cry for something better—more enlightening, inspiring? Fit to remould my world and kindle a future with hope? Perhaps it was a craving for a journey within, pointing to my inner lostness.

Could that have also been the case with my migrating ancestors, braving the terrors of the deep in search of new meaning and hope? Particularly my maternal uncle Thomas Breakwell of Birmingham, humble of origin and not without his frailties (he never married) yet a man of science and scholarship—but also of faith, imbued with the vision of a loving God willing into being a greater good for his creation, while seeking companions for the journey. Had I all unwitting wrapped myself in his mantle?

Joining new residents of Istanbul

Be that as it may, eighteen months after the China adventure with Sara-Jane I had responded to an invitation from Christopher and his wife, Yvonne, to join them in Istanbul for holiday travels in Turkey and Europe. In the northern summer of 1991 she had just completed the first year with a team of Australian teachers recruited for a two-year stint by the wealthy Koç Foundation conducting English-medium secondary schools in Istanbul, and Chris readily joined in the escapade.

It was destined to dramatically reshape his whole subsequent life, conferring on him a stellar academic career (but costing him a marriage). Since graduating from La Trobe University with Honours in anthropology in 1988, winnng the David

---

[41] St Paul's observation about his peripatetic preaching in 2 Corinthians 11:26, much of it in today's Turkey.
[42] Barbara Brown Taylor, American Episcopal (Anglican) theologian and preacher.

Myer Medal as the top student of the Humanities Faculty, he had been tutoring in sociology at the Lincoln Institute of Health Sciences in Melbourne, linked with La Trobe, but still on the cusp of finding his true *métier*. During the two years in Turkey with no specific brief (though he did write *The Very Beautiful Democratic Novel* which gained favourable mention from a publisher), it *found him* as he set about maximising his encounter with a radically different society via his already advanced understanding of anthropology.

They had a new apartment in the *Soyak Sitesi*, upmarket complex deep within the urban sprawl on the Asian shore of the Bosphorus. While Yvonne went teaching each weekday, Chris set about learning Turkish with a will, playing scratch soccer games with the young men of the estate and befriended by Fırat, son of a significant Kurdish land-owner from the eastern region of Anatolia, a capable and shrewd young man.

He was also generous: he lent us his car for a father-and-son expedition through dense and beautiful forests to the northern Black Sea coast of Turkey at Şile, and then along that lush mountain-framed littoral to Amasra and Samsun, both famed in antiquity. By contrast we stayed overnight in Zonguldak, a modern coal-exporting town, appropriately dingy but cheap. My Turkish actually worked in locating a suitable lodging with hot water! (In preparation for the adventure I had done a term of Turkish at Princes Hill evening college in Fitzroy.) Fortunately for me, under Kemal Atatürk, the Ottoman Empire's Arabic script had been replaced by the Roman alphabet, and the pronunciation seemed reminiscent of German.

Next day brought a long, circuitous journey 'home' through inland regions full of interest and often charm. But scarcely one valley from hell where the very effort to breathe had you choking. On every hand potteries belched forth pungent coal smoke—Turkey's 'Black Country' reminiscent of England's dreadful Stoke-on-Trent, and more than a match for the appalling Chinese cities we would later visit (living in one of them for months on end). Welcome to the tortured planet.

In the steps of St Paul

On the close of the school year soon afterwards, the three of us took bus from nearby Üsküdar (the classical Scutari) a city older than Byzantium (the original name for Istanbul) but situated on the Asian shore opposite, for a trip southwards along the Sea of Marmara coastline beyond Izmir (Smyrna) to Selçuk. There we booked into the '*Kangaroo Guesthouse*' run by a returned migrant. Nearby we visited the ruins of the Basilica of the Apostle John, a church built in the earliest centuries to mark the house where Mary the mother of Jesus was believed to have lived in the care of the 'Beloved Apostle' John, as appointed by Jesus from the Cross. Still extant is the stone baptistry for full immersion set into the floor.

Next day to the site of Ephesus nearby, now considerable if deserted ruins though once the capital of the Roman province of Asia, a bustling commercial hub claimed to be one of the largest cities of the Empire. For two years St Paul laboured there building up a church of Greek-speaking (Gentile) believers, until driven from the city in a riot instigated by the silversmiths' guild, threatened by the slump in profits from their graving of silver images of the goddess Diana (she of the 34 breasts!) who was widely worshipped in the near east. Indeed, one of the seven Wonders of the World had been the Temple of Diana at Ephesus, in ancient times a major seaport but today—thanks to earthquakes and the silting up of the Meander River—five kilometres from the sea.

Ephesus was my first encounter with a biblical archaeological site. We attached ourselves to a party of German tourists being guided around the ruins by the resident Austrian archaeologist working there for the past forty years. Certainly he could speak with authority (in German, naturally). We pictured life in the ancient world, with St Paul and the first generation of

Christians meeting in their house-churches, while the tumult of the great city throbbed outside. We took our seats high up in the well-preserved amphitheatre, picturing the performance of Greek comedies and tragedies far below, set against the backdrop of the city. We walked the stone-paved and guttered main street, picturing in our mind's eye the shops and dwellings still discernible from their ruins. We gazed in wonderment at the splendidly restored three-storey carved façade of the library of Celsius. We even sat over the holes in the long stone slab of the (very public) unisex toilet!

Restored façade of the library of Celsus

It was also there that St Paul wrote his first letter to the Corinthians, just across the Aegean Sea in Greece, and ancient rumour has it that St John wrote his peerless Gospel there too, besides his three Epistles. By contrast, one of the loftiest of Paul's letters, on the whole teachings of the Christian faith and how to live it out, was subsequently addressed to the believers there (his Epistle to the Ephesians). His touching farewell to the Ephesus church elders, gathered on the seashore, must rank with the most poignant writings from the ancient world.

Turkish delights

But on our return, it is Istanbul that now captures my imagination: its stunning location straddling the Bosphorus, narrow enough to be spanned now by two suspension bridges linking Europe and Asia. And on the European side the haven of the Golden Horn inlet deeply cleaving the cityscape that swarms up towards the mediaeval Galata Tower crammed with ancient and modern structures beyond which, from their elegant minarets, several grand mosques around the horizon aurally beguile worshippers. Like aliens from another world, a pride of over-dimensional white-gleaming ocean liners invariably guards the foreshore, incongruously exuding modernity, status, power. But a little further, as though squatting on the very waters of the Golden Horn, the two-storey Galata Bridge—traffic above, fish-mongers and diners below—brings you to the piers whence the fleet of stately ferries plough their inter-continental furrows.

Across the road crouches the Grand Bazaar, treasure trove of delights eastern and exotic ... to eat, to wear, to cherish, to present. Its evocative arcades and stone vaults display a richness unimagined by us Westerners sated by mass-produced but soulless baubles: wrought gold, precious stones, heavenly ceramics, rich fabrics, leather and furs, nuts, confectionery (Turkish Delight, of course), plus everything to titillate the palate and satisfy the inner emptiness.

Nearby the New Mosque ('new' in 1663—after all of sixty-six years a-building) competes for the faithful, and on the crest further around the curving shoreline rise the walled gardens and marble splendours of the Topkapi Palace complex, seat of the Sultans of the Ottoman Turks who in 1453 brought about the doom of the thousand-year Byzantine Empire, Christian successor to the Roman Empire. In the distant future Constantinople ('city of Constantine', who had declared the Roman Empire to be Christian) would be renamed as Istanbul ('city of Islam').

But even today the city's Christian history is not utterly forfeit: for a thousand years the world's largest church—until in the 16th century eclipsed by St Peter's Basilica in Rome—the Church of Holy Wisdom (*Hagia Sophia*, in Turkish perverted to *Ayasofya*) still rears above the skyline, while the Phanar, seat of the Ecumenical Patriarch presiding over the Eastern Orthodox Churches, as ever overlooks the Golden Horn.

Approaching the Blue Mosque of Sultan Ahmet, a good stone's throw from Ayasofya, and built to outdo it in size and grandeur by the famous architect Sinan (from a Christian family), we are struck by its six minarets and eight clustering domes. Inside we are overawed by the sheer space of emptiness under its vast silent domes, its rich carpets and its stunning ceramic tiles of rich blue. Ironically Ayasofya, since Mustafa Kemal ('Atatürk'—father of modern Turkey) a national heritage museum, still hosts scraps of ancient Byzantine paintings of Jesus that jostle with Islamic calligraphy from the 500 years or so of its role as a mosque. But today, in a serenity sadly unique among Muslim lands, their proximate co-existence appears not to outrage zealots of either faith. Compelling evidence of Turkey's bridging of east and west.

Nearby, dating back beyond both Byzantines and Ottomans, the ancient Hippodrome evokes Roman chariot races and carnivals, while a short ride along a bustling street by modern light rail brings us to the ancient water-supply cisterns, lying not far below the urban surface and still full of water, where recycled capitals from even older pillars, some with carved stone heads, have been pressed into service to support the vaulted roof.

Down the Bosphorus to the Sea of Marmara

Risking the most battered-looking electric trains I have ever known, we take a ride from Sirkeci Station (terminus of the fabled Orient Express) by the main ferry terminal, down the western Marmara coast skirting the ancient walls of Byzantium, some of which we scale and clamber along, our imagination running riot as we re-live the terrible days of the final siege of Constantinople in 1453.

Chris and Yvonne also kindly take me to one of their haunts, Büyükada (Big Island), a ferry ride beyond the Bosphorus and down the Sea of Marmara, which has cutely maintained its olde worlde charm by banning motor vehicles. We hail a horse and trap that jogs us euphoniously up to a hilltop Byzantine monastery, a favourite Sunday afternoon excursion affording believers of all faiths the opportunity of seeking a specific blessing by tying scraps of white message tape to the pathside bushes skirting the sacred site.

Elegant Bosphorus ferries

Since my hosts live on the Asian shore, one of the most abiding memories of Istanbul must be the ferry rides, shuttling back and forth from Europe to Asia while buskers ply their musical delights. The ferries themselves are works of art, self-possessed, white trimmed with gold, built on Clydeside, and significantly larger and statelier than the Manly ferries of my childhood. From the Bosphorus the views afforded of the vast global city are unrivalled, holding everything in a unifying perspective. But the life of the Bosphorus itself is absorbing—a *détroit* forever surging back and forth between the Mediterranean and the Black Sea, two vast primeval bodies of water lapping countries as remote as Portugal and Russia, Georgia and Morocco and, as we are told, flowing near the surface in one direction and deep below in the other. An analogue of time? Inevitably the incessant passage of shipping from either side of the recently defunct Iron Curtain captures my strategic interest. We are in the cockpit of the world: 'spot the flag'—Russian warships, Rumanian oil tankers, Western luxury cruise liners, Bulgarian tramp steamers, Turkish coasters.

Reaching the Asian ferry terminal at Kadiköy, beyond the monumental

Prussian-bequeathed eastern railway terminal of Hydarpaşa, at the bus station we jostle with a drove of commuters heading home to a range of exotic-sounding destinations. Ours is the district of Örnek. Thanks to my Turkish course I can at least pronounce the words more or less comprehensibly (as challenging as they appear to be, like everything else in Istanbul devoid of Indo-European background) and, on a good day, can even venture a basic question—perilous though, because likely to unleash a barrage of fast-flowing Turkish in response. But fun it certainly is: one of the great rewards of travel.

Sometimes, spurning a nicotine-choked bus with windows tight shut (from the national phobia of catching a cold, even in midsummer, yet spurning the greater risk of cancer) we take a *dolmuş* home—a sort of poor-man's taxi using a big, old beaten-up 'yank tank' seating about eight, where (in the day of high inflation) you swiftly passed your banknotes up to the driver via the other passengers, mobilising a heartening solidarity of wayfarers.

Traditional Kurdish hospitality

One evening Chris and I receive an invitation to dinner at Fırat's. To my surprise it turns out to be for men only. Our plates of delectable Kurdish delights discreetly pushed through a hatch from the kitchen by mother's hands—the sole contact we have with her. His father, still 'owning' a village in the east, is a journalist in Istanbul. Though on their own lands maintaining their feudal system, Kurds are refused any measure of autonomy, or ethnic or even linguistic identity (dubbed 'Mountain *Turks*') within the Turkish state. Denied aspirations towards nationhood in the Versailles Peace Conference that carved up the Ottoman lands after the 1st world war, the Kurds claim to be the world's largest people group without a country, now numbering 40 million, living in a contiguous area spanning SE Turkey, the NE corner of Syria, northern Iraq and western Iran. The Kurdish language is related to Iranian. In diaspora, many have now moved into the Turkish mainstream, though often viewed with suspicion because seen as disloyal. A resistance movement, the Kurdish Workers' Party (PKK) continues to wage a long but fruitless struggle for autonomy, mercilessly repressed by the Army to which all able-bodied young Turks are conscripted for two years. The contest devours a high proportion of the country's GDP.

Onwards to Paris—but not by the Orient Express

My first exposure to Turkey closes with departure by rail towards Paris, with the young couple on their first European visit– not by the Orient Express but the night train to the Bulgarian capital, Sofia, initially passing through Thrace, that small portion of Turkey located in Europe to which the Gallipoli peninsula is a bleak appendage. Of that long summer evening the only image retained is of a group of black-clad peasant women thrashing a walnut tree to harvest its delicious crop. We settle into our sleeping compartment and next time I open my eyes it is to behold a lush landscape backed by snow-clad mountains—Bulgaria, 'garden of eastern Europe', the one Balkan land untrodden in my 1984 odyssey. Random scenes from the following day flit before me: an imposing city square, now post-Communist but still bereft of traffic—but with a dancing bear. The modern Cathedral of the Bulgarian Orthodox faith, marked by a striking painting over the altar featuring women disciples among the Twelve at the Last Supper.

Then by 1st Class sleeper we move on: one night, one country. In Romania we stay with Father Mehedintu Sandi in Bucharest and are regaled by his street heroics during the overthrow of the hated Çeaucescu dictatorship eighteen months earlier. And so via Budapest in Hungary and Prague in Czechoslovakia to a reunited Germany, and my lone détour for the ritual visit to the Greßlers in Minden, and finally all three of us reunited, sitting up on an overnight train to Paris, tourist goal of the world, and for the young couple journey's end.

Now I come into my own as interpreter and guide, the only one who knows French and hardly unfamiliar with Paris. I revel in the role, living it all again through the eyes of two dear people lapping up western Europe for the first time. After breakfasting gallicly on *croissants et café*, we locate a good *logement* opposite the Gare du Nord railway terminal and set about 'doing' Paris on foot and by the Métro: the Arc de Triomphe, Champs-Elysees, Place de la Concorde, Musée du Louvre, the Seine and Ile de la Cité, the Left Bank, Notre-Dame de Paris cathedral, the Eiffel Tower. Drinking deeply from the fount of Western culture. But in the evening we attend a performance of Mozart's *Requiem* in the grandiose Church of La Madeleine—evoking the Parthenon in Athens—only to shame ourselves by being unable to stay awake. Soothed by the sublime choral music, Mozart's poignant last *opus* foreshadowing his imminent death. Ah, the magic of Paris by night! .Y.a.w.n... Snore.

We come to the parting of our ways: I travel on to visit friends Australian and British in England and Wales for further weeks, including by cross-country rail: Cardiff in Wales to Dumfries in Scotland and bus to Dalbeattie, while Chris and Yvonne turn towards their second year in Istanbul—and the first stirrings of separation.

Fast forward five years

Now 1996. Chris is back in Turkey, alone, undertaking fieldwork towards his PhD thesis in anthropology at La Trobe University, and now well advanced in acquiring the language. In Melbourne he had also been studying for a Bachelor of Divinity in the United Faculty of Theology. To our pain, on their return from Turkey he and Yvonne had separated and he had moved into a shared house, where one day we held each other tight and wept our eyes out. The two years in Turkey had ripped the lovers apart but had generated a new love—for Turkey itself. I had an urge to visit him there.

Denizen of Kuzguncuk

His rooms were in Kuzguncuk, a former Christian and Jewish quarter clinging to the steep hillside not far north of Üsküdar. In a forest park on its crest we sat to review the situation in an elegant tea garden beside an Ottoman mansion restored by the elected Islamist city council. He introduced me to his Turkish friends, old and young, and guided me around the historic suburb with its spectacular views over the Bosphorus from the hillsides, the former synagogue, the two Greek Orthodox churches and the Armenian church, a mini shoreside park, the corner shops with their tempting delicacies crowned by the almond croissant, my rich new discovery. Clearly he had found a new love for the place and its people. For his research he had already located several voluble and savvy informants.

The *Canberra* of Turkey

Now my imagination takes wings. Kuzguncuk clings precariously to the first hill above the Asian shoreline. But beyond, awaiting exploration, lies the hinterland of the country, not least the capital Ankara, one of its most ancient cities dating back to Bronze Age and Hittite times, and later capital of the Roman province of Galatia where a primitive form of Gaelic was spoken. It is centrally located in the Anatolian heartland[43]. On the dissolution of the Ottoman Empire in 1923 Ankara was designated by Kemal Atatürk as capital of the new Republic of Turkey. But at that time its population was a mere 35,000—comparable to Canberra's when we lived there in the 1950s.

But there the comparison must end: while the infant Canberra was born of an ill-tempered affair between two quarrelsome parents who later begrudged their offspring's support payments, Ankara was to become the favoured son of the heroic founder of the Turkish Republic, pampered darling of a brand new nation finally turning its back on the traditional cultural, religious and political polarities of the city of Byzantium /Constantinople/ Istanbul in order to embrace modernity. By 1996 the capital had begotten three million inhabitants—though today nearer to five—to become the second city of Turkey, home to the Government and the administration and all the foreign embassies. Situated at the height of our Blue Mountains summits but with a climate more extreme than Canberra's, Ankara is strategically located at the centre of the national highway and railway networks—today linked by high-speed rail and with its own underground Metro system.

In those days the journey from Üsküdar by luxury Ulusöy coach had taken

---

43   The eastern section of Turkey in Asia, stretching as far as the borders with Syria, Georgia and Iran. The term Anatolia is derived from the Greek word for 'sunrise'; cf. the similar Latin term 'Orient'.

five hours, more expensive than other buslines because reputedly safer, a vital consideration given the terrifying Turkish phenomenon on long winding hills of the three-lane highway, where the tussle in the middle lane between the downhill driver playing chicken with the overtaking climber is not for the faint-hearted!

Once safely there I stroll about Ulus, the old Ottoman centre around the antique citadel on the hill, and book into a cheap hotel (but no one seems to speak English) and then set out to explore the newer national area of monumental buildings and boulevards. This calls for some alertness, since the traffic shows scant respect for pedestrians (even if crossing on a green light!), not to mention the perennial obstacle course of footpaths under repair, with loose paving stones and injury-inducing holes in the asphalt minus warning signs, barriers or flashing lights at night. Back in Kuzguncuk when I had commented on this not unfamiliar scenario, Chris had expostulated defensively 'Dad, this is a *poor* country!" It recalled the whimsical German New Year greeting *'Guter Hals-und- Beinbruch'*.[44]

On the other hand Ankara, likewise on a bare windswept plateau, is not defined by the trees of our own purpose-built capital, whose very structure is now sculpted by myriad mature trees of bewildering variety, arising from the primitive urge to protect the city from the harsh winds with plantings that would enhance, but also lend some gravitas to our young capital. Since then Canberra has had an abiding love affair with trees, in which I had also become caught up on our windswept slope of Mt Painter.

Come evening, I take the pulse of Atatürk's well-patronised 'Youth Park', a large central green area with an artificial lake, rose garden, café-tea house and a Luna Park, open amphitheatre and swimming pool, and then admire the central railway terminal nearby, in art deco style, impressed to find the line to Hydarpaşa (Istanbul's Asian terminal) is electrified all the way. By 2016 a 'very fast train' is to cover the journey from Istanbul in four hours @ 160km/h, though almost double the Sydney-Canberra distance.

'Fairy Chimney' rock formations near Göreme in Cappadocia.

Next day I spend a memorable morning at the Museum of Anatolian Civilisations, housed in a domed Ottoman inn dating from the 15th century, lost

---

44   'Good luck!', literally 'Enjoy breaking your neck and leg!'.

in its magnificent displays of ancient artefacts, weapons and coins dating back to paleolithic and neolithic times (8000–5000 BC), the copper and bronze ages (3000–2000 BC), and the Assyrian, Persian, Hittite, Phrygian, Hellenistic-Greek and Roman civilisations. I conclude it would have to be worth going to Turkey if only to visit this museum. My father would have been enraptured at the archaeological wonders.

Moon landscape

Of course such a time scale puts my next destination into what seems only like yesterday's perspective: the early Christian cave-churches and rock refuges of Cappadocia (Turkish *Kapadokya*), scene of St Paul's first and second missionary journeys in the later years of the AD 40s. But late in the day, travelling not by donkey but by bus (the universal means of transport throughout rural Turkey), I head across a bare landscape to the regional city of Nevşehir and onto Göreme for an overnight stay.

By morning light I find the landscape simply mind-blowing—unique in the world, I suspect. Utterly arresting on every hand, even right in the town centre, are the amazing rock pinnacles touristically dubbed *'fairy chimneys'*, resulting from millions of years' erosion of the soft volcanic tufa.

Ürgüp

Through a long summer's day I go wild with my camera, moving around the town by taxi and later joining a tourist party to Ürgüp, Üçhisar, and Avanos, inspecting and at times entering the strange hollowed-out pillars, some of the larger ones used by the early Christians as churches and chapels, with superb but fading frescoes dating back to 300AD—not to be photographed because the flashes further drain the colour..

Here as everywhere I go in Turkey, I find the local guides abysmally ignorant of the thousand-year Christian history of their land. Any other tourist country would have TAFE or university courses on their own antiquities, if only to boost the economy, but I suspect modern Turks emotionally date their world from the Selçuk Turks' (Muslim) conquest in the 11th century—or even from the advent of Kemal Atatürk, in whose understanding the modern nation starts with a blank page in respect of any Christian history. No wonder one encounters so little understanding of our faith; rather, a (mostly benevolent) ignorance prevails, oddly at variance with the famous and unfeigned hospitality at the people's level.

At Avanos, after a hearty lunch in a hollowed out pillar, we get shanghaied to another pillar serving as a shop selling gorgeously crafted and fringed carpet squares and rugs. The assumption seems to be that all wealthy Westerners like us will buy one. I feel like saying, *"Sure, just roll it up—three metres square—and I'll carry it on top of my backpack."* I doubt that they sold a single carpet, so our guide got cold comfort from the age-old conspiracy of waylaying bemused tourists.

In the afternoon we are taken to the underground city of Derinkuyu, with its six descending levels, all carved out of the soft rock. There are many such cities in the area, some of them inter-connected by underground passages, and dating back to very ancient times but later used by Christians seeking refuge from persecution by the Romans. A huge stone could be rolled across the inside of the entrance, making it impregnable. Our guide claimed that up to 20,000 people could shelter or even live for protracted periods in Derinkuyu with its wells, granaries, food storerooms, kitchens, refectories, workrooms, study rooms and a sizeable church, some of which we inspected, aerated by narrow shafts. Stairways enable internal connection.

But in my somewhat claustrophobic imagination, it must rank with the deep mine under Broken Hill where without warning the guide (to be funny) turned off the lighting, striking absolute terror into our visiting party: could we ever get out again? Fortunately in Turkey we did not have to endure Stygian darkness, though in the past it must have meant a surreal life lived under grotesquely flickering torches.

As we drove off we passed a forbidding modern prison, totally isolated on the featureless plateau, clamped tight within its walled compound, reputedly for political prisoners—members of the Kurdish separatist movement, the PKK. I shuddered at that too. Certainly in this part of the world man's inhumanity to man has a long history. At day's end I recall lingering alone, gazing down into a moonscape valley at the changing patterns of colours and shadows projected on the spooky pillas by the westering sun. A memorable if somewhat.disconcerting image.

Saints of two world faiths

An evening's busride brings me to Konya for an overnight stay. In St Paul's day the city was called Iconium, where he lived for a period reasoning with the resident Jewish community and 'God-fearing' Gentiles (converts to Judaism) that Jesus was their true and long-promised Messiah, but with Barnabas was forced to move on to avoid stoning as blasphemers.[45]

In 1996 I find a city of over a million, with a massive mosque under construction in the centre (with Saudi oil money) and a tram network being introduced. I spend some time at the famous 'Green Tomb' of Mevlana Rumi, 13th century Persian poet, writer, philosopher and Sufi theologian, revered throughout the Muslim world.

Konya has the reputation of being rife with mysticism:, once known as the 'citadel of Islam', its people still said to be more devout than those of other cities. Konya was the final home of Rumi, whose followers in 1273 established the Mevlevi Sufi order of Islam there and became known as the 'whirling dervishes'. His epitaph reads:

> "When we are dead, seek not our tomb
> in the earth, but find it in the hearts of men".

He evokes a humanistic spirit, advocating reason, tolerance, goodness and awareness through love. Looking with the same eye on Muslim, Jew and Christian alike, his peaceful and tolerant teaching still makes a strong appeal to people of all faiths. Ruefully I recall the bold but fragile vision of our Multi-Faith Resource Centre.

Along the Aegean coastline

After an overnight stay in a cheap hotel my westward safari brings me to the port of Izmir on the Aegean Sea, in 1996 the second city of Turkey until the early 1920s known as Smyrna, a great cosmopolis peopled more by Greeks, Armenians and Jews than by Turks, and a flashpoint for the Greco-Turkish war with its appalling massacres and the Great Fire. By 1923 with the triumph of Kemal Ataturk, the Greek population had been expelled through a forced swap of Greeks in Turkey against Turks in the Balkans—to this day a source of ongoing tension, reflected in the division of the large eastern Mediterranean island of Cyprus into an independent (Greek-speaking) nation and the self-styled 'Turkish Republic of North Cyprus'—recognised only by Turkey.

One of the 'Seven Churches of Asia' from Revelation[46]

Swinging northward along the Aegean coastline and then cutting inland, late in the day I reach Bergama. On a ridge high above the town are the ruins of the once far larger classical city of

Pergamum, in St Paul's day administrative centre of the Roman province of

---

45 The episode is recounted in Acts 13:51—14:7
46 'The Revelation to St John' is the last book of the Bible (also called *The Apocalypse* = unveiling).

Asia, but unlike Ephesus a place of learning and culture rather than of commerce. It is the site of the secondlargest library of the ancient world. The city gave its name to *parchment*.

In the town square of Bergama I fall into conversation with a group of German tourists, one of whom invites me to join their coach party on a visit to the archaeological site above the town. Nothing loth, I take my place aboard, and soon find myself in a unique relic, the Asklepion, the ruins of a medical treatment complex renowned in St Paul's day as the world's first psychiatric clinic. This took the form of an enclosed stone colonnade almost a kilometre long, sections of which remain, with openings in the roof at intervals through which the physician walking above could relate to patients describing their dreams as they walked along below. There were rooms for sleeping and treatment, which included the interpreting of dreams, massage and herbal remedies. With its pools, mud baths and drinking from a sacred fountain (since discovered to have radioactive properties) the Asklepion was like a modern spa. Later patients are said to have included the 'good emperors' Hadrian and Marcus Aurelius.

But from a biblical perspective Pergamum has another side to it. In the last book of the Bible, we read that John the Apostle, exiled by the Romans to the offshore island of Patmos in the Aegean Sea, has a vision of the Living Christ who dictates to him a series of letters addressed to the 'seven churches of Asia'. The third one is addressed to the church in Pergamum. It commends its faithfulness and honours a church member, Antipas, martyred there but also deplores the dehumanising system of power holding the world in thrall 'where Satan's throne is'. The reference is to the power of evil embodied in the Temple of Zeus that crowned the city. It was the earliest temple built for the state-sponsored *worship of a man*: the Roman Emperor.

In Berlin in the 1960s I had admired the altar from this temple, richly decorated with sculptures portraying the struggle between the gods and the giants, between cosmic order and chaos. It is the most priceless treasure of the Pergamon Museum in East Berlin, where in 1871 it had been brought in fragments by a German archaeological team and laboriously reconstructed. Hitler had used it as the inspiration for his architect building the tribune from which he harangued the masses at the great Nazi rallies in Nuremberg in the 1930s, and on his defeat the Russians removed it to Leningrad, from where it was returned to Berlin in 1958.

The last night of my travels is spent at the resort town of Ayvalık with the island of Lesbos (Mytilene) just offshore. Judging by the street signs, German seems to be the local lingo: the warm coastal area is much favoured by northern Europeans. The region is without doubt the most prosperous area of Turkey that I have encountered.

From my lone odyssey I report in to Chris's flat in Kuzguncuk with a glow of achievement, from managing my trip in Turkish at a time when few Turks were familiar with any foreign language. Besides their natural friendliness the considerable overlap between the Turkish and German phonetic systems was doubtless a boon—not to minimise the understandable eagerness to lighten the pockets of 'rich' Westerners.

24
Pilgrimage to Controversy

Scarcely seven months later I was to find myself once again emerging from Istanbul Airport, heading for Kuzguncuk on another visit to Chris. It was the third of my four encounters with Turkey, but this time only for two weeks' holiday from the Cathedral offices in January 1997. That Turkish winter was a mild affair, akin to a Melbourne autumn. It came as little surprise to learn of his friendship with a young woman who lived with her family higher up the steep hillside overlooking the Bosphorus and kept a small shop where he would buy eggs one at a time so as to see her more often. Only on my last day did I get to meet Esma, but as she wore an ankle-length coat with tight headscarf and had not a word of English it had merely historic significance. More anon.

An unbeliever's pilgrimage

After a day or two, imbued with a sceptical curiosity, I set off alone on the ritual Aussie pilgrimage to Gallipoli—'pilgrimage' because it has now acquired quasi-religious overtones for younger Anglo-Australians eager to express devotion to their country. But now that the last survivors of the egregious military fiasco have passed on, the pilgrimage no longer has any rootedness in reality but, rather, has increasingly become the plaything of a supine media mindlessly backing Australian political nationalism—to question which amounts to sacrilege. This cultification has been dubbed 'political Anzackery'—which at the 100th celebration of the 1915 invasion would come into its own at a cost of $325 million (higher than the outlays by any other country[47])—and this by a new deficit-obsessed conservative government. So instead of Gallipoli being viewed as a reckless invasion of the Ottoman Empire (the Turkish nation did not exist until 1923), it has developed its own self-serving mystique purchased in the blood of the naïve colonial youth who responded to the Motherland's imperialist behest[48].

But why should Australian nationhood have been forged in that mad, predictable bloodbath rather than in the protracted negotiations by the various Australian colonial governments seeking common cause in a vision to found a new nation, and the achievements of the civil society in struggling to incorporate democracy and women's suffrage? If it was indeed at Gallipoli that our nationhood was forged, then it is no wonder that it has had to be reinforced through our headstrong involvement in every war initiated by the former British (and now

---

[47] Australian commemoration of the centenary of the first World War would cost taxpayers $430 million, compared to $90 million by the Government of the UK and nought by Canada.

[48] See *Defeat at Gallipoli* by Peter Hart and Nigel Steel, 1995. They are currently writing a further book on the myths surrounding the campaign. See their article "The Anzac myth exposed" in *Wartime* magazine, Issue 38, of the Australian War Memorial Museum, Canberra

American) empires, simply revealing how little independence we have achieved since 1915, even compared to our diminutive Anzac partner, New Zealand.

Moreover in so short a span as my lifetime, apart from World War II, almost every past war has come to be viewed in retrospect as a mistake, because not really related to our national interest, let alone our survival—the only justifiable reason for taking part in a war. Otherwise the bankrupt *'fight now or in your own backyard'* shibboleth prevails. Even the Great War (*'the war to end all wars'!*) that spawned Gallipoli has still found no wide agreement among historians on its causes. In the absence of agreement, conspiracy theories abound about international jockeying for power, the greed of arms manufacturers, or pitting the working class of countries against each other—thin justification for the deaths of 15 million human beings (combatants and civilians). Moreover the Anzac legend has been invaluable to later Australian Governments, including for John Howard's invasion of Iraq in 2003 without Parliamentary sanction in search of the non-existent 'weapons of mass destruction', which claimed 100,000 Iraqi lives and has since triggered the murderous rise of ISIL.[49]

Such have been the subsequent musings arising from my visit to Gallipoli in 1997, drawing on the insights gained there. Hearing the story for the first time from a Turkish viewpoint was to provide a salutary counter-balance to the propaganda imbibed year by year from Anzac Day ceremonies—as far back as primary school days. Before my visit I had never contemplated the possibility of an alternative viewpoint. Now an accommodation between the two understandings would be called for, leading to a personal judgment.

The silence of history

Why had no one ever told me about the reasons for invading Turkey? Or what precisely was being attempted, and why? Or the historical and geographical backgrounds? Let alone the role of the French, whose landing near Cape Hellas at the end of the peninsula was on a far larger scale and cost the lives of far more soldiers than our Anzac sideshow[50]. Who in Australia has ever heard that the French were at Gallipoli? Again, how were Gallipoli in the Ottoman Empire and Flanders in Belgium related? After all, *five times* more Australians died on the Western front than at Gallipoli. Indeed in the whole War, Australian casualties (killed and wounded) amounted to no less than 65% of all those who served—a hideous bloodbath! But to what end, and with what outcome?

But to return to my tale. With a ticket in my pocket to Çanakkale (*Chanákkalay*), the jumping-off point for a visit to Gallipolli, I board the bus at Istanbul's main bus terminal and settle back for a long morning's drive. Initially along the freeway crossing Turkey's unappealing European region, then heading left down the coast of the Sea of Marmara, through a drab wintry landscape. At the point

---

49 'Islamic State of Iraq and the Levant', or ISIS 'Islamic State of Iraq and Syria' or Daesh (an Arabic acronym)
50 In St Margaret's Church Eltham the memorial honour board is headed 'Great European War'.

where the Sea is narrowing to become the Dardanelles (the classical Hellespont, famously swum by Lord Byron) we pass through the uninspiring town of Gelibolu, which gives its name (in English, Gallipoli) to the peninsula, largely uninhabited beyond there, jutting out into the Aegean Sea between Turkey and Greece. A little farther along the strait, in parts no wider than two kilometres but like the Bosphorus at the upper end of the Sea of Marmara flowing deeply at two levels between the Mediterranean and Black Seas, at Eceabat we take to a large ferry to cross to the bus terminal at the regional capital, Çanakkale on the Asian side. But now on the wrong side of the Dardanelles I locate an English-speaking guide to Gallipoli well versed in telling the story to Australian and New Zealand pilgrims. It is a lucrative local industry.

Unexpurgated version of history

Recrossing the strait in his car, we climb by a narrow, winding road through an empty landscape to the ridge forming the spine of the peninsula. Looking down on the Aegean beyond, there is an extensive view up and down the coastline. Ali points out the southern tip, Cape Hellas, where the French and British contingents landed, both greatly outnumbering the Australian and New Zealanders in the minor 'Anzac Cove' fiasco. To the north along the gently curving shore there are mainly narrow beaches (virtually no tides in the Mediterranean) with the odd low headland in between. "See that beach in the mid-distance", he says quietly, "the British were playing cricket on the sands there while your fellows were dying here below us." Funny I've never heard that either. But it is too terrible to be a joke.

We examine the complex systems of trenches, still not completely eroded near the summit and further down the steep slope towards Anzac Cove on the shore below. "These were Turkish, these were yours. See how close they were to each other. They could hear each other talking. Only the New Zealanders ever captured the summit, you know, but couldn't hold it for long. The Australians never got to the top or clapped eyes on the Dardanelles." We go on to the Anzac memorial, museum and cemetery, and later to the Turkish monument and cemetery. Rows of crosses, then lines of crescent and star carvings, with names and ranks. Crushing to the spirit to picture the flower of youth mercilessly cut down on both sides. At Lone Pine you can look down on Anzac Cove, to which we then drive by a roundabout route. Slowly I wander along the beach kicking at the pebbles and bits of lead, imagining the landing and the hell that breaks out with nowhere to shelter. It's not really a cove, more a slightly curving line of tame shore, with wavelets rippling languidly, reminiscent of Dolls Point on Botany Bay where we used to picnic among the mossies when I was a kid. But when you turn back to look up to the horizon not far above, your heart sinks. How could anyone climb up there easily in peacetime, even without a pack and a heavy rifle? Clambering up and down deeply rutted gullies in such precipitous terrain? Catching yourself on the prickly bush creeping with crawlies, and under a rain of lead pouring down from above? How could any commanders have expected our virgin soldiers to capture that height, defended by dogged young Ottoman patriots (some of them from Christian regions of the Empire)—with their homes and loved ones at stake?

Ali explains. "Of course it was never intended, the French and British had far easier sectors to cope with. But in the night our scouts had moved the marker buoys set in the sea offshore by your advance naval party. The ship commanders were completely fooled. They landed your troops on the most impossible part of the coast". More news to me. "Probably the soldiers who died early were the lucky ones—on both sides—without having to go through the hell of it, and end up broken for the rest of their lives. They had a lot in common, you know. Many of them, poor farm boys from rural areas with no reason to hate or kill each other. But we were defending our motherland against invaders. I wonder what your boys thought they were fighting for". I wonder too: Empire, King, country? For adventure? For God?

The power of myth

The fact traditionally overlooked in our annual militaristic fiesta is that Gallipoli was an ignominious Australian and Allied defeat, said to be the first defeat ever of British Empire forces at the hands of a Muslim power. Indeed because of their over-riding loyalty to Islam, soldiers in the British India forces at Gallipoli who were Muslims had to be relocated to France. Back in Australia in the post-War aftermath of disillusioned, demoralised, traumatised and angry survivors battling with a stagnant economy and locked away in a truculent silence, the sick potential for hailing 'Anzac' as the heroic demonstration of mateship, initiative and self-reliance appealed to the political class. Since then this glorification of war has been officially nurtured, waxing and waning over the years until the last Anzacs had died (the final link with reality). Manifestly Gallipoli could have had nothing to do with defending our unknown country on the other side of the globe and in the opposite hemisphere.

But in my later reflections, both sadder and wiser: in its contemporary manifestation does it seek to create a sustaining myth for our society to compensate for the vacuum left by the de facto dismissal of Christian values from public life (sometimes mistakenly in the name of multiculturalism, despite its multi-faith aspect)? Does this amount to substituting Mars, vengeful god of war, for the faithful, holy and forgiving God of our fathers? Or again, is it to legitimise the frontier wars that culminated in the unheroic purloining of a continent and the unrequited dispossession and beggaring of its ancient peoples? Certainly this is still a weeping wound on our nation's soul that will not be not stanched by the band-aid cult of Anzac.

Moreover, in this centenary of the *débâcle* a novel thought has surfaced in the alternative media, that the British Empire need not even have got involved in a war with our kinsfolk, the Germans (as recently as Queen Victoria & her consort, Prince Albert von Saxe-Coburg & Gotha, the language of the English royal household was *German!*). The assassination of the heir to the throne of the Austro-

Hungarian Empire had nothing to do with England. Had England refrained—even at the cost of Germany winning the continental war—the rise of Nazism and Hitler, the London Blitz, the bombing of Coventry and the carpet-bombing of Dresden, the Holocaust and all the horrors of the second World War may well never have happened! If only....

What it did have to do with was a grandiose but flawed strategy of British Empire militarism. From Trojan times the Gallipoli peninsula guarded the entrance to the Hellespont. In his invasion of Greece in the sixth century BC Xerxes, king of the Medes and Persians crossed it, and later in the opposite direction Alexander the Great crossed it on his conquests of Asia as far as India. During the Napoleonic wars Britain and Russia blockaded it to put pressure on the Ottoman Empire, and in World War I the English warlords led by Winston Churchill hit upon the madcap scheme of capturing the Ottoman capital Constantinople—for the first time since 1453! History records his sick glee at the prospect of an invasion diverting attention from the stalemate of the Western Front in Flanders.

In March 1915 he dispatched an Allied naval force of 18 warships to breach the Dardanelles in order to join forces with Czarist Russia (then in its final years), only to be roundly repulsed by the Ottoman defences, which had mined the strait already fortified through castles built on both shores, one near Çanakkale dating back to 1450. Several British and French warships were sunk. Churchill's reaction was to launch a land invasion of the Gallipoli peninsula to wrest control of the waterway. Forces from Britain, France, India, South Africa, Australia and New Zealand numbering some 480,000 men joined in a series of landings along the Aegean coastline but the Ottomans were well prepared, with strong defence posts in place up and down the peninsula. After eight months of attrition ending in stalemate, the Allies had no option but withdrawal, leaving 60,000 dead, including 8,709 Australians and 2,721 Kiwis—and Churchill's credibility in tatters through his grandiose personal fantasy of invading the Ottoman Empire's capital. On their side, the Ottomans had lost 65,000. In all, the campaign had cost half a million lives

The ultimate victor

But there was a more significant outcome of the Gallipoli fiasco: the victorious commander at the Battle of Çanakkale (as it is termed by the Turks) was to make a far more significant contribution to his country's history than Gallipoli was to ours. For instance, what Australian has ever heard that, after the first days of utter carnage, Mustafa Kemal had personally led a deputation down to the beach at 'Anzac Cove' to propose a truce in order to bury the dead? But more: he would become the national hero who later, granted the honorific title *'Atatürk'* (Father of the Turks), would lead the revolution that consigned the 500 year-old Ottoman Empire to the dustbin of history, creating a new nation, the Republic of Turkey. It is not by chance that the largest Turkish mosque in Australia, by Auburn station in Sydney's west, is proudly titled 'Gallipoli Mosque'. By the main western line (to

Penrith, the Blue Mountains, western NSW, Adelaide and Perth) it is daily in the face of thousands of commuters.

'Dona nobis pacem, Domine'

In preparation for the centenary of Anzac in 2015 a 'peace coalition' had emerged in Melbourne spanning the Churches and pacifist groups and on 25th April a "Service of Lament, Repentance and Hope" was held in St Paul's Cathedral under the title *Truly, we will remember them.*

In the printed Order of Service the rationale was laid out:

> "To lament the destruction and waste of so many young lives, the pain and anguish of those who returned and of their families and communities; to repent of the ongoing war and violence in our world and in our hearts, and hear again the hope of God's gift of peace through the Crucified One; and to honour the courage and self-sacrifice of all who fought at Gallipoli by praying and working for peace."

Three stories were related, one of them focused on the Aboriginal wars. Quietly chanting *Dona nobis pacem, Domine*[51] while coming forward to light our individual candles for peace we could hear the skirl of the warpipes in the march outside the cathedral doors. We repented of the blindness of the Church leaders of the day who called upon the young men to enlist, preaching that conflict was purifying! We remembered the stretcher-bearers, the nurses and doctors, the chaplains on the field, and those at home with the courage to speak out as followers of the Prince of Peace. We also recalled the women who went to Iraq to act as 'human shields' under the 'shock and awe' bombing. *"Blessed are the peacemakers for they shall be called the children of God."* We affirmed our hope in God alone to renew the whole creation. Finally we sang,

> "Community of Christ,
> through whom the word must sound –
> cry out for justice and for peace
> the whole world round;
> disarm the powers that war
> and all that can destroy,
> turn bombs to bread
> and tears of anguish into joy."

To the Trojan horse

Back in 1992, sitting that evening in Çanakkale with a group of older Aussies at a foreshore restaurant watching the sun set over Gallipoli and swapping impressions of our day, there is talk of a group going to the ruins of Troy next morning, since

---

51   *Give us peace, O Lord* (Latin)

it is not so far away. The morrow sees us wending our way southwards down the main Aegean coast near one of Disneyland's Big Animals: a stylised wooden horse large enough to contain a sizeable detachment of Greek warriors[52]. The ruins are extensive though only vestigial, and since the 19th century have been the subject of much debate. The father of scientific archaeology, Heinrich Schliemann, wealthy but controversial 19th century Prussian entrepreneur and polyglot with a passion for the classical world, had financed large-scale excavations that revealed a stratum of ash containing a profusion of invaluable artefacts, above layers of earlier cities dating back beyond 1000 BC. Are they indeed the ruins of Homer's Troy?

Hearing an old man speaking German with an itinerant party of young people, I insinuate myself to listen. They turn out to be a university group from Georgia, a small Christian nation on the Black Sea coast north-east of Turkey. The German speaker, whose words are being interpreted into Georgian, is the supervising archaeologist who has worked on the site for a lifetime. Together we troop widely around the site, no longer a port but now well inland. So fascinated am I by the authoritative descriptions of the ruins that the setting wintry sun quite takes me by surprise. When the party departs by coach it suddenly dawns on me: how do I get out of here? The other Aussies, not having joined the young Georgians, are nowhere to be seen, the carpark is emptying out but I feel too embarrassed to ask anyone to take me—and where to? Disconsolately in the gloom I wander off down the road towards the main highway, wondering if the route buses run by night. Where am I going to spend a winter's night? *"O Lord, help!"*

A few minutes later a campervan pulls out past the Trojan horse and I resort to my old hitch-hiking stance. To my amazement it stops and an *Australian* voice asks where I am going. When I say Çanakkale (deliberately mispronouncing it) they reply *"Hop in, we're on our way north past there."* I am so relieved and so high: we do the raucous Aussie bit all the way, laughing and joking, swapping notes with the young couple.

Who said there is no God of grace who remembers our (Aussie) infirmities?

---

[52] A recent SBS television documentary floats the theory that the Trojan Horse may have been a siege engine drawn up close to the walls in order to rain heavy rocks against the gates.

25
To the Cradle of Civilisation

Back in Kuzguncuk with a story to tell, I respond to Chris' suggestion that I fly to the farthest area of Kurdistan, near the Turkish border with Iran, and on the way back meet him and spend our last few days touring together. He cannot afford much time away from data-gathering for his doctoral thesis, which involves the Turkish state's relationships with the Kurds. But I have to brave a Turkish Airlines flight in an antique Boeing 727, conspicuous for the three jet engines at the rear. A full twenty years earlier, back in my Canberra flying days they had vanished from Australian skies. We traverse the country from north-west to south-east, to land at the Kurdish city of Van after a long gliding descent across Lake Van, Turkey's largest. In 1997 a city of half a million located on a high plain, its notable landmark is an isolated rocky outcrop rising sharply from the lake shore, crowned by mega-ancient castle ruins.

Expedition to Mt Ararat

In the absence of English speakers I need to call on my rudimentary Turkish for booking into a cheap hotel but in the process learn that the owner's brother runs a service car for tourist visits. He takes me out to the castle ruins, where we clamber around the precipitous area, a great vantage point for overlooking the lake and the city, with a picturesque backdrop of a high snow-capped range. On a whim I ask whether he would take me to Mt Ararat and the deal is done, for $US25. In a large old Ford Customline we are soon on the road across the bleak plateau, relieved here and there by a stand of bare Lombardy poplars marking a creek. It will be a three-hour journey.

He turns out to be a genial host, with comprehensible English and we chat amicably about his life in the area. Like most of the townspeople, he is of course a Kurd. Although for centuries under the control of the Ottomans, the area has never had a Turkish majority. Before the invasion of the Selçuk Turks in the 11th century it was the heartland of the kingdom of Armenia, the world's first Christian nation (301 AD) with the oldest national church (Armenian Orthodox, founder St Bartholomew, one of the Twelve Disciples) based in the holy city of Etchmiadzin in today's Confederation of Independent States (ex-Soviet Union) just across the border bestraddled by Mt Ararat. The Kurdish population (Muslims) have also lived in the southern section of this region and also in parts of Iraq and Iran. A great figure, Saladin, a Kurd, was leader of the Muslim armies during the Crusades and became Sultan of Egypt, visited by St Francis of Assisi in 1219 on a vain mission of reconciliation.

But after 1920 Armenia was reduced to a miserable rump, in the Soviet Union, of a once sizeable country covering far-eastern Turkey, parts of Syria, and the southern Caucasus. During World War I the Ottoman Government had embarked on a systematic program of ethnic cleansing of its Armenians (Christians), accusing them of siding with Czarist Russia. It was unleashed on the very eve of the Gallipoli landing with the arrest of intellectuals and community leaders, and continued over the following years—the word 'genocide' was coined to describe the event—culminating in the extermination of over a million people, by massacre, evacuation, forced labour, deportation and death marches of women and children across the Syrian desert (to areas now under occupation by the ISIL 'death cult'). The remnant of Armenians was dispersed in a global diaspora (they have churches in Melbourne and Sydney that I contacted during the national groups survey of the 70s).

To this day the Turkish Government stolidly refutes this precursor to the Nazi Holocaust, though it has been recognised as such by 20 governments around the world, including Australia's. After the Nobel Prize-winning Turkish novelist Orhan Pamuk[53] wrote that a million Armenians and 30,000 Kurds had been killed by Turks he was charged with *'insulting Turkishness'*. His defence was *"What happened to the Armenians was hidden, a taboo, but we have to be able to talk about the past."* On pressure from the European Union the charges were dropped but Pamuk now lives in exile in the USA, a professor at New York's Columbia University.

A Kurdish village and Mt Ararat

As we drive northwards the great double-peaked massif of Ararat emerges from the mists, its top third gleamimg white in the wintry sun. At 17,000ft it is a

---

53   On a later visit to Turkey I would read his beautiful novel Snow (in English translation) set in the Kurdish city of Kars north of Van, telling the story of an expatriate poet coming home in the present day, only to be caught up in the murderous tensions between Islamists and secularists.

dominant but dormant volcano last known to have erupted 150 years ago, almost straddling the three-way Turkish border with Iran and the former Soviet Union republic of Armenia.

With Ararat looming ever more sharply in the middle distance we stop briefly for me to observe more closely a traditional Kurdish village, with its brown flat-roofed houses, recalling Chris' friend Fırat's background as son of a Kurdish clan leader who 'owns a village'. Maybe this one?

Before long we diverge from the route to climb to the İshak Paşa Palace, built on a mountainside in the 17th century as an administrative fortress by a Kurdish clan chief-cum-warlord loosely affiliated with the Ottomans, but now partially ruinous—yet wholly picturesque. Five kilometres further on we turn unannounced into the (unpaved!) main street of the regional capital, Doğubeyazıt, 15km short of the mountain, and with the feel of a set for a Hollywood western. But over a Kurdish lunch my new friend sheepishly explains that this must be journey's end, since the Government has closed Mt Ararat to tourism because the air force uses the depopulated Kurdish villages on its lower slopes for practice bombing runs. The inhabitants have fled into the town.

To the Iranian frontier

He placates me by proposing we go on to the Iranian border, 35km to the east. At the nearest publicly accessible point to Mt Ararat we stop for me to clamber over the incredibly alien great jagged blocks of black basalt that have poured down its sides as molten lava, lining the roadsides, interspersed with brambles. But he warns about the snakes with which they are alive. If this is the starting point for an ascent of the mountain, small wonder that the rumour of Noah's Ark being still up there where it came to rest has been neither proved nor disproved.

The Persian border is reached at a rocky, barren knoll marked by two flagpoles a few metres apart where the red flag of Turkey with the white crescent flaps beside the red, white and green flag of Iran. Differently uniformed, armed soldiers man the post on both sides. To me it looks like an exotic photo opportunity not to be missed but as I fiddle with my camera case an Iranian sub-machinegun is silently but ever so purposively trained on me. I get the message so merely take a mental snapshot to register the humourless moment. Perhaps this is the very spot where Oh Wie Tat, my old Indonesian-Chinese friend from Sydney University EU days, and a polyglot who had learnt Turkish for fun, once came unstuck in his lone travels. He was pulled in and denounced as a spy by an Iranian guard, bemused at the phenomenon of a wispy-bearded *Chinese* sage speaking *Turkish* on the borders of *Iran,* with an Australian passport:"*Kom zis vay*".

Confessing Christ

On the road back to Van our conversation grows more intimate. The driver asks if I am a Christian and then, what do I believe? I mention that I am a 'Christian *hodja*'[54] and explain that believers in Jesus have the assurance of being loved and forgiven and accepted by God. For Muslims, dogged by uncertainties about Allah's inscrutable will and their problematical performance, this makes a strong appeal. I suggest he read the life of Jesus in the New Testament, and he asks where he can get hold of one. Later back in Istanbul I cross the Bosphorus and find a Bible shop in the main commercial area of Beyoğlu, delighted to locate a *Good News New Testament* in contemporary Turkish and dispatch it to Van. This leads to a correspondence across the world over some years which sadly, falls by the wayside, doubtless through my neglect.

As we skirt the last arm of Lake Van he offers to take me to a special place, and pays a boatman to ferry us out to an island in order to visit the ruined 10th century Armenian church of the Holy Cross, once the focus of a monastery. He points out the architectural features and the remains of decorations and carvings, which intrigue me as I attempt to interpret to him their scriptural significance. Driving back to Van he says, "*You know, I've been bringing Westerners out here for years but today I've learnt more from you than from all of them put together*".

A perilous journey?

Dinner that night is a noisy affair in the hotel dining room crowded with jollifying Kurds and more discreet Turkish soldiers, mostly very young conscripts, reflecting the age-old tragedy of the region, with an occupying power ever dominating the local masses. Next morning I take my place in a trans-Kurdistan bus, pondering the advice from the Australian consulate in Istanbul to travel by air to avoid possible ambushes by the PKK. But there have been none lately and besides, I want to see the countryside up close and personal.

For an hour or two our bus winds along ridge and valley, always keeping Lake Van on our right, to the regional city of Tatvan on its western shore and then down through good ambush country of twisting gorges and blind bends to Bitlis, and on to a town with a strangely Victorian ring, Batman, and finally to the strategic city of Mardin safely ensconced on its hilltop under an ancient walled fortress overlooking the Tigris, where I meet up with Chris and we book into a cheap hotel. It is on the Ankara-Iraq highway, near the Syrian border but closer to Baghdad than to Ankara, overlooking the Mesopotamian plain and the Tigris River valley towards the site of ancient Nineveh. With a history of multiple civilisations dating back to 4000 BC the whole place is an outdoor museum. Until the massacres of 1915 this was a largely Christian Syriac area. To visit the last functioning monastery in Turkey we travel out to the once Christian town of Midyat and are kindly received by the venerable abbot who shows us around, particularly the ancient church with its treasures, daily maintaining its worship in the age-old Syriac rite.

---

54   Turkish term for the clergyman of a mosque.

Cradle of civilisation

Next day brings us to Urfa, awarded the honorific prefix *Şanlı* (Glorious) by Kemal Atatürk's government for services rendered to his revolution. But Şanlıurfa's fame vastly predates this. It was the ancient Edessa—over 9,000 years city of the Sumerians, Hittites, Babylonians, Assyrians, Medes and Persians, Alexander the Great and subsequent Hellenistic rulers, Parthians, Romans, Armenians, Arabs, Byzantines, Selçuk Turks, Crusaders, Mongols and Ottomans! Following the fall of Jerusalem and its destruction by the Romans in 70AD, the region north of Syria became one of the principal focuses of the Jewish dispersal, where the Christian Jews also brought their new faith. Thus it was perhaps the first significant concentration of Jewish converts to Christianity outside Judaea. It is likely that Matthew wrote his Gospel here, addressed to this community. Certainly by 150 AD the city of Edessa was an acclaimed centre of learning and of Christianity, with the 'Church of the East' which, before the advent of Islam in 638, had evangelised Persia, the Malabar coast of India, central Asia, Mongolia and parts of China. It even claimed to have reached the Pacific coast of China! But it was to fall victim to Tamburlaine's Mongol conquest of central Asia, and also dynastic change in China. Residual Ancient Church of the East communities still exist in northern Iraq, Lebanon and Syria, though now suffering persecution and avowed annihilation at the hands of Islamist State *jihadis*.

But Şanlıurfa is also a focus of Islam. A local legend claims the prophet Ibrahim (Abraham) was born in a cave here. In the garden of an ancient mosque we visit the legendary Pool of Sacred Fish where Allah turned the flames of Ibrahim's funeral pyre into water and the burning coals into fish, but we do not manage to see white fish—which would have opened our way into Paradise.

Received by the Turkish state

What is opened to us is entry into the administrative palace of the *Müdür*, Prefect of the province of Urfa, an official appointed by the Turkish state, not a municipal leader elected by the people. Chris is friendly with his brother, the *hodja* of the Kuzguncuk mosque, a charming but distracted fellow who supplements his income by selling the locals bulk supplies of quality water but is invariably caught short at the prayer times by the sudden outbreak of cacophonous calls to prayer from more punctual colleagues all around the horizon. The image of the good *hodja* panting uphill to his minaret to hoarsely rasp out his amplified call to prayer conveys to me a more winsome image of Islam than attending an inter-faith seminar! At the *Müdür's* traditional palace we are received with proper formality and shown into a dining room of Ottoman splendour where we sit cross-legged on sumptuous cushions on the floor, Chris and the Müdür conversing fluently. The main course served is an *aubergine* (eggplant) dish which I don't recognise, having till that moment never tasted the vegetable. Afterwards, wishing I still hadn't, I succumb to our kindly host's insistence that I take more—to find it quite gagable. Good that we have no language in common.

In the land of Abraham's birth

We travel out to Harran one of the most anciently mentioned places in the Middle East,[55] the city of moon worship from which God called Abraham, 'the Father of us all'—Jews, Christians, Muslims—to go forth in faith, not knowing where he was going, and led him with his wife and children and flocks and herds into the land of Canaan (Israel). In the next generation Isaac's son Jacob went back to Harran to find a wife, for whose hand he was compelled to serve his trickster father-in-law Laban for 14 years. At an archaeological site we see some scant ruins of the 9th century Islamic university where the ancient Greek scientific, mathematical and astronomical works were first translated into Syriac, and later into Arabic, destined to make Baghdad for centuries cutodian of the classics. It was the rediscovery of these by the West in the 15th century thst would provide the early stirrings of the European Renaissance.

The plain of Harran strikes us as miserable, parched country: we note a band of traditional-looking Arabs eking out a marginal existence with a few sheep—or are they goats? With their long shaggy wool/hair I am intrigued at the sight of them. Camera cocked, I creep forward to get a close-up and shoot. They look like an image for the Chinese 'Year of the Shaggy Beast' (sheep/goat?) but I never do find out which animal it is, neither in Harran nor in China—which makes Jesus' imagery about sheep and goats at the Last Judgment all the more compelling[56]. We are struck by the mudbrick 'beehive' houses (pointy hot-weather igloos?) where the Bedouin-like Arabs live, reputedly unchanged for 3,000 years.

---

55 Mentioned in ancient Sumerian clay tablets dating from 2300 BC, and in the Bible in Genesis 12:1–5. An inscription from 1100 BC mentions the abundance of elephants there!

56 Matthew 25:33

Painful letdown

For me, arrival at the next Anatolian city is dramatic. Alighting from the coach at the Gaziantep bus station the bottom step collapses under my (moderate) weight and I crash down hard on my bottom. Judging from the pain, something is damaged. Gaziantep (*Gazi* is another honorific) is known to me from reading the story of a Protestant Christian community there (then called Antaib), arising from American missionary work in the 19th century, originally among Armenians. We are directed to the old-established 'American Hospital', and meet the son of the original mission doctor fortuitously working there on a semi-retirement assignment. He establishes that my coccyx, bottom bone of the spinal cord, is badly bruised but not broken. I am deeply touched by the good Lord's provision: if you're going to meet with an accident in far-eastern Turkey, make sure it's in the one city where there is a missionary hospital with a native English-speaking doctor!

I am told to rest for 24 hours and spend the night in their care. In the morning the doctor (about my age) talks proudly about his father's lifelong devotion to the mission. In the 19th century Antaib was notorious for malaria. He shows me around the mission cemetery, touching for the number of young missionaries, men and women, who laid down their lives for the people. His own father is buried there too, but at the completion of a long life of missionary service. Sheepishly my doctor, his son, confesses to no Christian faith yet his residual values of service have led him there in semi-retirement. Over 100 years earlier his father's mission had established 'Central Turkey College' for the Armenian community, but the Ottoman genocide took a heavy toll, before and after the 1st world war. Today one of Turkey's fastest-developing commercial and industrial centres, Gaziantep also claims to be amongst the world's oldest continually inhabited sites.

Among civilisation's most ancient sites

It is the sheer romance of visiting these ultra-ancient sites that entrances me. Primeval *palimpsests* written on over and over again. Picturing people 8,000 years ago walking the very ground I am standing on—streets, squares, temples—trying to gauge what their life might have meant to them, what they ate, how they lived and were ruled, their beliefs about life and death and the hereafter. Such sites would have to be earlier than any extant European settlement, or even Chinese, reflecting the origins of human life in the 'fertile crescent'. On the other hand the timing is dwarfed by the habitation of Australia for at least the past 40,000 years, but there is scant possibility of inferring much from sites or implements about the inner meaning of Aboriginal life (though recently, contrary claims have been encountered based on the dot paintings now much in vogue among art collectors).

In St Paul's home base

And so to Antakya (ancient Antioch), by a long day's bus trip while the landscape grows ever greener and more fertile, with olive and pistachio groves, more closely inhabited and the towns more modern. We pick up an impressively engineered motorway vaguely reminiscent of the Italian Riviera, reaching the Mediterranean coastline near the point where it abruptly swings away southwards to edge Syria, and Lebanon and Palestine. But soon we turn off this main east-west artery, to climb up over a steep mountain range and pick up the new line of the coast southwards past the naval base and steel town of Iskenderun (former Alexandretta), with the limits of Turkey looming. Indeed we learn that this territory of Hatay, Arabic-speaking until today, had in 1939 been annexed by Turkey from the French colonial masters of Syria, occasioning decades of bitterness. After a long day's travel we crash for the night in a cheap hotel.

But next morning our expectations of exploring the antiquity of Antioch are dashed by Chris turning out to be too sick to leave the hotel. Ironic this, because the previous day he had thought my 'falling down the bus steps' somewhat amusing! So I nurse him all day, only in the late afternoon venturing forth alone for a cursory look around the neighbourhood. I walk beside the river Orontes, not very impressive, noting the vast age-range of the buildings. Antioch had predated Roman times, but by the beginning of the Christian era had become the third city of the Roman Empire, after Rome and Alexandria in Egypt. Several emperors had been stationed here, some bequeathing major structures: temples, theatres, colonnades, aqueducts, baths. Once the classical Olympic Games were held here.

Antioch also had a sizeable Christian community, and the New Testament has a good deal to say about it, noting that it was there that the believers were first called 'Christians',[57] arguably from the novelty of Jews and Gentiles forming one community of worship bridging the chasm of aloofness and mutual rejection sundering them from time immemorial. In turn this led to the despatch of Barnabas from the Jewish Christian leadership in Jerusalem to investigate the suspect innovation, which would clearly pose a precedent also for the new groups of Jewish believers in Christ springing up beyond Palestine, not meeting in synagogues but as *'assemblies'*[58].

Disappointing this scepticism, beyond the outpouring of the Holy Spirit on Jews from near and far at Pentecost, and then Peter's liberating vision on the rooftop at Joppa which led to the commander of the Roman garrison at Caesarea, capital of the province of Judaea, being baptised as a brother, together with his family and associates. Peter's conclusion *"So God has broken through to the other nations"* opens the way to the future worldwide chains of assemblies that we call the Church. Acting on this new openness to God's purposes for *'the nations'* (the wider world), it is from Antioch that Paul from nearby Tarsus (and former learned rabbi but also Roman citizen) and Barnabas are subsequently commissioned to undertake the first missionary journey ever recorded, westwards through Turkey as far as Iconium (today's Konya).

But over a number of years a series of earthquakes was to shake Antioch,

---

57   Acts 11: 19-30

58   The Greek word Paul uses is *ekklesia*, in the early versions of the English Bible wrongly translated as 'church'.

inflicting huge damage which, coupled with the opening up of new trade routes eastwards, would lead to the decline of the city once characterised as the capital of the East, with a Christian population of 100,000 cited by St John Chrysostom in the 4th century. Along with Jerusalem, Constantinople, Alexandria, and Rome, it would itself become one of the five original patriarchates (regions led by a Patriarch) of the Christian Church. Until today, one of the major Eastern Orthodox churches is called the Antiochian Orthodox Church, of which many Australian Lebanese are members, with parishes throughout the Commonwealth, some dating back to the late 19th century, several of which I had encountered during my survey of ethnic organisations.

Our Anatolian safari closes with a bus ride retracing our route back to, and then along the motorway to Adana, another neolithic site and also mentioned in Homer's *Iliad*, formerly part of the Roman province of Cilicia and now the largest city in the south-east of Turkey. From there we fly back to Istanbul and, leaving Chris to resume his gathering of research material, I am soon winging my way to Dubai and Melbourne.

Never again can the Turks and Kurds of Broadmeadows be merely anonymous migrants.

26
Nurturing Multicultural Ministries across the Churches

Late in 1998 my four-year role at the diocesan headquarters fell victim to my own self-confidence when I responded to Bishop Curnow's invitation to all program managers to seek a performance review. Unwittingly I was to become mine own executioner! Cheerfully I prepared the reports and the documentation required. Came the day when, having examined these, the Bishop—acting at the time as Diocesan Registrar (OiC Administration)—called me in for interview, accompanied by two members of my advisory committee. As I had expected, the Bishop expressed his appreciation and even admiration for my diligent and creative efforts over the past four years. Then to my dismay he added, "So you'll be finishing up next month". Stunned silence. My friends, both of them normally forthright and articulate, sat there gobsmacked. With hearty handshakes all around we were shown out, to troop stonily across Swanston Street for a coffee. Toying with the idea of some conspiracy with the Bishop, testily I asked them why they hadn't spoken up: they replied feebly that they couldn't think of anything to say!

Return to Canberra?

End of an era. So what to do now, healthy and active as I was, at the young age of 66 and enthusiastic for further service for the Kingdom. Oh, oh—where could we live now? We owned a house in Canberra. So was it time to return and resume life in Moss Street? But how dull and cloying! Besides, if I anticipated continuing in ministry, there would be no prospects in the Diocese of Canberra-Goulburn. Never having been Anglicans there we were quite unknown. In any case I was beyond the retirement age for parish clergy.

Pondering the dilemma and praying, soon a different option loomed, upon Marjorie's appointment as Pastoral Worker in the English/Cantonese-speaking parish of St Michael & All Angels Bennettswood (in East Burwood, some 16km east of the city centre). I could also make a commitment to share in the ministry with our friends Rick and Jessica Cheung. Early in 1999 I was informally named Associate Priest, with the role of complementing the vicar's ministry among the original but now ageing and dwindling Anglo congregation, thus enabling him to concentrate on building the Cantonese congregation—the parish's hope of the future. This commitment would continue until my ultimate retirement from active ministry eight years later in 2007 at the age of 75, completing a ministry of 21 years in the Melbourne Diocese—the same period as in the Public Service.

The Christian ministry had proven a profoundly transformative chapter of my life, involving three signal changes: of career, of denominational affiliation and of city of residence. But manifestly God's good hand had been guiding us through the transitions. Since we had originally envisaged our 'accidental' association with the Anglicans on arriving in Eltham in 1984 as merely a 'holiday' from the Uniting Church, we retained formal membership in the Uniting Church, and for years I remained a member of the Victorian Synod's Migrants & Refugees Committee, meeting monthly at the UCA headquarters in Little Collins St. Members included some eminent parish clergy, some of them former missionaries, plus a number of ethnic clergy on loan from sister Churches such as the Tongan Methodist Conference.

Of prime concern was the struggle by the ethnic clergy against what they considered the cultural imperialism of the mainstream leadership, despite the publication at national level of a groundbreaking manifesto entitled *The Uniting Church is a Multicultural Church*. This was precisely the outcome that our Anglican General Synod Committee had sought through the policy document we had prepared for the national Anglican meeting, but I have never heard whether that policy was ever adopted by subsequent General Synods.

It was only at the end of the two-year ITEMS project that the prospect of throwing my lot in with the Anglican Diocese had taken shape, triggered by Archbishop Penman's invitation to work with him and his subsequent surprising suggestion that I should be ordained. Once inside the ecclesiastical building—even if it were by a back door—I faced the challenge of *unlearning* my lifelong Methodist/Uniting Church lore and replacing it by traditional Anglican understandings, especially of worship. A task not to be under-rated, linked as it was with acquiring a true sense of identity to match the occupational transition from Canberra-based bureaucrat to clergy trainee—at the tender age of 53. Certainly when I joined the group of Anglican theologs at Trinity College in 1986 I had been a very raw recruit. A drastic reworking of my self-image was called for.

A novel development: 'ethnic congregations'

On the death of Archbishop Penman, though now committed to Anglican parish ministry, I did not want to lose my hard-won community perspective nor any potential influence on cross-cultural development in Melbourne within the other Protestant Churches. Completion of the ITEMS Project and my subsequent work within the diocesan HQ had kept my community antenna up and tuned in. Earlier, as a member of the UCA Migrants & Refugees Committee I had persuaded my contacts within the Melbourne Office of my old Department of Immigration to launch a survey of all the ethnic congregations in the city—a pale if localised reflection of my National Groups Survey of 15 years earlier.

Already by the mid-1980s, besides the Uniting Church, several other denominations had also established congregations of particular ethnic groups, in particular the Baptists with their archaically styled 'New Settlers Federation', the Lutherans, the Churches of Christ, the Salvation Army, the Catholic Diocese and even the Jehovah's Witnesses. But too often this gesture had proven patronising: in effect minimising expectations by sidelining ethnic congregations, rather than rethinking the holistic ministry of the Church *in the presence of* ethnic clergy and leaders, whereby everything might be up for review. In the Uniting Church it was through some theologically sophisticated clergy returning from missionary service that a fresh look was now being taken at how that Church as a whole might relate to the changing character of Australian society.

I used to wonder whether this patchy denominational activity in cross-cultural ministry might be stimulated more widely by pooling experiences across the Churches. But in what context could such exchanges occur? While several of the Protestant Churches had a residual commitment to the 'conciliar' ecumenical movement (that is, to the Victorian Council of Churches), their interest was focused more on overseas aid and development issues rather than mission within our multicultural society. Other denominations (Baptist, Presbyterian, Lutheran, Wesleyan, Pentecostal) had no such cross-links with each other.

Building inter-Church connections

In 1992 the Baptist Union's cross-cultural fieldworker, Rev. Charles Wilcox, a former missionary, had convened a meeting of representatives from all the major English-speaking denominations to explore common problems of leadership and resources for cross-cultural ministry, but with no real authority and no continuing structure. Within the next few years this group would be reconvened and formalised with support from John U'ren, of the School of World Mission based in Whitley College. Subsequently the first chair of missiology in Melbourne was to be held by Whitley's Professor Ross Langmead, whose interest and collaboration had provided the necessary financial and personnel support for this initiative.

In banding together to form the *'Inter-Church Network for Cross-Cultural Mission'*, the voices long crying in the wilderness against their own denominations' unwitting (though sterile) *'Anglo-Saxondom'* might now draw upon each other's energies and insights. It seemed clear to us that change would not come overnight but only in the longer term as more clergy trained in multicultural ministry took their places leading congregations. As the only paid worker across all the Churches who had been tasked with promoting such a retraining emphasis, it was strategic for me to become involved from the outset. I became the founding secretary of the Network—a congenial role of supporting the leader but without incurring the prime responsibility for which I was manifestly unsuited, as I had learnt 30 years earlier in the fiasco of the Sydney Teachers' College EU. Constitutionally I had always been a 'words man' rather than an 'action man', a supporter rather than a leader.

Achievements of the Inter-Church Network

Over the next 15 years or so the Inter-Church Network would meet as a ginger group of up to 20 clergy, deliberately hanging loose from any structures, denominational or ecumenical, with the modest goal of 'leavening the lump': monitoring developments across all the Protestant Churches, compiling a database of churches and leaders interested in cross-cultural ministry, keeping track of ethnic congregations linked with the denominations,[59] publishing *Multicultural Horizons*—a 'Newsletter & Digest', courtesy of Whitley College, and organising in-service education opportunities for clergy.

In the public realm an early initiative was the organising of two regional adult educational courses, running over three or four nights in suburban centres (Moonee Ponds and Kew) to offer lay people and clergy from all Churches a balanced training experience through speakers, discussions, videos, and ethnic testimonies. For each course I gave the introductory lecture and in all some 200 people participated.

But undoubtedly the Network's most distinctive public activities were quarterly pastors' breakfasts held in churches all over Melbourne where there was a multicultural ministry. Over a breakfast prepared by the church according to its own ethno-specific cuisine, the pastor would describe his ministry and vision. Some of these ministries were to Japanese, Chinese, Koreans, Russians, Germans, Spanish/Latin Americans, Slavs, Arabic speakers, Vietnamese, Indians, Horn of Africa people, Karens, Pacific Islanders, Aborigines as well as multi-ethnic ministries. Over the years several hundred people attended these breakfasts. Two major occasions were at Harvest Bible College and the upmarket Rydge's Hotel in Richmond (generously funded by a benefactor). These occasions were a delight, both for the richness of their ethnic texture and for the warmth of their common humanity, universally redeemed in Christ. A veritable foretaste of the heavenly banquet! And a feast of new ideas and stimuli.

The largest-scale projects undertaken by the Network were the convening of two day-long Melbourne-wide Pastors' Seminars at Whitley College, several years apart,[60] seeking to attract higher-level denominational leaders and persuade them of the scriptural claims of cross-cultural mission within their strategic planning and allocation of resources. These were widely judged to have been valuable for communicating the vision to denominational leadership and for triggering appropriate new responses.

The ultimate pledge of the Network's authenticity was its diverse ethnic composition. Early on we recognised that our leader should be a person from an ethnic background, variously an Ethiopian evangelist, Paulos Djini, and a Chinese minister, Wai-Kwong Sun. I always felt as much at home among like-minded enthusiasts from all over as in my own Anglican circles, maybe more so. In the process several of the inner leadership group became amongst my close friends.

Over recent years, the decline and ageing of the mainline Anglo denominations has been to some extent offset by the intensely multicultural character of the emerging Pentecostal mega-churches. In our increasingly cosmopolitan society

---

59 At that time Baptist c.30, Uniting 16, Wesleyan and Churches of Christ 9 each, Lutheran 8, Presbyterian 8, Anglican 4 (but 31 by 2012—half of them African) and Salvation Army 3.

60 On '*Encouraging Churches in Cross-Cultural Mission: Tackling the Dilemmas*' in 1995 and '*Multicultural Church is Possible: Embracing Kingdom Visions for Multi-Ethnic Melbourne*' in 2001.

this highlights the need for multicultural ministry and mission activity to be normatised by every denomination seeking to maintain its relevance. To promote this conviction, after wide-ranging consultation, the Network published in 2000:

> ### A MULTICULTURAL MANIFESTO TO THE CHURCHES OF VICTORIA
>
> *It had a glance at the past*—in gratitude for the great souls who had sought to reach out across boundaries of race and culture—but in penitence for acts of violence, cruelty, and neglect and for arrogance and racial superiority.
>
> *It addressed the present*—the diversity of the society but not of our Churches, the growth of ethno-specific churches and multicultural churches, but the maldistribution of resources and of training opportunities.
>
> *And it surveyed the future*—we live in a post-Christian, pluralist society: a missionary environment. So we call for affirmative action by church leaders and decision-making bodies in regard to:
> - appropriate theological curricula and training
> - reforms to empower NESB people through involvement in decision-making, and recognition of the gifts they bring
> - their access to church facilities, financial and human resources
> - encouragement for the use of a multiplicity of languages and appropriate forms of worship
> - support for 'incarnational ministries' among the marginalised and vulnerable (including asylum seekers and refugees) motivated by unconditional love
> - an appeal for Christians of all backgrounds and Churches to work together for God's Kingdom
>
> *It concluded* "Knowing the transforming power of God's love, we commit ourselves to addressing these issues in our church life, in the living power of the God who acts."

The *Manifesto* was also laid out in liturgical form for use in covenanting services.

Late in 2008 after a period of quiescence the Network was formally wound up and I wrote the appropriate letters of thanks. Judging its pioneering role to have been a positive factor in the changing climate across the Anglo Churches, and in the light of the normatising of our society—in both the policy area and in actuality—as irrevocably multicultural, we felt privileged to have played a strategic role in that evolutionary process.

Role of the ecumenical movement in Victoria

But over the years all this activity had run parallel to the efforts of the Victorian Council of Churches, through its Commission on Living Faiths & Community

Relations, which had originally brought me to Melbourne to seek such outcomes—not so much at the grassroots level as in theological training, which had spawned the ITEMS project. Over those 20 years I had continued as a member of the Commission, initially as a paid worker and later as one of the nominated Anglican representatives.

The reasons for this complementary (rather than competitive) activity lay in the different composition of the ecumenical movement and the Inter-Church Network for Cross-Cultural Mission. Whereas the Network was basically composed of evangelical Churches sponsoring ethnic congregations at grassroots level, the ecumenical movement in Victoria comprised all the Churches from the Roman Catholic and various ethnic Orthodox Churches to the 'mainstream' Anglo denominations.

But significant absentees were the Baptist, Presbyterian, Lutheran and Pentecostal Churches, which declined to join the ecumenical body, perhaps suspicious of its (now dated) liberal theology or fearing to compromise their independence and freedom of action. This reluctance had long generated a degree of tension within the *national* ecumenical body, the Australian Council of Churches, which I had encountered way back in my work with the ACC's Multicultural Commission in Canberra. Indeed when the ACC, the roof body of the ecumenical movement was being restructured in 1989 to become the National Council of Churches in Australia (now the NCCA), Archbishop Penman had agreed to become its initial President on condition that the Roman Catholic Church (at national level) become a member and also that formal attempts be made to incorporate the evangelical denominations. But with the Archbishop's untimely death only the first of these stipulations would be realised. Sad, because today the ecumenical movement, with its liberal theology and fading dreams of organic unity, looks increasingly dated and jaded, while much of the Christian activity in our community is small-scale and localised—though vibrant.

VCC's Commission on Living Faiths & Community Relations

During my 20 years' membership of the Victorian Council of Churches' Commission on Living Faiths & Community Relations (I suspect as quite the longest-serving member in the Commission's history), it brought together some significant figures: clergy, Catholic sisters, experts in the fields of theology, sociology and migration besides the well-meaning but often less informed rank-and-file denominational representatives. Mostly the Chair would be a socially-oriented theologian.

Aside from its monitoring role, from time to time the Commission would undertake a creative initiative: while I was still working with the ITEMS Project during the Victorian Sesqui-Centenary Year, it fell to my lot to compile and produce a 55pp handbook called *Accents of Faith: the Churches of the Victorian Council of Churches*. I have a copy of a letter to the VCC from Archbishop Penman observing that "It will be a marvellous resource for prayer and encouragement in our mutual shared ministry". To encourage wider understanding of each other, each of the

15 Member Churches (denominations) provided a brief essay on their Church—historically and in Australia—in some cases written in their own language as well as in English: Greek, Romanian, Coptic, Aramaic (by the ancient Assyrian Church of the East from northern Iraq). As editor it was my task to plan, design, and arrange for publication of the book, commissioning the essays and in some cases organising their translation.

Its appearance was timed for the VCC's 1985 Annual General Meeting (a two-day conference) on the theme *'The Church is Multicultural'*, assembling over a weekend in the Romanian Orthodox church in Carlton. The book opened with letters of commendation from the Governor of Victoria and the Premier, John Cain, and concluded with a directory of Christian activity in Melbourne in the fields of immigration & ethnic affairs, acknowledging the Victorian Government's grant to the VCC for the ITEMS Project and the support of the Commission on Living Faiths & Community Relations. At the Annual General Meeting I spoke on the ethnic scene and the ITEMS Project, besides organising the discussion groups on related issues.

During the 1990s the focus of this VCC Commission was shifting more towards inter-faith relations (my old bugbear—*'been there, done that'*), although none of the members had been involved with the Multi-Faith Resource Centre years before. There was a corresponding decline of interest in the cross-cultural ministry scene, conceivably because the denominations themselves had taken up the challenge. But I maintained that 'community relations' was a perennial issue because of societal factors such as the 'Asian debate' triggered by Pauline Hanson and her One Nation Party, and the advent of Black migration from Africa. But several strong voices were calling for the promotion of inter-faith dialogue as the Commission's major focus, seemingly oblivious to the social reality that, in the suburbs where there was a significant presence of newcomers from several faith backgrounds (such as Dandenong), it was virtually only the Christians proposing the encounters. While it was of course a sound humanistic project to spread knowledge and understanding of other faiths, Muslims (the largest other faith group) had no interest in learning about Christianity, for them a 'superseded, inferior and corrupted' religion. Neither had I ever heard of any Buddhist interest in discussing beliefs for instance with Hindus. I tended to conclude that it was merely a romantic dream that cross-faith groups of *grassroots practitioners* might be interested in seeking mutual contact. On the other hand there was a significant Council for Christians and Jews in Melbourne working on a meaningful agenda, beside a high-level Christian/Jewish/Muslim dialogue group, both of which I had been earlier associated with.

After attending about two years of monthly Commission meetings mostly preoccupied with this dilettante interest in inter-faith dialogue to the detriment of social justice aspects of migration, inter-ethnic relations, and refugee policy concerns, I wanted out. My voice seemed superfluous. So I explained my position and resigned from the Commission which, 20 years earlier, I had been employed by and accountable to, and which had changed our family's history by bringing me to Melbourne. But of course by then it was a new day: there was no collective memory of my earlier activity. I received a formal acknowledgement of my resignation, with a polite expression of thanks. This also represented a poignant end to my association with the ecumenical movement, to which I had dedicated my zeal for a pivotal year in Canberra, and subsequently severed my link with the Australian Public Service (except for my ongoing pension!) in order to move my family to Melbourne to work in a frontier role. But it had ended in some disillusionment. That I had in fact outlived my relevance came as a sobering realisation. But of course my real focus had long since shifted from inter-Church relations to the privilege of serving God through ministering to specific congregations of Anglican Christians.

Belated entrant to university teaching

By a surprising turn of events, about this time I received an invitation to teach a semester course on *Religion in Australian Society* at the Australian Catholic University's campus near Monash, standing in for the regular lecturer. I had to devise and teach the course, a compulsory subject for young people training for the teaching profession—and more academically oriented than the ITEMS course. I enjoyed doing the historical research and preparing the teaching material which also drew on my lived experience. Two generations younger than me, the class seemed to lap it up. After half a lifetime's involvement in adult education this experience represented the fulfilment of a long-held conceit about one day becoming a 'proper' university teacher.

Publications

Over the years in Melbourne I had frequently written both Christian and secular publications:

- *The Cultured Pearl: Australian Readings in Cross-Cultural Theology and Mission,*
- Victorian Council of Churches, 1986, 294pp (Christian Book of the Year 1987);
- *Accents of Faith: the Churches of the Victorian Council of Churches*, compiled and edited for the VCC, 1985, 55pp;
- *Seeds Blowing in the Wind: Review of Multicultural Ministry & Mission*, Anglican Diocese of Melbourne, 1993, 133pp.;
- *Journeying On Together: The Inside Story of a Bicultural/Bilingual Church in an Australian Suburb*, St Michael & All Angels Bennettswood, 2001, 85pp;
- A chapter on 'Cross-cultural Ministry in the Australian Anglican Church' in the book *Multicultural Ministry: Report of the First International Network Forum convened by the National Assembly of the Uniting Church; 2000*
- An article 'How Multi-Cultural is God in Australia?' in *AFES Graduates Fellowship Papers on Biblical & Current Questions*, Issue 32;

- An article 'The origins of multiculturalism policy' in *Australian Mosaic*, journal of FECCA (Federation of Ethnic Communities Councils in Australia);
- Articles on 'Christianity and the Struggle for an Australian Identity' and on 'Jerusalem and Judaea and to the Ends of the Earth', both in *On Being*, Christian monthly magazine;
- Articles on working-class ministry in the Anglican newspaper *Church Scene*.

Marjorie had also burst into print several times, on 'Hard Labour in the Vineyard' in *National Outlook*, a Christian monthly magazine, and 'Seven Years in Broadmeadows' in *Church Scene*.

Beyond our own writings I had edited several books: two for Chris and one for Banu; two for Fr Anthony Paganoni (one of c. 400pp.); and *Refuge on the Roper* plus an early draft of *Gumbuli of Ngukurr* for my friend and former colleague, Murray Seiffert.

So the long Melbourne years had been distinguished as much by networking with diverse people through wide community linkages beyond the Anglican Church as by our commitment to the parishioners we had loved and served day by day. Of course as we have grown older, especially now well beyond retirement, community activism has perforce given way to an ongoing identification with issues rather than a practical involvement (other than every day signing half a dozen public petitions on-line). But the connection with our ageing fellow-Christians becomes ever more meaningful.

27
Family Matters!

What of life at home? In 1997 Christopher had brought Esma to Australia on a prospective spouse visa, and the two moved into the Richmond vicarage where we were living while I was Director of Cross-Cultural Ministry for Melbourne Diocese. Nicholas was for the moment based in Quito, Ecuador learning Spanish, Sarah-Jane in Korea teaching English, and David staging his 'Full-On Theatre' shows around the country and visiting remote Aboriginal communities. Esma faced the huge challenge of learning English from scratch: she seemed literally to have not a word of the language. I tried to apply what Turkish I had acquired but it was a dour struggle all round. By then Chris was writing his doctoral thesis for La Trobe University full-time, based on his painstaking research in Turkey over several years, on the interplay of the Turkish Republic with its Kurdish population, within the common framework of Islam.

We arranged for a leading layman from St Mary Magdalene's Dallas, Alan Aylward, a civil celebrant, to conduct a marriage ceremony in the Vicarage lounge room and garden, with a handful of guests, followed by afternoon tea. Soon the couple were able to move temporarily into a flat in the nearby high-rise estate whose tenants were in Turkey.

Losing the inner-city dream

But late in 1998 the sudden end of my stint in Cross-Cultural Ministry with the Diocese had brought with it the implication that we needed to locate accommodation elsewhere, although the landlord, St Stephen's parish, seemed quite relaxed about when. We had greatly enjoyed inner-city living in that vibrant setting: the cosmopolitan variety of cuisines on tap along the three parallel shopping strips of Richmond, the coffee shops of South Yarra just across the river, the Prahran weekend market, the bike paths upstream and downstream. One Sunday afternoon Chris and I had ridden along the riverbank right through the downtown area of Southbank as far as the Bolte Bridge before turning off to reach the overseas passenger terminal at Port Melbourne. Other days I had ridden upstream to Dight's Falls near Clifton Hill where the tidal river ends at a rock barrier, once a great Aboriginal meeting ground and close to where John Batman and tribal spokesmen concluded the 'treaty' to be subsequently repudiated by the Governor of New South Wales. I took my bike by train to Brighton and rode around the bay foreshore to Moorabbin. On a famous occasion at Flinders Street station I had narrowly averted being locked overnight in a train being shunted to the Burnley railyards when I had leapt back in to retrieve my orthopaedic cushion just as the doors closed behind me. Fortunately being in the front half of the train I was able to hammer on the wall of the driver's cab. Appropriately I was abused and deposited at East Richmond, an unscheduled stop.

A merciful provision—and a new role

Another time just before New Year, walking through the Swan St shopping centre, I had sensed some flecks swirling across one eye. At the community health centre my doctor, a former Sydney EU member, immediately got me into the Eye Hospital in East Melbourne where there was only one surgeon on duty over the holiday period, but reputedly the best in Melbourne. By laser surgery he reattached the threatening detached retina, observing that if I hadn't seen him then, within the week I would have lost the sight of the eye. *"The eyes of the Lord are upon those who revere him"* (Psalm 33:18).

Another great blessing was the birth in the Women's Hospital of our first grandchild Raphael Emre in April 1999, with Marjorie in attendance. At 67 we were late entrants into the ranks of grandparents. Helping in the search for a name meaningful to both cultures, we proposed the archangel who was Hebrew patron of love and of travellers in the apocryphal Book of Tobit. (In Turkish the archangel is *Israfil*, while Emre means '*agape* love'.) Appropriate, because by then we were both ministering in the Bennettswood parish of St Michael & All *Angels*, chief of whom were Michael, Gabriel (in Arabic *Gibran*) and Raphael.

Marjorie had hoped we might find a house to buy in Richmond but the costs of inner-city property proved exhorbitant: $1m for a refurbished but ancient mean, single-fronted terrace house! So how far afield would we need to roam? After our Canberra years I cavilled at the boring flat chequerboard pattern of most of Melbourne, and recalled from our years at Eltham the wooded ridges of the north-east.

Buying into the *Garden of Eden*

So in March that year, having finally sold our beloved family home in Canberra at 26 Moss St, Cook for a good price we bought outright a pleasant, partially two-storey house at 41 Sackville St, Montmorency in a beautiful garden setting on a wooded hillside, terraced on some seven levels with natural rock walls and bricked paths. It proved an uncanny replay of our house in Cook (built about the same year) but with a lush garden, shaded by some 30 major trees, both natives and exotics (liqidambar, ash, maple, birch, dogwood, sycamore, hawthorn, cypress, catalpa, pistachio, Chinese elm, lemon, apple, fig, prunus) as well as colourful hibiscus, rhododendrons, camellias, daphnes, and azaleas, all interspersed with treeferns, clumps of bamboo, yucca and a great variety of flowering ground covers, chiefly the luscious plectranthus, and with grand, sweeping lawns. Truly the garden setting was ravishing—a true work of art glorifying the Creator.

As seems to have happened several times when house hunting or selling, we had met with immediate success. Early in our search, one Monday morning I had happened to notice among *The Age* real estate reports that a house in Montmorency had been withdrawn from auction sale at the last moment. Soon we were being driven there by the estate agent, who explained that the seller belonged to some religious sect and had suddenly felt uncomfortable with the Saturday sale. On Lower Plenty Rd, cruising down the long hill towards Eltham, half-way down we dived off to the left into a small roadside valley. My heart sank: I'm a mountain man. But no! The twisty road rose up the far slope and we got out to discover an attractive house well above the road level, looking down across the valley. (I noticed that on the opposite side of the street the roof-tops of the houses were about road level.)

We were met at the door, elegant with its red figured glass, and walked into the entrance hall and the lounge, with a large two-storeyed family room visible beyond, obviously a newer addition. I had to repress the urge to say, *"We'll buy it"*. The more we inspected it, house and garden, front and back, the more certain I became. When we finally sat on the back terrace to consider a price I said to the lady, *"We're Christians too, retiring from living in parish houses and now buying our own. You're Seventh Day Adventists, aren't you?"* That clinched it. She settled for a lesser price than the agent had estimated, delighted that God had provided for us all, and that Christians would continue to look after her beautiful home and garden.

The joy of grandparenting

There we were to live for ten years, mostly spent working in the Bennettswood parish half an hour's Sunday drive away. Before long Chris and Esma rented a house near Montmorency station and village shops, where we often did our grandparental duty of baby-sitting. How sweet the memories of rocking baby Raphael to sleep as Esma did, nestled between her lower legs as she reclined, while I sang to him, *"Jesus loves me, this I know/For the Bible tells me so"* and prayed for his future wellbeing, faith and happiness. Or I would wheel him up to the station to meet his mother coming home from English classes in the city, talking to him in my pidgin Turkish, "Look, the train's coming. See Mummy?" In fact she was learning English more quickly and better than any student I had ever known. As Chris had said, she's very clever.

His little family were parishioners of St Phillip's on Hoddle St, near the Collingwood Town Hall. It was there that one of the high moments of my life saw me baptizing my first grandchild after a morning service, by special arrangements with the vicar. I had been surprised when Esma, a nominal Muslim, had agreed to this—though as I poured the water over his mass of wavy black hair she rushed forward to rescue him! It was Easter morning 2000 and it was his first birthday. Rich celebration of new beginnings!

Rewards of scholarship

The other momentous event in that period had been Chris lodging his doctoral thesis after several years' work and the subsequent award of his PhD at Latrobe

University, with him decked out in the flat black doctor's hat and red gown, hired for the occasion, and afterwards the photos of him holding baby Raphael with Esma and our family. It had been my privilege to edit the book based on his doctoral thesis[61], published in Oxford—dour struggle though it had cost me to acquire the new and opaque 'tongue' of anthropology.

His first professional commission was a one-year in-house anthropology consultancy in the Collins Street national HQ of Rio Tinto, the world mining giant. On one project he was despatched to the Baluchistan province of SW Pakistan, reporting on a minority ethnic group's dispossession from a newly proclaimed conservation park. His entry into the world of academe came about with his appointment as lecturer in anthropology in the University of Canterbury, in Christchurch, New Zealand.

Several times over the next few years we were to visit the family in their town house in Ilam close to the university, assisting with Raphael, later buying him his first two-wheeler training bicycle and helping him learn to ride it. In turn he 'helped' me get their garden in order. In 2002 Esma would invite Marjorie across the Ditch to help care for the family while she was in hospital for the birth of Gebran James—Arabic form of another archangel, Gabriel (Turkish, *Gibrail*), who at the Annunciation proclaimed God's purposes to Mary.

In our several subsequent trans-Tasman visits we undertook brief safaris in the Canterbury province, to Hanmer Springs, the port of Lyttelton, Akaroa on the remarkable Banks Peninsula formed by two ancient volcanic cones, and one longer tour of the North Island visiting all the significant places and sites to which we had not been able to do justice in our family campervan tour 20 years earlier. On our final visit we spent a few days on a holiday break with the family at Greymouth beyond the Southern Alps on the west coast, driving over in two cars.

On Chris' appointment to Macquarie University in Sydney in 2005 they would set up house in nearby Epping, becoming associated with West Epping Uniting Church. Later he was to become Senior Lecturer and head of the Anthropology department (largest in the Arts Faculty) and in 2013 Professor.

Family tradition: grasping opportunities

Some years earlier we had driven briskly from Melbourne to Macquarie University to be present at Sarah-Jane's graduation in Arts. Afterwards during refreshments the Chancellor, Judge Michael Kirby, a Justice of the High Court of Australia, had kindly chatted with us all. Likewise we had attended Nick's graduation in the Wilson Hall as Bachelor of Arts and Law of Melbourne University, and again for the presentation of David's Diploma in Acting from the Drama School of Melbourne College of the Arts, linked with Melbourne University.

With Marjorie's and my degrees in Arts, and Marjorie's two diplomas in 'Social Work', and 'Community Development' and mine in Education, it

---

61   *Kurdistan: Crafting of National Selves*, Oxford, Berg, 2008

represented significant social progress over two generations to have all four of our children also now holding tertiary qualifications. We had come a long way from the quarries and coalmines of Scotland and the Hunter, and the silver/lead/zinc mines of Broken Hill. Maybe I clinched it for the previous generation by also graduating Bachelor of Theology in Melbourne University's Wilson Hall in 1996 at the age of 63.

Award of *Medal of the Order of Australia*

But on a different plane altogether was the award in October, 2000 at Government House of the Order of Australia Medal (OAM) by the Victorian Governor, Sir James Gobbo, with Marjorie, Chris, Esma & Raphael accepting the invitation to attend the ceremony. The award cited my *'contribution to the development of our national policy of multiculturalism and to cross-cultural ministry within the Anglican Church of Australia'*. As he pinned the medal to my breast, Sir James whispered, *"That was a great paper you wrote for Al Grassby"*. He would know, since as a young Italo-Australian lawyer he had been associated with the 1970s campaigning for ethnic recognition in the burgeoning multicultural society.

Among the congratulations received were letters from the Governor of Victoria, the Premier Steve Bracks and the leader of the Opposition Denis Napthine, the Minister for Immigration Phillip Ruddock (citing only the *secondary* focus of my contribution to the Anglican Church!), the Head of the Immigration Department (with an oblique hint to my link with his Department), local Members of State Parliament and Federal senators, Professor Jerzy Zubrzycki, the SBS, Dr Mark Lopez, the Mayor of Banyule City, and Church dignitaries from the Archbishop to regional bishops and several parishes and a Uniting Church theologian, besides personal friends. In the *Diamond Valley Leader* there was an article with photo (*'Cultural crusader'*) and later a feature article in *The Age* entitled '*The man who dared to write the 'm' word'*. To be recognised in one's own day—an unlikely if gratifying scenario.

Family's contribution to the community

Today our four children grace a range of community-oriented professions. I am proud of the contribution they are making to the wellbeing of our society. Sara-Jane trains adult migrants in Sydney's largest ESL-teaching network, Navitas. She has garnered extensive experience of teaching English: in Oviedo in Spain, Prague in the Czech Republic, in South Korea, and in Charlotte in North Carolina, USA. Christopher is professor of anthropology at Macquarie University. Nicholas, a former officer of the Immigration Department and the Quarantine Service in Canberra, now conducts his own migration agency, *Visaustralia,* facilitating the migration of professionals from Mexico; and David leads his own Full-On Theatre company mainly working in schools, including in remote Aboriginal communities. We are proud of them all both for their commitments and their achievements. With us, all share the vision of a more just and humane society.

In 2009 we had the joy of another family wedding when Nick asked me to conduct the ceremony in Canberra for him and his bride, Dominiq Hein, whom he had met in Mexico City, though she had studied in Australia at Monash University as well as at a Canadian university. By the shores of Lake Burley Griffin on a glorious summer's day, it was to prove a stellar occasion, launched by Dave acknowledging our debt to the local indigenous elders, and with Marjorie presenting an insightful and practical homily, followed by feasting and dancing in the adjacent Yacht Club at the elegant reception with our extended family and many of our lifelong friends.

The couple have since presented us with two dear grandchildren, Hughan Patrick and Valentina Lucienne, blue-eyed blonds of five and four, being raised bilingually. So now there are three generations of Hughans in the family: grandfather, father and son. One of the greatest joys of my maturer years has been to hear both Chris and Nick unself-consciously exercising their bilingualism with partners and children. *Viva el bilinguismo!*

28
Under the Spell of the Old World

My boyhood had been spent in a home redolent of our British origins. From very early on, I knew that my people had come from Scotland and that our 'Australian-ness' was still somewhat provisional. The ties of Empire were strong and always officially promoted. We were loyal to the Motherland and were affectionately disposed towards her maternal role in maintaining a grand worldwide Empire bringing civilisation to *'lesser breeds without the law'*. Of course we were also taught about our own progressive nation—but we sensed it a bit amateurish.

A world of European empires

The proof of Empire was there on our schoolroom wall in the technicolor maps. In 1939 the world map consisted of empires and lands of diverse colours: red (British—and by far the most extensive, amounting to a quarter of the world's landmass), green (French), yellow (Spanish), mauve (Portuguese) with random shades for other countries The remainder of Continental Europe was of variegated shades, but some of these countries also held overseas possessions (Netherlands, Belgium, Denmark, Germany, Italy). Jointly, Europe dominated the world, and its Western and Christian civilisation was the world's norm, to which ultimately even the most benighted of souls would one day aspire, if not actually attain.

Beyond Europe few countries were independent: USA (the colonial power over the Philippines), the Soviet Union, China, Japan (the colonial power over Korea), Turkey, Saudi Arabia, Iran, Thailand come to mind, and of course Latin America—but the Latin societies were in *economic* thrall to the USA, no doubt a cheaper and more effective means of extracting profits from them than through physical occupation.

Arguably the sole positive outcome of World War II had been the demise of empires (colonialism), though they were an unconscionable time a-dying, the process marked by protracted local conflicts as independence movements all over the world fought it out with their well-armed colonial masters: in India/Pakistan, Algeria, Malaya, Indonesia, Korea, Vietnam, Laos, Cambodia, Congo (still riven), Kenya, Tanganyika (Tanzania), Nigeria, Ghana, Sierra Leone, Ethiopia, Sudan, Mozambique, Angola and many other parts of Africa, Bangladesh, Burma *et al.* Even Australia had a colony in Papua-New Guinea until the time of the Whitlam Government (the double-barrelled name resulting from Germany's colonising of New Guinea and New Britain (north-east) and the UK's colonising of Papua (south-east), both before World War I).

Changing sides

During the 1950s, the first decade of the painful de-colonising process, like a loyal son of Empire, I had been emotionally identified with the old regimes resisting the independence movements: *("What ingrates the rebels are for all the development bestowed by the benevolent colonisers")*. Of course I was totally ignorant of the issues involved—essentially political—relating to freedom, equality, human dignity, civil and human rights, and an end to the exploitation, violence, cruelty and oppression which bleeds a colony white for the enrichment of an unfeeling motherland.

So these two antithetical understandings of colonialism defined the political spectrum running from 'reactionary' to 'progressive'—that is, from holding the fort in order to maintain one's own privileges *vs* actively seeking the wellbeing of others whose needs are being ignored—in democracies a spectrum dubbed 'right' and 'left'. That such stirring issues should have escaped the attention of my contemporary generation of evangelical Christian students and graduates (as well as me) now seems incomprehensible—indeed reprehensible! It was only in England in the early 60s where the issues (physically) appeared more stark that I had gained enough understanding to redefine my life-position—as I now see it the only Christian stance to adopt: *'Who would Jesus exploit?'*

Of course my studies had been politically neutral: languages, history and culture of two or three European civilisations, past and present. Perhaps my university days were too close to the devastating impact of World War II with its numbing legacy of destruction and calamity, for alternative radical thinking to have gained much traction. Only in my high school years had the United Nations been launched and it was initially preoccupied in resolving international crises of colonialism.

But now in 1950 the first stage of the Cold War was being played out. The Korean War was being waged by our soldiers, supporting the South Koreans backed by the USA and other UN contingents, and opposing the North Koreans backed by newly Communist China and Russia. Oddly, the armistice of 1953 continues to the present day, i.e. the War has never officially ended! But elsewhere, with the restoration of peace and the focus on the rebuilding of Europe, we had to wait a decade or two before radical reforms were in the air, let alone implemented. This was the period when we took ship for Europe where it was all happening.

'Back home in Bonnie Scotland wi' my ainfolk'

I remember being thrilled at discovering my spiritual home, getting in touch with my roots—drinking of the nectar and relishing the fruits of the family tree!—and getting to view my colonial homeland from an external, Empire-wide perspective. And quintessentially so when we made the pilgrimage to our revered Scotland.

In 1959, naïvely predisposed to approving whatever I encountered, it had been love at first sight with the civilised landscapes of Britain. The countryside was magical: nature and human settlement blending in a perfect harmony a thousand

and more years in the making. After the untidy grey-greens of Australia with the tortured outlines of gumtrees its ordered verdure was stunning, its autumnal foliage glorious, the crops bountiful, the essentially human scale of it all comprehensible at a glance. In later travels beyond the UK we were to discover the obvious kinship of styles across Europe, variations drawing on a shared ecological, cultural and architectural patrimony—though not without national distinctives.

So through our five years of living and working in England and Germany, exploring some sixteen countries—and speaking three languages—my absorption and delight in Europe had never slackened but had if anything grown more intense. As ethnically European, and heirs of a thousand years of recorded history and cultural interaction, we wanted to go deeper in exploring our origins in their broader historical & cultural context. Indeed if left to my own decision-making I may well have opted to spend my life in Europe, even in Germany. I felt truly at home, and strangely liberated. Since then, though living happily and (I trust) productively in Australia, contributing to our evolution into a multicultural society—albeit with tragically unfinished business with the original Australians—I have maintained my love affair from afar with that dynamic and ever-evolving continent, in the 24 years between 1984 and 2008 paying five visits, four of them travelling alone.

Though Britain was mostly the goal, and Ely invariably one of the way stations, I also nurtured the relationship with 'our' Minden family as well as roaming further afield on the Continent. Probably the most wide-ranging of the five safaris was late in 1993 when I cashed in on the advent of an airline new to Australian skies, Gulf Air, which initially offered return flights to the UK for under $1000. Doubling back by train and ferry to Calais I drove the brand new Citroën CX5 awaiting me on the docks through northern and eastern France, the west of Germany, and ultimately to Spain and Portugal in order to visit Sara-Jane for a week-end in Oviedo in her first English-teaching post.

Fields of blood

My initial focus was on the battle sites from the two world wars: in 1940 with the Nazis over-running France, the desperate evacuation of the British Expeditionary Force from Dunkirk, not far from Calais, assisted by a makeshift navy of private craft. Then a short drive to the World War I battlefields of Flanders and the Somme straddling the French/Belgian border. Unimaginable today the agony and horror of those four years of military stalemate, so starkly evoked by visiting the appalling war cemeteries and the Menin Gate at Ypres (like a mini-*Arc de Triomphe* but written all over with thousands of names of the Allied fallen, from all parts of the Empire), and the memorial to the 1200 Australians killed in the world's first tank battle at Villers-Bretonneux (today with its *Café au Kangourou*)—all compelling testimonies to the pitiless slaughter and the colossal senselessness of war. My visit coincided with All Souls' Day with cemeteries crowded by mourners, but when I asked a group of French widows where the Germans were buried they affected to say they'd never thought about that. As fallen invaders, were they dumped in unmarked mass graves or respectfully repatriated to their *Vaterland*? Who knows?

Tour de France

Journeying on in real time brought the twin delights of using French in normal everyday life far removed from *La plume de ma tante*, plus avidly succumbing to the pastrycooks' wickedly tempting confections on display in every village high street *confiserie*, complemented by the succulent chocolates for which northern France and Belgium are notorious—but this in a period of my life when my rangy build justified such dietary lasciviousness.

Beyond an overnight stay in historic Amiens, chief city of Picardy with its 13th century cathedral, the largest in France, I moved on to Strasbourg/Strassburg in Alsace, famed for its red sandstone cathedral (for 250 years the world's tallest building), and now a UNESCO world heritage city straddling the French/German border, seat of the European Parliament and many of the instrumentalities of the European Union. Onwards to the charming Vosges mountains west of the Rhine in the region of Alsace-Lorraine (in German, *Elsass-Lothringen*) for centuries a political football between French and Germans, and finally to the national museum of the French railways (SNCF) at *Mulhouse/Mülhausen*, a protestant city—in France!

Returning to my car it dawned on me that I had made no record of its numberplate, while in the gathering dusk every second vehicle in the broad carpark looked like it. A panicky prayer later I recalled something I had stowed on the back window sill and by a laborious process of elimination retrieved my faithful steed. Dopes travelling alone can sure make it hard for themselves.

That's why I later picked up a British student hitch-hiking along the alpine road from Grenoble to the ski resort of Chamonix, at whose request I shared my understanding of the Faith. Then taking the U-turn back westwards across the river Rhône at Lyons, third city of France, the route led through the once-volcanic Massif Central, isolated upland region in the southern half of France, to one of the country's largest cities, Toulouse, home of the aerospace industry and the Airbus. And on to the elegant city of Pau, long favoured by wealthy English visitors for the beauty of its location close to the great Pyrénées mountain chain forming the border with Spain. After evening worship in the oldest (and dimmest) church I had ever attended—its architecture 11th century Romanesque—the ancient priest and I shared experiences of parish ministry on opposite sides of the world. Next day, as a mountain man how could I resist the opportunity of driving the Citroën up to one of the highest villages within the rugged, snow-capped Pyrénées range before wending my way down to the Atlantic coast and on into Spain.

To España

A long morning's drive, initially along an *autovia*, enabled me to traverse the Basque country and its capital of Bilbao which has an active separatist movement (ETA) angrily aspiring for autonomy. (Thankfully not while I drove by.) The Basques, whose language shares no external links, are said to be one of Europe's oldest peoples. But the cities of Spain's northern coastline are quite industrialised and unappealing, with coalmining a major activity, encouraging me to swing inland to visit the 13th century cathedral of Burgos. But in vain: inexplicably I found it locked up. Bent on reaching Sara-Jane's lodging by nightfall I was scooting along a winding highway when I fell foul of a motor-cycle policeman announcing that I had crossed the unbroken centre line and needed to follow him to the nearest automatic teller machine, where I had to withdraw a sizeable pile of pesetas—which he shamelessly pocketed and rode off, leaving no documentation, let alone a receipt. Guilty as I undoubtedly was, as a foreign (i.e. French) driver I was probably fair game. But Sarah's warm welcome a little later made it all worthwhile.

It was a revelation to see our firstborn operating confidently in Spanish, based in a private commercial college run by an overbearing Brit. Proudly she showed me around her Hispanic world, the old city of Oviedo, capital of Asturias with its ancient churches, some dating back to Visigothic times of the 8th century (cf. the few surviving Saxon churches of England), and the mediaeval cathedral with its off-centre single spire. Also we drove down to the nearby coastal resort city of Gijon (with its intriguing Spanish pronunciation *Híhon*).

Portuguese Sunday

On Sunday we embarked on a longish drive into Portugal, heading inland in order to cut off the north-west corner of Spain. Crossing the border we found that country visibly poorer, with tired-looking small towns in a rather dried-out landscape, at one point deeply dissected by a small river straddled by an antique bridge. By afternoon it was evident we were not going to make it to the capita Lisbon, in time for Sarah to reappear at work next day, so we settled for visiting Oporto, the country's second city. Driving across a high-arched double-decked bridge over the Douros river in the centre of the city (designed by Gustave Eiffel who built the Tower in Paris), we were struck by its dramatic location, along a curving estuary lined by stately city buildings. The region is celebrated for its port wine production.

Oporto from Douros river bridge

Turning northwards into the highway up the Atlantic coast we ambled along the beachfronts with all the Sunday afternoon excursionists so that by the time we cleared Portugal to re-enter the top corner of Spain it was time to seek an overnight lodging. As it happened we found a modest but comfortable hotel in the centre of Santiago de Compostela, a richly historic city at the north-west corner of the Iberian peninsula, and fabled goal of *'El Camino de Santiago'*,[62] the mediaeval pilgrim walk from France along the north coast of Spain now enjoying fresh vogue worldwide among questing Christians of many denominations. In recent years we have known several middle-aged Australians who have 'done' it, and some actually claim on foot!

Regretfully, having spent the night in the hotel on the Cathedral square, we had to make off early for Oviedo, setting a cracking pace all the way, at one point on the north coast road for kilometres driving through a huge plantation forest of young Tasmanian bluegums. Like all eucalypts we noticed overseas, they looked amazingly healthy and vigorous as though not subject to nasties, but these trees were planted so close together that probably by now all their trunks might well have merged into the world's most solid (and picturesque) wooden wall several kilometres long!

Retirement safari

Thirteen years later, in 2006 at the age of 73, my other memorable lone European safari would become affordable on discovering Servas, an international hospitality co-operative, part of the developing worldwide 'sharing economy' whose members commit to offering two nights' accommodation gratis to members visiting from abroad. On the recommendation of an established local member and interview by a selection panel I would become accredited and access compendious membership lists from several French-speaking and German-speaking countries.

Crisis of retirement

As it unfolded, the trip took on the character of a modern-day pilgrimage (albeit by train!), within the context of a minor faith crisis triggered by my ultimate retirement from church ministry. Somewhat dubious about God's concern for my situation I had sought advice from a spiritual *guru*, a mentor of Christians in ministry, confessing my urge to travel again to Europe alone in order to renew acquaintance with cultural treasures, including languages, while at the same time boggling at the cost outlay on personal pleasure in a world of want. We reached a compromise: "Go in peace—but on return give the equivalent of the full costs of the trip to overseas aid". At ease with the suggestion, I couldn't get to a travel agent quickly enough. In the event, I recorded every *penny/pfennig/centime* of my expenditure on travel, food, accommodation, petrol, gifts and everything else. And of course lived like an itinerant pauper—or pilgrim? But once back home I

---

62 In Spanish 'Santiago' means St James, the apostle whose tomb in mediaeval times was believed to be there.

would experience the purest joy in dashing off cheques to Christian and secular aid agencies such as *Médecins sans Frontières* (Doctors without Borders), Save the Children, and the Leprosy Mission, to the tune of some $3,000.

Turkish interlude

At Tullamarine while waiting for take-off I had the inspiration of booking a side-trip from my destination of Frankfurt to visit Christopher and his family on a field assignment in Istanbul. It was a delight to see him so much at home in Turkish, even though at a social occasion he handed me a sharp rebuke for my ignorance in proffering my hand to a devout Muslim woman who would have been defiled by *haram* (sinful) contact with an infidel—not to speak of a male! Sheepishly withdrawing the offending paw I felt quite unnerved at her unflinching gaze. More positively memorable was the interpreter role played by grandson Raphael, then aged seven, in ordering me coffee and almond croissant in a village shop in Kuzguncuk. In a tea garden overlooking the Bosphorus Chris explained the substance of his later book on republican/Islamist tensions, and took me to a mass rally of the Islamist party in a football stadium, where someone asked him what side his Dad was on, since (of course unwittingly) I was conveying contradictory messages by sporting a Muslim beard with a republican cap!

Revisiting my spiritual Heimatland

The return leg to Frankfurt was absurd: to satisfy the requirements of my ticket I had to fly Istanbul/London and then London/Frankfurt. Circling interminably high over SE England, I have never forgotten the awesome spectacle, as though in a living atlas, of the revolving cradle of the British Empire: the metropolis, Surrey, Middlesex, the Thames estuary, Essex, the North Sea, Kent, the Channel coast, Sussex.... Finally making it from Istanbul back to Frankfurt, continental Europe's busiest airport, I set off on the long and scenic train journey down the Romantic Rhine, one of the world's great rivers, through a cultural landscape long fashioned by human hands and deeply influencing German composers, writers, and artists. For hours the train wound its way around every bend of its steep valley past soaring vineyards, historic castles on many a hilltop, gabled villages clustered round their spired church, the fabled rock of the *Lorelei* with incessant river traffic in both directions, and later through major cities like Bonn, Köln (Cologne) and Düsseldorf, alighting at Duisburg.

Awaiting me were Josef and Dorothea Scherkl, likewise veterans of the Routeburn Track in NZ, who brought me to their small home town of Moers for three delightful days. He was a minor industrialist and she the accountant of their family washing-machine factory. Together they drove me around their secluded (almost backwoods) region between the industrial Ruhr District and the Dutch border, made up of farmlands with still-functioning mediaeval windmills, ancient churches and small towns that seemed to have escaped the destruction of both world wars, including the home town of one of Henry VIII's surfeit of wives, Anne of Cleves.

After Sunday mass we spent a long afternoon at an extended family gathering in the countryside enlivened by my spirited discussions with a youngish priest—the area is entirely Catholic, a feature of the German scene dating from the Peace of Westphalia which ended the Thirty Years War in 1648, leaving a patchwork quilt (to this day) of Catholic and Lutheran domains across Germany. Afterwards they kindly took me to their weekender in Piesport, a picturesque village nestling among the vineyards in the steep Moselle valley, renowned for its wines. Next day our departure was by a long morning's drive down the tortuous but picturesque Moselle valley between vine-clad hillsides (a mini-Rhine) to the city of Koblenz where it joins that noble stream.

Hospitality of a dear clergy friend

Entraining there, a further *Deutsche Bundesbahn* journey across the Rhineland and Westphalia towards Minden took me first to Bielefeld where I stayed with Pastor Dieter Schwerdtfeger and his deaconess wife Ursel. His retirement ministry was at 'Bethel', a pioneering residential Lutheran community some 150 years old, for mentally handicapped people, where Adolf Hitler was publicly defied in the name of Jesus Christ for his plan to send mentally handicapped people to the gas chamber, and where the first charter of the anti-Nazi 'Confessing Church' was drawn up in 1933, the year he came to power.

In the nearby university town of Detmold, Dieter and I visited a rustic village created by assembling and faithfully furnishing ancient farmhouses, historic barns and farming implements, where you got to ride in a heavy dray drawn by two draught horses, with me perched beside the driver hearing the story. For me equally novel was to encounter a *'raptor lookout park'* where giant eagles, set loose among the hills, returned voluntarily to 'perform' for their keeper. In 2014, at the age of 90, Dieter is still active and a great traveller, with perfect English and French. A wonderful man and remarkable role model.

Guiding *Germans* around their own capital!

Then across Westphalia, 'homewards' to Minden and the Gressler clan's extravagant hospitality during a week revisiting people and places, on this occasion culminating in a road trip to Berlin in a grandson's VW people-mover. Who said diesels can only chug along? On the *Autobahn* system with no speed limit we kept up with the Porsches, with the GPS SatNav system (new to me) warning of traffic blockages up to 25 km long and suggesting options for bucolic *détours*. Since neither Gressler son Friedhelm, nor grandson Frank had ever been to their country's capital, I had the ironical task of suggesting sights and locations from my previous four or five visits dating back over 35 years!

The one site new to me was just outside the city: the Palace of the Prussian

Kaisers (kings and later, emperors culminating in Kaiser Wilhelm II, loser of World War I) at Potsdam. During the long decades of post-WWII partition, the vast palace complex—a Teutonic Versailles—being within Communist East Germany had long been neglected but was now undergoing a protracted restoration, set in its splendid gardens featuring a 'Chinese' pavilion (an unconvincing figment of a European imagination).

By 2006 the capital had long been re-unified, with the *Reichstag* (Parliament), a bombed-out ruin since 1945 finally restored, extended and functioning democratically as the Bundestag, and few signs of the war in evidence. Indeed looking down on the integrated capital from the radio/TV tower it was difficult to discern where the Wall had divided the two Berlins, with many landmarks restored to their previous glory and new ones emerging in contemporary styles. Checkpoint Charlie was now a tacky tourist site in a back street, while the location of Hitler's suicide bunker cowered behind a wall covered with historic texts and images denouncing Nazi times. I felt too embarrassed to read much of it with my two young companions standing by who had no experience (nor even much knowledge!) of the War.

Our base became a modest three-bed room in a family's private flat close to a restaurant in a leafy square where each day was heralded with a gargantuan breakfast on the sidewalk. We took in the Berlin city sites: the throbbing glitz of the *Kurfürstendamm* with its broken-toothed war memorial church, the monumental Brandenburg Gate giving onto the stately avenue of lime trees *Unter den Linden*, the Bundestag by the Museum Island in the river Spree with its memorial to East Berliners shot dead swimming to refuge in the West, the President's baroque castle, the newly reopened Lehrter Bahnhof (rail terminal), also visiting the Olympic Stadium where in 1936 Adolf Hitler had opened the infamous 'Aryan superiority' Games. Too soon it was time to head down the *Autobahn* for the art city of Dresden on the Elbe, far to the south.

To the agonised 'German Florence'

Before the tapestry of German-speaking principalities, duchies and kingdoms were woven into the *Deutsches Reich* ('Realm' or 'Empire') in 1871, Dresden had been capital of the Kingdom of Saxony, a Protestant city celebrated for its baroque architectural and cultural glories (*'the German Florence'*). But in three nights of fire-bombing in February 1945 the city had been reduced to rubble by repeated waves of Allied carpet bombing, triggering a hellish holocaust that claimed the lives of no less than 25,000 citizens, more than are said to have died in Hiroshima!. It was later denounced as a war crime—*'the German Hiroshima'*—and that, in a city of small strategic importance. Being spared until then had led the citizens to conclude that Dresden would become the headquarters for post-war Allied occupation.

Now in 2005 it was a bitter-sweet experience to revisit the city for the re-opening of its splendid baroque *Frauenkirche* (Lutheran) Church of our Lady, after 60 years faithfully restored in all its marble glory, crowned by the dome whose cross is of pure gold, the gift of a remorseful British people. Queuing for an hour to enter and marvel at the breathtaking marble majesty of the interior, faithfully restored to the last detail, we must have felt like the original 18th century worshippers entering their glorious new church for the first time, especially when with the peal of an organ a worship service began in that heavenly setting. We found ourselves sharing in worship with a congregation drawn from the four corners of the earth, giving thanks for the reconciliation of enemies as well as the rebirth of a Dresden icon. I found myself transported to another world—one of the most precious of all my memories of Europe. Afterwards I spoke with the church official supervising the visitors and was taken up under the dome to look down on the baroque wonder of the circular interior, thronged with visitors from all over Germany and beyond.

Die Frauenkirche Dresden

In stark contrast, my companions had bought tickets for a production at Germany's most celebrated opera house, the restored Semper Opera. To my disappointment it turned out to be a new American work, *Dead Man Walking*, sung in English, amounting to a 'musical' conversation between a death-row inmate and a compassionate Catholic sister. To my relief the opera was not altogether bereft of melody.

Next day we admired other architectural landmarks, the most celebrated, *Der Zwinger*, the royal palace complex of galleries and pavilions built in the extravagant Rococo style of late baroque. We also joined the well-heeled throng promenading along the Elbe backed by the classical facade of the palaces. Not far outside the city in the foothills of the *Erzgebirge* (Ore Mountains) we experienced a dramatic lookout perched high above the river where it cuts through a sandstone gorge in an area pretentiously named *die Sächsische Schweiz* (Saxon Switzerland), somewhat reminiscent of Echo Point in the Blue Mountains but on a smaller scale. Finally there came the madcap dash to bundle me unceremoniously into the express for Vienna, the Austrian capital. In between lay a wing of the Czech Republic which the train sped through without stopping. Close of the Gressler chapter of my European wanderings. Enter the first of my Servas hosts.

By the Blue Danube

He met me off the train, a charming polyglot and polymath just retired from a Viennese classical *Gymnasium*, whose wife was still teaching in a school in Bratislava, capital of Slovakia just across the Danube—accessible by 'international tram'! They were classics, straight out of the *Inspector Rex* TV series. Admirable lefties, former trendies who had lived for a time in a commune in America, having travelled everywhere, met everyone, learnt everything, incredible hosts who on the second night left me in charge of their *olde worlde* apartment in the centre of Vienna while they drove off into the country, but not before telling me where to find their personal papers and financial treasures, so I wouldn't untidy the place rifling through their secrets! (Manifestly, they were also fine judges of character.)

That day he had walked me around some of the stunning sights of Wien, the *Stefansdom* (St Stephen's Cathedral), the Spanish *Reitschule* (Riding School), art galleries and museums, the 'Blue' Danube and the Prater with the *Riesenrad* (the original giant Ferris wheel in the riverside pleasure grounds). On first meeting him I had announced that, while I *could* speak English, I was going to pretend I couldn't—a charade we rigorously maintained throughout my short but unforgettable stay in his magical city. One of the greatest weekends of my considerable travelling life.

A moment of pure grace

My journey westwards with the *Österreichische Bundesbahn* (Austrian Federal Railways) to Innsbruck near the opposite end of the country was transformed by grace, through fellowship with an older traveller who turned out to be a Protestant church elder. Alone in the compartment, the further we went the deeper our intimacy grew: our family life, our church work, our understanding of the world and our hope in Christ. Come lunch time he produced his bread rolls and wine. Simultaneously we grasped its significance, and spreading it on his attaché case between us we broke bread to share an informal but heartfelt Lord's Supper as the train glided on. A moment of pure grace. As he was leaving the train we spontaneously hugged each other and he suggested I might like to note the ancient Puffing Billy locomotive beside the next station. A few moments later, reaching for the expensive camera from my carry-bag on the seat, I found it missing! As I went into a panic I spied it, hidden from sight well back beneath the seat where I would never have thought to look when reaching Innsbruck. Grace upon grace. Maybe... though retired from formal ministry... I was still safe *'under His wings'*? Lesson One.

The two days in the Austrian Alps were exhilarating. My quarters were under the steep-pitched roof of a Servas family's chalet on a mountainside looking up to the Brenner Pass, surrounded by chocolate-box alpine peaks. It was painfully beautiful, accessed from Innsbruck via a suburban *tramline* winding high around the valley slopes. Nestling by the ancient bridge over the Inn (as its name indicates) the city must enjoy one of the most beautiful locations upon earth, with towering alpine peaks rising range upon range to close the northern horizon. But I had to admire them from the postcards because during my stay they were perennially wreathed in cloud!

Literally enraptured

The sheer power of the alpine vistas! They recall a majestic experience from an earlier lone European safari when fulfilling a lifelong ambition of going high into the Alps, after an overnight stay in the unimpressive Swiss capital of Berne, and then taking the *Lötschbergbahn* heavy-duty private railway to Interlaken, set between two lakes at the foot of the Bernese Oberland. From there I took a rack & pinion electric railcar high up to Kleine Scheidegg village, over which towers the famous north face of the Eiger, a forbidding wall of black ice-flecked rock, crowned by a tapered snowclad peak rising to double the height of Kosciuszko. The first sight literally took my breath away. Dozens of climbers have died scaling the sheer North Wall but though a Korean expedition was said to be attempting it that day I could make out no human figure moving on the massif's perpendicular flank.

Following a track to crest a slight incline under the mighty wall of rock I came upon a small greensward laced with yellow meadow flowers—itself a minor touch of heaven—beyond which you would need to be a mountaineer. To scan the grandiose peak rearing starkly above me a mere fifty metres away I threw myself down into the lush grass. At once I fell captive to the power of that vista At first imperceptible, an uncanny sensation was creeping over my soul: as though I was no longer me but rather ushered into a glorious world of heightened sensibility. It was as if I had never truly lived until that moment of blinding clarity. Intoxicating, ineffable—an out-of-body experience where time had no meaning. Literally *enraptured*! How long I lay there gazing heavenwards, 'lost in wonder, love and praise' I cannot tell. I was out of this world, in a heaven sublime, utterly indescribable—drawn into the infinitude of a Creator revealing Himself through the majesty of His creation.

Reluctantly dragging myself back to re-engage the real world, at Kleine Scheidegg I took to the railcar again, but this time tackling the further downward slope. During the long winding descent to the alpine resort town of Grindelwald on that sunny though chill afternoon, suddenly out of nowhere came a sharp assault by an ice shower for minutes clattering noisily on the roof and windowpanes, literally shaking the car. The darkling world was frightening in its mystery. But just as soon was it gone, leaving a query about its reality.

Far down the valley in Grindelwald I sought an overnight stay and located a homely lodging correctly deduced to be run by Seventh-day Adventists. I felt the least I could do to express my appreciation of that wondrous day was to accompany them next morning, a Saturday, to their worship service—deeply devotional, a precious treat for a lone wanderer so far from home.

Glories of the *Romantic Way*

To resume: from Innsbruck in 2007 reluctantly turning my back on the Austrian section of that magnificent alpine chain in order to resume my travels with Servas hosts, I headed northwards into Germany by *Deutsche Bundesbahn* train through the foothills and across Bavaria, another of the earlier German kingdoms (and to this day perceived as distinctive in its strong Catholic identity), traversing the capital, Munich *(München),* where in 1961 I had attended a summer school for German teachers, and Nuremberg *(Nürnberg)* where the trials of the Nazi war criminals were held at the end of World War II following the revelation of the Holocaust. Resisting the temptation to alight I continued to Augsburg, a Bavarian city of culture famous for the Augsburg Confession of 1530, a definitive statement of the 28 Articles of the Reformation doctrines agreed upon by Protestant princes and church leaders for presentation to the threatened and threatening Catholic Emperor. This ultimately led to Lutheranism being granted legal status within the Holy Roman Empire, antedating the 'Thirty-Nine Articles' of the Church of England by a few years. The focus of much of that history was St Anne's Church, a 14th century monastery which in 1545 became the city's principal Lutheran church. I lingered long, admiring its artistic treasures and scanning the visual displays of its Protestant journey, also praying fervently for the troubled family I had visited in Istanbul.

Afterwards there was a memorable moment in a bookshop when, attempting to take advantage of the vastly reduced sale price for a major German dictionary, at the counter I was informed the price was only available for members. At once the lady behind me announced she would buy it on her card, and promptly handed it to me at the special price. Truly, a great benefit of fending for yourself in overseas travel is the kindness so often encountered at the hands of ordinary people. Beats hermetically sealed conducted tours hands down! Lesson Two.

Beyond Augsburg, for the only time in all my Continental travels, I forsook rail for road, joining a long-distance coach along the *Autobahn* and then the *Romantische Strasse*. I had opted for cross-country travel through an amazingly unspoilt area of Swabia and Hessen whose picturesque small towns were mercifully spared by the war. But also by the previous 500 turbulent years of intra-German history. In their mediaeval authenticity Dinkelsbühl and Rothenburg ob der Tauber recall cardboard cut-outs for some exotic film—ancient cobbled streets lined by vertically-challenged half-timbered houses with high-gabled roofs, artisan signs hanging outside, curious names of hostelries[63] and bans on motor traffic all conspiring to project you centuries back into a more benign world, though the roofed and fortified walls encircling Rothenburg also conjure up phobias from the past. Before the bus resumed its journey I had sauntered 100 metres along the top of the defensive perimeter without sighting a single invader.

Finally at the end of an idyllic drive through the golden afternoon, engrossed with chatting with the driver of the now empty coach, I was kindly deposited near the *Babelfisch* youth hostel in Würzburg, booking in as the most senior guest—by a mere 40 years!

---

63   e.g. Blue Goose, Golden Vulture, Heaven's Ladder, Angry Ant, Thirsty Pelican, Musical Cat *et al.*

Next morning again I discovered a city of absorbing interest. What is it about German cities? They never look like anonymous country towns but distinctive mini-metropolises, perhaps because they were all capitals of some fiefdom. Würzburg is in Franconia, land of the Franks who also colonised France. Its venerable six-arched stone bridge over the Main is lined by statues of saints and notables and above the city rises a hill topped by a castle and palace. But all had been painstakingly reconstructed, as I learnt from a remarkably restrained museum specifically recording the city's total destruction by Allied bombers in World War II, on one night that actually eclipsed Dresden in the degree of utter destruction wrought, and exacting a proportionally higher death toll. The graphic record chooses to focus on the human misery, pain and loss—making a more heartrending impact by its restrained language (with careful English translations) and its sober summation. It should be compulsory viewing for warmongers and sabre-rattlers.

The following day brought me by train to the German nodal point of Frankfurt, thence swiftly to Paris via the *Deutsche Bundesbahn* and changing to the TGV high-speed super-express of the French National Railways *(SNCF)*.

Switch languages and launch the wonderful French Servas interlude.

Homage to Brittany

I had determined to head immediately to one chosen region of France in order to immerse myself in its geography and culture through some intensive encounters with kind-hearted hosts. My goal was Brittany, the north-west corner of the country jutting out into the Atlantic, unique for its Celtic heritage and story, the 'Wales' of France. Its language of Breton is still widely used and officially promoted by a nationalist movement seeking greater autonomy. Indeed there are moves emerging towards a 'Celtic common market' of Brittany, Cornwall, Wales, Scotland and Ireland. To date a signal achievement is a cross-Channel shipping line from Plymouth on the edge of Cornwall to Roscoff in Brittany.

After another peaceful night in a youth hostel, before departing Paris I served as an interpreter for a (non-French-speaking!) Canadian at the Gare de Montparnasse, and then headed off by SNCF electric-hauled train for the historic city of Poitiers, in the 8th century marking the northernmost point of the Muslim Moors' advance into France. A few moments after meeting my Servas host, a professional man, he pronounced that I was the only English speaker he'd ever met without *'cet accent ridicule'*. It augured well for the French chapter of the trip. Though he had to leave for work early next morning, his lively teenagers sketched out for me a picture of high-school life in today's *lycée*.

Beyond a brisk walk around Poitiers' ancient city centre with its mediaeval houses and churches I thought it best to move on towards the Atlantic coast at La Rochelle, then changing trains for Nantes, near the mouth of the Loire and the region's largest city. To my surprise I was confronted with a network of trams of the same design as Melbourne's latest (also of French descent). Impossible not to be impressed with the modernity and efficiency of French public transport—and its high technology generally—though for some reason we hear little of it in Australia. Is it our inherited Anglo-Saxon prejudice, even jealousy? Nantes is justifiably rated as one of the world's most livable cities, outstanding in its green credentials.

Then broaching the wide peninsula of Brittany, bent on meeting my next Servas host family, I reached Vannes just inland from the south coast. Since they had told me to wait for them in the small square by the railway station (but without mentioning a time), I took my stance, hopefully scanning every passer-by. Some three boring hours later, and weary with studying the cobblestones and flowerbeds but unwilling to start reading lest I miss them, I was on the point of re-entering the station to check the next train out of town when I was hailed from a car. A hearty teacher guy whose wife was also a teacher muttered something about being delayed (after all, "it *was* Friday afternoon") and took me home. They were a thoroughly modern family, with exuberant teenage kids, one of whom even surrendered his bedsitter in the basement for me. By coincidence that evening happened to be the annual 'street party' of their cul-de-sac, and I was appointed an exotic sort of guest of honour from kangaroo-land. I hung around the barbecue and circulated a bit among the festive group of buddies but after the initial welcome sensed I was a super-numerary and excused myself. Naturally they were bent on making the most of their wine-fuelled celebration.

Next morning the family headed off somewhere and I was turned loose, but not before responding to the doorbell that announced a Jehovah's Witness on crusade. I felt I could hardly invite her in so heard her spiel on the doorstep and then launched into a counter-blast of orthodox Christianity focused on several of her perverse claims. We declared it a nil-all draw. Wandering into town, I was surprised by its ancient market square with Germanic-looking, half-timbered and gabled houses—in their crookedness fraternally propping each other up. A veritable Gallic Dinkelsbühl. But further on was an impressive 18th century *château* now seat of the regional administration, and sections of earlier turreted town walls. In antiquity the Celtic tribes of Armorica (Brittany) had fallen victim to Julius Caesar, involving a naval battle off Vannes as well as the conquest of the Veneti people in 56BC—as he would imperiously crow in his *Gallic Wars*, studied in Latin classes at Canterbury High.

To the end of the earth

What a delight the westward train journey would then become, pictorially and linguistically, as we threaded our way along the southern (Atlantic) coast of Brittany, now gazing down from high-arched viaducts on a picturesque fishing village tucked away below in a rocky cove (the stuff of tourist brochures), now pausing at an ancient granite township cuddling its moss-streaked church, sometimes with lush farmsteads stretching inland. I loved the place names: Douarnenez, Quimper, Paimpol, Saint-Thégonnec, Guingamp, Quiberon, Plougastel, Concarneau,

Plouharnel-Carnac—some of them kith and kin of Cornish or Welsh names. It didn't feel like France at all.

Soon the main line ended and we transferred to a diesel train, smaller but equally well-appointed, almost elegant. The single track now wound around tighter curves, with even quainter village stops, finally to link up with the main line running along the northern coast, and glide into the terminal at Brest in the administrative *département* of Finistère (= end of the earth). It is a major port, the westernmost in France, once the transatlantic terminal now largely rebuilt after the heartless wartime bombing—by the Allies!—because of the large Nazi *U-Boot* base whose lethal submarines were taking a hellish toll of the transatlantic convoys of men and *matériel*.

Waiting for me were my Servas hosts, a charming and serene couple—but French rather than Breton—Jean recently retired and Jeanne-Marie still teaching English in a city *lycée*. They agreed to my linguistic *tour de force* whereby no English word would escape our lips. They were staunch Catholics and Jean turned out to be an amateur theologian, so we talked at some length about faith and parish life and the radical changes introduced in the 1960s through the *aggiornamento* of the Second Vatican Council, such as abandoning the use of Latin in the Mass for the local vernacular (but French, not Breton, as I discovered on Sunday). Brittany is known for the fervour of its religious life and its conservatism about the survival of distinctive customs and traditions, especially in these westernmost areas. Jean drove me to some of the most ancient churches of the district where carvings of the disciples and other biblical figures adorn tall and elaborate free-standing mediaeval crosses, called *Calvaires*.

They were marvellous hosts who quite spoilt me by their attentiveness. Jeanne-Marie showed me around the port, both naval and commercial, which happened to be hosting the visit of a fleet of tall, square-rigged sailing ships, and then through the modern Cathedral which, like Coventry's, rose from the ashes after the bombing. For some years afterwards Jean and I would maintain an e-mail correspondence on theological matters—the first truly spiritual link I ever enjoyed through the French language, since (unlike in the case of German) all my university studies had been in a secular, humanist context. We even talked of the couple coming to stay with me in Melbourne as an Australian Servas host but in the event they opted for New Zealand.

On the pink granite coast

But the best was yet to come: my final stay in Brittany brought the greatest delight. As with all the other hosts, I had selected them according to the interests they listed in the directory and e-mailed my request. It triggered an invitation to join a middle-aged couple living near Lannion, the regional town behind the gorgeous 'Pink

Granite Coast' of the English Channel. Leaving the Paris express at Plouaret on the main north coast line, I took the rail motor on the short branch line to Lannion to find my host waiting. He was a charming man, editor of the regional newspaper with its firm commitment to promoting the revival of Breton language and culture, whose wife was the social worker with the professional fishers' association. As such he was an authority on everything Breton. Intriguingly, the name Lannion came from Breton words for 'land of Huon', a *Seigneur* (Lord) from the Arthurian legends, reflecting the link with the Scots Gaelic 'Hughan'. Maybe we were related!

At any rate we clicked instantly. He drove me to the old quarter with its historic town square of half-timbered houses and shops, winding alleys and ancient chapel, before the brief drive to their home in the hinterland, set in a productive garden with an apiary. Later, appropriately armoured, I was shown how to gather the honey from the hive. But how enthusiastically did he respond to my real interest in Breton autonomy! His people were not the country's original Gauls conquered by Julius Caesar but rather, descendants of refugee Britons fleeing across the Channel in the face of Anglo-Saxon incursions into England in the fifth century AD. At the time it was called Little Britain. I learnt the sorry history of decline and near loss of the language, increasingly under siege from Napoleonic times and banned in schools until as late as 1960, but now undergoing revival (while still listed by UNESCO as an Endangered Language). Quite a number of bilingual public schools had been initiated, place names were likewise bilingual, and the statistics were trending in the right direction. He demonstrated to me the Breton-language television channel and a radio station, which of course they both understood, and they took me to a neighbouring town for an evening of open air folk dancing in native dress with music played on traditional Breton instruments. Charming—and heart-warming.

Sunday morning I went to (French-language) mass in the Lannion parish church, high above the town, and afterwards made so bold as to beg a copy of the contemporary missal/hymnbook from the priest. Wandering around the churchyard later I was struck by the number of children's graves, above which one headstone commented pathetically *Ici repose un ange* (Here rests an angel). In the afternoon they drove me to the nearby coast at the modern beach resort of Perros-Guirec with its pink granite rock grotesquely sculpted by the Atlantic swell entering La Manche (the English Channel). Finally, bidding farewell to Brittany over a memorable outdoor dinner, we watched a golden sun plunge into the western sea from a pink rocky promontory at Trégastel.

Amazing postscript

About a month later, in China, participating in an American Independence Day dinner in Chongqing's most expensive hotel, the chef-in-chief was brought out from the kitchen in his high cook's hat to be honoured for cooking a genuinely Western meal (otherwise unthinkable, despite aspirations and claims by Chinese chefs). Not only was he a real Westerner, but he spoke with a French accent. Chatting with him in his language, I asked where he came from. One guess: Lannion! On hearing I had just been visiting there and had loved it, he presented my table of Western teachers with *another* crackling turkey laced with cranberrry sauce. Gratis!

Chartres' glorious cathedral

The train trip out of Brittany as far as Rennes, significant city and historic capital of the Duchy of Brittany, proved something of an anti-climax, with a change of rail line to meet my final Servas hosts at Chartres early in the afternoon. A dear middle-aged lady was waiting and we drove to her village nearby through waving fields of golden grain—the area is known as *'the granary of France'*. Both professionals, she and her husband were urbane and much travelled, having lived in Madagascar and other overseas French territories in his role as senior finance official. In Chartres he was chief administrator of Finance for the *département*. Until he came home I earned my keep by picking bushfuls of blueberries in their garden towards their *cordon bleu* hospitality.

My purpose in selecting Chartres for my swansong arose from one single factor: the 13th century Chartres Cathedral is the supreme example of Gothic architecture in France and the best preserved. I purposed to do it justice. From afar its twin towers soar majestically over the rippling wheatfields—an indelible image of my French travels. But on arrival its over-dimensional size dwarfs the entire city at its feet.

Its survival in World War II is credited solely to one American officer who challenged the command to destroy it as harbouring Nazi units, after infiltrating behind the enemy lines to establish that the claim was indeed false.

Determined to shun the tourist's all-too-fleeting scan I dedicated a day of my life, not only to exposing myself to its beauty and wonder, but to absorbing—and experiencing—the sense of awe and holiness generated in pilgrims through eight centuries of worship. A remarkable aspect is its unique capacity to recapture its mediaeval atmosphere through the exquisitely preserved architecture and glowing stained glass, including a wonderful circular 'rose window', and the external sculptures. I worked my way around the towering nave (main central section), marvelling at the power and intricacy of the symphony in stone, studying the themes of the stained glass windows[64], the statues, the wood carvings and the memorials. History hung heavily.

Utterly engrossed, as never before, in the many cathedrals that have fascinated me in Europe—including 'our' cathedral at Ely which was earlier (being mostly of romanesque architecture with its rounded arches), on that summer day time lost all meaning. Yet I still had the exterior to admire in detail. Hours later when I finally reported in, my hosts mentioned that on summer evenings a unique light show was presented, with the cathedral painted in dappled and ever-changing shades that softened the architectural features and enhanced the sense of awe. They were kind enough to take me back to experience the magic, well before the innovation of Melbourne's 'White Night' or Sydney's 'Vivid'.

At the time of my visit I failed to appreciate the significance of a labyrinth set in tiles in the floor, but with the growing interest in 'walking the labyrinth' today, in contemporary texts we find many references to the Chartres labyrinth as paradigmatic.

In the Ville-Lumière

The weekend that followed enabled me once again to pay homage to the *Ville-Lumière* (City of Light) that is Paris—capital of the world! Revisiting cherished sites, sauntering down the Champs-Elysées, crossing the Seine by the extravagant Pont Alexandre III, circumambulating the baroque splendour of Les Invalides (resting place of Napoleon) not far from the Eiffel Tower, dining solitaire at a sidewalk café, and being near run down by a silent horde of roller-bladers swiftly appearing out of nowhere, taking over the whole road and pouring past in their hundreds on their

---

64   The famous deep blue ('Chartres blue') of many of the windows has never been reproduced, its formula lost beyond recall.

Friday evening *Tour de Paris*, then taking the Métro to a cheap but not nasty hotel in the pleasant 19th *Arrondissement*, to struggle up to the fifth floor (heavy suitcase, no lift). *N'importe*. Ah, to be in Paris. *C'est la vie!*

Come Sunday I attended morning service at the main *Eglise Protestante de France* and afterwards had a spirited conversation with a man who turned out to be Pentecostal at heart, and who that afternoon took me to their meeting in a former cinema in the industrial quarters east of the city. Typically Pentecostal, it was crammed to the doors with a multicultural throng. The visiting preacher was a (very old) gypsy evangelist, whom I afterwards asked to pray for my Istanbul family.

Next morning one of the lenses from my glasses had come completely adrift. *Quelle horreur!* My landlady mentioned an optometrist's nearby, but the notice on the door said 'CLOSED MONDAYS'. Before my heart had time to sink, I was startled to see the grille in front of the door clunking into action. Ten metres away a lady was putting the remote back into her handbag, then pushed me aside to enter the shop and disappear. While I watched the drama, mouth agape, she returned to ask what I needed, explaining that there were only a few seconds available to operate the grille but that anyway, since it was a non-opening day, she had no authority to let anyone into the shop. I explained my dilemma: I was leaving the country in the next hour or so. Again she disappeared inside with my glasses, soon reappearing with them intact. To my question *Combien, madame?* she smiled: service was free. Hmm. Before you call I will answer you. And "Your heavenly Father knows your needs". Amazing timing. Lesson Three: relax, you are eternally loved.

Under the Straits of Dover

Before long at the Gare du Nord I was photographing the super-streamlined electric locomotive heading the TGV's *Eurostar* bound for London. TGVs are currently offering the world's fastest regular rail service, with speeds up to 320 km/h (while also holding the overall world speed record of 575km/h) and now include a double-deck version. There has never been a fatality. By 2014 there would be a discrete TGV network covering all of France and extending into the neighbouring lands, actually making a *profit* of $A2bn annually! In a country the size of NSW the trains often provide more convenient and faster door-to-door service than airlines. I noticed they were full of businessmen working from the on-line terminals throughout the carriages. So as the transformation of the 19th century railways proceeds everywhere (except in Australia) French trains are now being exported worldwide (including slower suburban versions to Melbourne). Noteworthy that in committing funds to build infrastructure, while Germany has long opted for building *Autobahns* (though their trains are no slouch), France is taking the opposite tack—with a more responsible green future in mind.

Before the TGV glided on its way, I had made so bold as to ask a *gendarme* on duty, how come he and his colleagues were all so polite nowadays, when in my earlier visits to France they were all.... er, so *ruggedly surly?* He took it in good part, grunting that it was because of all the bloody politeness seminars they had had to undergo under the European Union. So much for the celebrated French *politesse.*

In two and a quarter hours of careering wildly through the nondescript Flanders countryside, including past Armentières[65] where *'Mademoiselle'* came from, diving recklessly into the Channel Tunnel ('Chunnel') to emerge into the miniaturised but lush English landscape, rocket through Kent and finally cruise into Waterloo Station, we had changed worlds. But on board we were still in France: what sweet revenge when the charming young lady, over the train's PA system, announced *her* welcome to the UK– in French! *'Bienvenue en Angleterre'*—at Waterloo (Napoleon's nemesis)!

---

65 The most famous song of World War I was *Mademoiselle from Armentières, parlez-vous?* in an English/French mishmash (and from WW II *Lilli of the Lamplight*, in similar German).

29
'Farewell to Old England Forever'

Not having a Servas directory for England I was left to my own devices, but had arranged to hire (almost borrow, so cheap was the rate) an elderly car from the Ichthus Motor Mission in South London, a Christian service agency also part of the sharing economy based on using donated cars for missionaries on furlough. As a parish minister I had requested a favour and been accepted, albeit at the lowest level. That represented a jalopy unsuited to serious use over a period, an ancient and sorry-looking Renault. The plan was to visit some lesser-known parts of Britain, particularly Cornwall and Wales with their Celtic history, following my experience of Brittany.

Setting off into the sunset, the first time I used the sun visor it fell off into my lap!. Nerve-wracking doing battle (but quite out-gunned) with the late-afternoon peak hour traffic in an unfamiliar car of perverse pedigree, driving on suburban trunk roads, congested and unknown, meandering to various points of the compass without a map (which I had naïvely assumed would be provided), looking for the main exit roads south-west into Surrey. The pace of the traffic also daunted me, having no clue about what the old beast was capable of, and averse to lashing her under uncertain conditions. In the end I had to pull into a service station for a briefing.

In the wilds of Sussex

My goal was a missionaries' retreat centre in the locality of Chelwood Gate, a curiously isolated part of West Sussex, though only some 60km south of London. After finding the outer ring road, geography fell into place and things brightened up. But after nightfall, creeping through the tight roads and cramped villages of rural Sussex and checking in pubs, one of which later turned out to be quite close to my goal, I found the place name still ringing no bells, though finally someone thought they might have had heard of it, not too far down so-and-so road. I found it hard to believe that people to-day could be so parochial—or were they (even though not seeing my jalopy) having fun at my expense as a colonial? Or was that paranoid? Maybe they were the counterpart of the near-Neanderthal local yokels who used to turn up from the Fens in Ely on market day? I had always believed the counties south of London to be so *sophisticated!*

1066 and all that

Late in the evening when I knocked at the door of a large house by the roadside, two old Canberra friends from our home fellowship in Cook twenty-five years earlier, Mal & Margaret Prior, were surprised at my tracking them down by night in the wilds of West Sussex. Holidaying in the UK, they were minding the place in the absence of the manager. Next day, not having a car, they were glad to join me in chancing a drive to the site of the Battle of Hastings, actually 11km inland from the coast by a town named Battle, where in 1066 *Guillaume le Conquérant* (William the Conqueror) triumphed over Harold II, King of the Anglo-Saxons, forever afterwards making our language a *mélange* of Germanic and French: e.g. *beginnen/commencer*—for domestic and learned discourse respectively. The battlefield is still a wide grassy terrain with commemorative pavilion and explanatory panels. After a daylong indecisive struggle, if anything favouring the English defenders, William's troops had feigned flight only to turn it into a triumphant attack on the king, backed by large numbers of bowmen, mortally wounding him. As a demonstration of his piety, William built the first Norman abbey in England on part of the site, the ruins of which we inspected.

In the afternoon we drove down to the coast at Hastings, the town where the TV series *Foyle's War* was set, and ambled along the pebbly, sandless beach where a local fishing industry, in the absence of a harbour, depends on quite large boats being laboriously winched up onto the beach every evening. Driving along the strip of coastal villages to Hove we headed inland and back to base via different by-ways.

Westward ho!

Departing the following morning I tried out my hunch that you could traverse England east/west and north/south without recourse to the numbered and lettered main road networks. Picking my way laboriously across country on minor and rural roads through comfortable villages in rustic settings, heading for Winchester with its Norman cathedral, I finally resorted to the south-western motorway, but was immediately horrified at the speed and aggression of the trucks threatening to run right over the bumbling Renault. Retreat being the better part of valour, never again did I travel on a motorway until the last day, when returning what had after all proven to be my tottering but faithful steed back to its south London stable.

My route had crept through the south-west counties: Wiltshire, Dorset (the Wessex of Thomas Hardy's novels that I would read in China), Devon and Cornwall, admiring cathedrals (Exeter, and Truro—in late 19th century 'Gothic revival' style), beaches (Dawlish), ports (Falmouth), *Doc Martin*-type fishing villages and *Fawlty Towers* hotels, culminating (necessarily) near Land's End at Penzance—but noting how little had survived of Celtic Cornwall's language or culture. Snuggled down overnight in a Penzance YMCA hostel (secure from marauding pirates and smugglers), next morning I located in the tiny village of St Sennen Cornwall's 'first and last' parish church, closest to Land's End with a sign proclaiming it was founded in 520AD. On its bleak windswept moorland its pitted granite had ever withstood the Atlantic gales, and a thousand years later a warning bonfire would herald the advent of the Spanish Armada.

Checking out the terminus of the original Great Western Railway back in Penzance, nationalised as 'British Rail' from World War II until Iron Lady Thatcher, I was surprised to discover two privatised companies sharing the station, offering travel to London or to Wales, one of them French-owned (Stagecoach). Even on Britain's remotest corner globalisation had left its grubby fingerprints.

Striking (unsurprisingly) eastwards I opted for the main road hugging the north coast overlooking Bristol Channel which leads on to the wide estuary of the river Severn. From Cornwall and west Devon you cannot see the Welsh coast opposite. But it is an engaging scenic route, with rugged cliffs, deserted small sandy beaches with 'almost-surf' and occasional cute villages. Later it becomes a little more civilised except now backed on the landward side by the wide area of Dartmoor—by no means barren but an unproductive tract of poor soils, with wild ponies running about. In the gathering gloom, hurrying to reach my goal and driving through a forested area I narrowly missed a large stag that leapt out of the brush right in front of me.

A heart-warming sojourn

My goal was Lee Abbey:

> "Located on the rugged, hilly coastline of Exmoor National Park with woodland and cliffs overlooking the sea, Lee Abbey is home to some 90 people from about 20 countries, offering guests the opportunity to connect with God's creation of streams, forest, farmland and moor. A 'thin place' where God is felt to be very near. You can breathe in the good air and feel that you have come home and found rest and nourishment in a driven world".

(From a promotional brochure)

Though knowing no one I had booked in for a weekend to seek relaxation in that beautiful setting with its inspiring Christian atmosphere and company. It is one of the few Christian communities to have survived from the vogue of the 1970s when, with others from O'Connor Church, we had flirted with the idea of forming such a residential community in Canberra—but lacking a coherent mission. In its holiday setting, Lee Abbey's mission is to offer hospitality, activity and teaching to guests throughout the year focused on deepening Christian faith, knowledge and commitment. Churchgoers of all ages from around the UK join with younger people from many overseas lands, sometimes first-generation Christian converts such as a young Turkish woman I met, with the family name of Çalık! Sensing an opportunity to make a link to bless our daughter-in-law we swapped addresses and later wrote to each other a few times but without such an outcome.

Apart from the weekend of joyful participation in charismatic worship and teaching, complemented with discussions in a friendly small group of mature-age people (and of course the sociable mealtimes), memorable for me was to wander through a genuinely primeval forest in its summer splendour—despite all our years of living in England a unique experience.

Celtic dreaming

Sunday afternoon saw the under-powered Renault battling a huge flow of homing traffic heading eastwards, later crossing the Severn estuary by a high suspension bridge to arrive in Wales, 'Land of my Fathers'[66], and stay briefly with a medical couple from Sydney University EU who had spent their professional lifetime in Cardiff, the Welsh capital. Himself of Welsh background, Les Hughes was professor of surgery at the University. Seeking to reconnect with my grandmother Gwyllimia John's Welsh heritage and language, I was taken to an open-air folk museum formed by relocating representative buildings from around the Principality: a reconfigured Celtic settlement, a working blacksmith's forge, weavers' and potters' displays plus water mill, toll booth, schoolhouse, non-conformist chapel, all authentically evoking the Welsh spirit from its lengthy past. I also spent an afternoon in the Museum of Wales, where I was stunned to learn that in ancient plate tectonics today's Welsh landmass had actually formed part of *southern* Africa before 'migrating' north!

Having inspected Cardiff Castle on an earlier visit, one day I was kindly driven to Monmouth Castle and the majestic ruins of the 12th century Tintern Abbey despoiled by Henry VIII in his anti-Catholic rampage, then on to the quirkily named Symonds Yat, a high rock ledge in the Forest of Dean dramatically overlooking a deep, looping gorge of the River Wye, boundary between Wales and England. It was the last time I would see Les and Marian who did not live long afterwards. From the time that we had linked up with them again in the early 60s in England, their first daughter the same age as Sarah-Jane, they had been good friends and generous hosts.

Bent on circumnavigating Wales, scarcely known from those earlier years, I left Cardiff via one of the picturesque but ruined coal-mining valleys evoked by the film of my childhood *How Green was my Valley* to Merthyr Tydfil, formerly a large ironworking and coal-mining town. Everywhere signs in Welsh and the road directions bilingual. Chapels, dour in appearance and deliberately unpretentious in style—Wesleyan, Methodist, Baptist, Particular Baptist, Independent—were commoner than churches, reflecting Wales' 19th century evangelical revivals.

At the head of the valley, crossing the gaunt Brecon Beacons with crags as high as the Blue Mountains, at Les' suggestion I had made for the small market town of Hay-on-Wye, remarkable as the 'book town' of the UK with some 30 second-hand bookshops in a modest high street, in several of which I lingered long, finally buying a monumental History of Railways to lug home. (I mused that Bungendore might set itself up in the same league, as adjacent to our national capital and on a major and well-trafficked highway.) Between there and Worcester, though on a main road, I had to cross the Wye by a privately owned toll bridge—a weird anachronism.

---

66   First words of the Welsh national anthem

A purposive *détour*

My itinerary led back into the adjacent English county of Worcestershire in order to visit Peter Hopper, a colleague from King's School Ely. Now he was in semi-retirement in a mini-parish on the outskirts of Worcester, where I once had the honour of reading the Gospel in a St Mary Magdalene's Day service. He also introduced me closely to the 11th century Worcester Cathedral of his diocese, founded in 680 AD and still picturesquely surveying the Severn river, and where he still shared some responsibilities.

Next day he and Barbara drove me through the charming landscapes and honey-coloured stone villages of the Cotswold Hills to Oxford, on arrival lunching in a venerable hostelry whose doorways threatened to decapitate tall colonials, on the banks of the Cherwell where the egregious Toad and his cohort of Ratty, Mole and Badger held court in my favourite Year 7 text *Wind in the Willows*. We meandered along High Street bordered by several of the Colleges, architectural and historical gems at the heart of the University, venturing into a couple open to vulgar inspection of courtyards and dining hall (such as Trinity College, my theological *alma mater* in Melbourne), and admiring the circular and domed Bodleian Library until stricken with horror at the monument outside Balliol College to Anglican Bishops Ridley and Latimer, burnt at the stake there under the (Catholic) Queen, Bloody Mary in 1555. In Oxford's Cathedral (really the chapel of Christ Church College, largest and most aristocratic of the Colleges), there is a memorial to John and Charles Wesley, my spiritual ancestors and heroes, in 1725 ordained there to Anglican Orders before—unwittingly—founding the worldwide Methodist Church. Another memorial recalls the subsequently Catholic Cardinal John Henry Newman and John Keble, founders of the 19th century Oxford Movement that ushered in the artistic and ecclesiastical impulses of high-church, Anglo-Catholic worship.

Enjoying geriatric company

Bent on resuming my Welsh safari, I steered the rattling Renault north-westwards into the remote border county of Shropshire through the 'literary country' of Wenlock Edge, celebrated by the poet A E Housman and set to music by Vaughan Williams. Beyond that range of hills reared the Long Mynd[67] a broad upland tract of treeless moorland with deep internal valleys in one of which lay my goal for the night, a Youth Hostel in a National Trust wilderness area where I had made an internet booking. The climb was to become a mini-epic, by the only unpaved road I had ever driven on in the UK, closed in winter but in summer progressively degenerating into two wheel tracks across the grassland, up hill and down dale, quite bereft of traffic other than the roaming black-faced sheep. Just when I had concluded I was lost and there could be no civilisation beyond, the track wound tightly down into the wonderfully-named glen of Ratlinghope where a large old

---

67 The word is from Old Norse, meaning 'mountain'.

farmhouse bore the YHA sign[68]. I was welcomed to an old-fashioned English dinner (they don't come older-fashioned!) by three retired old codgers from Newcastle-on-Tyne who go trekking every summer (the Lake District, Yorkshire Dales, etc.) ravenous after their long day's 'ramble' in the Shropshire Hills. Despite deploring my recourse to a motor vehicle (as exaggerated as that might sound) they offered an amiable reception and we spent a pleasant evening spinning yarns about our lengthy stories lived out on opposite sides of the globe.

Next morning, seeking to push on towards the Welsh border through that empty 'hick country'—the like of which I had never imagined could exist in England—I literally ran out of 'road' so had to retrace my climb back over the range, re-entering civilisation at Church Stretton, a pleasant market town where I bought some gifts to take home.

In the 'Land of my Fathers' (mother)[69]

Beyond lay the land of my father's mother Gwyllimia John and of Marjorie's mother's father Thomas Reece (originally Rhys?), designated by the first town of Welshpool and confirmed by wild mountains and sparsely inhabited valleys as I traversed the Principality to Llanfair and Dolgelly, reaching the Irish Sea at Barmouth on Cardigan Bay. Here the whole hinterland is a national conservation park. I was intrigued by the small Welsh towns of uniformly-aged and weathered grey stone buildings, often fronting cobbled streets. In one I had peeped into an ancient Anglican church, and swapped notes with a lady preparing vases of flowers for next day's services.

The Welsh had been Celtic Christians for centuries before the pagan Saxons invaded and, while the 19th century revivals had seen Anglicans outnumbered by the combined members of the various non-conformist Churches (Methodists, Baptists, Independents, etc), today the 'Church in Wales' has again reasserted its standing as the largest.

Boggling at the outrageous name of the hamlet and tiny railway station of *Llanfairpwllgwyngyllgogerychwyrndrobwllllantysiliogogogoch* (unsurprisingly, the world's longest place name)[70], near Bangor I touched Menai Strait spanned by Thomas Telford's pioneering suspension bridge in iron from as early as 1826 to link the large island of Anglesey with the north-westerly corner of Wales.

Linguistically I was now clearly in a foreign country, with never an English place-name to be seen but everywhere only polysyllabic Welsh names, all of them unpronounceable by anyone unschooled in the language. But the odd thing was that everyone was speaking English, to each other as well as to outsiders! It appeared to be an occupied country where the victors had ruthlessly imposed their language and culture to the point of swamping the local inhabitants. Only the land

---

68		Youth Hostels Association
69		Name of the Welsh National Anthem
70		Meaning "The Church of St. Mary in the Hollow of White Hazel Trees near the Rapid Whirlpool by St.Tysilio's"

had proved unconquerable, its towns and villages clearly not English, nor its wild, untamed vistas, nor even the appearance of the small, dark Celtic population. I mused what might have happened by now, culturally and demographically, if a victorious Japan had occupied the coasts of eastern Australia in my early childhood.

Crashing for the night in a well patronised youth hostel in a one-time farmhouse up a stiff climb beyond Bangor, Sunday morning saw me back in town for a worship service at St Deiniol's Cathedral. Though founded by Deiniol as a monastic abbey in 525 AD it was quite literally a 'low church': deliberately lacking the usual spire, in order to avoid presenting a conspicuous target for marauding Vikings offshore, but since the 12th century much rebuilt. As I was leaving, the next service was beginning—in Welsh.

Dating from the Roman withdrawal from Britannia after the sack of Rome by the Goths in 410, the sense of a Welsh identity had emerged among the Celtic tribes, with rulers styled Prince of Wales. But in 1277 the English king, Edward I, completed the conquest of Wales and subsequently appointed his firstborn baby son 'Prince of Wales' (still the current though meaningless tradition), launching a forced program of domination through population transfers of English to newly planted towns and the introduction of the English legal and administrative systems. A typical pattern of domination by marauding foreigners.

Today Wales (*Cymru* in Welsh, pron *'koom-ri'*) is one of the Modern Celtic 'nations' and since 1998 the National Assembly for Wales exercises authority over a range of local policies. At present about 20% of the population of three million still speak Welsh, especially in the northern and western areas that I visited.

Significantly, it was the translation of the Bible into Welsh as early as 1588 that had proven a powerful factor in keeping the language alive. Since 1993 the law has required that Welsh and English must be treated equally. Indeed, there are still enclaves where English is taught as a foreign language! Road signs in Wales are in both languages, often with Welsh first, e.g. *Caerdydd/Cardiff*. There are Welsh-language television and radio services, offered by both the BBC and commercial channels. A quarter of the schoolchildren study in Welsh-language schools, though élite private schools hold themselves aloof, cf. the racist reference in the nursery rhyme *'Taffy was a Welshman, Taffy was a thief'*. As everywhere, globalisation (the unchallengeable universal rule of Mammon) is sounding the death knell of localism and voiding the dreams of the common people.

Reluctantly pointing my historic steed England-wards I set off to traverse the Snowdonia conservation region of north Wales, a rock-strewn wilderness of gaunt, purple-brown peaks, bereft of vegetation but despite winter snows, no skiing mecca. Alas, as I drove upwards towards the highest peak the weather closed in and I soon gave up the attempt to coax the wheezing beast to the invisible summit of Snowdon, accessed by a rack-and-pinion railway, at 3,500ft the highest point of Wales (and England). Instead I settled for rummaging about in the Festiniog quarries for fragments of the perfectly smooth, centimetre-thick grey slate, in which my childhood home at Dulwich Hill was roofed.

A modern English riddle

Soon the Welsh signs were no more and the return trip south-east through England drifted into anti-climax, dribbling along with Sunday afternoon traffic on main roads now supplanted by motorways—but leave those to the *German-origin* Jaguars and Rolls Royces! Indeed, toddling along with ample time to check out the oncoming traffic, there was scarcely a vehicle to be seen that was not built in Germany, France, Italy, Sweden, Korea, Japan or even America, not to mention the Czech Republic. An occasional UK-built Vauxhall (but actually a rebadged German Opel) would pop up. Whatever had happened to the once proud British automotive industry? The Rolls Royces, the Jaguars, Bentleys, Rovers, Alvis, Armstrong Siddeleys, Humbers, Singers, Standards, Triumphs, Hillmans, Sunbeams, Morris, Austins, MGs, Morgans and the rest? Killed by the unions, claim some. Not as profitable as playing with money, say others. Does British national pride (*'British and best'*)—or the urge to create—no longer resonate?

Heartrending parting

The sands of time were sinking: my appointment with Qantas loomed, but still granted a small window of opportunity: recrossing the Fenland dykes and canalised rivers, to reassert a precious and lifelong Christian friendship with John and Eileen Smith near Ely, now long retired and watching grandchildren mature but still archetypally English (while driving a German Audi). In the next day or two they took me to visit an original Dickensian workhouse in Norfolk (appalling place) and a Christian aged care facility nearby. But all too soon, farewell, probably for ever—in this world. So be it. The best is yet to be. As I love to sing in the Welsh pilgrim hymn translated *Guide me, O Thou great Jehovah*:

> "When I tread the verge of Jordan, bid my anxious fears subside
> Death of death, and hell's destruction, land me safe on Canaan's side."

Then off on the last leg of my final European odyssey, south to Cambridge and briefly re-acquainting myself with a glance at its glories before venturing warily onto the London Orbital that crosses the lower Thames by a lofty new suspension bridge, the capital's answer to Melbourne's Westgate Bridge. I edged my way back through cramped south-east London suburbs, finally to creep into the Icthus Motor Mission's garage at Forest Hill and gratefully reclaim my deposit. *"Thank you, my doughty steed"*. And *"Farewell to old England forever."*

30
'A Wilful, Lavish Land'

Back in 1999, for the first time in 15 years settling into our own home, and now irrevocably committed to remaining in Melbourne, we had come to cherish our quiet sylvan retreat in Sackville St, Montmorency, with a large undulating park only 50m away, memorable for Christmas afternoon family cricket and children's delight in the swings and roundabouts. We were grateful to God for the comfortable and elegant house with its excellent facilities, to which we had added central heating.

Terraced Garden of Eden

But our large terraced garden had instantly become of particular wonder for me: *"other men had laboured and I had entered into their labours"*[71]. It took months to identify many of the exotic plants, watching for them to perform in due season. It wasn't just a jumble of assorted growths but a symphony of form and colour, with recurrent themes in different corners. Much thought, and huge costs, must have gone into planning and building the rock terraces, some with huge bluestone boulders not found locally, and in choosing the plantings. Now the onus was on me to uphold—and even extend—the beauty and transmit it to the next generation.

The Millennial Drought

Alas, by a sad irony, our ten years there would coincide exactly with a dreadful ten-year drought, the worst in Victoria's history, since dubbed 'The Millennial Drought'. It took the first few years for the public to recognise that something serious was happening to the climate. The story was being graphically told in the falling figures for the water storages north and east of the city. There would be long summers of dry and often extreme heat, followed by mild winters of mostly waterless grey skies. The weather maps on TV indicated that the rainbelt had moved to the south of the continent, so that it seemed to be incessantly raining over the oceans while the southern third of Australia languished.

At first only pessimists like me seemed to appreciate its significance, while the professional optimists of the media peddled their bland reassurances: the dry El Niño weather pattern wouldn't continue for long. But my favourite ABC radio compère, Jon Faine, began to tell it like it was, querying whether the 'possibility of isolated showers' so often forecast would ever bring 'real rain', pointing out to Weather Bureau informers, reluctant to concede anything about climate change, that the continued absence of the long-familiar patterns amounted to the advent of a wholly new pattern, perhaps destined to become the norm. The Bureau (now

---

[71] John 4:38

under government instructions, according to conspiracy theorists) persisted in minimising the impact, reassuring us all that such protracted droughts were not unknown. A number of States committed to building desalination plants, Victoria's particularly controversial for its capacity and projected cost.

For me the evidence was before our eyes: the sparkle was long gone from our beautiful garden, the lawns becoming parched and the bushes drooping—yet it didn't much respond to sprinkling. I had engaged a professional gardener, Ken, to come every fortnight to help me and advise on priorities, and to extend the existing underground sprinkler system. Ultimately there were five, two of them under the front garden, and the three at the back with a time control system, but often there were mishaps of burst connections or blocked outlets only discovered the morning after. Also, it was becoming expensive: the water bill began to soar but how could you let a mature 30-year-old garden languish so forlornly on your watch?

Then the knockout punch was landed: harsh water restrictions imposed made it illegal to water lawns at all, sprinklers were banned, only handheld hoses permitted, with watering systems to be run for two hours only on certain mornings and evenings, soon tightened further with odd and even-numbered houses banned from garden watering on alternate days. However there were some slight concessions for elderly people which I seized upon, at one point shouting back to a glaring passer-by, *"I'm over 70!"*

By now the old-established Dutch elms lining Melbourne's classic boulevards were struggling, some dying. Throughout the Garden City many parks were degenerating into dismal dust bowls. At the Botanical Gardens, our top tourist attraction, massive rainwater tanks would be installed, while the hugely expensive desalination plant was begun on the West Gippsland coast at Wonthaggi.

On further continuing years of drought, sinister indications began to appear in our garden: our maple trees, both the large Canadian ones and the many dainty Japanese miniatures, would start losing their leaves halfway through summer. Next spring the leaves would be tiny and sparse, with whole boughs looking dead. To give them a fighting chance we pruned some back but in vain. My re-sowing of the front lawn had proved a failure. Precious memories of lying on the lush front lawn with Raphael, admiring the overarching foliage and the fleecy clouds above faded. As green turned to dust-brown the 'lawn' became too bare and too hard to lie on. One year Melbourne's rainfall was practically on a par with Alice Springs'! Normal winter rains failed, and summer rains came mostly in erratic and violent thunderstorms: at one point Diamond Creek ran a banker across the low-lying land around Main Rd bridge.

In our garden the first trees to die were the young birches, expatriates too far exiled from their native Scotland, Scandinavia and Siberia. Then the Canadian maples, mature trees several of them, showed less and less spring growth and before long were moribund or dead. We chopped several down to remove the curse. I was starting to despair: you weren't permitted to water enough to sustain life in the larger trees. I used to rationalise that the restrictions were inappropriate for such extensive and copious gardens as ours, but only designed for a standard norm. So my solution was to resort to surreptitious night watering using the sprinkler systems, hoping no one would notice. There were stories doing the rounds of feuding neighbours denouncing each other. I wasn't too sure about one of our neighbours. Then one night (predictably) I forgot to turn the front system off and next morning the roadway was awash. It would only be a matter of when.

Celestial conflict

It was as if the times were out of joint. Within nature itself a war of attrition had broken out—a protracted civil war, where the attacker, drought, was holding the other side, life and growth, to ransom by depriving it of the basic resource of water. Or was it all engendered by humans? You couldn't stand by, lamely invoking neutrality. The eight- or nine-year struggle—and the moral degeneracy it was engendering in me—was getting me down. As a Christian I suffered from guilt attacks: if you simply *'trusted God and did the right'* (as the hymn put it) the garden would die, and besides—hadn't God put us in charge of creation, to tend the earth? To obey God or Caesar? I had invested love, care and money into that garden but the odds had become too high. In the end I rationalised that the only honourable thing was to get out. We put the house on the market.

Asylum seekers

Where to this time? Somewhere in the north-east, with a small flat garden but ideally still with a view. Possible? Maybe it was time to 'downsize' to a unit in a retirement village, as several of our contemporaries were doing? We looked into the prospects, all of which seemed to imply consuming our lifelong savings and destroying our children's patrimony. But now there was a new factor. Esma and the boys had stayed on in Istanbul after she and Chris had decided to separate during a protracted visit there, and the boys had spent a term or two enrolled at an international English-medium school not far from her new quarters at Kısıklı, on the Asian side of the Bosphorus near Üsküdar.

But on her new resolve—expressed during the visit we paid in 2008 to keep relationships alive—to return to Australia for the sake of the boys' future, Chris would be bringing them to stay with us on his fathering visits from Sydney every second weekend and through the school vacations. We would need a three-bedroomed house.

For weeks we scoured the NE region from Heidelberg to Research, Yallambie to St Helena, Watsonia to Greensborough and Eltham, inspecting a bewildering variety of quasi-suitable homes, mostly older than our house in Sackville St. But it seemed crazy to be going backwards by contemplating buying an older house. Yet the newer ones were remote from suburban centres and transport. Finally with auction day for 41 Sackville Street looming but no house to move into, we began to wonder whether we shouldn't buy the very next property that seemed vaguely suitable.

Auction day proved a non-event: the small knot of people hovering gauchely in the front garden turned out to be mainly local nosey Parkers, with only two or three couples interested in bidding, and that desultorily. After a few awkward minutes during which the reserve price we had agreed upon was not reached, the sale was called off and people drifted away. Peering out of the upstairs window (banned as we were from attending the event!) we mused, what does this mean? Or rather did I feel a guilty frisson of pleasure because I loved the house and garden and now we would be staying on? Came a knock at the door. The agent reported that one couple had made a further offer—at the reserve price unknown to them. They were shown in and minutes later owned the house, which they professed to love, coming back next day to have technical issues like watering and heating systems explained to them.

Grace abounding

Like the Internet generation that we were becoming I now spent hours scanning estate agents' websites, inspecting properties from my desk chair—appearance, age, aspect, floor plan, location, garden and of course, price. None appealed on all counts. Maybe I had become too pernickety—but was it too much to expect economics, practicality and aesthetics to fall into alignment ere long?

One wintry morning in 2009 they did, with the unanticipated solution popping up of generous floor space with tight garden size, embodied in a house built in the backyard of another. Less land meant considerably less price. *Eureka!* Cursory inspection from the outside confirmed that it was newish, positively sparkling, and well located with a view across a wooded valley reminiscent of Sackville St (though never again the grandiose panorama from Moss St, Cook). When the agent, in the owner's absence, led us up the front steps to the elevated front deck and invited us in, a glow of midwinter warmth from the central heating welcomed us, while polished wood, large floor tiles and carpets invited treading, as we admired elegant drapes at the windows, quality appliances in the kitchen, and well-appointed bathrooms. Below was a double garage with a small room used as an office, and the well equipped laundry. Outside was a modest garden bravely surviving the drought, edged with a variety of small hedging trees and feature bushes: the property amply met our specifications. Swiftly the deed was done, obviating the agony of an auction. We had bought 66A Eucalyptus Rd *'off the hook!'* Moreover, in the whole suburb built in the 70s we had unwittingly bought the 'youngest' house—by a good thirty years—built on a subdivided block in a practice since repudiated for the area.

Burnished terror

Over our previous ten years at Montmorency the Great Drought had done its worst. Then came the horrifying climax. On 7th February 2009, a day straight from hell with 47°C heat and north-westerly gales of 120 km/h (in my 76 years by far the greatest heat I had ever experienced), fire tore through a broad band of bushland along and beyond the crests of the Great Divide north of Melbourne, from Kilmore in the west and across the tableland of Kinglake to Marysville in the east. It would become the worst fire day in Victoria's history, exacting a toll of 173 lives lost, plus over 400 seriously burnt, and would ultimately lead to a group action in court which ordered the negligent power company to pay $300 million to the survivors.

In the late afternoon of that Saturday, emerging from an (air-conditioned) China prayer meeting in Box Hill, we were appalled at the lurid burnished copper of the northern sky and, as we drove home, from the heights of Doncaster were able to see the whole northern horizon 30km away ablaze, under a vast plume of off-white, red-smudged smoke surging towards the harsh blue zenith.

Mercilessly driven by the gale, the fire devoured the tinder-dry bushland as though it were soaked in petrol. Many people died in their homes, deceived by the fire's spread at over a kilometre a minute, others died 400m ahead of the firefront from the sheer heat. Others again died in the impenetrable smoke on the roads, some of them blocked by massive fallen gumtrees. In Kinglake East whole streets of houses fell victim, oddly leaving one or two untouched by the fiery maelstrom. Two churches were destroyed, in Kinglake and Marysville, the Vicar of Kinglake saving his life by taking refuge in a concrete drainpipe under the road.

Had there not been an unforeseen windshift in late afternoon it is likely that the fire would have leapt the Yarra near Warrandyte, not far to the east of Eltham, to ravage the leafy streets of Melbourne's suburban east. Would Montmorency and Eltham also have been in its path? But this quirky wind sheer from north-west to south-west which spared Melbourne doomed Marysville to virtual annihilation.

It was a real if small town, not a straggling linear settlement like Kinglake, and charming with its deciduous streetscapes, coffee shops and antique dealers, a haven of peace. In season you could also hire skis for the region's Lake Mountain snowfield. The resort was known for its beautiful walks beside waterfalls, streams and through gullies of tree ferns and cool bushland to Steavenson Falls, floodlit in summer evenings, and the nearby Taggerty River. The urban focus was the 'Cumberland', historic luxury tourist hotel with charming gardens of enormous foliage trees. where I had enjoyed several Eastern Region clergy conferences meeting over three collegial days. Marjorie and I had also stayed from time to time at *El Kanah*, a favourite Christian retreat centre, where tragically a young woman mission worker perished through misunderstandings about her evacuation. Both these places, of such happy memory to us, were razed and 53 Marysville residents burnt to death in their homes. In the two residential centres 2,100 homes were destroyed and Marysville was left an ash field. Subsequently claims were made that the fires had released the equivalent of 1,500 Hiroshima atomic bombs!

Like all Victorians we were devastated by the power and depth of the tragedy, giving liberally to the relief appeal which raised many millions. Some weeks afterwards we drove up the tortuous road from Hurstbridge to Kinglake, appalled at the totality of the destruction on every hand. At one point, needing to check our route back down the range via an informal track, I asked a couple of young people in a garden before noticing a burnt-out house. They were planting a memorial tree in honour of their parents.

Drought gives way to floods!

Finally, in September 2010, the long-promised La Niña weather pattern made its comeback—with a vengeance! Across eastern Australia the heavens opened. Unprecedented rainfall brought flooding across the plains of western Victoria, inundated for months on end. Then on Christmas afternoon of 2010 a massive localised hailstorm sent torrents pouring through the lower storey of our house (on the hill!), even washing out the railway line in the centre of Eltham. Our insurance cover came to the rescue. Next, parts of South Australia and New South Wales were stricken but finally, for two months until January 2011, tropical deluges swept repeatedly across Queensland, swamping all the major river valleys up and down the coast, triggering a state of emergency and wreaking a death toll of 45—many even around Toowoomba on top of the Great Dividing Range! The Brisbane floods proved to be the worst for 150 years, with parts of the central city flooded, resulting in total disruption. As the western floods moved interminably across the flat outback, long-dry riverbeds ran a banker and then overflowed, inundating vast tracts of the inland, so that Lake Eyre, largest 'lake' in Australia, became an inland sea and for months an attraction for tourist flights. In the Scriptural promise of renewal, *'the wilderness was blossoming like the rose'*.

For us, the irony seemed to be that, no sooner had we fled Sackville St to escape garden-destroying drought than the rains had begun. On the other hand now I have time for more creative pastimes than incessantly sweeping brick paths and patios of gum leaves and other debris, a way of life at Montmorency. My parting shot had been to make a complete photographic record of my beloved if bedraggled garden.

In the wry words of Dorothea Mackellar's poem *My Country* learnt in primary school: *'a wilful, lavish land'*.

31
Bicultural Parish

In our later life we were to spend eight engrossing years of 'semi-retirement' from the age of 67 in 1999 working in the parish of St Michael & All Angels' Bennettswood in the east of Melbourne, near Deakin University's campus at Burwood. In 1951 the church had been established as an offshoot of the Burwood parish, in a new suburb being built on dairying land along the main road to the Dandenong Ranges and the outer east. The first modest church had been built in 1957, when a weatherboard dairy farmhouse became the vicarage and later the parish office and meeting rooms.

Suburban saga

In 1971 a new church linked to the earlier building, now become the parish hall, had been built, wide rather than deep in its configuration, whitewashed outside and in and featuring dark timber beams, with a large wooden cross backed by a red stained-glass window as the focus of attention within. The high clerestory windows behind the congregation, facing north along the full width of the building, projected a dazzling sun into the eyes of the preacher on some winter Sundays, his face shining with radiance of the early saints. The building had a good homely feel about it: modest, modern but not trendy. In fact it accurately projected the tone of the parish community: honest, solid, with neither affectation nor great aspiration. The people were mostly from the lower echelons of the middle class: tradesmen, technicians, middle administrators, a couple of teachers and small businessmen. Friendly, open, respectful—good people.

But by the late 1990s they were in decline, both in numbers and in energy. Their heyday—and the church's—was well behind them. Memories of the dynamism of earlier decades had faded, when the church would be comfortably filled morning and evening and a Sunday School of 100 scholars included an overflow into the scouts' hall down the hill. Many of the early leaders had moved on—variously. Expectations now were slight and current needs basic. The children had married and moved elsewhere, not replaced by newcomers since the suburb had finished growing, now just ticking over and ageing. Moreover St Michael's seemed never to have sought to reach out to the unchurched of the area. Rather its atmosphere was clublike. Strictly speaking, it identified with neither the Anglo-Catholic (High Church) nor the evangelical streams of Anglicanism but hovered uneasily about 'the middle of the candlestick'. There were no children or young families, so the forty or so survivors had little expectation of better times ahead, at least in this world.

New parish appointments

In 1998 Marjorie had responded to Rev Rick Cheung's suggestion of applying for the position of Pastoral Worker in the parish, and on an interview with a lay committee, was duly appointed on a modest stipend. A further rich chapter of her life was looming. In the new Hyundai Excel bought as a second car on leaving Dallas she took up the task with a will. And after a few months of driving to church with her on Sundays instead of attending the St Stephen's Richmond service ten metres from the vicarage door, I also threw in my lot with Rick and Jessica Cheung and early in 1999 was appointed Associate Priest (virtually honorary, for lack of parish resources—I was still working through the weekdays in the Anglican Centre).

The Cheungs were from Hong Kong. Some eight or nine years earlier, for a few months, Rick had helped us at Dallas (voluntarily) so now it was time to repay the favour. Our friendship was deepening. I was godfather to their two boys, Dietrich and Calvin. As a senior secondary school student Rick had come to Australia and become a Christian and had subsequently studied for ordination. He had been the minister of the Chinese Chapel in Little Bourke St, Melbourne's Chinatown, where he had also planted a separate congregation speaking Cantonese (the *lingua franca* of South China and Hong Kong and also of many 'Overseas Chinese'). It was the time when an influx of Cantonese speakers from Hong Kong reflected their apprehension about Red China's looming takeover of the Colony beyond 1997—a fear to prove unfounded by 1999 because of the latitude accorded by the central government to the 'Special Administrative Region', under the principle of 'one country, two systems'. So much so that many migrants returned home to resume their profitable activity.

On transfer from Little Bourke St, encouraged by the Eastern Region Bishop, Rick had brought the new Cantonese-speaking congregation to St Michael's Bennettswood, where they met in the afternoon or late morning as paying guests of the parish. Before long their numbers would grow to the point of matching or even outnumbering the host congregation, and after some years they would become joint owners of the parish with a common administration and a common purse, though it still operated in the two languages. In reality all except the elderly Chinese could speak English more than adequately but naturally preferred to worship in the 'language of the heart'.

While his English was quite idiomatic, by then Rick had felt the need for assistance in ministering with cultural relevance among the elderly Anglo congregation, old enough to be his parents but with no shared life experience. From the outset we formed a ministry team of two clergy and two pastoral workers in our wives, for the next eight years meeting weekly for prayer, mutual support, and planning. This proved a choice period of our lives, bridging languages and cultures in our joint ministry, and ultimately conferring on us the serendipitous discovery of China. From early on it became heartening to see the way the Anglo 'Traditional Owners' were adjusting readily enough to the presence of the Chinese around their church, always excepting one old soul who reputedly had announced, "I'm not coming back while the Chinaman's there"—and never did. But for the real believers there was nothing exceptional about it: the Early Church was like that—as indeed is the Kingdom of God. Besides it would have been difficult not to warm to Rick, whose theological understanding and depth was prodigious and sincerity patent, with his quite stylish English, albeit at times marked by such *singular* exclamations as *"Oop!"*

Bilingual ministry

Rick had also been instrumental in persuading the Bible College of Victoria to establish a Chinese Faculty where duly accredited degree studies could be undertaken via Mandarin, the official language of China, thus providing a stream of qualified pastors for the burgeoning Chinese Churches of Melbourne. For years the lectures were given on weekdays in the St Michael's church buildings until the entire College (since renamed Melbourne School of Theology) moved to new premises in Wantirna South. But as the numbers attending worship slowly declined the two English-language morning services were coalesced into one, freeing the late morning time slot for the Cantonese service, rather than gathering in the afternoon. Occasionally I would be invited to preach, which implied sitting through an hour or so of incomprehension, interspersed with hymns sung to familiar tunes. Finally Jessica Cheung would act as interpreter as I preached, itself an art form for both parties: how much to say in one language before pausing for the other, while not losing the ongoing thread? And the further challenge of not using idiomatic English, nor trying to be funny or punny, but down-to-earth and translatable. It sorted out the twin intertwined strands present in all public speaking: of style and content (the form and the substance), offering opportunity for enhanced simplicity in communication. Every time a salutary experience—at least for the preacher!

Conversely, after completing a theology degree at Ridley College with the aim of joining Rick in ministering to the Cantonese congregation, Jessica offered for ordination and I was appointed by the Diocese as her supervisor at St Michael's for a year, as she undertook the various strands of ministry within both congregations in order to meet diocesan standards. Relationally, I found it a challenging assignment.

Perhaps two years into our term at St Michael's the Vestry recognised the need for the English-speaking congregation to consider its future—and the clouded future of the parish (at that point still bifocal). For three Saturday mornings running, Rev Andrew Livingstone, a guru in church planning and development and then vicar of Greensborough (destined to become our own worshipping community upon ultimate retirement), led a group of leaders—and anyone else interested—in imagining alternative futures. A raft of proposals with potential for bringing newcomers into the parish life were elicited for further consideration. Among them, the one to find favour came from Marjorie, that we launch an English-teaching program for newcomers, bearing in mind the church's proximity to Deakin University, at the time greatly expanding its proportion of Asian students.

Saturday English classes

After a few planning meetings the new initiative was launched, co-ordinated by Marjorie and staffed mostly by parish members, some of them former teachers, but also with devoted enthusiasts such as a young Indian Fijian who discovered her latent gift and is now a paid TAFE tutor. It would proved an instant success.

Before long Saturday mornings in term time would see some 40 learners milling about the church facilities, using every conceivable nook and cranny for classes and small groups, and drawn from a wide variety of backgrounds: older European migrants who had never really learnt the language, Chinese grandparents brought here to look after their grandchildren while both parents worked, post-doctoral fellows from China undertaking short courses, and many Asian undergraduates from a variety of countries. There was always an impressive buzz of purposive excitement about the Saturday mornings: the variety of interesting and enthusiastic learners reflecting such a wide range of ages, cultures and statuses. At a morning-tea break one day I asked a burly Pacific Islander, a mature man, what he did at home, to be told he was the Prime Minister of one of the smaller island republics!

For years I experienced the sheer pleasure of teaching the second highest-level class, meeting in the church, which at times included a young Spaniard, a Japanese young lady, an older Greek migrant, a Chinese computer expert doing his second PhD, a Korean couple, a Taiwanese—the ages ranging from the early 20s to grandparents. Among them were a married couple who have since become our closest international friends, (Mr) Chun Huang and Dr Ya Wang from Shanghai, a former engineering lecturer married to the director of a medical research institute. As children, both had had links with Christian schools, broken when the Red Army had taken over. In turn they brought other friends to the class, one of whom had a grandson of about nine who could play the piano. At the end of each semester we would have a celebratory gathering of all the classes and teachers in the church, with cultural contributions from various talented students and some simple Christian input or choral item. We taught songs such as *'I am, you are, we are Australian'* and at end of year some Christmas carols and did a Nativity play. The diminutive boy pianist sat to play what I expected to be *'Twinkle, twinkle, little star'*—which turned out to be a Beethoven sonata, performed flawlessly! Sadly, though, he was typical of many of the children of upwardly mobile Chinese who literally have no play time, being tutored in the afternoons and over the weekends. No Western child could (nor should) survive such a regime but in China it is typical for those aspiring to university places in the face of such immense competition. Small wonder that over recent years the top-performing students in the final Victorian public examination mostly have Chinese names, while many of the parents specifically move into the catchment areas of the best high schools.

In the inter-semester breaks we held regular staff meetings, and soon recruited Jan Shattock to lead the professional segments. She had been of great support during my work at the Anglican Centre in encouraging parishes to grapple with their local multicultural community by initiating English classes. After our time in the parish, she was to become both Marjorie's successor as paid pastoral worker and to this day also the co-ordinator of the Saturday English classes

On a couple of occasions Marjorie and I took my class away for a few days to clergy holiday cottages at Point Lonsdale or at Cowes on Phillip Island, delightful for the cross-cultural interaction between Anglo-Australians, Chinese and an Indian Fijian lady, Ruth, especially when the Chinese hilariously claimed that her morning greeting, *Namaste*, bowing with her palms together, sounded in Mandarin like *'Your mother is crazy'*. It was while sauntering along a beach with my arm around his shoulder that Chun would observe, "I never imagined the day would come when I would have a real Western friend". Precious memory. After breakfast we would have language practice in the form of reading and discussing a simple story from the Gospels that I had written in learner's English. Likewise for each Saturday's class I would write a passage of simple English on wide-ranging themes from everyday life, as well as using material from AMES, the government's Adult Migrant English Service, gathered from their Box Hill teaching centre or from Sarah—shades of my remote past in the Language Teaching Section of the old Commonwealth Office of Education and my final days with the Immigration Department preparing more sophisticated materials, not to speak of teaching senior English at the *Altsprachliches Gymnsium* and the *Mädchenlyzeum* in Minden—the theme had been a recurrent one through my life.

Ministry to our fellow-elderly

But as stimulating as our language teaching initiative at Bennettswood proved to be, it was after all only a Saturday extra to our weekly pastoral and preaching ministry among the English-speaking congregation. Our old Dallas teamwork now came into its own, with Marjorie leading a monthly 'faith nurturing group' among the (equally) elderly ladies, apparently filling a spiritual gap that had always existed beyond the merely beneficent activities of the Ladies' Guild. We both found the parishioners warm-hearted and responsive to our pastoral visiting in their homes, and sometimes in hospitals, as we got to know most of them more intimately. The only German in the church, recipient of a heart transplant when I had visited him intensively in hospital, subsequently presented to the church a gold-plated cross he had fabricated. I had it listed in the Diocese register as a parish treasure.

One Chinese family, the Chu's, belonged to the English congregation; their daughter Jenny a finalist in the ABC's *'Young Performer of the Year'* award who also played the piano elegantly for the church services. A couple of other Chinese ladies also swapped to the English-speaking congregation, all the members cheerfully gathering after the Sunday service in the living room of the old farmhouse, which now also housed the office for the Chinese faculty of the Bible College. Nearby in the church grounds a large portable classroom block had been brought in by the

College, which on Saturdays afforded an excellent teaching space for Jessica's large elementary class for newcomers to Australia.

Yet try as we might, introducing contemporary hymns and songs and preaching our hearts out, Rick and I never really managed to crack open the reticence of the old St Michael's veterans to embrace the possibilities of spiritual renewal. One 1st April I announced at the start of the service that we had arranged for ABC Radio to come and record the service, so they should sing their very best. Dangerous stuff really, you could kill some older folks with sick April Fools' jokes. But regularly and faithfully they performed their allotted tasks, so that the church ran smoothly and predictably, while the numbers held up, except for the occasional bereavement such as the oldest member, Bill Pyatt, aged 96.

After ministering there for several years, one day Marjorie observed to me that the men of the church didn't seem to have any special focus, or even to know each other all that well. We hit upon staging a men's breakfast, initially catered for by the women, and marvelled that so many men rolled up. It was to launch a tradition still extant after 15 years, whereby every month a team of retired men: food shoppers, cooks, table-setters, servers and washers-up produce an elegantly-served breakfast for 20 or so of their mates. I christened it 'Mike's Mates' (after the parish name). Each month a speaker from some community agency, mostly but not always Christian, brings a presentation, both verbal and pictorial, covering a great range of topics: *inter alia*, by missionaries serving in several lands (Japan, Indonesia, Chile, Tanzania, the Outback), about the Prison Fellowship, the life of General Sir John Monash, Rick (once a pharmacist) on healthy eating, on problems of building an oil installation on the Caspian Sea in Kazakhstan, on the 'peak oil' crisis, and also undertaking guided visits to the Vicroads Traffic Control Centre, the Air Force Museum, and the Guide Dogs for the Blind animal training centre. Mates' own travels have also been featured: around Australia, to the Holy Land, in the steps of St Paul, in Vietnam, my own travels in Germany, France and China and later, our several months' of English tutoring of English. The group has also made charitable offerings to a number of Christian agencies. Occasionally to give the 'servers' a day off, we all adjourn to a nearby café for a more expensive, more sophisticated though less hearty breakfast.

Jubilee publication

Holding our youngest member (a Chinese toddler), the 96 year-old Bill Pyatt had featured on the front cover of the slim book that I put together for the parish's jubilee in 2001—a charming if photo-shopped image. A contribution to the social history of Australian localities, we lodged the requisite copies with the National Library in Canberra. The blurb on the back cover concludes,

> "St Michael's is now home to a new community, Chinese Christians from Hong Kong and they form the growing edge of the parish. Two services are offered on Sundays, one in English and one in Cantonese. Through the week two rounds

of social, caring and faith-nurturing activities follow. All is linked through a joint leadership drawing on a common purse. But the one God is worshipped and served, the God who speaks all languages—in accents of love. The people of St Michael's intend to journey on together, with the God Who journeys with all people of faith."

The process of gathering memories and historical records had been overseen by an ad hoc committee that invited the pooling of parishioners' memorabilia. These feature heavily in the first of the book's three sections: *'Journeyings Past'*. The second section *'Journeying Now'* brings descriptions of the current scene within the two congregations and the Chinese faculty of the Bible College and the third, *'Journeying On'*, anticipates possible futures as envisaged by a 'think tank' especially staged by the two language groups: the pros and cons of being a bilingual/bicultural parish, our common links (in faith, worship styles, but also in our very fallibility and quirkiness—including the famous Cantonese unwillingness to get hands dirty (work for servants), so that the parish garbage was always cheerfully put out by an older Anglo parishioner with a servant heart, a retired academic from Melbourne University! What was instructive was to have seen the elderly company of middle-class suburbanites (the Australian heartland) thawing out from their subconscious yet instinctive racism through having normal contact with Chinese siblings in Christ. The power of the Gospel seen up close.

Finally Rick and I each had a last word: I suggested that, despite our dislike of change with advancing years, we might resonate with God's 'divine discontent' with the way things are in the world, and embrace the need for 'Kingdom action for change' while cherishing what we had achieved together. Rick issued a salutary warning about the risk of allowing our 'sacred cows' to become our collective 'Golden Calf' of idolatry! The book's last 'word' was a photo of Marjorie and two other women ESL teachers (one now teaching in Bangladesh) standing collegially on a footbridge over a local tributary of the Yarra with four Chinese women students. Togetherness. Worth a thousand words!

University English tutoring

With the advent of Jessica Cheung's initiative of a multicultural evening service for international students from Deakin University we turned a new page. Offering a simple basic-English form of worship led by a Chinese team, and later by Jan Shattock with interpreter, we saw numbers gradually grow, including mature-age post-graduate scholars from the People's Republic with whom Marjorie and I particularly connected. After the service we would adjourn to The Cottage for a potluck East/West dinner and further conversation. It was to open up a whole new focus for our later lives.

Jessica's appointment as honorary student chaplain at the University saw us also accredited as English tutors. I had not set foot in the buildings of the former Burwood Teachers' College since the Unesco Seminar forty years earlier in

1967. Every Friday afternoon we would each gather a small circle of scholars and undergraduates from Chinese-speaking countries to practise everyday conversation, an opportunity not otherwise available to them, though they had passed the requisite language exam to qualify for entry but (not unnaturally) mixed mainly in their own circles throughout their courses, some of them even creating their own Overseas Christian Fellowship.

It seemed that, as international student numbers had grown exponentially, the days of Christian Unions seeking to cultivate friendships across cultures were past, along with the leisurely pace of study and the high jinks. Victims of the marketplace mentality that knows the price of everything but the value of nothing?

In April 2007, with major changes in the parish life and leadership looming, we moved into full retirement. By then the Regional Bishop had concluded that St Michael's was not strong enough to maintain its parish status and was ripe for merger with a neighbouring parish. We were affectionately farewelled in a parish dinner amid fervent expressions of appreciation and love. For us they had been wonderful years, tranquil after the tumult of parish life in Dallas—demographically a quite different setting—but now we had been able to build more intensive relationships focusing on our own vintage of Anglo-Australians while supporting a parallel ministry among Chinese, upwardly mobile, talented and hardworking. With a number of them, despite the language barrier, we had also been enriched by warm relationships. And of course the choicest bond of all was with dear Rick. It augured well for the real retirement years looming.

These years would be spent as lay members of All Saints parish in Greensborough, a large and thriving Christian community where we enjoy fellowship with sincere believers, and in particular the splendid modern pipe organ and the brilliant organist (who occasionally gives recitals and directs oratorios) setting the tone of the early morning service with older members. Though I no longer play much part in assisting with the worship services, Marjorie has varied roles including leading a home Bible Study group . I keep my languages fluent by mentoring a young German-Australian who has become a Christian, and participating in a home Bible Study group of the French-speaking Church.

Postscript

Some six months after we were farewelled from St Michael's, the parish was twinned with the neighbouring parish of St Theodore's Wattle Park, and renamed St Thomas' Burwood to be based in the expanded Bennettswood plant. (Jesus' disciple Thomas was a twin.) Initially reported as doubting of Jesus' resurrection, he became the founder of the ancient Mar Toma Church in south-west India.

St Theodore's minister, Chris Appleby, became the new vicar and energetically set about realising the vision for a new building, finally opened in 2013. It incorporates the old St Michael's church as the core of a greatly expanded building featuring two worship spaces for simultaneous services of the two language groups, a roomy public area suitable for parish dinners and other gatherings adjacent to many specialist rooms: a professional kitchen, offices, basketball court and bathroom. All exuding style and flair. What a grand setting for creative ministry to the new multicultural generation, including the raft of overseas students at Deakin University. And what drive it embodied on the part of the vicar, matched by the depth of financial commitment by the people, compared to the mere holding operation of our day. It's called *Leadership*!

32
In the Land of the Rising Sun

It had been a case of love at first sight. Outside St Paul's Cathedra, as the llamas came abreast of me, imperiously mincing along the tramlines, I was entranced—a veritable epiphany! Myself somewhat long of neck, I found the elongated llamas' necks a thing of elegance and beauty as I watched the parade heralding the opening of the 1997 Royal Melbourne Show. They were making their own unique statement on the Show's irresistible attractions.

To Ecuador—via Japan!

It became a moment of decision: my 'yes' to Nick's persistent appeal to come over and visit him in Ecuador. For the past year or so he had been living in Quito, acquiring Spanish in one of the cheapest yet safest republics in that agonised continent. It would ultimately lead to his founding a migration agency in Mexico City (*Visaustralia*) for recruiting Spanish-speaking professionals to swell our burgeoning economy, not to mention meeting his future wife.

By then, unbeknown to me, the day of Immigration Department officials being posted to the major 'source countries' to select appropriate candidates had long since evaporated in the welter of privatisation, replaced by myriad private agencies, some led by shonky go-getters. In Nick's case he had degrees in Arts and Law, and had worked with the Immigration Department in its Canberra head office until becoming disillusioned with the Government's inhumane asylum seeker policy. But of course privately he had been latterly pursuing a love affair with Latin America and its Spanish language, of which he had become a thoroughly competent speaker, later being interviewed on Mexican radio about the prospects of life in Australia's safe and orderly society. One of the greatest joys of my maturer years has been to hear both Chris and Nick unself-consciously exercising their bilingualism with partners and children.

With travel prospects to Central & South America looming I sought advice from a community travel agency created to outflank the profit-making ones by providing more creative and economical solutions. I discovered that the cheapest flights to South America were via Japan! While Marjorie preferred to stay put, son David opted in, though constrained by time limits to forego the Japanese leg. In turn this presented a golden opportunity for accepting a long-standing invitation to visit Richard Hosking, my old SUEU friend, in Hiroshima. After 23 years as professor of English he was retiring. Self-exiled from Australia because of homophobic attitudes he was bent on writing the final chapter of his story in London, where earlier he had lived for decades. He had been among our Christmas visitors in Ely and Minden, and had taught us all we knew about homosexuality.

Driverless transit and 'Bullet Train'

Landing at Osaka with Japan Airlines I was impressed at my first encounter with Japanese whizz-bangery: the driverless train that swiftly conveyed passengers to the distant terminal. The big Toyota taxi, driving on the left as they do, deposited me at the *Shinkansen* ('Bullet Train') station, without the drama of being ripped off New York-style. They say you can leave your wallet on a park bench and go back later to find it still there. From Osaka thirteen 16-car trains are scheduled *every hour* (four minutes apart) to carry commuters to Tokyo, at speeds up to 300 km/h! But I headed in the opposite direction, southwards, to cover the 280km to Hiroshima in little over an hour. Passengers unable to understand the language on the PA system are advised to get off at the exact time scheduled for arrival—no way the train will not be on time! But I was struck by the machine-gun intonation of the upcoming stations by a female voice: *Fukuyama...Okuyama...Hiroshima* with each monotonous syllable equally sounded out without emphasis or stress. I was to learn that this is how the whole language functions.

But given that Japan is such a mountainous country, as a touristic experience I found the journey somewhat disappointing: to maintain the bullet speeds the line has to run at about the same level throughout, which involves tearing across all the small plains at higher than rooftop levels, interspersed with racing through equally long tunnels beneath the intervening ridges. I experienced it all as a bit unreal: was I really there? Or was it all just happening on the TV screen of my window?

Welcome to Hiroshima

Richard met me at the station and drove me to his apartment in a new circular tower building (what else could it be but new—in Hiroshima? Later he pointed out the one building in the inner-city area that had survived the nuclear holocaust.) Of course the city's name will forever conjure up the horrific end to the 2nd world war with the dropping of the world's first atomic bomb in August, 1945.

His home was a sort of museum of Japanese art, with small rooms and a minute kitchen. Beds were a low wooden rack with futon mattress. Beneath the tower, tenants' cars were stacked two deep and about eight wide in a mechanised rack which at the press of a button shuffled them around to deliver your car to the point where it could be driven off.

My week in Japan proved to be one of the most stimulating of my life. Not only had I no knowledge of the country or its highly distinctive culture, but my mind was closed against acquiring any. Like any patriotic Australian boy of my era I had mindlessly absorbed the information served up by the Government's wartime propaganda machine: it was our patriotic duty to hate the Japanese. And in adulthood I had never experienced any desire to query it. To be sure, terrible atrocities had indeed been committed, against civilians as well as military, in the name of the unspeakably heartless Knights of Bushido. So it was a crash course that I undertook that week, drinking deeply from Dick Hosking's fountainhead of knowledge of all things Japanese. He was a thoroughly competent Japanese speaker and cultural interpreter, widely respected for his warmth of humanity that spanned the cultures, and after 23 years it was now his period of final farewells. Of course it was a highly inconvenient time for me to be there, so he had no option but to turn me loose to fend for myself—but with his expert guidance.

Liberated from a lifelong hatred!

One cold day, coming back to his flat from the city by tram, a moment of redemption befell me: an old man sitting next to me suddenly asked, *Was I an American?* When I said *Australian* he mentioned the brave Australian soldiers he had fought against in the New Guinea jungles. Next he asked me (in clear English, a rare phenomenon in Japan), *Was I a Christian?* I said I was a Christian pastor and he replied that he was secretary of the Hiroshima Baptist Church We were brothers! The tram reached its terminus and we all alighted. We walked across to the footpath where, moved by a powerful impulse—and probably a very non-Japanese thing to do—I hugged him. For a long moment we two stood there intertwined while fifty years of pent-up hatred of the Japanese leached out of my soul. We smiled as we parted, and he crossed the street one way and I the other. At the same instant we both turned and waved to each other, before I stumbled off in tears. Liberated! *Reconciled by the blood of the Cross.*

At 'Ground Zero'

From that moment I saw Japan through new eyes. We might be as divergent from each other as any First World countries could be, but we shared a common humanity I had been taught to deny. Now it was time to visit the Hiroshima Memorial Park and Museum, on 'Ground Zero'. I walked there from Dick's flat, around a riverbank and through splendid winter gardens enlivened by coloured berries and what looked like ornamental purple cauliflowers surrounding the mediaeval Hiroshima Castle, authentically rebuilt and ringed by its lake. The Memorial Park is on the riverbank, surrounded by an entirely new city. The first encounter in the tranquil garden setting is with the Peace Bell, a massive item set at head level, which visitors are invited to sound by drawing a long wooden beam backwards and releasing it. The prayer is that the long-quivering *boooom* will encircle the earth, *"planting the seeds of peace in the hearts of men"* (as the Unesco Charter has it). Only then do you move into the draining experience of the Museum's record of that fateful Monday, 6th August 1945.

At breakfast time on that summer morning indiscriminate death and destruction was wreaked upon the unsuspecting population by the world's first atomic bomb, dropped by an American B-29 bomber, the *'Enola Gay'*. It killed some 80,000 people, by year's end swollen through injury and radiation to 160,000, over 40% of the city's population. All of them collateral damage, victims of an explosive energy that seared everything within a few miles, flattened the city below with a massive shockwave, set off a raging firestorm and bathed every living thing in deadly radiation. Maternity hospitals, kindergartens, school classes, department stores, as well as military barracks and depots, transport links and port installations—all randomly pulverised. The city was obliterated.

The sole surviving building in the city centre

I spent almost the whole day in the Peace Memorial Museum studying the appalling photographs with text in a huge variety of the world's languages, and listening to English versions of interviews with survivors, sensing a compulsion to identify with the victims and crippled by my own compassion in the face of the monstrous tragedy of war which knows only losers. The Museum recounting the story in graphic and horrifying detail belongs to the world, not just to the people of the city, nor even to the Japanese nation. And it addresses the world to '*shore up the defences of peace*'. The Peace Flame in the Memorial Cenotaph is to burn until nuclear weapons are banished from the earth. The worldwide Council of City Mayors for Peace, dedicated to their elimination by 2020, is chaired by the Mayor of Hiroshima.

This heartfelt prayer, from a Hindu source, is prayed at noon worldwide by many earnest people and has been set to beautiful contemporary choral music by an English Christian composer, Margaret Rizzo. It is one of our most cherished recordings.

> **Universal Prayer for Peace**
> Lead me from death to life, from falsehood to truth.
> Lead me from despair to hope, from fear to trust.
> Lead me from hate to love, from war to peace.
> Let peace fill our heart, our world, our universe.
> Let peace fill our heart, our world, our universe.

Grassroots encounters

Next morning I went to the university with my host, sitting in on a class and afterwards meeting the students. Dick had taught them about the singing of

Psalms in English churches, a rarified cultural icon that he loved. In the evening (with me in tow) he was guest of honour at a students' informal farewell dinner in a city restaurant, marked by a level of fun and intimacy that mocked my stereotype of a Japanese national aloofness from foreigners. He had mentioned to me that the contemporary population of Hiroshima is almost entirely from outside the area, since the original survivors of the atom bomb had left the city, fearing being shamed with their children as pariahs because of their exposure to radiation.

Another day Dick drove me out into the city's mountainous hinterland. Immediately I was entranced by the beauty of the countryside, even under the rigours of winter—in summer it must have been heaven itself with a small-scale ordered beauty not unlike England's. Except that our lunch destination proved uniquely Japanese—a Shinto shrine with a goddess statue in a pond nearby that I mistook for an oriental Virgin Mary—but with tables outdoors for serving traditional foods where the area beneath the bench-seats (normally Japanese dine squatting near floor level) were enwrapped by thick insulated blanket-like enclosures warmed from within. Though a very cold day, with our legs snugly warm and of course wearing heavy jackets it was ... invigorating! (in a masochistic sort of way).

Second nuclear target—'Christian' Nagasaki

Finally I was packed off on my quest to the world's other nuclear target city of Nagasaki, involving a further journey by *Shinkansen* to the extremity of the main island of Honshu, then through an undersea tunnel to the island of Kyushu, emerging near the port city of Hakata and terminating shortly afterwards at the main centre of Fukuoka. Needing to change from the Bullet Train to the narrow-gauge Kyushu rail system, on the main concourse I surveyed the large electronic destination indicator. My heart sank: there was not one Latin letter in the entire display. Crestfallen, I gazed in bewilderment. Where to go from here? In the instant a well-dressed businessman (who else travels in peak hours?) came straight up to me and asked in good English, *"Where do you want to go, sir?"* When I told him Nagasaki, he said, *"Come with me"* and we went to the booking window. He bought me a ticket and presented it to me, waving away any attempt to repay him. Another great leap forward in my respect for the Japanese.

A two-hour trip through the rural landscapes of Kyushu brought me to the historic city of Nagasaki, closest Japanese port for trade with China and Korea. It is the oldest open-port city for foreign traders in Japan and one of the most beautiful, with a great natural harbor bordered by wooded hills and protected by several islands at its entrance, with heavily populated residential and commercial areas spreading for kilometres up the valleys and along terraces up the hillsides.

I reported in to a Catholic guesthouse to which I had been recommended, located near a large high school run by the Jesuits. My overnight host was a kindly old Spanish Brother speaking reasonable English. To my surprise he explained that Nagasaki owed its origins as a seaport to Portuguese merchants early in the 16th century, and in 1549 had been visited by the Spaniard St. Francis Xavier, founder of the Jesuit Order who brought the first missionaries to the country. Christianity had spread quickly from Nagasaki, so that by 1580 there were two hundred thousand converts in Japan despite the opposition of Buddhist priests and local rulers. However in 1596, after a sizeable number of feudal barons and *samurai* became Christians, along with tens of thousands of peasants and townsfolk, the *Shogun*[72], wary of the Spanish colonialism that had taken power in the Philippines after converting the population, had banned Christianity. A brutal campaign of persecution had followed, with thousands of converts across Kyushu and other parts of Japan killed, tortured, crucified in the sea, or forced to renounce their faith. Best known are the 'Twenty-Six Martyrs of Japan' crucified in Nagasaki, nine of them missionary brothers from several countries including Mexico[73] and India, and 17 Japanese laymen, three of them boys.

It was to be a moving experience next day to make a pilgrimage to the memorial erected on the site of their martyrdom. But despite repression and persecution down the intervening centuries, in 1945 Nagasaki was still the most Christian of Japanese cities, with 10% of its population Catholic.

Significantly, the 1597 persecution had arisen not from any religious motivation but for nationalistic reasons and the preservation of political power. Subsequently Dick was to share with me his conclusion from his 23 years of sympathetic observation and relationships with students, that (apart from worshippers of the foreign Christian God) *"The Japanese don't have a spiritual bone in their body"*. Recently it was re-echoed here by a current CMS missionary couple from Japan who reported that the country's Christian population was actually in decline. The Japanese remain devoted to their Shinto traditions of animistic nature spirits linked with nationalistic fervour—quite alien to any concept of a Supreme Being. According to another description, Japan might be considered the most modern feudal state in the world.

Ironically, although Nagasaki was a leading industrial centre for the production of armaments, military equipment (Mitsubishi) and ship building, it was only a secondary choice of target for the second atomic bomb, decided by weather factors on the day, three days after the destruction of Hiroshima. The atomic blast at 11am generated a heat of 3,900° C and winds of 1,000 km/h. which together wreaked total destruction over a square kilometre, centred on the Mitsubishi armaments works—and the valley where most of the Christians lived.

Even more so than Hiroshima, its buildings were made of wood. But being a city of valleys and intervening hillsides, it was not totally obliterated. Mercifully, a few days before the bombing the schoolchildren had been largely evacuated, but on the

---

72   Generalissimo, the *de facto* hereditary military dictator of Japan, nominally under the symbolic authority of the Emperor (a god). The Portuguese viewed him as the King, while viewing the Emperor as the Pope.

73   As the Mexican-born friar was about to die on his cross, he is reported to have foretold that one day Nagasaki would be destroyed by "a ball of fire dropping from the sky"!

other hand, the inhabitants included many conscripted Korean and Chinese workers and British Commonwealth prisoners of war.

The Cathedral, the largest Catholic church in the Orient, was utterly destroyed in the nuclear attack, at the time filled with worshippers gathered to pray for a speedy end to the war! The bomb killed almost half of the city's Catholic community, leaving altogether 70,000 people in Nagasaki dead, with several hundred thousands more dying subsequently from illnesses related to radiation.

Another anguished day

I spent the bulk of the day at the Nagasaki Atom Bomb Museum built in a garden setting at the epicentre of the blast. Comparisons are of course odious, but I was right to visit Hiroshima first. Perhaps two museums within a few days offer a surfeit of horror too much for the soul to endure, or maybe the museums' shock tactics are counter-productive. Suffice it to record that the spirit pervading the Nagasaki Museum struck me as petulant or even accusatory, though perfectly understandable. The old nationalistic impulse in Japanese life again? A refrain encountered several times on the descriptive panels had it: *"O that the 9th August 1945 had never been!"*

Naturally, but could that not also be said of the entire human project of war, hatred, cruelty and depravity? *"O that the Japanese attack on Pearl Harbour / the Changi POW camp / the Thailand railway / the Kokoda Trail / Dresden / Stalingrad / Gallipoli / the Somme / the US Civil War / the Battle of Waterloo ...the Battle of Thermopylae .... had never been"? O that our rulers were not hubristic war-mongers! O that oil barons were not heartless! O that banks didn't foreclose on the poor ! O that the Aborigines' lands had never been raped!* Where does it end? *O that we didn't belong to a fallen race?* Of course the sad reality is that we are all contributory architects of our own fate for which we must accept personal responsibility, not least the Japanese who launched the Pacific War. And unwittingly, we are all crying out for redemption.

Until the 70th anniversary of the end of the war, Japan had offered no formal apology for launching a conflict in which 10 million Chinese, 2 million Koreans and three million of their own died, apart from the losses of the Western Allies. The Chinese bitterness over this is still visceral, as we would discover in China. And then again, to whom is the plaintive cry addressed? Virtually every reader of the repeated text on the Museum exhibits had no hand in the calamity, and those who might have, may long since have repented of its enormity, if only from fear that the nuclear genie will never be got back into the bottle.

By comparison the Hiroshima Peace Memorial Park (note the semantics of the name, compared to 'Atom Bomb Museum') engages you at a deeper level, eliciting identification and compassion, and appears to have progressed further down the stages of the grieving process (to re-embracing life) than the Nagasaki Museum (still in the phase of angry denial). However, 16 years after my visit, the Museum's website now records—but I sense rather woodenly:

> The citizens of Nagasaki pray that this miserable experience will never be repeated on Earth. We also consider it our duty to ensure that the experience is not forgotten but passed on intact to future generations. It is imperative that we join hands with all peace-loving people around the world and strive together for the realization of lasting world peace.

In the end I turned away sickened at the horrors, to seek communion with nature. Near the city centre, with its busy traffic and trams, I discovered a cable car transporting you to the tranquil crest of a high ridge overlooking the harbour, the sea and the offshore islands. To be sure, even in its midwinter garb, and in proximity to one of the most blighted spots on earth, still a beautiful land!

STOP PRESS

No less than 70 years after the dropping of the atomic bombs has it come to my notice (through the media) that the American fire-bombing of Tokyo in April 1945 incinerated 100,000 people, more than the initial death toll from Hiroshima and Nagasaki combined!

In the Tokyo raid 300 bombers dropped half a million cylinders of napalm (jellied petrol) on an urban area primarily of flimsy wooden construction, exacting *the highest death toll on one occasion in human history!* Most of the deaths were of women and children, since the men were largely absent on military service. In the last months of the war *500,000 people* (for the greater part civilians) died in 'carpet bombing' raids on Japanese cities. The (Christian!) USA has never issued an apology nor made reparation. And few of us were even aware of it.

At the world congress on global warming

Next day taking leave of my generous host, Dick Hosking, I made for Tokyo by the *Shinkansen* but stopped off about half-way to check out Kyoto, a city of over a million, for 1200 years the ancient imperial capital of Japan with traditional temples, shrines and palaces set in beautiful gardens, but also to get the feel of an international conference meeting there at the time, which would produce the Kyoto Protocol of 1997 on Greenhouse Gas Emissions. The modernistic Kyoto station turned out to be also a shopping mall, with department store, theatre, restaurants, and the city Underground Metro hub below. From the moment I emerged from the station I found the whole city abuzz with vitality and excitement—for the moment the world capital of the people's alternative movement. Unlike Tokyo which I visited later (the archetypal urban jungle), Kyoto combines an elegance of architecture and *décor* with its grid pattern of charming natural vistas and dignified streetscapes. Mercifully, its original choice as the target for the second atomic bomb (in order to finally crush the proud Japanese spirit) was amended, to Nagasaki's everlasting loss.

Impossible to resist joining in the incessant parades of chanting environmental activists from around the world, holding aloft banners proclaiming the best of human aspirations for the future of our planet. What a warm feeling of solidarity with the world citizenry of concerned people, truly brothers and sisters! Then I was delighted to notice an Australian group 'speaking truth to power', and joining in with the front ranks and chatting with some elderly demonstrators, I eventually got to hold aloft one side of the wide banner advising John Howard to find the courage to sign the draft Protocol. He never did, although in 2008 it was among the first actions of the new Labor Prime Minister Kevin Rudd, renewed in 2013 for a further commitment period until 2020—though the Liberal Party is committed to withdraw, as Canada has done.

Encountering Buddhism & Shinto

It was in Kyoto and later in Narita, the town close to Tokyo airport, that I explored some exotic temple complexes, both Buddhist and Shinto. In Kyoto alone there are said to be literally thousands of Buddhist temples and Shinto shrines, sometimes side by side within the same complex. Shinto worship focuses on the water gods, the god of prosperity and good health, and millions of nature gods to be found everywhere. Invariably the temples are set in splendid traditional Japanese gardens with gorgeous seasonal foliage and blossom trees, expressing the oneness of nature and the intimate links between the mind and the senses.

In Narita, the approach to the temple complex offers a traditional streetscape of shops, restaurants and stalls selling traditional crafts, foods and souvenirs. As you enter the temple area, courtyard after courtyard opens out before you. Engrossed I spent a whole morning admiring the traditional gateways, visiting the temples, including a three-storeyed pagoda dating back over a thousand years, and the modern Peace Pagoda and smaller shrines, observing worshippers (individuals or in family groups rather than a congregation) purifying themselves at fountains, bowing deeply in adoration, making offerings, burning incense, while monks ceremonially struck resounding gongs and drums, deeply intoning chants. It is said that elements of Buddhism and Shinto have become intertwined in Japanese worship practices, mingled with elements from folk religion. But Western secularism has also made its inroads, with soppily commercial versions of Christmas, St Valentine's Day, Mother's Day and other money-making occasions punctuating the calendar. What's new? As in the West, the over-arching divinity is Mammon—a failed god for offering a source of meaning.

Postscript

During the stopover on my long journey back to Australia from South America I would close the touristic gap represented from having by-passed Tokyo earlier. In the brief time available I could only take the local train from Narita airport and cover part of the city *from below* (to avoid the impossible snarls with surface level transport). There is a wide network of underground lines, from which I bobbed up at various points, memorably the Ginza, famed shopping street blazing with neon and commercial frenzy. I could only hope to gain some 'feel' for the metropolis through observing the peak-hour commuters on the trains, in itself a fascinating study, to be commended to Japan watchers. Fun *under* the antheap!

33
Love Affair with Llamas

After spanning the interminable North Pacific from Tokyo overnight, I spent all of two hours in Canada, admiring the distant fir-clad horizons beyond the airport lounge and, during the approach and beyond take-off, enjoying extensive views of Vancouver Island, with Victoria the capital city of British Columbia on the island and the city of Vancouver (perversely) on the mainland, backed by snow-capped ranges. Judging from this cameo alone, Canada appears a beautiful country indeed.

Sadly disillusioned

But scarcely the next country, the United States, whose border we crossed within a few minutes of take-off. In a surprisingly short span of time we had run out of forest and mountain peaks, and were over hungry-looking rugged, yellow-brown landscapes, apparently devoid of civilisation and charm, reminiscent of the central areas of Australia. And so it continued for hours as we headed south for Mexico City. I was quite disillusioned, having always thought of North America as a green paradise. One small town I observed attentively (though from a great height) seemed to have only one green area in it, a sports oval on the main street. The backyards were uniformly bare and brown. A Broken Hill? Undoubtedly useful for making cinema Westerns.

Remoteness above the earth makes mock of borders, and when I finally decided we must be over Mexico (similar terrain) we were in fact already in our descent pattern for landing at Mexico City. I say 'we' because son David had met me at Narita Airport, and we were together for the rest of our Latin American odyssey. Spurning the officially commended (and therefore more expensive) conventional taxis, we grabbed a VW Beetle cab (long after their kin had disappeared from Australian roads, though still being built in Mexico) and covered the 5km to the centre of the world's largest city—as they claim locally. Later we were warned that the VW cab drivers had the quaint habit of taking you to their corrupt mates' garages where they relieved passengers of their wallets and valuables, before beating them up and throwing them onto the streets. Maybe after all, the officially sanctioned taxis were a worthwhile investment in security. At the time I had never envisaged the Mexican reality of a virtual civil war incessantly waged between drug barons and the authorities (themselves often held to be implicated), nor the level of criminality on the streets. Mercifully, in our few days there we witnessed no such affray.

Mexico City—pioneer in town planning

Rather was I impressed to learn that a central section of Mexico City was the first metropolis in the world to be laid out on the principles of modern town planning, claimed to be the model for the subsequent reshaping of central Paris by Baron Haussmann, characterised by wide boulevards, long and straight—their buildings, cafés and shops evoking a new type of urban scenario in place of the dense and irregular medieval alleyways breeding crime and ill-health. Near the centre of Mexico City is a great wide but shallow figure of X where two immensely long boulevards intersect: *Insurgentes* and *La Reforma* in an area called Zona Rosa. Nearby we located a cheap lodging and, sauntering about the district were captured by the colourful life of the streets. We also came upon some huge urban parks, one celebrated for its sculptures.

But apparently the inspiration for theprinciples of town planning went back to the time of the Aztecs, pre-Columbus. The Spanish *conquistadores* built their colonial city centre on the foundations of Tenochtitlan, capital of the Aztec empire, located on an island in a lake, later drained. Its central feature had been an extensive plaza, lined with public buildings such as temples, large and smaller pyramids, the royal palace, halls, baths and schools, all astronomically aligned on sunrise at the summer solstice. Hernan Cortés, brutal leader of the Spanish conquerors obsessed with the lure of gold, marvelled at the size and character of the city he captured in 1521, arguably then with its 200,000 people the third or fourth largest city in the world. As a triumphalist statement he deliberately built the Cathedral of the Assumption of the Virgin Mary on the site of the *Templo Mayor* where unspeakable ritual sacrifices of children and teenagers had regularly been offered. With its broad façade in Spanish Gothic architecture it is the oldest and largest Roman Catholic cathedral in the Americas. But when we were there it was closed for repairs—believed to be sinking into the mud of the ancient lake! The revenge of the Aztecs?

Panoramic view of the Plaza de la Constitución (Zócalo) and Cathedral

One evening at dusk, on the Plaza de la Constitutión before the Cathedral we were part of the tourist crowd attending the ceremonial lowering and furling of the giant red, white and green flag of Mexico by a crack Army unit. The square is popularly known as Zócalo *('base')* of a plinth commemorating independence but which was destroyed and never re-erected. With its 112 million people, the world's largest Spanish-speaking country has never become independent of the patrician party that forever dominates the scene while—behind the façade of 'democracy'—largely neglecting the writhing masses.

Under a corner of the square is a Metro station, part of a huge underground railway system with multiple lines and distinguished by truly elegant stations in the key city locations making extravagant use of marble and statuery, reminiscent of the Moscow underground.

Houstons in Houston

We were taken aback to learn that the most economical way of flying south to Quito, capital of Ecuador, was by first flying *north* with an American airline to… Houston! This afforded the opportunity of marking the connection with Scottish migrant Sam Houston, in the 1830s president of the independent nation of Texas. But we never did get to see the boom town because of my parsimony (reinforced by Christian scruples). Outside the Houston terminal I had a laboured conversation with the policeman on duty, to learn that there was no public transport of any kind to the city, quite a journey: for the couple of hours we had to spare, taxis there and back would cost $US54. 'Laboured' because we both had to repeat everything we said, since initially the other could not understand. As Churchill once said, "two nations separated by the one language".

It was a long slow flight in an ageing and rather shabby US airliner (how spoilt we are in Australia by the high quality service with state-of-the-art aircraft). Slow also because on the way we landed at Panama City, but at night so that we didn't get to see the Canal. My only memory of the flight was the sun setting over a swampy, jungle coastline of the Yucatan peninsula of Mexico, doubtless infested with man-eating alligators!

The night landing at Quito was hair-raising, with a curving approach between steep urban hillsides fringing a rather narrow valley. The airport seemed to be in the middle of the urban area. As we moved out of the plane I mentioned to the pilot, an older American, that it seemed a challenging landing by night. *"Yep, she sure is tough"*, he drawled. How truly he spake: some years afterwards a whole planeful of passengers perished at a botched landing!

We were warmly welcomed by Nick, driving us in his paediatrician girlfriend's car to where he lived in an impressive villa in a wealthy quarter high on one of the hillsides. With a Canberra mate Bernie he'd been taken in by a patrician family bent on practising their English, their property surrounded by elaborate walls and guarded at night by security patrols whose task was to blow repeated blasts of their whistles on the hour, right through the night, to indicate the coast was clear. Every time it woke me up I felt newly reassured!

The indigenous scene

Welcome to South America, immigrant continent with its gaping chasm between an established well-to-do minority of Hispanics and the multitudinous poor (many wretchedly so), mostly of indigenous Indian origin (in these Andean countries, mostly Quechua).

A sharp contrast with the scene in our own immigrant continent. The distinguishing factor in 'the Lucky Country' was the huge disparity between the size of the continent and the tiny, thinly-spread indigenous population made up of hundreds of small language groups of rudimentary technology rendering the conquest so much easier, by comparison with South Africa, New Zealand, Canada and the USA. Under the spectre of the 'Yellow Peril' and our location on the edge of a teeming Asia it has led to continuous, concerted programs to increase the overall population size for security reasons. But the deal offered to migrants stands in gross contrast to the mean-spirited attitudes displayed towards the small numbers of original Australians whose alienated land is our prime national asset, and who have simply been discounted (until 1967 even *uncounted*!). But maybe we stand near the threshold of a more ethical deal based on redefining the constitutional balance. A minimal step in that direction is the trend for churches and community installations to prominently locate a plaque like the one unveiled (at our initiative and largely, expense) in 2013:

> All Saints Anglican Church Greensborough
> acknowledges, under God,
> the Wurundjeri people
> as the traditional custodians of this land, and is
> committed to work for reconciliation and justice.

In the rural areas that we traversed in Latin America I was comforted to see the heart-warming link between the indigenous people and their gorgeous llamas—most becoming to both of them. Often we would see Indian groups waiting by the roadside with their llamas standing by (hoping for tourists' largesse for the photo opportunity). Delightful creatures, as well as indispensable to the local lifestyle, with their versatility as beasts of burden and riding mounts—not to mention their steaks!—and their gentle, non-argumentative temperament. Surprising how tall they are: I could look them in the eye, thanks to that wonderful elongated neck—as well as my own.

Recent research on continental drift has established that, with the original breakup of 'Pangeia' (the whole-world super continent), North and South America were widely separate, pointy land masses which over aeons drifted into closer proximity. Relatively late in pre-historic time their extreme points came together to form the isthmus of Panama, permitting a migration of fauna, whereby the llama population of North America moved southwards, to flourish in the Andean lands.

Capital city by the equator

Proudly we were shown around Quito by Nick and Bernie, a teacher also from Canberra, both adept at interpreting the city and the country to us. Ecuador is a small, democratic republic straddling the Andes and the tropical Pacific coast, in the north-west section of South America, between the larger countries of Colombia to the north and Peru to the south. As its Spanish name indicates, it lies across the equator, affording the regularity of sunrise at 6am and sunset at 6pm every day in the year. But the heat and humidity associated with the tropics are mercifully absent from the upland areas where Quito is situated, so that its average temperature is a balmy 24 degrees every day. It is the world's highest capital, set on a volcanic Andean plateau 2,800m (9,350ft) above sea level, far higher than the summit of our puny Mt Kosciuszko.

The region formed part of the extensive Inca Empire also straddling parts of Colombia, Bolivia, and Peru, conquered in the 1530s by the Spanish military adventurer Francisco Pizarro, spurred on by lust for gold. Some three hundred years later the Spanish dominion would be overthrown in a colonial rebellion that began in Quito and soon spread across the continent, led by patriots such as José de Sucre and Simón Bolívar. (At the time of our visit the Ecuadorean unit of currency was called the *sucre*, replaced in 2000 by the US dollar!).

We were not surprised to learn that over 70% of Ecuadoreans are of mixed race *(mestizos)* and only 6% Hispanics—landholders and businessmen who largely controlled the country's governance and economy. Hence in 1997 no less than 40% of the population lived in extreme poverty, dogged by ill-health and illiteracy. Though the vast majority are Roman Catholics, the faith of many in poor or rural areas has always been intermingled with strands of indigenous religions (syncretism). Today among nominal Catholics, Pentecostalism is making significant inroads. It remains to be seen how this may affect the social structure of the country over time.

Nick and Bernie's benefactors, Cesar and Mariasol, were mutually exchanging language tutoring. David and I also had a room in their villa, opening off the central colonnaded swimming pool. With the freedom of the kitchen conferred on them, Nick and Bernie largely fended for themselves, though our arrival was marked by a welcome family feast served in our honour. Nick showed me around the locality—historic sites, shops, transport. He warned me of the dangers of the streets but, sceptical about the warnings, I wandered about alone (since David had collapsed with jetlag and a bad gastric upset and Nick had his daily round to attend to), walking miles across Quito exploring and visiting landmarks like the 500-year-old cathedral and a splendid museum of Inca and colonial history. On one of the ridges edging the city I discovered a huge parkland area covered with a mature forest of gumtrees! Beyond its summit I looked down upon the deepest valley I had ever encountered, arguably deeper than the Jamison Valley in the Blue Mountains, but quite urbanised below. On a grand scale, these Andean regions.

"Cotapaxi's out!"

Early one morning the rousing cry went up. At over 19,000ft, one of Ecuador's dozen Andean volcanoes, it is also one of the world's highest, so much so that it is rarely visible because of its perennial cloud-wrap. But now, gleaming white in the morning sun, the lone peak reared starkly out of the horizon about 30km from Quito, and practically on the equator. We swung into action. In his borrowed car Nick drove me across the plateau and up the mountain's lower slopes, but as we crawled into the highest car park the motor expired from lack of oxygen. With our breath 'coming in short pants' we fairly staggered up the sharp slope to the hut on the snowline, Nick pushing me along from behind. Laced by glaciers the snowy peak towered above us, but without special gear and high-altitude training any dream of climbing higher was idle. In the hut, as recommended, we sipped coca tea. Then as we ventured out onto the slopes, challenging weather and altitude, a sudden icy squall assaulted us. As we clambered over an unsteady jumble of volcanic rocks, without warning a harsh swirl of sleet pelted into our faces, blotting out the world, clattering harshly onto the scree. We could only turn our backs to the darkening shower and hunker down. Just as quickly it passed over and the sun shone wanly on the acute-angled wasteland. At far more than twice the height of Kosciuszko, you felt utterly puny, powerless in the face of nature's might. It is the highest altitude I ever attained on earth.

Curiously, until the early 19th century, another Ecuadorean volcano, Chimborazo, at 20,500ft was believed to be the world's highest mountain. But the day closed with Nick and me lolling luxuriously in a hot-springs pool at a nearby valley resort, gazing up at the snow-capped peaks above. Real living!

Cotopaxi

Visiting the 'Middle of the World'

Another day the Quito family drove us to the equator, near the market town of Cayembe where a small settlement had capitalised on its unrivalled location by modestly styling itself Mitad del Mundo (*Middle of the World*). Inside and below the large chunky monument marking the equator, we visited an ethnographic museum of the peoples of the area. It is also a historic site recalling the measurements made by a French scientific expedition in 1736 that demonstrated that the world is not perfectly round but bulges at the equator, giving rise to the introduction of the metric system. We took a longer route home, along the *Panamericana*, part of the vast (and still incomplete) highway system linking Alaska to Chile, characterised as 'the longest road on earth' and in Ecuador impressively engineered in coping with the deep valleys scarring the Andean plateau.

I was amazed to learn that, as recently as 1942, Ecuador had lost a good third of its territory (though mostly impenetrable and uninhabited lowland rainforest) through aggression and military defeat at the hands of its southern neighbour, Peru. At about the time of our visit hostilities broke out again with naval and air warfare, leaving Ecuador compelled to acknowledge the new border at the point earlier seized by the Peruvians. But in 2007 a popular leftist leader, Rafael Correa, would be elected President of Ecuador and subsequently re-elected twice. His administration would succeed in rebuilding national morale, tackling the high levels of poverty and unemployment, winning significant legal and international actions to re-order the burden of national debt, and also breaking the media monopoly. In 2013 he enjoys the highest level of approval of any leader in the Americas.

Riding a bucking bronco

Our departure from Quito was a tad unorthodox. Nick and David were perched on the roof of a carriage of the *Ferrocarriles Ecuatorianos* Quito-Guayaquil 'express' with me chickening out inside. It had become a major tourist gimmick to climb onto the roof for one of the Great Train Journeys of the World, a folly tolerated by the rail authorities (while disclaiming any responsibility). Some young bloods even had the bravado to stand, risking the worst as the carriages swayed about drunkenly or suddenly plunged into a low-roofed tunnel! That sunny morning the carriage roofs were well populated as we lurched out of the terminal to head coastwards, by a major descent down the western flank of the Andes via many tunnels and a spectacular zig-zag built by American railway engineers (on a grander scale than the one descending the western escarpment of the Blue Mountains). On a stiff gradient cut into the mountainside, the train would creep forward for a few hundred metres, then reverse as far, ever downhill, backing and filling, to the cacophony of a grinding and squealing of brakes and the throb of the diesel loco. Actually the following year was to see the closure of the railway because of washaways from El Niño flooding, with this section still not reopened in 2013.

Resuming normal progress in one direction, we found the views ever-changing and stunning: small farmsteads on terraced hillsides with gnarled Quechua workers chipping away at their crops, all backed by steep mountain slopes where the scant trees clung tenaciously to the terrain. Then lower down to sad-looking small towns, where the single track ran right through the main street, with poultry birds squawking out of the way, people carrying enormous burdens, and urchins racing us on both sides as we crept along while, all around, the moving pageant surged about us of crowds of the craggy-faced elderly and the brilliant hues of young women's clothing, crowned by the characteristic round-topped black hats of the Andean tribes. Classical images of Latin America!

But we had also swapped climate zones: the temperate zone of the Andes gradually giving way to the torrid zone on the wide coastal strip as the thermometer climbed and the humidity increased. Now many of the roof-riders were deserting their posts to seek shade below, perilously climbing in the windows as we swayed along. I was rapidly losing interest in exploring further: scorching humidity wasn't what we had come to South America to experience. At a larger town we decided to bail out rather than travel on to Guayaquil, which is actually Ecuador's largest city and the seaport from where you can embark for its Galapagos Islands 1,000km out in the Pacific. So we scouted about for long-distance buses heading up inland to Cuenca, and were fortunate enough to find seats, given that it was Christmas Eve of 1997.

Friendship betrayed

I found myself next to a white-collar family man going home for the holiday, who kindly indulged my mish-mash of Spanish and Italian. Earlier I had been gratified to discover that I could read Spanish well enough from my evening classes in Italian some thirty years before (based on the Latin that is their common ancestor) and that its pronunciation was not greatly dissimilar to Italian.

During the three-hour ride our relationship blossomed to the point where, arriving at Cuenca's bus station, he offered to locate a large taxi to take us to a hotel where he had suggested we could spend Christmas. He dived off into the crowd while I marshalled our considerable luggage. But the boys were already booking a small taxi, and off-handedly dismissed my intention of waiting for my erstwhile companion. Much against my better judgment, I was bundled into the front seat of a smaller vehicle which soon had us in the centre of the city. But disaster loomed.

While unloading the heavy baggage from the boot, I had intentionally left my carry-on bag where I had been sitting. But before I could retrieve it the taxi took off, with me vainly bellowing for it to stop. David likewise took off on foot and virtually caught up with it at the next traffic lights before it sped away. Was it unwitting or an intentional absconding by the driver? I had been feelingd enough about betraying the kindness of a friendly stranger without the dawning realisation that the bag contained—fortunately not my travel documents—but my whole photographic record of Japan captured on seven rolls of undeveloped film, particularly focusing on Hiroshima and Nagasaki! I was angry, ashamed—and inconsolable. To apologise and seek help I called the phone number given by my friend and was told he would call back next day, Christmas. Also the Taxi Co-operative, contacted by the hotel management, assured us they would locate the bag, but later it turned out that the driver had been an unauthorised stand-in for a Co-operative member.

An *un*merry Christmas

That Christmas still looms in my memory as the most meaningless ever. All day long I hovered alone in the hotel room sweating on my friend's call. It never came. Understandably, on returning to the bus station in a larger taxi, he would have felt alienated by my disappearance. And of course he had come home to spend a precious Christmas with his family. My further efforts to contact taxi-drivers proved equally fruitless. Not until evening did we regroup for a belated Christmas dinner, and that in a Chinese restaurant. Afterwards on the Cathedral square with the boys I consoled myself by observing the Christmas spectacle of myriad coloured balloons being released into the cool night sky, each borne aloft by a burning candle suspended beneath.

On the other hand I was captivated by Cuenca's seemingly modern, though actually very historic grid of tight little streets lined with buff-coloured buildings of uniform height and appearance, now rated as a Unesco World Heritage site. With over a quarter of a million inhabitants it is Ecuador's third largest city, set at an altitude a little higher than Mt Kosciuszko's, vouchsafing perfect weather year-round. For countless ages it had been home to a culturally advanced indigenous people until captured by the Incas, only themselves to be defeated soon after by the Spanish *conquistadores* in the 1530s.

On the trail of the *conquistadores*

Our rather protracted farewell to Ecuador was inflicted by bus, all day rattling southwards through forested country along progressively worsening roads as the country petered out, with a few stops at nondescript mountain towns and the larger centre of Loja, before pulling up at the Peruvian border. The instant improvement of the road quality in the larger and better-resourced neighbour was tangible, until the long day drew to an end with our arrival at Piura, the first city in Peru founded by *conquistador* Francisco Pizarro (1532) and the third Spanish-founded city in all South America. Our arrival in the semi-arid region, in the rain-shadow of the Andes, was greeted by an unseasonal cloudburst that had us wading knee-deep through flooded streets to an overnight hostel in what appeared to be a former gaol, with two storeys of small and austere rooms opening off inter-facing covered balconies.

Peru being a far larger country than Ecuador, next day we emplaned for the capital, Lima, well down the coast to the south. Our goal was the heartland of the ancient Inca kingdom at Cuzco and the enigmatic remains of Machu Picchu on an Andean mountain top. But Nick wandering off on a private 'reccy' in the airport at Chiclayo, where we called along the way, had managed to miss the plane. In the pre-mobile phone era, how to meet up again 'somewhere in Latin America'? On arrival in Lima, David and I had taken a taxi across the city towards the Pacific coast at the elegant beachside suburb of Miraflores, settling into comfortable accommodation for New Year's Eve. By morning, when I came back from a New Year paddle in our common South Pacific Ocean, inexplicably Nick had found his way to rejoin us!

We flew on to the second city of Peru, Arequipa in the far south, founded by Spanish colonists in 1540, in a dramatic setting dominated by a ring of three isolated volcanoes rearing out of the plateau, each up to 19,000ft high, the closest of them El Misti trailing its perennial plume of smoke. At once I fell in love with the fine architecture of the colonial buildings framing the historic city centre (now also a Unesco heritage site) built of white volcanic stone, and fringing the main Plaza de Armas before the Renaissance cathedral which sadly was to lose its towers in the disastrous earthquake of 2001. Many other churches are among the most beautiful colonial buildings preserved. Of indelible memory was the afternoon I spent exploring the early-colonial convent of Santa Catalina, a beautiful but depressing walled mini-city shrouding a sad 'world within a world', where daughters from generations of noble Spanish families were locked away lifelong as religious devotees, surrounded by stunningly beautiful paintings and other works of art.

In Quechua territory

In order to visit the prime attraction of the region, the incredible Colcha Canyon more than twice as deep as the Grand Canyon of the Colorado, we next succumb to the lure of a two-day minibus tour (taking our lives in our hands). In a tired old VW Kombi, the long journey for me becomes almost unbearable, since I occupy the backmost seat with no space to straighten my bent right leg (a challenge during an orchestral concert, let alone for a whole day's bouncing over mountainous gravel roads) as we snake our way ever upwards. At the higher levels devoid of vegetation and close to the snowline the track is lined intermittently with curious little pillars of gathered stones precariously stacked one upon another, six or eight high. More sinister is the appearance of memorial crosses, sometimes decked with recently decayed flowers, marking the site of a fatal accident. After 30 or more of these poignant protests, sick at heart, I renounce the morbid count of that 'toll' road.

At the summit I stagger out thankfully to scan the desolate prospect of treeless ranges before we essay the descent into the valley of the Colcha river beyond. At the first downward glance I am appalled: it is akin to a perspective of the ground from an airliner—but in our overcrowded Kombi *we* are committed to the tortuous descent on four wheels, sliding around endless loops and zigzags, some of them at an alarming gradient. Will the brakes be up to it? Conversation ceases as the driver battles with gravity while the motor roar its protests in low gear behind us mute but white-knuckled spectators.

Once on the valley floor we relax, admiring the ancient pre-Inca farming terraces on every hand, evoking the new world of crops that had greeted the astonished colonists from the old world. Among them maize (corn), potatoes, tomatoes, capsicums, chillis, jalapeño and of course chocolate and tobacco. It is claimed that half the modern world's food supplies have originated in the Americas. Along the broad and fertile valley floor bounded by ever-steepening hillsides, for hours crossing and recrossing the Colcha river, we finally reach our goal at a point where it has carved its way through softer sediments to hollow out a narrow canyon, ever-deepening into an unbelievable and terrifying abyss. With no safety railings you edge forward with pounding heart and finally lie face down to gaze into the mighty void. While overhead in broad sweeping circles glides the mighty Andean condor, largest of land-birds, black and white, with three-metre wingspan, and as much a tourist drawcard as the canyon itself. Nothing modest about the scale of the Andean landscapes!

But the rest of the trip slumps into an anti-climax: booked into a slightly upmarket hotel in the poor regional town of Chivay (the *v* pronounced as a *b*) and whose Quechua people reflect its pre-Columban origins, we are informed without apology that the evening's scheduled folkloric entertainment is cancelled. Disconsolate I wander off, lingering in the oldest church, buying some tawdry items from an Indian woman hawking outside. Next morning we face a replay of the daunting odyssey, but in dappled sunshine splashed over the valley's tight patchwork of stone-edged, terraced fields as a soothing prelude to the terror of the heights.

Once back in Arequipa as we stiffly clamber out of the minibus I am blandly asked by the travel agent, in English, did I enjoy the excursion? As I reply my eye falls upon the van's front tyres—as bereft of tread as a baby's bottom! Visions of the cross-lined road and the sliding descent rise before my eyes. I mutter something about such a situation in my country likely to lead to an arrest. More appropriate would have been a prayer of humble thanksgiving for our protection.

To the Inca capital

By a more predictable conveyance, we now head off by train north-east to Cuzco en route for Maccu Picchu, although the Peruvian State Railways tracks must be rather bumpy, judging from the crazy dance of the carriages at times seemingly about to uncouple and go their own wilful ways. Laboriously we ascend to the *altiplano* (high plains) around Lake Titicaca straddling the Bolivian border, the world's highest navigable lake, but before reaching it we swing away to the north to the junction city of Juliaca. Despite its considerable population it has a sort of 'wild west' feel about it, with poor Indians living in makeshift shanties trackside. Then during a long afternoon we bounce around, tracking across the empty landscape at a height of some 12,000ft. At one wayside halt Nick ventures off to check something outside but without warning the train moves off. Nonetheless, *voilà*—at the next station he is already waiting for us, having hitch-hiked a (paying) pillion ride on a motor bike. At least his Spanish had stood him in good stead.

To our immense relief, close of day finds us drawing into the Cuzco terminus where the train disgorges its cargo of hundreds of backpackers and other tourists, to be besieged by lines of touts with competing offers of overnight accommodation. The guide we accept leads us to a taxi which deposits us at a pleasant family home not far from the city centre. Our hostess turns out to be a warm-hearted Seventh

Day Adventist Christian who a year later sends us a Christmas card recalling our stay. Admirably she provides for our needs: comfortable beds, hearty breakfast, good advice duly laced with appropriate warnings. As the launching pad for Maccu Picchu-bound adventurers the ancient Inca capital has itself become a celebrated (and dangerous) tourist trap. A day or two later in the waiting room for the Maccu Picchu train I joke with a blond Nordic couple who look as if they've 'got their backs to the wall'. I am taken aback at their reply that it is the safest posture since being struck down without warning, from behind, while publicly walking along a main street the night before, and relieved of all their valuables.

But for me, our two days in Cuzco prove to be sheer delight, memorable less for the clarity of the chill midsummer air at over 11,000ft than for the tangible sense of the Inca presence on every hand. We are intrigued to experience that, unlike other conquered cities in Latin America, Cuzco retains much of its pre-Columban feel. Indeed, it is based on the capital of an earlier people dating back to the 13th century, who were conquered by the Incas only a few years before the advent of the Spanish *conquistadores* in 1533. Two years later, after a long siege, the city was retaken by the Incas under their great hero Manco but could not be held in the face of the superior European firepower. The captured Inca emperor Atahualpa, sentenced to execution by burning but offered his life if he were baptised, famously asked Pizarro whether as Christians, the Spaniards would likewise go to heaven and, being assured that they would, opted for death and was garrotted. By poetic justice Pizarro was later assassinated in a factional revolt of his army.

Rather than being destroyed by the Spanish, the emperor's palace and the recently built Temple of the Sun God were incorporated into the church of San Domingo and the Archbishop's residence. But the Inca (and pre-Inca) city plan is still there, with the streets at times lined by immense blocks of fine-grained grey granite jointed together without mortar, so precise was the masonry fit. My Scottish stonemason grandfather would have been hugely impressed. Actually, some of the colonial buildings superimposed on them have since fallen victim to earthquakes, only serving to highlight the strength of the Inca architecture beneath, still unscathed.

Surely one of the Americas' seminal historic sites, Cuzco would become the centre for Spanish colonisation (and the spread of Christianity!) in the whole Andean region. Little wonder I linger in that Dominican church and convent, seeking to identify the Inca elements, originally including walls plated in solid gold and silver, looted on sight by the Spanish adventurers, thought to number no more than 200 men.

Later, jostling with the throngs of Western tourists, I can scarcely tear myself away from the grandeur of the nearby Plaza de Armas with its late-Gothic cathedral on one side, built out of Inca stonework and on another side the larger and more opulent baroque Jesuit basilica with its goldleaf-wrapped altar built on the site of the emperor's palace. By night the atmosphere of the pulsating square is electric, the sense of history compelling, the vista across the broad Plaza with its illuminated fountains and gardens adding mystery to delight. On the far sides the Plaza is flanked by stone colonnades dating from early colonial times. We learn that it often hosts flamboyant fiestas and carnivals in which the nation's proud pagan past collides colourfully with solemn Catholic rituals, even more ancient.

Unsurprisingly, Cuzco has since been declared a Unesco world heritage site, as well as 'Archaeological Capital of the Americas' and without a doubt, the area has become the prime goal of tourism in Peru. Suddenly embarrassed, one senses the tawdry ordinariness of Australia's cities.

Nick's friend Bernie having now rejoined us after overcoming visa difficulties, we opt for another short tourist excursion, this time venturing out onto the Andean slopes overlooking the city to Saksaywaman, a fortress destroyed by the Spaniards but whose vast solid walls still tower above you. We are told that many of the huge polished granite blocks of varied (unmortared) interlocking shapes (weighing up to 200 tonnes) are so closely spaced that not even a single piece of paper will fit between them. Further on, we are delivered to a lofty panoramic spot where a number of Quechua women in brilliant hues of blue and red, with high black hats—their faithful llamas tethered in the background—entice us for a paid photo opportunity. With llamas in the offing, what resistance can I offer?

Mystique of Machu Picchu

But the country's greatest drawcard of all now awaits us, the 'lost city of the Incas', Machu Picchu complex of ancient ruins still shrouded in mystery enwrapped in a riddle, perched high on an isolated mountaintop, a morning's train journey away. The narrow-gauge line has no connection with the mainline into Cuzco, departing rather from its own station high above the city, via another zigzag descending into the adjacent valley. We jog along modestly, past urban houses each sporting the sacred guinea-pig tile at the roof-corners, tracing the valleys and the Urubamba river. Among the trainload of young Western tourists there are a few conspicuous local people with heavy packs. Along the way the three boys alight at the point where the Inca Trail heads off over the Andean ranges, to enter Machu Picchu from the rear after a three-day hike.

The greatest architectural achievement of the Inca civilisation, variously believed to have been created as a worship and/or retreat site for the emperor Paccahuti in the 15th century before the Spanish invasion, but mysteriously abandoned barely a century later, forgotten—perhaps a prey to smallpox or civil wars? Wrapped in forbidding rainforest terrain and crowning an almost inaccessible mountaintop, it appears never to have been completed and remained unbeknown to the *conquistadores*, being rediscovered only in 1911 by Hiram Bingham, an American academic historian turned archaeologist—prototype of the latter-day Hollywood hero Indiana Jones. A few years after our visit the UNESCO World Heritage site would be popularly voted one of the New Seven Wonders of the World. At the site archaeological research goes on apace.

From the train station in the river town of Aguas Calientes (*'Warm Waters'*) you take a bus up the sheer mountainside and pay to enter the site. At once I am captivated as much by its atmosphere as its dramatic location, at a height greater than Mt Kosciuszko's summit, overlooking the Urubamba River hundreds of metres below. In a trackless and uninhabited area now once more reclaimed from the jungle, the partly restored ruins cover an unevenly levelled mountaintop overshadowed by two imposing crags rising even higher. Around the edges of the site huge granite terraces, built without iron tools, descend the steep slopes, unique for their remarkable drainage system safely diverting the run-off from the huge rainfall on the mountaintop site. Undoubtedly the terraces were once used for growing the royal crops of maize and potatoes—and grazing llamas.

A small section of the site

But clearly it is the sheer quality of the architecture and its excellent preservation, as well as its breathtaking mountain setting, that has rendered Machu Picchu one of the world's most celebrated archaeological sites. The vista is truly grandiose: the mountaintop has been sculpted with giant walls, grassed ramps and terraces all interlaced with stairways and streetscapes. In the Inca style the walls of the buildings are also made without mortar from locally quarried stone. It forms a grandiose complex, a sort of natural outdoor cathedral, in its breathtaking beauty comprehensible at first glance. But it has now come to be understood that its purposes were not military or defensive, but rather related to appeasing the deities of the sun, earth, mountains and water by an élite community of Inca royalty, served by a large corps of virgins, together perhaps a thousand souls. Contemporary Inca paintings figure the actual mummified body of the 'still-ruling' god-king Paccahuti, son of the Sun, being carried in ritual procession through the streets of his capital Cuzco (a ceremony subsequently 'christianized' as the annual festival of Corpus Christi.)

The three most celebrated structures are the *Room of the Three Windows*, the *Temple of the Sun* and the *Hitching Post of the Sun*, all located in the non-residential, sacred section of the site. These are set in alignment with four mountain peaks that mark the cardinal points of the compass, the highest point crowned by a huge altar-stone whose outline mimics the shape of the mountainous horizon behind it, when the sun's rays at the summer solstice fall on a granite slab associated with ritual child sacrifice. Nearby, groups of ruined buildings, some ranged around a central square, reveal a variety of shapes, sizes and purposes, including a bath-house linked with an elaborate and precise aqueduct system from a higher spring. As you wander through entrance halls and inner recesses, now all unroofed, your imagination takes wings: what was the purpose of each one? And what were their occupants' concerns—social, hierarchical, ritualistic?

In glorious cool sunlight I spend a long and evocative afternoon, drawn ever deeper into reverie and imaginative exploration. In such settings what is it that lifts one's spirit so far beyond the mundanity of life? I fall to musing about similar transcendental experiences over the years, at the Pyramids and Sphinx, at Stonehenge, looking down into the crater of Vesuvius, gazing up at the north face of the Eiger, on the Mount of Olives, the Galilee lakeshore … at Gallipoli … Dachau! Are they somehow akin to the 'thin places' of Celtic spirituality—whether beautiful or terrible—portals for glimpsing a world beyond?

Finally from the southernmost extremity of the site I decide to climb by the Inca Trail to the crest of the ridge from where the approaching boys will catch their first breathtaking view of their goal, laid out below them. I am thrilling with excitement as I stand gazing down on its totality. Then for a while sitting on a large stone I have the brainwave of addressing them by a welcoming message laid out in tiny but conspicuous white pebbles at a turning of the track: '*Welcome! Jim was here*' and finally smirk off back down to the ruins. But the wheeze falls flat: dog tired from their exertions on the mountain trail they notice nothing. By the time they arrive the day is declining fast but I gallantly play the expert guide, briskly covering much of the site before all being shepherded out at closing time. In a simple but eminently adequate hostel on the bank of the Urubamba river at Aguas Calientes we spend a tranquil night soothed by the music of the fast-flowing waters on their journey to the Amazon two countries and thousands of kilometres away. Surely the music of babbling mountain waters offers one of the purest of life's delights.

Islands *floating* on the world's highest navigable lake

Next morning sees us on the morning train bound for the third destination of our South American safari, the poverty-stricken nation of Bolivia, in the heart of the Andes, land-locked, as large as NSW. Changing trains (and rail gauges) at Cuzco, again we sway and bounce around for hours on the world's second highest railway (after the Qinghai to Tibet railway in China) across the treeless *altiplano* back to

Juliaca, from where we take bus for Puno, the last outpost of Peru on the shores of Lake Titicaca It is a surprisingly large city, stretching from its original hillside site down to the plains around the lakeshore. It is known for its large livestock market, trading in llamas and alpacas as well as less exotic breeds.

One morning, leaving the boys to their own devices, I hail a pedal rickshaw to take me down to the marina where I come across excursions advertised to the 'Floating Islands'. Intrigued I take ship. The ferry ride takes about fifteen minutes to reach the nearest islands out in the huge lake, at 12,500ft altitude the world's highest commercially navigable lake, 200km long and 80km wide and in parts almost 1,000ft deep. As well as the larger real and mountainous islands in the Lake, it is said there are over 40 'floating islands' on which the local indigenous people, the Uros, have lived for centuries, originally places of refuge from the conquering Incas. These are artificially created from layers and layers of floating *totoro* reeds woven together, that grow abundantly in the shallows, and are anchored with reed ropes attached to stakes driven into the floor of the lake. The dense roots interweave but rot away fairly quickly, so new reeds need to be added to the top every few months. I am surprised how soft and spongy the ground feels underfoot, at first footfall rather alarming. The Uros keep guinea pigs, rabbits and ducks and have even constructed ponds for fish farming. Their huts, canoes, and even a watch tower, as well as most of the craft objects that they sell to tourists, are all made from the *totoro* reeds, truly the focal point of their existence. However my purchase is two jumpers of soft white alpaca wool, wonderfully warm and boldly patterned with black llamas. One I have kept, naturally still my 'best'—and warmest.

But it is in Puno that I suffer the only bout of panic, ripening into outright fear, that I have known in all my travels, before that day or since. I cannot recall what triggered it: reading that Puno was the most dagerous city in Peru? Or hearing of further bashings of tourists on the streets? Or being taken for a resented *gringo* (American)? Perhaps our trip has gone on for too long and home is calling. Suffice it to confess that, while the boys do their own thing, I spend our last day in Puno skulking in our accommodation, with the cloying fingers of fear massaging my heart. *I want to live!*

Our bus journey out of Peru takes a long morning, gyrating around the many twists and turns of Lake Titicaca's shoreline, but often climbing high above the brilliant deep blue expanse stretching off towards the horizon without a ripple. At one point I am amazed to look down on a large, red-and-black-funnelled steamship making its way across a broad arm of the lake. Later we would learn that it is the *SS Ollanta*, built in England in the early 1930s and reassembled in Puno. Previous steamers had been incorporated into the Peruvian Navy. Briefly we pause at the resort of Copacabana which, although within Bolivia, is on the western shore and soon after, we come to a narrowing arm of the lake which we cross on a small ferry, and then cut inland while Titicaca generously opens out again on our right.

In Bolivia, on the roof of South America

On the bare high plains of Bolivia, in the middle of nowhere the first promise of human habitation finally looms: a prominent roadside sign *Urbanización* marking a large building site. Shortly afterwards civilisation greets us at the dreary and sprawling city of El Alto ('the Tops'), as we draw up at a large railway terminal. Only then do I 'get it': actually we are already in the Bolivian capital of La Paz (in formal Spanish *Nuestra Señora de La Paz*, Our Lady of Peace) but unable to see the city proper because it is far below our field of vision. But it suddenly unfolds as we begin a sensational urban descent. The first glimpse takes my breath away. In reality the city centre and two thirds of its population live in an unimaginably deep Andean valley, 3,000ft below El Alto on the *altiplano* where the other third live. Together the vertically segregated population blocs are home to more than three million inhabitants, of bewildering variety: Quechua, Aymara and many other Amerindian peoples, Hispanics, Blacks, Orientals and mestizos. So much so that the country's official title is the '*Pluricultural Republic of Bolivia*' --- with its 37 official languages!

La Paz is the highest *administrative* capital in the world, as distinct from Quito which is the world's higherst *legal* capital. Oddly, Bolivia has two capitals: the legal (constitutional) capital at Sucre—like the country's name itself honouring the two great liberators from Spanish domination in 1825, Simon Bolivar and Antonio Jose de Sucre. La Paz, the far larger city, is the seat of government, hosting the National Congress and the Presidential Palace.

But Bolivia is one of the poorest and least developed countries of Latin

America. Less than 10% of its population are of European ancestry. Hence immediately noticeable is the broader social gap between haves and have-nots than in the other two South American lands that we have visited, doubtless reflecting both its history and its geography. From the time of the Spanish conquest immense wealth was extracted by slave labour from the silver mines and repatriated to Spain, but on the other hand the first stirrings towards independence in Latin America occurred in Bolivia. Once far larger, in the 19th century the country lost half of its territory to surrounding nations during wars between the newly independent republics, suffering the loss of its entire Pacific coastline and ports. Today tin has replaced silver as the country's main product, though undoubtedly the workers are still exploited.

Indeed throughout the 20th century the situation of the indigenous labourers in the mines and large estates amounted to a timewarp of outright feudalism: excluded from access to education, economic opportunity or political participation by governments controlled by small economic and social élites. At the time of our visit in 1997 the military dictator Gen. Hugo Banzer was president, propped up by the American CIA[74] actively providing finances and training to the Bolivian military. But in the 2005 election a *mestizo*, Edo Morales, would become the first indigenous Bolivian head of government, winning the presidential election by a clear majority on a program of economic reforms, nationalisation of gas resources, greater civic equality and a new Constitution aimed at giving more power to the indigenous majority. At the following election he and his Movement for Socialism would be re-elected with an increased majority. Outcomes since have included greater economic progress and a decrease in ethnic inequality (reflecting incoming Democratic Party policies of US Governments and the reining in of the CIA).

Exploring La Paz

In the totally urbanised valley of La Paz, whose streets curl up the lower slopes (the higher up the slope the poorer the inhabitants), we settle into a modest tourist apartment, surrounded by 19th century buildings, with parks, squares, stately public edifices, the cathedral and the National Congress all close at hand. For me the city has a good feel about it, small enough to be graspable nor yet without its elegance. Perhaps it is indeed *a city of peace*. Soon I decide I like it.

Near our base is a bookshop run by a Catholic order of sisters where we hold some heartening conversations in their English and my Italian-Spanish, both halting. Come Sunday, I head off to a Protestant outreach group that I have discovered, with services in Spanish and English, led by American missionaries. That afternoon, passing the city gaol, I observe a modest rally outside the entrance by a group bearing banners of the local Pentecostal Church. They appear to be relating to the visitors coming and going, mostly indigenous in appearance (as

---

74 Central Intelligence Agency. In 1967 the legendary revolutionary leader Che Guevara had been killed in Bolivia by a team of CIA officers attached to the Bolivian Army.

indeed many of the Pentecostals themselves are.) Like latter-day Wesleyans—in their day also known for their compassionate gaol visitation.

One afternoon we join a tourist excursion to the Valle de la Luna (Valley of the Moon) on the outskirts of the city, a weird surreal landscape where erosion has worn away the soft rock of a mountainside, leaving a tangled waste of bleached and multi-coloured stalagmites, but on a far smaller scale than the 'fairy chimneys' of Cappadocia.

But finally sensing it is time to go home we book our tickets to Los Angeles with Lloyd Aéreo Boliviano, the national carrier, leaving on a night flight from the high airport near El Alto. Just as well we had no idea of its astonishingly accident-prone record. Commencing our long journey north-west we head .... south-east! To Santa Cruz ('Holy Cross'), the airline's hub in the large southern city. Finally the ten-hour flight deposits us *"In California in the morning"*, as my Dad used to sing. Leg One and a long and sleepless night behind us, we contemplate the two immeasurably longer legs with Japan Airlines still to come: spanning the width of the Pacific to Tokyo and then the length of the Pacific to Melbourne. Gulp!

Longest flight on earth

The next interminable day (or two days if you accept the calendar's verdict about crossing the International Dateline) is spent in a dozy stupor six or seven miles above the featureless Pacific Ocean. By the time David and I disembark at Narita International Airport near Tokyo after the 11-hour flight (Nick having left us at Los Angeles to return to Mexico) we are punchdrunk. Had I considered the implications of a continuous journey of no less than 32 hours from La Paz to Melbourne (half a day longer than a flight from, say Dublin to Dunedin and approaching the time you would take to fly around the entire globe), I surely would not have alerted Marjorie to my expected arrival date and time. All I am aware of that night in Tokyo airport, with my brain addled by sleeplessness, is my 65 year-old body gone on strike, refusing to contemplate a replay of the terrible day behind us. Mercifully I am able to defer my onward flight for 24 hours but David heroically opts to fly on. Alerting a disappointed Marjorie to the implications of my freak-out, I am ferried to the closest international hotel and crash into oblivion.

Next morning, mercifully back in our own time zone, I rise refreshed after a proper night's sleep. Blinking out the window I am astonished to discover the hotel surrounded by lush Australian bush but which on closer inspection turns out to be a forest of massive bamboo stalks (trees actually), botanically the world's largest grass. Back in the northern hemisphere, it is a clear day of wan winter sunlight, inviting good use to be made of it. So on a good ten seconds' contemplation I leap at the opportunity to salvage something from the loss of my seven rolls of film on Japan, and head off on foot for Narita suburban station to catch a train to Tokyo. On the way I am mugged by the splendid Buddhist temple complex I have already described.

And as we would have said in the 1950s, after watching the continuous round of short films at a city newsreel theatrette, while reaching for our coats, *"This is where we came in"*.

34
The Lure of Cathay

My late-born love for llamas largely languishing, the last love-affair
of my longish life looms larger, luring me longingly to Lotus Land.

Nurtured from the bud of my first trip to China with Sarah in 1989, only now—in my seventh decade—would the romance burst into open bloom, triggered on a whim by my offering to join a Christian party of language teachers heading there in 2003 to conduct a short refresher course in English at the Chongqing Institute of Technology. The co-ordinator was Jan Shattock, parish pastoral worker and returned missionary from Borneo theologically trained at Moore College in Sydney, where of all places she had been attached to St Saviour's Punchbowl. In later years she had become qualified to conduct officially recognised courses of training adults in 'the teaching of English to speakers of other languages' (TESOL), and at the diocesan HQ we had worked closely together during those years. Annually during the northern summer vacations she had been leading a small party of teachers to China. In the absence of a formal ESL qualification I had recourse to my Dip. Ed. and experience of teaching English in Germany. But alas! Our plans were thwarted by the epidemic of swine 'flu that swept China that year. *Oink!*

Issued with a Chinese *'Expert's Passport'*

But come next winter, our plans had ripened to the point where a team of seven (only two of them men) had been gathered, accredited, briefed and trained, and authorised by the Chinese consulate in Melbourne to exercise their skills, acknowledged by the issue of an *'Expert's Passport'*, standing beside our Australian passport in gaining privileged entry and a public role in the People's Republic of China. Today it ranks among my most treasured mementos.

During the preparation sessions our briefings had stressed the necessity of relating with professional integrity to the adult Chinese learners of English in our teaching destination, and respecting the political orientation of the People's Republic. Any attempt at Christian witness would be a breach of protocol likely to have future groups excluded. Our group represented the first contact made with the Chongqing Institute of Technology by our sponsoring agency, MSI Professional Services, which arranges assignments in China by professionals in medicine, agriculture, business and English teaching (many of them 'overseas Chinese'). It is a lineal descendant of the famous China Inland Mission founded in 1865 by the pioneer English medical missionary, Dr Hudson Taylor, but forced out by the Communist regime in the early 1950s.

Brimming with excitement—though appalled at the furnace we stepped into on disembarking at Chongqing, one of the three infamous 'ovens of China'—we were welcomed by Ronald Sun from the Institute's International Office and driven in their minibus along an interminable freeway to access the metropolis via an impressive bridge over the Yangtze—in Mandarin not called that but rather the *Chiang Jang* (Long River). Indeed it is the world's third longest river and Asia's longest, sourced from the glaciers of the Tibetan Plateau

In the 'megalopolis' of Chongqing

Chongqing [*pron. Choong-ching*] rates after Shanghai and Beijing as the third city of China, with an urban population of 10 million and 31 million in the 'Chongqing Municipality'—an emerging megalopolis. By locals it is dubbed *'mountain city'* or *'foggy city'*, set at the confluence of two mighty rivers, the Yangtze and the Jialing, surrounded by moderate ranges. The skyline is evocative of Manhattan's. From the time that Marjorie and I would subsequently spend there, totalling seven months, we could well claim to know Chongqing better than any major city in the world except Sydney and Melbourne.

Skyline of central Chongqing, taken from the south-east hills. Jialing R. on right.

Yet as familiar as it would become, its exotic allure would never cease to delight us as wetravelled about by the Qinggui [*Ching–gway*], the new overhead/underground monorail mass-transit system, and by taxi on Sundays to the 'foreigners' church' that assembled gratis in the luxurious Hilton Hotel, courtesy of the manager—as well as our weekend explorations by bus of the tourist spots in the encircling mountains.

But particularly would we get to know our local suburban area of Yangjiaping [*'the Yang family's home on the plain'*] on the mighty Yangtze some eight kilometres downstream from the city centre. Our Chinese *alma mater*, the Chongqing Institute of Technology, dated back to the war with Japan (1937–45) as the training college for ordnance manufacture for the Nationalist Army of Chiang Kai-Shek and later the Communist People's Liberation Army. With the Japanese occupying the whole eastern third of China, the wartime capital had been moved to Chongqing (then written Chungking). So much I clearly remember from primary school days during the war, ever an enthusiast for maps and exotic countries.

Also dating from wartime are today's subterranean shopping arcades running for hundreds of metres beneath the main streets of Yangjiaping, originally bomb-proof munitions factories. A weird nether-world of mini-shops where all manner of food and clothing is to be had at quite literally 'bargain basement' prices. But given the extended shopping hours seven days a week, we used to wonder whether the salespeople ever saw the light of day.

As the wartime provisional capital of the Republic of China, at that time Chungking had been a tangled jumble of steep, often stepped streets clambering around the ridges and riversides, lined by flimsy wooden houses. Under Japanese bombing the carnage from the ferocious blazes was terrible. The war with Japan, and later the civil war against the Communists, were conducted from President Chiang Kai-Shek's villa overlooking the Yangtze, while a long sandy island in the middle of the river provided the airstrip on which both US General Stilwell and British science head Dr Joseph Needham landed, bringing moral and practical support to China as a wartime ally.[75]

Chongqing's explosive growth as a federal territory and the national development zone for the west of China has seen it emerge as a major centre of heavy industry, particularly producing cars, trucks and motor-cycles.Cars and traffic are certainly well catered for in and around the city, with impressive urban freeways, cloverleaf intersections, fly-overs,tunnels and no less than six mighty bridges across the Yangtze in the city area, many of bold contemporary design. And everywhere awash with traffic—all of the vehicle made in China. The cars are all European and American makes built under licence while the trucks are locally designed. One is called the '*Great Wall*'.

Teaching—but learning far more!

In 2004, on my first visit to Chongqing, our team's contribution was modest, offering a three-week refresher course in English for lecturers in technical subjects (invariably simply called 'teachers'). Those hoping to undertake doctoral studies were required to pass a stiff test at national level in written and oral English. We found the campus of the Institute of Technology *(Qi Gong)*, accessed through an arched and policed portal off the main Xing Sheng Lu (Rd), to encompass a little world of its own, hilly and extensive with many internal tree-lined streets whose buildings varied greatly in age, styles and purposes: modern multi-storeyed teaching blocks with white-tiled external walls and towering dormitories for men and women, securely safeguarded (all universities in China are residential, obligatory for all students), a down-at-heel student bathhouse, a health centre with doctor and nurse (which I would later need to patronise, despite lack of a common

---

[75] The history of the period is brilliantly evoked in Simon Winchester's biography of Joseph Needham, *Bomb, Book and Compass*

language), technical workshops and factories, besides a number of dining-halls and kitchens, some for staff (plus the few richer students). It was like a mini-suburb in its own right.

Most charming was the original classroom building, the only example of traditional Chinese architecture on the campus, its green ceramic pan-tiled roof upturned at the corners and overlapping splendid wooden eaves picked out in several colours. In the residential zone of the campus informal stalls sold fruit and vegetables, adjacent to shops selling cakes and buns, stationery and a unisex hairdresser's. Apart from the classrooms, the undoubted focus of student life was a sportsground (innocent of any grass) with soccer field, running track and small grandstand, adjacent to the crowded men's basketball courts where endless practice and impromptu games surged on by day and night, despite the poor lighting.

Later we would learn that, China-wide, in order to graduate, students are required to attain strict standards in physical capabilities and athletic achievements (though we picked up hints and nods about ways of circumventing requirements—a not unusual feature of Chinese life). Of greater significance is the total centralisation, again China-wide, of the curricula for the three levels of education, all of them laid down from Beijing and of course all reflecting the nation's communist ideology. Marxism is a compulsory subject at secondary and tertiary levels, though experienced as boring and poorly taught. On the other hand Chinese universities know nothing of the 'academic freedom' so highly prized in the West. Reflecting this centralised control, all universities are graded five-yearly by inspection teams from the Education Ministry in Beijing. As a result of this occurring during our third visit, the Institute's rating of no. 254th in China was upgraded and it became the Chongqing *University* of Technology, one of 14 universities in the city!

But of course during the initial three-week visit in 2004 our team of mature-age language teachers could learn little of student life or about the Institute's courses and amenities, since it was long-vacation time and the campus was a ghost town. Nevertheless we all felt culturally and linguistically daunted: none of us had any Chinese language or familiarity with the culture. But I couldn't even get my bearings, since we were mostly shepherded about together, without much freedom to encounter the world outside the gates (I think for convenience rather than sinister reasons). Not able to see the sun because of the perpetual haze of pollution, I never did establish the points of the compass, normally my instinctive reaction to a new location. (Scarcely could I even register that we were in the northern hemisphere where the sun, rarely if ever seen, moves across the heavens 'in the wrong direction'—to our southern way of thinking.)

Guests of the Visitors' Centre

We were housed in individual rooms in the Visitors' Centre where subsequently Marjorie and I would also live. It was a securely locked-off and patrolled modern four-storey building of guest rooms, each with bathroom and a tiny kitchen, and fortunately equipped with air-conditioner/heater and wired for computing, plus a communal laundry with rooftop drying lines. Our team dined in the adjacent teachers' and visitors' refectory building, enjoying the excellent cuisine specifically prepared for our party, carefully abstaining from serving the customary horrors of bits of strange animals, including dog and rat. On the first weekend a Communist Party Congress was held on the campus, reflecting the Institute's long-standing identification with the Party. This made us a bit edgy, prone to believe that the walls had ears. We fluctuated between a tense prudence or joking openly about it, sometimes addressing the 'hidden microphones' during our daily devotions and prayer times before sallying forth.

On the other hand on arrival we had been greeted by a long red banner draped across the façade of the language-teaching building proclaiming in English and Chinese that *"the Institute warmly welcomed the overseas English-teaching experts"*. Not that any real arrangements had been made about how we would expertly teach, such that the first day was wasted in exploratory discussions between our leader Jan and the Institute authorities, since we were the first team of 'foreigners' (*read*, Westerners) ever to offer a voluntary program—always a perplexing proposition for the hard-headed Chinese to contemplate: *"What game might the foreigners be up to?"*

Breaking down barriers

Inevitable hiccups aside, I believe we made a useful contribution to the 40 or so teachers who had sacrificed two weeks of their summer vacation to improving their English. Later we found they had paid the Institute a tidy sum for inclusion in our voluntary program! Some of them had acquired extraordinary English names, conferred by past teachers: in the group were a March, April, May and June. Each morning, using an American English-teaching compilation, Jan or other professional ESL teachers would present important aspects of English usage, and the rest of us would practise with small groups of learners, often introducing classroom games and competitions. Sometimes we would humorously mimic proverbial Australian expressions, e.g. *Being up the creek without a paddle.* They were impressively earnest but in time thawed out, trying to 'get' our Australian wavelength. Singing helped the process:

> "Give me a home among the gumtrees
> with lots of plum trees
> a sheep or two, and a kangaroo,
> a clothesline out the back,
> a verandah out the front
> and an old rocking chair".

We also taught them (as a purely literary exercise) a version of St Paul's poem on love from I Corinthians 13 with Chinese melody and English words, which they found powerfully appealing, Chinese society not being on that wave-length but focused instead on a heroic self-sufficiency and a strict reciprocity. And Chongqing being off the beaten tourist track, with no Westerners to be seen on the streets, virtually none of them had any experience of meeting—let alone learning from—native English-speakers, nor encountering any other teaching style than textbook-based monologues delivered to classes of 60+ by teachers whose proficiency in English was sometimes dubious. Even the professor of English was wary of us because of her lack of confidence in oral communication.

Through the afternoons the seven of us would each take our regular group of six or so teachers for conversation practice, without formal prescriptions but randomly discussing issues of interest, often with a humorous approach. Once in my group we progressively built up an impromptu tale of intrigue and heroism, with each participant in turn lending a new direction or twist, and faulty English being corrected by colleagues. This process often brought to light some surprising and amusing East/West intercultural moments—real learning for all parties, while building a permissive atmosphere of learning from each other. For them a new experience but stimulating for us all. In human-relational terms at least, the short course seemed to be a hit.

Encountering the wider community

Sometimes in the afternoons after class the students would take us off-campus to show us around Yangjiaping. One afternoon a small group of us walked to an outlook point over a broad sweep of the Yangtze with its traffic of heavily laden barges, and then climbed down over railway tracks (the main line from Shanghai to Tibet) to visit a small but ancient Taoist temple on the riverbank. No one offered any explanation and I wasn't game to ask. Another day I was taken to an expensive teashop where an ancient Greek warrior in full armour incongruously guarded the door. I was ignorant enough to ask for coffee. Without turning a hair they shelled out the equivalent of ten dollars for a cup—probably worth nearer $15 today! It taught me that, at least in 2004 in remote provincial centres, coffee was virtually unknown among ordinary Chinese. After all, what they drank was traditional China tea: mostly tasteless, weak 'green tea' like warm water.

Our host, the International Office, was also generous in ensuring that our stay was memorable. Some evenings we would be taken out by the Office staff in the minibus: the first occasion for an evening cruise up both the Jialing and Yangtze rivers, marvelling at the brilliant illuminations in the city centre at Yuzhong. One weekend we were driven out of town, through a long tunnel under a mountain range, to a spa where we were issued with rods for fishing in the custom-built ponds, afterwards dining in summerhouses on our catch. Needless to say, I was not among the few who landed a (tasteless) carp. However afterwards, while a few of our team went for a swim, I found myself singing along with our International Office guide, Ronald Sun—my only experience of *karaoke*. That moment of fraternal solidarity would stand us in good stead for subsequent visits.

Another sultry evening we were driven to the spacious marble square before the Great Hall of the People, thronged by thousands of townsfolk of all ages dancing in huge groups to amplified music, ballroom and traditional and modern, with some kind souls inviting us to join in, and breaching every conceivable distinction. The night invariably closed with the *Auld Lang Syne* melody booming out over the square. Rabbie Burrrns would have been nonplussed: in every imaginable dimension the contrast with Scotland could hardly have been starker. But on those sultry nights it amounted to simple and unsophisticated mass entertainment—enjoyment as well as exercise, the wholesomeness of which appealed to me as much as the beauty and grace. I was entranced. People power!

Stifling climate—but warm Christian contacts

On the other hand, putting it mildly, the incessant heat of Chongqing by day and by night proved distressing, soaring from 30° in the early morning to 40°+ through the day. For the two central months of summer this pattern was said to hold without relief, day after day. Certainly during our stay there it was unvarying apart from one dramatic night which produced a spectacular, torrential dump of rain accompanied by truly frightening lightning and thunder. In the small hours I got up to witness the spectacle, to find myself being hugged for protection by a domestic worker girl of about 20, probably from an ethnic minority group, cowering fearfully in my arms. For a moment while time stood still, beyond words and across every conceivable human distinction, we were bonded by awe at the power of heaven.

But by day the heavens were not discernible, wreathed in an opaque cloud of chemical smog which cut off the view at about 100m or less in all directions. Conditions in Chongqing were recognised as bad, thanks to the belt of heavy industry on the outskirts, but by no means the worst case in China.

On our Sundays (for most workers in China also a day off) we sought out a place of Christian worship, gallantly assisted by the International Office with its minibus, for them an exotic mission. After first taking us to a large Catholic church our driver located a central cinema standing in as meeting place for a Three-Self Church (Protestant) congregation, pending legal difficulties being resolved over the use of its newly built office block in the city centre with church facilities in the top storeys. Although we had no common language I was thrilled with the first encounter with Chinese believers, with robed choir, familiar order of service, sharing 'the peace', and known hymn tunes. Afterwards we swapped notes with several good English speakers.

The following Sunday we worshipped with a crowded congregation in a 'real' church building overlooking the Yangtze which evoked a more charismatic rather than 'Presbyterian' style. Being warned by the MSI leadership not to seek out groups from the 'underground church' for fear of incriminating them, we were content to contact these officially sanctioned Three Self Churches (self-governing, self-supporting, self-propagating) tracing links with Protestant missionaries, and always strictly monitored by the government. We heard that both these 'wings' of the Chinese church were growing significantly, though not without official pressures, at times amounting to lengthy imprisonment of some of the underground church leaders.

At the end of three weeks our course closed with a formal award ceremony at which each teacher had to speak on a topic of their choice. These ranged from the workings of an internal-combustion engine (absorbing!) to the unintended environmental threats posed by the (then impending) Three Gorges Dam lower down the Yangtze, mostly given in creditable English. Many testified to their head knowledge of English now giving way to loosened tongues. We were elaborately thanked by the organisers and given many gifts from the teachers, so that we departed both honoured and sung.

Fast train to Beijing

While the rest of the team headed for the airport three of us, Jan, Tineke and I entrained in the modern, comfortable air-conditioned coaches of the Beijing Express, travelling First Class at very economical fares. It turned out to be another Great Train Journey of the World, for most of the afternoon ascending a splendid river valley with superb landscapes of rustic villages, from way above looking down on rural roads and bridges backed by wooded mountains until, nearing the summit of the ranges, plunging into tunnel after tunnel after tunnel. Experiencing then, and throughout our visits, the superlative quality of China's modern infrastructure led to reflection about what our own land could be like if serving the public good could became the driving force of infrastructure spending instead of the tawdry need for an élite minority to make profits out of everything. After all, what monetary profits accrued from building the Roman roads of Britain or the Great Wall of China?

When we awoke next morning after a comfortable night in our seats transformed into beds, we were racing—electric-hauled—across the vast plains of North China, interesting rather than picturesque, with brick farmsteads and down-at-heel villages on every hand, backed by cornfields (no longer rice paddies—too far north) and interspersed with occasional shabby-looking factories. By early afternoon our 24-hour journey (China is about the same size as Australia, though much of its west is also uninhabitable desert) had deposited us right on time in one of Beijing's two railway terminals, a human antheap. Agog at standing in one of the world's most strategic centres, we took the new metro underground to our backpacker accommodation not far from Tiananmen Square and the Forbidden City, triggering that same eerie sensation I experienced standing on Moscow's Red Square at the height of the Cold War in 1963, now updated by memories of the gruesome Tiananmen Square massacre of Chinese student activists a few years earlier in 1989.

Walking the Great Wall

Bent on getting the best out of our three days in the 'Northern Capital' (the literal meaning of *bei jing*), we opted for the priceless ancient and historic attractions rather than the modern city, global metropolis though it be. Primal among these was the Great Wall of China at Mutianyu about two hours' taxi ride through the suburbs. Unlike many a famous site it amply lived up to expectations—and beyond. Running the gauntlet of hawkers and souvenir stalls you climb steeply up to the Wall running along the summit of its ridge. Immediately its grandiose scope and dimensions take your breath away: in its dark grey granite stretching away in both directions, climbing, descending, curving across the rugged terrain, paved on top with lighter coloured stone, sometimes with steps on the remarkably steep slopes that it masters, sometimes with lesser outriders as defensive buffer zones and, a little way off rising out of the wall itself, a sizeable watchtower and troop barracks that we inspected. Of course it reeks of history, some sections of it elsewhere dating back two centuries before the Christian era.

Your imagination takes wings as you envisage hordes of screaming Mongols (descendants of the terrible Genghis Khan who conquered more territory than any man on earth, stretching from north China to Hungary) dying under showers of arrows fired off by the gallant defenders crouching behind the battlements. But in the mid-17th century the Wall would finally be breached by the Manchu invaders, seizing Beijing and establishing the Qing Dynasty's rule over all of China for the next 250 years until deposed by Chiang Kai-Shek's Nationalist forces, themselves defeated by Mao Tse-Tung's Red Army at the end of the 2nd world war. The 'last emperor' would spend his life as a captive of the Party, as Marjorie and I would later learn from a famous Chinese film of that name. But contrary to a common claim, science has established that the Great Wall is *not* visible from outer space!

Majestic Summer Palace

Our next Beijing day, which we fully dedicated to exploring the vast complex of the Summer Palace gardens, was to prove a day of wonder and delight. The Chinese Versailles—both palaces are comparably remote from the capital (some 15km) and were created in the same era for the pleasure of absolute rulers by conferring the grandeur of royal gardens, vistas of natural beauty, elegant water features and monumental buildings. Used as a retreat for the imperial court fleeing the suffocating heat of Beijing's Forbidden City, the Summer Palace was declared a World Heritage site by UNESCO in 1998, as

> "a masterpiece of Chinese landscape garden design. The natural landscape of hills and open water is combined with artificial features such as pavilions, halls, palaces, temples and bridges to form a harmonious ensemble of outstanding aesthetic value."

Entering the extensive domain among a crush of local summer holidaymakers our first goal was Longevity Hill, a long and stiff climb amongst a stunning variety of grand pavilions, palaces and temples which rewarded us with the surprising discovery of an expansive and charming lake beyond. On the highest point rose the Tower of Buddhist Incense crowning the Temple of the Sea of Wisdom. Sweeping naturalistic gardens then ultimately led us down to the lakeshore, lined with willows and mulberry trees, and remarkable for a sculptured twin-decked marble boat, traditional in form and life-sized, and a white marble bridge of 17 arches rising up to the centre and then equally elegantly descending.

Nearby, at one end of the Long Gallery, we jostled with a myriad of plebeian visitors for a local fast-food lunch—in vulgar disregard for the shades of the Dowager Empress for whom it was created in 1750, as an artistically wrought and decorated open wooden colonnade three quarters of a kilometre long, paralleling the lake shore, affording an 'outdoor' stroll even in seasons of rain.

It is hailed as the most perfectly designed classical feature in the entire complex, though such connecting galleries are a feature of the architecture of the period. To cap it off, every beam is richly carved and adorned with brilliantly-coloured paintings, many reflecting the colours and profusion of the surrounding gardens.

'Hush-hush Square' and the Forbidden City

Our final day was spent in the historic zone on and around Tienanmen Square, the huge forecourt to the Forbidden City, and Beijing's major focal point for tourists, especially Chinese, for whom its charming name ('Gate of Heavenly Peace') stands in shocking contrast to the image it conjures up for the rest of the world—would 'Portal of Hell's Fury' be more appropriate? Later Marjorie and I would glean from our tutorial groups in Chongqing that the 1989 massacre of perhaps two thousand students seeking reforms was just starting to seep into public consciousness—as late as 2005. The square is now one of the world's largest, expanded to accommodate massive military parades, flanked by the Great Hall of the People (Congress) on one side and the National Museum of China on the other, both in heavy Soviet-style architecture. But for us it exuded a feeling more of sterility, noting the heavy presence of police and security, though somewhat softened by children flying kites, and knots of Chinese tourists posing for the obligatory photo under Chairman Mao's immense portrait outside the entrance.

But what undoubtedly draws the eye onward is the classically Chinese monumentality of the Gate of Heavenly Peace beyond the square, guarding the entry into the Forbidden City, in its bold red—ever the colour of celebration in China—dating from the mid-17th century. Its high walls protect the broad pagoda-like structure, with its three tiers of roofs featuring the traditional upturned corners.

It is the guardian of the world's greatest and best-preserved walled complex of ancient Chinese buildings, ringed with a wide moat and offering vista after vista of forecourts with successive palaces of emperors whose reclusive dynasties together span 500 years, steeped in abstruse mandarin protocol and stultifying imperial ritual, each palace an architectural gem with its own paved forecourt with ponds, bridges, sculptures, temples (but quite innocent of natural greenery), a remarkable walk-through museum of architecture, but with interiors still inaccessible to the public. 'Forbidden' still holds sway, so that you feel tantalised at being close to, yet still sundered from the inner world of these age-long dynasties. If anything, you get a sense of being a boorish intruder mischievously trespassing where you had no right to be. So the inner world of the 'inscrutable Orientals' remains inaccessible. I found the culture gap simply unbridgeable.

After the tiring day's exploration in the heat, covering many kilometres on foot, in the evening we went to a performance of the Beijing Acrobatic Circus, courtesy of our hostess at the backpackers'. The offering was enthralling for the unimaginable skills on display, drawing on a Chinese tradition dating back for millennia blending athleticism with artistic perfection and demonstrating the harmony of mind and body. The whole day had brought us face to face with the historic depth but also the essential otherness of Chinese civilisation, for me leading to the tentative perception that it presents an alternative model of being human. But the concept of evolution taught in Chinese schools—that as *homo sinensis* they have evolved to a higher level than *homo sapiens*, evidenced by being less hairy—is of course dismissed elsewhere as scientific hocus-pocus.

Brash Westerners

And that's where we bailed out, catching the overnight Shanghai express after a tense dash to the central station in a taxi driven by a diffident woman apparently unfamiliar with the area, who had dropped us off way short of our goal, necessitating our on-the-spot hiring of a guy with a bicycle cart for our luggage. Frantic by then, I fear we left a trail of mayhem behind us, brash Westerners that we were, scything our path to the departure platform through the perennially seething crowds. Once settled into our comfortable sleepers in the classy express as it glided off on its long journey, I heaved a guilty sigh. But I knew I'd be back.

Genesis of a vision

For our two nights in Shanghai we slept in the Visitors' Centre of Tongji University, one of the best in the country, its extensive campus marked by impressive buildings and top-class sporting facilities. It was at next morning's early dawn that the inspiration first took hold of me to put pen to paper on my life's story, all of twelve years ago... and counting!

In the world's most cosmopolitan metropolis

We were hosted by Min, daughter-in-law of my favourite English learners from St Michael's Enlish classes, a married couple Chun Huang and Ya Wang (in China, wives retain their family surnames—always placed first). We were treated to lunch at one of the best-known (and I fear, most expensive) restaurants in the city, China's largest and most cosmopolitan metropolis—claimed to be the world's most populous—and boasting the longest history of Chinese contact with Europeans from many different nations. After our gourmet lunch in the restaurant, uniquely set atop small low bridges zig-zagging at right angles across a broad and cool pond with goldfish and lotuses, we strolled along The Bund, China's celebrated waterfront embankment, its 19th century European buildings skirting the Huangpo River within the delta of the Yangtze, and looking across to the daring skyscrapers of Pudong.

Next day we were driven by minibus out into the countryside through a flat landscape teeming with lakes and rivers to the charming tourist centre of Suzhou, dubbed the 'Venice of the East', to cruise by oriental gondola along its urban canals. Alas! I found the heat so oppressive that I foolishly opted to stay in the air-conditioned vehicle and missed the highlights. Noticeable on our return journey were the numerous churches, in Western architecture, reflecting the area's long exposure to the Faith.

Dining together that evening in a restaurant close to the university I was surprised to hear a student couple at the next table speaking German. Irresistibly drawn, I introduced myself in the same language, to learn that Tongji University had been established in the early 1900s by the German Government and was widely known for its German courses. The student romantics were sharing a farewell dinner before the *chinesisches Fräulein* took off on her scholarship in Vienna.

As *we* took off next morning from Pudong International Airport (now linked to the city by the innovative German 'magnetic-levitation' train) we seemed to be flying over the ocean—until the far side of the mighty Yangtze estuary hove into view.

Big country China, with big rivers, big cities, big crowds—and a big sense of destiny.

35
Old China Hands

Back home, though once more engrossed in our ministry at St Michael's Bennettswood, my imagination was still on the wing. Far over the horizon in China: memories of people and images of places had captured my dreams—waking and sleeping. China's strange power to seep into your heart held me captive. China's very 'otherness' was mesmerising, yet the people we had got to know fully shared the depths of our common humanity. Not merely exotic (in the shallow touristic sense of 'Gee whiz'!), but in its very being, China proffered credible alternatives to our Western ways of being human. *Yin and yang?*

Pondering a return

My reporting back to Marjorie had led us to muse whether together we might somehow be able to make a more significant contribution than my input to a tutorial team under the MSI cachet, visiting for only three short weeks. Unlike the other members of the previous summer's team, we enjoyed the freedom of semi-retirement. Though now over 70, we were still fit, active and (for the most part!) *compus mentis*. At St Michael's I had no formal terms of employment: no issues about weeks of leave available or holiday pay, let alone on being indispensable to the ministry there. Rather than being assigned by the Diocese to the parish I was little more than a longer-term volunteer, more or less a self-employed amateur not dependent on the meagre honorarium. To be sure, Marjorie had been engaged as a remunerated pastoral worker, part-time, but now she too was at the point of retirement. Maybe we could transfer ourselves northwards for a season...

The thought was father to the deed. I leapt into print, writing to Dr Xie Fei, Director of the Chongqing Institute of Technology's International Office, who had been the team's principal host the previous year. But by now, according to the Chinese strictly reciprocal system, he was indebted to us by virtue of Jan Shattock's arranging accommodation for him in Canberra with a (Christian) family for his three-month guest attachment to the ANU. On his way back to Canberra from a visit to Tasmania he had been guest of honour at a dinner convened in Melbourne by our team of the previous year, and in his final gallant words of thanks had assured us that we would all be welcome any time at CQIT.

But my letter had been greeted with a protracted silence. The dream was fading. Then one day came an e-mail indicating that the International Office, rather than arranging for us to become super-numeraries in the English Department, was interested in our tutoring small groups of lecturers seeking to qualify for doctoral studies, plus students majoring in English in their final year. With a serious prospect now in view, we wondered about the Christian auspicing of a China visit. To us at that stage freelancing seemed unthinkable.

We had kept in touch with MSI through regular involvement in a monthly China prayer meeting, attended also by some other members of the former Chongqing team. Now we learnt that formal accreditation needed to be obtained via OMF (Overseas Missionary Fellowship). The standards for their workers, even short-term ones, were formidable, if not heroic. I concluded that frankly, we would not qualify.

A bold initiative

So we went ahead independently, negotiating dates and duration and housing arrangements. Besides a Chinese Visa and a Residence Permit for Foreigners, we would each require a *'Certificate for Foreign Experts Working in the Fields of Culture and Education'* (in the form of an additional passport, in red, embossed in gold) to be issued through the Chinese Consulate in Melbourne on the motion of CQIT's International Office. But these documents cost me a wait of some hours in a queue snaking in from the footpath outside the Consulate's Toorak mansion, while running the gauntlet of the permanent demonstration mounted by Falon Gong supporters outside the gate, handing out materials with impunity but repudiated on the 'Chinese soil' inside.

We planned to arrive in early spring in March 2005, for three months, flying in to Hong Kong and a few days later to Chongqing, and departing before the onset of the midsummer heat that had been so trying the previous year. It would be Marjorie's first overseas travel since our traumatic return from England in December 1963, over 40 years earlier.

Her introduction to the Orient would see her immersed in the maelstrom that is Hong Kong, with its humidity, teeming crowds and commercial frenzy, while she got the beginnings of a feel for China[76] . For a day or two we stayed with Darren Prentice in his poky flat in the downtown area of Hennessy Road, Wanchai on the island, with its antique English double-decker trams, while he showed us around. In 1984–85 he had lived with us in Eltham, and since that time had been having linguistic adventures teaching English in Japan and now in the New Territories of Hong Kong. He encouraged us to plan our departure by taking the hydrofoil at Kowloon, across the harbour on the mainland, speedily threading its way among the shipping littering the wide estuary of the Pearl River, to the huge *nouveau riche* commercial and manufacturing city of Shenzhen, from where we emplaned for Chongqing.

Homecoming?

For me, what joy to be back in Chongqing for the second time in two years, and once again welcomed extravagantly at the airport by Ronald Sun, deputy to Dr Xie Fei in the International Office, an excellent English speaker and a 'really nice man'.

---

76   By 2005 Hong Kong had "adjusted amicably enough to its status as a semi-autonomous region of the People's Republic of China.

On the interminable trip by CQIT mini-bus along the freeway to the city I resolved to make it my business this time to orient myself properly to the confusing lay-out of the metropolis, assembling the various pieces of the urban jigsaw cluttering my mind from the frustrating three weeks of the previous visit.

We were delivered to the CQIT campus at Yangjiaping and shown to our furnished suite on the third (top) floor of the Visitors' Centre. Our Chinese home opened off the balcony running the width of the building and was spartan without being primitive: a good-sized living room and a bedroom, a tiny kitchen with a cool 'induction cooker' (unheard of by us), microwave, fridge and electric jug essential for boiling all water, otherwise undrinkable, plus chinaware and cutlery (no chopsticks!), a small bathroom with shower and cockroaches—and a proper 'sit-down' toilet (we had dreaded the 'two-footprint style')—and access to a laundry on the roof with washing machine and clothes-lines. Perhaps best, it had two air-conditioners/heaters, television, and internet connection. It was cleaned by service staff. And it was free. My proposal to the International Office had been that we came as professionals but volunteers, and would meet our own airfares if the Institute would offer us free accommodation.

From previous MSI leadership we had learned that the concept of volunteering has no antecedent in Chinese history, neither in political nor religious life. Society functions on self-interest and reciprocity, while our faith focuses on One who renounced all for the sake of others, teaching that *"It is more blessed to give than to receive"*.

Early in the piece a meeting was convened for us in the Institute's boardroom with a large group of lecturers interested in improving their English, especially the spoken language, in order to qualify for access to higher study in an English-speaking country. I tabled the list I had drawn up of topics that might be explored in practising English conversation: professions, the modern world, government, the arts, culture, festivals, sports and entertainment, etc. and explained the advantages of small-group dialogue over formal classroom instruction. Some 30 responded by enlisting for the adventure, leaving the International Office to draw up schedules and locations. The English Department also arranged for about the same number of their final-year students to be involved, (separately) in twos or threes. We would be based in the older three-storey classroom building in the heart of the teaching area of campus, the one with the authentic Chinese turned-up roofs and traditionally painted eaves, but austere within with its bare concrete floors and drab *décor*. We would both operate in the largest room, with our groups of threes and fours at opposite ends. Further, the Office appointed a personable senior student, June, as our 'minder' to help us in adjusting to life in China.

'No proselytising!'

But first both of us had to sign a formal agreement not to teach the Bible nor take students to church—its style and appearance betokening a local interdiction rather than a central government edict. Not wanting to fall foul of any authorities, of course we took it seriously, though we judged that it need not exclude our giving frank answers to any questions genuinely raised in the context of our English discussions. And of course Westerners were generally held to be 'Christians'—whatever that was thought to mean. So in practice, while we avoided contriving discussion of religion (ours or theirs) we never shunned any significant ethical, philosophical or religious question that cropped up spontaneously. To us that demonstrated greater integrity.

Two examples. At Easter time I mentioned that around the world the public holiday of Good Friday was being observed, one of the two most significant days in the calendar, when few people worked. "Why is it called '*good*'?" came the question. "We were taught that was when Jesus *died*". And then somewhat later, when a student mentioned it was Grave Sweeping Day, out of genuine interest I asked what that implied. It led to a lively discussion of who still actually believed in the folk tradition, related to appeasing recently dead relatives. One by one the three sophisticated girls admitted, cautiously, sheepishly ... yes, they *did* believe in their parents' observance of the day, despite the Marxist overlay in which they had been schooled all their lives.

Weekly routine

Before long we had swung into our routine: awakened at seven by the rousing marching song ringing out across the campus. Breakfast in our quarters on the cornflakes and toasting bread discovered in the new French department-store *Carrefour* ('Crossroads'—its pronunciation by Chinese mangled as *Jialafor*), which also stocked milk, NZ butter, cheese, and real bread, all at ridiculously low prices. From a departing Westerner we had acquired a toaster (unknown in China). Then before nine it was off to our groups, which mostly continued in 30-minute blocs until lunchtime. At 12:00, back up the hill to 'Grandmother's Kitchen' (bearing the sign in English), occasionally joining other Western teachers or members of our dialogue groups who would kindly enable communication with the staff. In particular we became friendly with a charming little waitress as innocent of English as we were of Mandarin, but she soon learnt our sign-language preferences. A favourite dish was scrambled eggs and tomatoes, presumably an interloper into the Chinese cuisine. Then with the whole Institute, we would enjoy free time until three o'clock when the martial music would stir us once again into action, finishing at five or six o'clock. Here and there through the week we had odd half-hours off. Even so it became a stiff routine for 70-year-olds to maintain cheerfully, given the emotional energy needed to bridge the wide gap of culture as well as age. Later we were surprised to learn that the young Western teachers engaged formally carried less than half of our workload!

But once a week we did have a whole afternoon free and would go exploring, mostly around our district of Yangjiaping, an urban growth centre with a station on the *Qinggui*, the newly inaugurated overhead/underground mass transit system, accessed from the large (though irregularly shaped) 'square' by an open-air all-weather escalator. We also enjoyed exploring the shops, especially the three department-stores (five the following year!) one of which offered a sophisticated cafeteria to which we often repaired.

One-stop shopping

From the day that *Carrefour* opened, with literally hordes of wide-eyed patrons (including us) shuffling shoulder-to-shoulder through its huge floor space, we became devoted shoppers thoroughly conversant with its layout. So large was it that a team of runners on rollerblades were on call to field customers' queries. Not so much a Western department store as a vast supermarket selling everything imaginable: clothing, footwear, home wares, appliances, electronics, cameras, stationery, toys, bicycles, as well as groceries, meat, fish, frozen foods, dairy products, fruit and vegetables—its crowning glory a genuine French *confiserie* (bakery). The prices of everything were derisory: at first you felt guilty ripping off the natives, until you internalised the new price regime—in time to be shocked out of your brain on returning to Oz. Without speaking a word of Mandarin we could provide for all our needs under the one roof. Just slightly different from Hudson Taylor's day...

For money we simply pushed our Mastercard into an automatic teller across the square outside the Bank of China where we opened an account, and out would pour piles of RMB *(renmin bi,* commonly called *yuan)* @ six to the $A1. Outside its marble portico the bank boasted an impressive brass stand embossed with the immortal English legend *'Proper dress refuse come into'.*

Unforgettable moment

It would be on that same square, on our return visit the following year, that Marjorie's greatest China moment would occur. Emerging one evening from a restaurant dinner with our lifelong friends Laurie and Margaret Wigney, French and German teachers whom we had recruited to join in our tutoring program—though new to the Orient—we found the square awash with dancers and alive with music. She couldn't resist lingering, gazing longingly at the circle of elderly couples moving gracefully in ballroom tempo. Then she noticed a little man whispering in his partner's ear. They parted and he floated over towards her smiling, arms outstretched in rhythmical invitation. Unhesitating, beaming with pleasure, as the band played on she took her place as his partner—mute, yet at one with the circling company in the dance of life.

Before long our familiarity zone began expanding well beyond that square and Yangjiaping, as we explored the downtown areas of Chongqing around Jiefang Bei (='*Liberation Monument*') ten stations away via the *Qinggui* and then on foot. By now we had realised that lack of Mandarin did not need to restrict us. Direction signs and street names, underground stations, buses, shops and installations such as food courts of major shopping centres, cinemas, even an ice rink were all accessible through English letters *(pinyin)* as well as the Chinese characters.

Of course virtually no one could really speak English (it was idle ever to address anyone face to face), but foreigners were invariably received hospitably, if only for their potential input to the local economy. But that is to underrate the genuine openness and friendliness of people in community settings, such as the Bank of China staff when I lost my Mastercard—before long it turned up, handed in by a customer!—or even taxi drivers whom I learnt to direct in Mandarin through the tangle of streets back to our quarters in the Institute's extensive grounds: *"Left here, next right, back gate, stop here, thanks. How much?"*.

A particularly favourite haunt became the multi-storey Xinhua bookshop in the city centre with a large English-language section which, besides teaching materials, also sold collections of literary classics such as Thomas Hardy's Wessex novels imported cheaply from the UK. I was able to placate my terrible ignorance of English literature by reading three of them. Actually you could sit in the shop reading all day long without being challenged to buy. It was said that people had educated themselves that way at no cost: the beauty of a semi-public utility concerned as much to develop people as to make profits.

Home life

Back at the flat, from lack of a familiar stove we cooked in the simplest way the foods bought at one of the supermarkets: thankfully now including coffee. But we would also patronise one of the local restaurants offering a menu in English, enabling us to roam more adventurously over the Szechuan cuisine on celebratory occasions—occurring not infrequently.

Hazards of dining out

The most redoubtable dish was *'Chongqing Hotpot'* but only once were we unwittingly lured into trying it by a well-intentioned host bent on blessing us by introducing us to the best-loved local dish *'known all over the world'*. Once was too much: it is cooked in the restaurant by the diners themselves in a pot of soup stock bubbling away on a gas ring let into the centre of the table, into which dubious specialities (thinly sliced meats, seafood, vegetables, tofu, plus unrecognisables) are tossed, and cooked up into a devil's brew of green and red peppers and chili. The title *'hot'* is an irresponsible under-statement: both in temperature (boiling) and also in flavour (to the point where lips, mouth and tongue become instantly numbed at the assault on the tastebuds), so that you dread your host urging you on to ever greater follies, as you blubber away pretending you're not really crying, though your eyes are streaming with tears and your tastebuds are destroyed. The locals seem to have no comprehension that anyone could find it alien to the point of repugnance, so the charade goes on that everyone loves *Chongqing Hotpot,* especially during the damp winters.

Of course dining out is what everyone does in China at the drop of any hat (hence the plethora of eateries everywhere), doubtless reflecting diffidence about revealing how mean and crowded their own quarters are. Many times were we wined and dined by the lecturers, including the International Office, by way of thanking us—the old challenge of coping with volunteers. On such formal occasions I finally tumbled to it that the eldest person has to take his seat first (invariably me) while at the end of the meal we never ceased to marvel at the brutal abruptness of our hosts' collective departure, the moment somehow instinctively sensed by them—but never by us, caught maybe in the midst of a sentence! *Whatever happened—where did they go?*

At home our evenings were enlivened by television, flicking around the seventy or so channels (including several duplicates of other channels) screening varied Chinese fare: historic drama from ancient times, the nerve-grating Chinese opera with howling sopranos, the war with Japan, and the heroic days of the Maoist struggle to set up the People's Republic, the 'Long March', modern love stories, game shows and sports coverage. But our favourites (because of their English subtitles) were the Hong Kong thrillers starring Jackie Chan, that india-rubber comic hero battling for the right. Of course for us the most popular channel was CCTV's English language service, bringing bulletins of world news mornings and evenings from a Chinese perspective, plus documentaries about cultural and tourist topics little known to the West. One news presenter turned out to be the former weatherman from the ABC: so far from home a genial Melbourne face in our living room!

Plumbing the depths of each others' lives

As we got to know our 'customers' our discussion groups were turning out to be absorbing—for all involved. We were sharing our experience of life: our homes, families, friendships, ambitions (invariably termed *'dreams'* by Chinese), hobbies and interests, understanding the history of our two nations and their place in the world, patriotism, imaginable futures. One girl student reported "Marjorie is very loving, and Jim knows a lot". *Touché*. Again, while we never went fishing for political attitudes and loyalties, sometimes these would spontaneously surface, triggering our respect—and discretion. Once mutual trust had been established some younger teachers in particular would at times evince renegade opinions, though there were also a few Party zealots around. A surprisingly frank comment on the socio-political situation in Xinjiang, homeland of the restive Muslim Uighur minority people, was voiced by a former People's Army officer turned lecturer who, on returning from a 40-hour train journey to visit his parents at Moon Festival recalled, *"Whenever I looked into their eyes, they were burning with hatred for me because I am Chinese"*. What a privilege to be given access to their inmost convictions, often expressed the more freely in the foreign language, maybe because of its aura of semi-unreality for Chinese.

Come the beloved August Moon Festival at harvest time, we were taught about the myths and customs still practised—reflecting the moon worship of ancient times—featuring coloured festival lanterns and the universal favourite, the (fairly tasteless) round mooncake made with red-bean paste and duck-egg yolk, gifts bestowed within the family. Parted lovers and family members, gazing upon the same full moon, would feel closer. But today, thanks to industrial pollution and smog in the 100 or more Chinese cities with populations over a million, the moon is scarcely seen at festival time any more than the sun by day! Sadly, my scanning of the night sky from the vantage point of our apartment's roof failed to identify any trace of the celestial absentee. The impenetrable murk had eclipsed thousands of years of romantic association, originally with a religious sanction. Technology triumphant?

From early on we were coming to perceive the rich potential of the *de facto* exchange that we had inaugurated: our language against their experience of the life and culture of China—sinology, of which we offspring of European colonialism were palpably ignorant. And not only of the contemporary scene but of the astonishing four thousand year cavalcade of history that our partners drew on. We heard for instance of the many dynasties of Emperors *(Huangdi)* who presided over this history, as well as offering a dating mechanism utterly unlike our Western division of history into *Before Christ* and *Anno Domini* (in the Year of our Lord)— itself a legitimate point of departure for explaining the Western Christian construct of history.

We soon realised that most of our interlocutors had no concept of our history dating system ('Columbus 1492') but could only speak in terms of the '*12th year of Emperor Tongzhi of the Ching Dynasty*' for example, not appreciating how little that would convey to us. For their part they had small inkling of the several powerful historic cultures of the West and their empires (Hellenistic, Roman, Spanish, Portuguese, French, German, Dutch, British, etc.) nor of their inter-relationships in time or place—let alone their linguistic linkages. I used to claim that historically there was strictly no such language as English but only a rough amalgam of Germanic and Romance languages, the former describing everyday life and the latter coving learned concepts.

Experiential learning

Of course our most significant learning is frequently experiential: For instance I was about to learn of the community health system by getting sick, following an over-rich lunch of roast duck as guests at an upmarket restaurant overlooking the Yangtze. Next morning, retching and crippled with stomach cramps, I was pointed to the Student Clinic on the campus located in an unprepossessing older building and staffed by a tiny team of medical aides and a doctor, none of whom had any English. Fortunately our student helper was on call. First I had to be registered before meeting a lady doctor, who kindly prescribed (and supplied) a foul-tasting medicine and tablets—and a morning off.

I learnt that in China there are no private doctors' practices or clinics, nor virtually any pharmacies, though there are shops selling herbal and 'alternative' medicines. Health is of course socialised: sick people report to the local hospital on foot or are taken there by family or friends—we heard of a group of young men students one night carrying a sick mate overhead to the large and modern-looking Yangjiaping Hospital. We never noticed any ambulances, though presumably some must attend serious road accidents. Hence Chinese hospitals are huge, teeming, multilateral institutions, featuring hard-pressed outpatient departments where swathes of suffering humanity wait for hours in cheerless and spartan settings.

One Saturday morning early in our first visit we were driven in the International Office bus to a hospital across town to undergo the compulsory but rather cursory physical examinations required of all foreign experts. Then late in the piece we participated in a celebratory dinner with a visiting MSI team of Christian medical specialists from Australia, Singapore, and the UK who had been demonstrating new approaches and technologies in a major hospital. Though lone rangers, we sensed a warm solidarity with our fellow-Christian benefactors of China. The country has such a capacity to woo you –winning heart and mind.

Through our discussion groups we were to learn much of recent history, for instance of the experience of our teachers' parents during the turbulent days of the Maoist revolution that spelt the end of the Nationalist government of Chiang Kai-Shek and the founding of the People's Republic of China in 1949. We heard for example of the privations and doggedness of the Communists' Long March, the subsequent upheaval throughout the countryside with makeshift village trials and summary executions of feudal landlords, of the near-starvation suffered by millions in remote provinces, of the Great Leap Forward, the barefoot doctors, backyard steel production, Mao's *Little Red Book* and the Cultural Revolution that saw multitudes of the urban intelligentsia sent to learn the life of the masses by shovelling pig shit in remote communes which afforded them neither appreciation nor respect.

While several of the younger teachers still had peasant parents farming a tiny private plot as well as working on larger farms, they themselves had seized the opportunity of escape through maximising the educational opportunities never before available. So my unusual Australian experience of transcending working class background was quite eclipsed. This had also been reflected at the national level under the widely respected Chairman Deng Xiaoping introducing the capitalist economy *'with a human face'*. And also by our student partners' own struggles to achieve entrance to tertiary study on merit. To our astonishment, we learnt that virtually none of them had opted to study at CQIT but had all been allocated their place there on merit, relative to the 750 nationally ranked universities and tertiary institutes across the nation.

The world's largest tertiary education system

We were intrigued by some unusual aspects of student life made mandatory nationwide for all men and women in tertiary institutions: attaining compulsory standards in physical capabilities and athletic performance (though we picked up hints about winks and nods for circumventing the requirements—said to be a not unusual feature of Chinese life); participation in elementary military training; and a morale-building talent quest in popular entertainment run competitively across the faculties all over China. In the first weeks of the academic year, all freshers (girls as well as boys) did day-long exercises in military skills such as marching, parading and physical training—no weapons, though all clad in military fatigues of greenish khaki. Later in the year some of our student friends invited us to attend finals of the talent quests, mostly featuring would-be pop stars singing Western-reminiscent songs, compèred by a personality guy we both knew, Bowie, who also turned out to be leader of the elective Students' Council and a Party man (accidentally?). Then in the winter semester, mini-Olympics came into their own, full-time for days on end, introduced by competitive marching teams from every faculty, clad in various hues. Sitting near the Institute's executives on tiers of seats we politely watched some finals of events.

Across the Institute's classrooms and practical workshops there was said to be a marked rigidity about the teaching style and the course content, laid down China-wide from Beijing, reflecting the nation's ideology. Marxism is a compulsory subject at secondary and tertiary levels, though experienced as boring and poorly taught. Although one of 'my' teachers lectured on the subject she was coy about it, declining to be drawn into a discussion, but my impression was that she sat lightly to it. On the other hand Chinese universities know nothing of the 'academic freedom' so prized in the West. The emphasis is rather on filling heads with data than developing critical thinking or creativity. When we tried to convey these Western concepts, mostly they fell on deaf ears, as being quite unimaginable in the local environment. Only a few more reflective and philosophic souls expressed wistful regrets.

Reflecting this centralised control, and following the five-yearly review of the Institute by an inspection team from the Education Ministry during our last visit, its rating of no.254th in China was upgraded and it became the Chongqing *University* of Technology, one of 14 universities in that city. On the other hand, because China-wide all tertiary students live on campus, the largest buildings were single-sex high-rise dormitories, though a huge building under construction (on a duckpond!) during our first visit would turn out to be the new library. Nonetheless it seemed clear that for everyone, university life was a rich and memorable experience, creating fraternal bonds (invariably deemed 'classmates') to last a lifetime, judging by the experience of our Chinese peers from the English classes at Bennettswood.

"What do Christians believe?"

One day out of the blue an older lecturer, Ted, asked me what Christians believed. Providentially alone with him that morning since his discussion group mate had failed to show, I felt open to explaining the Gospel, subsequently buying him a bilingual Bible from the new Three-Self Church office block in the city area at Jiefang Bei. Later it occurred to me that it might have been a set-up by the Party machine to catch me out, but if so the continuing warmth of the International Office towards us both could scarcely be feigned. In response we were invited to dinner in his apartment—something virtually unheard of in China. Ted introduced us to his wife and small daughter, and also to his parents-in-law, all bowing deferentially and offering us a great array of Western chocolate bars acquired for the occasion. (Most Chinese actually dislike confectionery!) Around the dinner table we had to depend on Ted's skills as an interpreter and afterwards, producing his new Bible, he asked me to read something to his family. I chose to read Jesus' parable of the Good Samaritan after which he read it aloud in Mandarin and proceeded to preach an impromptu sermonette. He explained he was stressing the significance of Christ's surprising teaching on such a central issue for human community. When we returned the following year he was in Canada on a posting. Since then we have prayed that he might have taken the opportunity to make contact with Chinese Christians.

About that time I also bumped into Jack, a world-weary commerce teacher encountered the previous year with Jan Shattock's team, who had asked me about Christian belief. Likewise I bought him a Bible and one evening in the teachers' dining hall over a dinner for two explained the Gospel.

There was also the occasion when a lecturer, Mary, shared with me her distress that her husband, working in Shanghai, now had a mistress. We often encountered the surprising scenario of a married couple, for reasons of job security, working for many years in cities remote from each other (while professing to be happily married) and getting together once or twice a year at the major holiday seasons.

In the first weeks of our return visit the following year a librarian, April, who also remembered me from the earlier team program, asked us to teach her about the Bible, explaining that she was a Christian but without church connections for political reasons, given the Institute's standing as a bastion of the Party. For the remainder of our three months we had dinner with her once a week before repairing to our quarters to work through simple-English Bible studies that I had devised. Memorably, on one occasion she hailed Marjorie heartily with her skewed translation of the traditional greeting among poor peasants, but which came out as *"Have you been eaten?"*

I reckoned such chance encounters to be providential, and consider I had honoured the agreement we had signed, since I initiated no Christian topic but responded to a genuine question—to have ignored which would have seemed disrespectful. Rather they represented heart-to-heart moments of precious intimacy, spanning the two cultures with universal truths.

Then in the lift one day, noticing a woman teacher wearing a cross, I asked whether there was a Christian group meeting on the campus. Her affirmative word led to my having lunch with the leader she identified but his limited English and also his wariness at getting involved with Christian foreigners led to no further outcome. Recalling the note of warning struck by the MSI leaders before my first trip to China not to mess with underground churches, I renounced any dream of making local contacts.

'Tell me about Christian'

But in a conversation session near the end of our second spell a final-year automotive engineering student, Xing Jie, asked blandly, *"Tell me about Christian"* He explained that on the invitation of some young men recently encountered on the basketball court he had attended a free dinner at a local tourist hotel, where he had heard about Jesus. His hosts turned out to be a group of Chinese-Americans on a mission trip, mingling incognito with the basketballers while witnessing to Christ. At the dinner he had responded to their presentation of the Gospel and had become a Christian. His partner in our conversation also seemed interested. We spent the final couple of our discussion sessions sharing faith insights before our paths diverged: he found a position in Wuhan, a large industrial city further down the Yangtze.

But remarkably, our paths were to cross again two years later, in 2008 in the city of Foshan (='Buddha Mountain') near Guangzhou, to which Xing Jie had later moved from Wuhan, and where we were also staying with a dear couple, Joseph and Lisa whom we had met at St Michael's Bennettswood. At his request I had had the honour of bestowing the (English) biblical name Joseph on him, but despite our tutoring he had not passed the stiff IELTS English language exam in the four requisite skills of listening, speaking, reading and writing, leading to their brusque rejection as skilled migrants. On their sad departure from Melbourne they had blessed us with many valuable items which we use to this day. Back in China Joseph, an engineer, set up a factory in Foshan in the Pearl River delta to manufacture sophisticated electronic spa baths for export. As typical in China, not having guest accommodation (or under the 'shaming' system reluctant to receive Westerners in their lodgings), they had booked us into a good hotel and proved excellent guides, particularly of the famous Taoist temple in the city centre. How we enjoyed the warmth of their Christian fellowship, dear family of Christ.

On Sunday they had taken us, with Xing Jie and a friend of his, another CQIT graduate already a Christian, to a Three-Self Church service which went on interminably, since the visiting preacher was a Mandarin speaker who had to be translated into Cantonese. Jocular though it sounded for everybody else, the sermon said nothing to us in two languages! Afterwards we adjourned to our hotel room where Joseph and the two young men spent further hours exploring and explaining the Christian faith for Xing Jie's benefit. Though again unable to comprehend a word, we were on holy ground. Also for Joseph it proved deeply significant: he told us later that he dreamed of becoming a teacher of the faith.

Alas, that visit was to be our last opportunity to see Joseph and Lisa face to face. In 2008 the Global Financial Crisis on the other side of the world would destroy many of China's booming export markets just as they were sending their first spa-bath products to Holland. Before they could gain a toehold in the European market the demand for luxury goods vanished overnight. Unable to service their loan requirements they were bankrupted, in the world of Chinese business the ultimate shame. They were also mortified to have lost our modest investment in their enterprise, despite our honest dismissal of the issue. To make it worse Lisa, an accountant and tertiary English teacher, found herself stood down in favour of a lesser-qualified person who had unconscionably checked out her salary level and then offered to work for less! And this in the *people's* Republic? But in our *capitalist* economy with more ordered wage rates: unthinkable!

Foreigners' church

But back at CQIT in 2005, for us non-speakers going to church on Sundays meant a taxi ride across Chongqing to the Hilton Hotel (in Mandarin pron. *Hyérr-ton* as I would carefully enunciate.) Mostly the driver would nod affirmatively but occasionally one would look blank, whereupon I would have to point loudly at every large overhead destination sign along the tortuous 20-minute cross-city route bearing both Chinese characters and English *pinyin* letters. Virtually without stopping, we would negotiate several congested roundabouts (no less tangled than on weekdays) where an elaborate game of bluff and counter-bluff was the order of the day—at that time there were few traffic lights in downtown Chongqing—to finally cruise downhill beside the early morning Yangtze emerging from the murk, spanned by a mighty suspension bridge still under construction, and turn off at a rat-run I had learnt which saved a longer way round, sometimes unknown to the driver. Then my *vast* (!) Mandarin vocabulary would come into its own, pronounced as if there were no such thing as tones in the language. Never did we encounter anything like the New York taxi syndrome of robbing you blind with a smile.

A moment of pure grace

In fact we found the local service people amazingly honest: once when I deliberately paid a bonus to a peasant shoeshine woman outside the Institute's gates she handed it back! Apparently a matter of honour, conceivably because she knew we were not vulnerable tourists but honorary locals. But on our next trip I would experience the most touching moment of my whole China exposure, on a whim pushing a sizeable banknote (maybe a couple of days' local pay) into the top pocket of an exhausted labourer sitting under a shade tree, leaning on his bamboo shoulder-pole on the ends of which he had been carrying washing machines into a new department-store—and fast asleep. His mate noticed it and gave me a smile. A couple of days later, as we crossed the square again, I noticed his mate nudging him and discreetly pointing me out. Taking the hint, I went over and clasped his hand for a long moment of grace as we searched each other's eyes without a word. Our cross-cultural smiles were more eloquent!

Arriving at the five-star Hilton on Sundays, to be greeted by the resplendent commissionaire opening the taxi doors and bowing, we would make our way across the marble hall to take the lift to where the foreign Christians met for morning worship. Tea and coffee would be offered by a uniformed attendant, all smiles. The first Sunday we went there I was disgusted that foreign Christians would meet in such an opulent setting (did the 1st century Christians meet in the Governor's palace?) until we heard that it was offered entirely free by arrangement with the manager, accompanied by gratis tea and coffee served on arrival by Hotel staff. The worship was non-denominational in style, led by a charismatic pastor from Adelaide, Leon, a former Uniting Church minister. He was also the headmaster of an international Christian school for expatriate children and some of the other worshippers were on his staff.

The congregation of some 25 'foreigners' represented a good range of backgrounds and roles: American, Canadian and Australian tertiary teachers, Singapore and Malaysian businessmen, some with spouses and children. Soon we got to know everyone and formed warm friendships (one still continuing after eight years) and later we would both be given the privilege of preaching. After the service the whole international company would troop over the road to a somewhat upmarket restaurant for a shared lunch, the pastor playing (non-paying) host, after which some of us would undertake an afternoon activity together.

Battling with the Sunday crowds one day we were taken to the quaint village of Ci Qi Kou *[Ji Chi Ko]*, a tourist trap not far from the city, rising up from the Jialing River by a stepped street full of traditional crafts and workshop displays, crowned by a Buddhist temple. A wisp of memory recalls well-dressed burghers promenading with their pet bird in a small cage. Another Sunday afternoon with an Australian English teacher who spoke some Mandarin, we crossed high above the Yangtze by cable car and inspected an old quarter of the inner city under redevelopment, impressed that two churches had been spared the total razing. We also discovered a momento of the 'concessions' granted in the early 20th century to European powers: the '*French* Naval Barracks' on the bank of the Yangtze opposite the heart of the city, now a hotel and restaurant, but once base for a flotilla of gunboats safeguarding French interests up and down the river, journeying 1,500km from Shanghai through the Three Gorges and also vainly seeking an inland waterway from Shanghai to French Indo-China (now Vietnam, Laos and Cambodia).

Visiting other universities

Another weekend, on the invitation of a Malaysian-Chinese couple who taught English at the Posts & Telecommunications University in the mountains above the city, we enjoyed staying in their university guesthouse, marvelling at the quality and modernity of everything, especially the sporting facilities, making our CQIT look like an academic slum. In that attractive town, across the river from the city, there was also a large, long-established church complex to which they belonged. We were surprised that the university permitted them to use the Bible as a university English-teaching text. This visit brought our first inkling that the Chinese tertiary education system consisted largely of specialised universities as well as the regional multi-faculty ones. Chongqing's 14 tertiary institutions included separate specialised universities for business, modern languages, politics, science, military medical technology, teacher education and later we would visit the University of Oceanography in Qingdao. Some of these universities boasted superb facilities beyond the standards to be found in their Australian counterparts.

Exploring our neighbouring metropolis of Chengdu

During the week-long Moon Festival in our first year we had the opportunity of becoming acquainted with the University of Sichuan (Szechuan in the old notation) the mountainous province surrounding Chongqing. A morning's bus trip along a freeway brought us to the provincial capital Chengdu, a metropolis of eight million—rivalling Chongqing in population—where we stayed for several days in the university guesthouse set among gardens on a spacious campus where several of the students kindly shepherded us about. Though such facilities seem to be normative in Chinese universities for accommodating visiting scholars, we were privileged to be ruled as eligible. During our China safaris we could therefore stay in several such guesthouses, in comfortable settings and at moderate rates, courtesy of our 'expert' status. Of course our accommodation at CQIT was also in such a facility, the poor relation of those elsewhere.

Our host for the Chengdu visit was a lady from 'Youth with a Mission' in Canberra running an English course for tourist industry workers as a Christian initiative. On Sunday we joined with the fellowship for foreigners meeting in her quarters. The city population includes ethnic Tibetans, not expatriates but reflecting the wider distribution of Tibetan people and culture across much of south-western China. We were taken to a street of traditional crafts where we saw a demonstration of silk-making, one of China's many creative gifts to the world. Exploring the city area on foot, we were struck by the anachronism of a huge statue of Chairman Mao, arm upraised in blessing under which we were requested, as a couple of foreigners, to pose with a little girl for an exotic photograph. Such statues, once universal in China, have dwindled sharply in recent years.

Nearby in the People's Park, a large monument turned out to be honouring the martyrs of the 'Railway Rights Movement' massacred in 1911 for going on strike against the Qing dynasty's sell-out policy to Western commercial interests, which was to trigger the revolution leading to the inauguration of the Republic of China under American-educated Dr Sun Yat Sen. We were attracted by an elderly group of music-makers hugely enjoying playing their instruments, not as buskers, but with great naturalness and for sheer pleasure—perhaps a lost art in our ever so 'sophisticated' society.

It reminded us of the admirable example set everywhere by elderly Chinese gathering morning by morning for informal physical exercises in public places, often to taped music. Spontaneous citizens' initiatives in lieu of the programmed commercial attractions of the West. But the most memorable feature of our week was a visit to the Panda Research Centre on the city's outskirts, where animals are bred in captivity against the day when they may go extinct in the wild. Several of the delightful but shy and somnolent creatures were on display at close quarters, unlike their relations at Yangjiaping Zoo in Chongqing, who rudely slept through our visit.

Official acts of grace

As the weeks melted into months we felt more and more identified with our own *alma mater* and appreciative of the respect accorded us by the International Office. One day we were called in and each presented with a pile of banknotes as high as a bowl of rice, with the explanation that they had decided to reimburse our travel costs. Our embarrassment was compounded by being asked to count them aloud, to our and their satisfaction. It looked like the counting house of King Midas. But during a visit to Foshan a few weeks later we had insisted, practically at gun point, on handing them over to Joseph and Lisa as an investment in their new manufacturing venture which lacked capital. It could achieve so much more in China than any use for it in Australia. We had never expected to see it again. And of course it had been an act of pure grace on the part of the International Office enabling us to bless dear Chinese Christian friends. But how mortifying for them to lose it through no fault of their own.

In addition to our tutoring program, and in response to wider invitations to address specific groups, we presented illustrated lectures on Australia, of which little was known but keen interest manifest. I also screened a large number of photos taken a few weeks earlier in Germany and France. Marjorie gave an address on her profession to the students of a newly launched Social Work course. From time to time we would put in an appearance at *'English Corner'*, a feature of all Chinese universities, affording relaxed opportunities on warm evenings for private conversations in the open air, preferably with native speakers. We had teamed up with a number of these, mainly Americans on the regular staff of the English Department, sharing irreverent restaurant dinners with them, swapping amusing stories of life in China and ribbing each other about our national foibles.

For us the crowning privilege was to be invited to address a meeting of emeritus professors of the University of Chongqing, the city's foremost academy, on *'Retirement Life in Australia'*. It was arranged by a former Professor of Russian whom we had met in Melbourne while visiting his daughter then doing post-graduate medical work, a dear and kindly man. Partly in English and partly in translation, the ensuing discussion session among the 20 or so retired men and one or two women proved the liveliest and best-informed encounter of our Chinese experience, continued later in the professor's family apartment in a gated high-rise community in nearby Shaping Ba, Chongqing's most up-market suburb a long bus ride from poor old Yangjiaping. But their naughty little spoilt granddaughter epitomised what we had often heard about the *'little emperors'* in wealthy families, whose doting hopes focus on the one and only child—naturally unable to cope with such adulation.

Actually what was notably missing from our memory of Chinese streetscapes was *where were the children*:—the future of this nation of well over a billion? The single image of schoolchildren that I retain was of a tight little playground of a modern primary school glimpsed far below from the 12th floor of our tutoring tower. Of course in the great cities the 'little emperors' were too precious to be allowed to roam outside in streets pulsating with traffic, motorised and human. Besides, beyond school hours, children from educated families were doubtless coping with the extra study and paid tutors arranged by doting grandparents. The pattern is familiar enough here in Melbourne, where many older Chinese children seem strangers to leisure (let alone the opportunity to generally 'muck around' like Anglo kids—albeit today with gadgetry), but rather endure protracted coaching or music learning after school and at weekends. On the other hand, check the incidence of Chinese names in the lists of top performers at the VCE. Their contribution to the Australian future may well influence our national identity.

Stunning tempo of development

During our first stint at CQIT in 2005 we had learned of plans for its relocation to the southern outskirts of the city. On my expressing interest in the project the International Office took a few foreign teachers to visit the site, which involved a tedious half-hour journey through bleak outer areas, then through a tunnel and across a mighty bridge over the Yangtze. The site was unimpressive. Everywhere hills were being bulldozed to create flatter terrain, on which foundations for new buildings were already emerging from the mudheaps. It would become study base and home to 12,000 students from all parts of China, taught by a faculty of 1500 professors and academics.

Amazingly, on our return visit barely twelve months later, we were able to participate in 'English Corner' on a courtyard of a newly established campus, welcomed by our students from the previous year now living in multi-storey dormitories set in landscaped gardens! In today's China not only do major new buildings seem to mushroom overnight, thanks to a massed workforce under intensive management, but mature trees get transplanted in the form of tall trunks shorn of all branches, their roots bagged within a cubic metre of soil. At first sight I scoffed at such folly, surely offering no hope of regeneration. But eighteen months later we were driven through avenues lined by mature deciduous trees, resplendent in their springtime garb, having not only taken root but grown—both taller and bushier! In Australia utterly unthinkable, yet typical of the fertility of the three great valleys of the Yellow, Pearl and Yangtze Rivers, cradles of a civilisation four thousand years old. Was it the very fertility of these valleys that had laid the foundation for China's status as the world's most populous nation?

Our second stint climaxed in an award ceremony where again the lecturers had to make a public presentation by way of demonstrating their newly acquired fluency. The most memorable contribution, from a beautiful and clever lady engineer, opened with the remark *"When I began this course, though I had been learning*

English for many years, I was dumb, I could not speak". The brilliant presentation that followed admirably evidenced her transformation.

Our modest contribution towards educational development

In our closing weeks I had put on paper an outline of our approach and methodology for the International Office's use. Subsequently we heard that it had been written up by CQIT's Professor of English in an article published in a Chinese journal of English studies, demonstrating the advantages of using native speakers in leading small discussion groups in tertiary institutions, rather than as formal teachers before classes of 75. I would like to think we had made some modest contribution to that vital area for China's future: of enhancing English proficiency in the use of the diplomatic world's *lingua franca*.

Less serious were my two outrageous contentions canvassed (tongue firmly in cheek) in the discussion groups for bridging the yawning cultural chasm between East and West: firstly, replace the multitudinous Chinese characters (which have to be laboriously mastered one by one, each serving as a separate word) by an alphabet as used in the rest of the modern world, using *pinyin* as a springboard—as flawed as it appears to be. Revolutionary notion!

But even more outrageous: liberate the numberless army of kitchen workers from the lifelong bondage of cutting all food into bite-size chunks to pick up on chopsticks, thus recruiting the teeth as workers, while blessing the cutlery industry supplying *knives and forks*, again like the rest of the world. But in the Middle Kingdom[77]—centre of the world—unthinkable.*"Let them eat cake"*—on chopsticks! Sadly, as far as I've heard, no changes have eventuated.

---

77   The name of China today (*Zhong Guo= Middle Kingdom*) dates back to 6th century BC. The word 'China' is believed to have originated from the name of the Qin Dynasty (*pron. Chin*) in the 3rd century BC, while 'Cathay' (*Kitai*) dates from the time after Marco Polo's adventures, but originally designated the land of the Mongols, a northern people who later conquered the whole country. The Yangtze River marked the border between 'Chin' and 'Cathay'.

36
Two Sinophiles on the Loose

Sometimes our intensive weeks of term-time tutoring would be offset by weekend excursions to local beauty spots in the mountains around Chongqing. Come cherry blossom time in spring we were urged to visit an extensive formal parkland in the hills above the city, on a pristine Saturday morning jostling with crowds of thousands marvelling at the fleeting splendour of the blossoms. In a daze of beauty on every hand we were still learning the public role of foreigners: people would openly point us out to their children as exotic oddities from another planet[78], sometimes mutely bidding us to stand by them for a photo. At first I never knew whether to feel honoured or embarrassed—or even resentful: Exhibit A! Then over lunch sitting on a low garden wall, a dear elderly couple kindly offered us a choice delicacy from their own lunchbox, a petrified-looking chook's foot! Graciously I acknowledged the gift, affecting to nibble it with relish until the opportunity arose of slipping it discreetly in among the broad-leaved foliage. Afterwards, waiting in queues hundreds of metres long for a bus ride back to town, we were kindly ushered to the front as foreigners, though I had to stand all the way downhill, watching in unbelief as the driver deliberately and repeatedly chose to cut blind corners on the wrong side of the busy but narrow mountain road—a protracted suicide bid with a busload of innocents!

Out and about in Sichuan

Beyond our own initiatives in exploration, we were beneficiaries of a number of free excursions for foreign teachers organised by the International Office, reflecting their commitment to international understanding, sometimes from a Party perspective such as the visit to Guang An in Sichuan Province, Deng Xiaoping's home town. The town has become a showpiece of contemporary China, with clean, generously laid-out streetscapes, impressive schools and parks, and the Deng family home nearby now a museum and virtually a shrine. Truly he seems to have been a heroic—if diminutive—figure, twice purged but making a comeback and widely esteemed among the people. The only blot on his copybook was the order he allegedly issued to People's Liberation Army units brought in from remote areas to shoot the student protesters on Tienanmen Square. But knowledge of this has been widely withheld from the public.

Once while Sarah was teaching English in South Korea she visited us during an Easter break and together we undertook a day trip to the UNESCO World Heritage site of Dazu to see the remarkable three-dimensional Buddhist rock sculptures dating from 650AD under the Tang Dynasty. Descending into a rocky

---

78   Early reports from Chinese adventurers (like Marco Polo in reverse) evoked disbelief on claiming to have encountered foreigners with orange hair and green eyes!

ravine featuring large open caves we were confronted by a massive sleeping Buddha carved into the rock wall, reclining on one side and flanked by quite horrendous warnings of the torments of hell in the form of three-dimensional stone demons flagellating guilty sinners—utterly alien to the Buddhism projected by Western devotees which declines to be named as a religion (merely a philosophy), let alone proclaiming a concept of Judgment Day. When we raised this with our English-speaking guide he eschewed any knowledge of traditional Chinese religions, explaining that he was a Christian!

On the way back to Chongqing we fell foul of the cheap commercial trick whereby the tourist bus turns aside without warning to provide a captive audience for a spruiker of traditional medicine, decked out in white doctor's coat, interminably extolling (including to non-Mandarin speakers) the virtues of herbal products. On principle we declined even the medicinal baths freely on offer.

Museums, exhibitions, galleries

But a source of delight became the dozen or so museums gracing Chongqing city with their splendid collections of historical and cultural artefacts. Over the six months of our two voluntary stints at CQIT we did justice to most of them—treasure troves for opening up for us the richness of China's heritage. Mostly they provided a brief English summary of the exhibits, except in the Calligraphy Museum where we had to apply our own primitive taste to assessing the various merits of the widely divergent styles of characters.

But judging from its strategic location across the main city square from the Great Hall of the People, the top attraction was Chongqing Museum (*aka* Three Gorges Museum) whose spectacular interior immediately caught our imagination—not to speak of the exhibitions, especially the circular 3D cinema literally taking you on a boat trip down the Three Gorges prior to the controversial project, then under early construction, of damming the mighty Yangtze where it breaks through the mountains in three narrow rocky canyons far down-river from the city. You looked above to the ships' bridge behind you where you wanted to respond to the captain's cheery wave before gazing back at the ship's wake and then to the sides where the towering rock walls edged ever closer.

Other exhibits featured priceless cultural relics: documents, paintings, sculptures, porcelains and coins from the ancient dynasties and earlier, even from the Kingdom of Ba centred on Chongqing about 1,000 BC, reflecting the evolution of the history, culture and life styles of Sichuan from ancient times to the modern day, well matched by displays of the folk arts of the ethnic minorities of south-west China in their brilliantly-coloured traditional dress. Particularly graphic was the photographic record of the ordeals suffered by the people of the city under the heavy bombing during the War against Japan (1937-1945), when Chongqing was China's provisional capital.

This crucial period of 20th century Chinese history, with the crumbling Nationalist Government under intense pressure, not only from the Japanese invaders but also from the gathering force of socialist workers in rural areas under the leadership of Mao Tse-Tung, is evoked in a historical cross-cultural museum that we visited near the city centre in memory of the 2nd world war American General Joseph Stilwell. It is a magnet for streams of Westerners, especially young American tourists. In 1942 Stilwell was sent to Chungking *(sic)* as a Chinese-speaking military diplomat to effect liaison with Generalissimo Chiang Kai-Shek and his forces, poorly trained and supplied, and low in morale. He became chief of American forces in China and Burma, his headquarters in that building, and forged a solid friendship with the Chinese people—though less with Chiang Kai-Shek. In 1944, after setbacks in Burma he built the Burma Road between India and China and organised a massive airlift *'over the hump'* (the Himalayas) to bring in military supplies through China's back door. Post-war Chinese historians have viewed him as a hero for his principled and dogged opposition to Chiang, which was to favour Mao's rise to power. In the residence we saw his uniform and manuscripts and many personal items, and in the garden a monument featuring his bust and an epigraph in President Roosevelt's handwriting.

On the outskirts of the city at the foot of a mountain, Gele Shan, we were taken to the Revolutionary Martyrs' Cemetery and museum where, on the day before the Nationalist leadership fled from Chongqing in 1949 some 300 Communist prisoners were massacred by Chiang Kai-Shek's retreating forces. What implacable hatred and unspeakable vindictiveness, evoking the Nazis four years earlier hanging Pastor Dietrich Bonhoeffer three weeks before the war ended.

More gratifying to my passion for geography was the afternoon we spent with two women students in the Chongqing City Planning Exhibition, dramatically located under the great square of Chaotianmen, on the tip of the confluence between the Yangtze and Jialing rivers, where tourists embark for the Three Gorges boat trip. Quite mind-blowing was the gallery's centrepiece: a scale model no less than 30m square of the future Chongqing city area, viewed from a gallery around it, presented in total and painstaking detail. At last the chance to grasp the inter-relationships between the chaotically located quarters of the city, constrained by two winding river valleys separated by intervening hills and all framed by ranges of mountains.

There were also displays of developmental plans for many towns within the extensive and mountainous Chongqing 'Municipality', in 1997 excised from Sichuan province, measuring all of 500km by 100km. It is one of five metropolises in China administered directly by the central government (cf. Canberra), the others being Beijing, Shanghai, Guangzhou and Tianjin, a vital factor in affording access to major financial resources for development. The contrast with Australia's pusillanimous commitment to building infrastructure is quite shocking until you factor in the capacity of 1300 million to pay, compared to our 23 million. Still, with the profit motive minimised, the Chinese government's commitment to national development remains inspiring. Around you on the gallery level were ingenious exhibits recounting Chongqing's story: there is evidence of human habitation dating back more than 100,000 years in the Yangtze and Yellow river valleys, and other exhibitions looking ahead to future transportation projects and the completion of the Three Gorges scheme.

Our visit to the Planning Exhibition also brought the opportunity to grasp Chongqing's role in national development, especially though the graphic presentations, often in 3D. Over the centuries its location on the two large rivers had fostered its emergence as a major trading centre and later treaty port, so that today the city is the economic hub of western China. Its diversified economy flags major industries in food processing, car making, chemicals, textiles, machinery and electronics. It also produces most of the motor cycles in China. Once we encountered an *Australian* businessman in the Pizza Hut in Yangjiaping (much more upmarket in China) who regularly travelled over there to buy motor-cycles for his Perth dealership.

Not surprisingly Chongqing is the world's largest municipality, with 31 million people (well over the population of Australia), 10+ million of them in the urban zone. In the next decade or so, given that every year eight million peasants are forsaking the Chinese countryside for the major cities, the urban population is expected to double to twenty million.

But as we found to our discomfort the climate is off-putting: top winter temperatures averaging 6°C, and summers invariably hot and humid with temperatures averaging 33°C over many weeks, while cool changes are unknown. For the three weeks of the team visit with Jan Shattock the daytime temperatures were almost constantly 40°. Most of the rain falls during summer, and foggy conditions are the norm. The city is nicknamed the 'Fog Capital' of China, but during our visits the daily murk was more attributable to industrial pollution than good clean fog. During our first three-months' stay in springtime we saw the sun/moon on one occasion! On some days from our twelfth-floor teaching rooms in the new Library building we could barely see the ground! And the Moon Festival proved a fiasco. Small wonder that our Wigney colleagues, used to European teaching conditions, could scarcely cope with the unrelievedly depressing environment, although by our second three-months' stay we had noticed considerable improvement resulting from some of the heavy industrial plants being banished to the city outskirts.

Multicultural China

Our final *'Eureka!'* came the day we discovered the Ethnographic Museum, scarce publicised but actually of absorbing interest, brilliantly displaying its historical and anthropological riches—Chongqing's most priceless three-thousand year treasure: its people! Originally from a local minority race they were replaced centuries ago by population drafts of Han Chinese, the overwhelming national majority then fleeing invasion from the Mongols further north. The museum brilliantly canvasses the classical challenge to community educators of believing in—and proclaiming—

the benefits of a multicultural society comprising more than one heritage, but with all equally honoured and sung.

If China still has some way to go in ensuring equal life opportunities for its 55 ethnic minorities (8% of its population), Australia's record *vis-à-vis* our Aboriginal peoples pales into horrible insignificance. For example in Beijing there is a University of the Nationalities for minority peoples, guaranteeing that they are not discriminated against because of their restricted capacity for competing with the mainstream. This is not to set the bar to tertiary study lower but to encourage participation in a specialised form for customarily excluded competitors. Taking due account of the immense cultural differences between the tribal minorities of China and the indigenous people of Australia, nevertheless I felt on familiar territory. Probably the unifying factor among all such peoples is their daily experience of prejudicial treatment at the hands of the 'self-legitimating' mainstream.

Indeed, the day I write this in 2014 there has been a random mass slaughter at Kunming Railway Station inflicted by Uighur separatists from far-western Xinjiang at the opposite end of the country, Muslims demanding recognition through independence. But doubtless the one feature starkly distinguishing them from the country's other 54 ethnic minorities (and certainly from the Buddhist Tibetans) is their commitment to violent *jihad*.

Xinjiang and the 'semi-autonomous territory of Tibet' *(Xizang)* in the south-west of the country, are the only administrative areas of China where the Han majority is not predominant. Elsewhere the minorities are minor indeed. But in 2006 Tibet—fabled though largely inaccessible land in the clouds—at over 4,000m the highest territory on earth, had been linked essentially for strategic reasons to the rest of the country by an amazing railway 2,000km in length, in parts rising to an elevation of over 5,000m (16,600ft), the highest railway on earth, 500km of it laid across the permafrost. The train (without any doubt the World's *Greatest Rail Journey*) actually passes through Chongqing twice a week—even through Yangjiaping!

To Tibet by train?

Agog at the prospect of our visiting Tibet by train I scoured the internet. Everything was there and the costs were within our budget. It would have to prove the crowning adventure of my life to cross the cold, high outback of China, savour the tragic drama of the Buddhist Tibetans oppressed in their sacred city of Lhasa *and* travel on such a train—knocking our 'Ghan' into a faded cocked hat! Ere long the plan had fallen into place: on finishing our second stint at CQIT we would go home via Lhasa. I took our plan to the International Office, who would obtain the tickets and make the necessary reservations. They greeted it coolly … but hold on: weren't we their favourite foreigners! Sensing it was a political issue I pushed them harder: I wondered what game they were playing. It turned out that a little earlier a Chinese man of our age had died on the train of a heart attack induced by protracted exposure to the altitude, although the train cabins were pressurised like an aircraft's. Subsequently the authorities had ruled people over 70 ineligible to travel. We were both 74.

Excursion to paradise

We countered by raising the possibility of a visit to Jiuzhaigo [pron. *jewj-I-go*], described by someone at the international church as ravishing: a recently discovered 'valley of nine [Tibetan] villages' (as the name means). They lie nestled among the pristine Minshan mountains rearing beyond the northern edge of the Tibetan plateau in the northernmost region of Sichuan. Until 1975 quite unknown and inaccessible, it was becoming a sensational tourist mecca, now also for Westerners. From Chongqing we could fly 300km north to the regional town of Huanglong (=*Yellow Dragon*) and then travel by bus to the area only a few years earlier declared a UNESCO world heritage site. We would be part of a Chinese group undertaking a conducted tour.

Soon after being farewelled from CQIT by our benefactors we took to the air but well into the flight, as the jetliner went into its descent pattern, I fell to wondering anxiously how we could possibly land in a terrain of forbidding peaks and wooded valleys stretching unbroken to the horizon. No need to worry: this is China, land of stunning infrastructure. Until the very moment when the plane had the runway safely beneath its wheels we were always over impossible terrain. But on disembarking it became clear: two mountain peaks had simply been sliced off to fill the intervening valley and produce the only flat land within the four horizons!

From the airport the bus wound *downhill* to the town, pausing at the top of a ridge where two yaks were tethered as a photo opportunity (charming, if contrived). On entering the airport terminal at over 11,000ft we had been confronted by an ominous notice: "*Buy oxygen canister now*". Thankfully we complied: the last thing a one-time asthmatic needs is air too thin to breathe.

Immediately it was the surrounding architecture that intrigued me. I couldn't quite place it: certainly non-Chinese, but of course we had never been in Tibet. Indeed the whole area was populated by Tibetans, round and rosy of cheek but black of hair, and all wearing vivid traditional dress. The wooden buildings struck me as equally exotic, as much for their architectural forms as for their bold colour scheme of scarlet and deep blue.

An hour in the coach brought us to Huanglong Valley, where a series of small lakes quite took our breath away for utter beauty: gleaming lustrously in the afternoon sun in a variety of unbelievable colours—from light blue, to turquoise, to dark green—ever contrasting with the stark white of limestone ledges and formations, some of them steaming with hot springs, and on every hand the shorelines clad with the early-autumn tints of foliage trees and azalea blossoms native to the area. Could heaven be more ravishing?

Tibetan glory

Good question, more tantalising as our party set about a longish foot-slog up the river valley, criss-crossing the noisily cascading stream as we gained altitude. Finally Marjorie began to feel uneasy—first sign of altitude sickness—despite swigging away at the oxygen canister. She located a seat. Still feeling young, eager and energetic I valiantly pressed on, observing that practically all the Chinese in our party had now fallen by the wayside—perhaps merely a comment on motivation. But had I made the journey from Australia to turn back before attaining the goal? Even if it did require ever more outlay of energy and resolution—and also more frequent pauses (to admire the texture of the forest, of course) the higher we climbed.

Meanwhile signs along the way in Mandarin and English mathematically monitored our ascent. In non-communicative company with a few young bucks, the oxygen and I slogged on to a point (if not quite at the head of the trail then certainly not much lower), from where a majestic prospect opened out in the middle-distance: sun-flecked virgin forests on either bank.

The tumbling cascade in the foreground now assumed the principal role while the backdrop slid into place—the dramatic vista of a jagged-toothed snowfield at the summit of the Minshan Range against the border of the Gansu Province. As I stood there panting, it recalled Switzerland rather than any hitherto held concept of China. Committing it to my camera, I resorted to the life-saving canister once again before managing to tear myself away from that sublime view. But this was merely the beginning of our trip, with Jiuzhaigo proper still to come!

The next two days were to bring sequences of scenic glories unimaginably eclipsing one another. That first afternoon, from Huanglong our coach wound its way for two hours along a new but deserted road (this is China?) through undulating emerald pastures and across richly timbered slopes. Later it would come as no surprise to learn that one third of China is uninhabited—even uninhabitable, like so much of Australia. Finally with the sun's slanting rays lighting up a pristine river valley in their late-afternon glory, we passed through a decorative portal to enter a model new-town environment barely twenty years old. Jiuzhaigo! Ripples of excitement quivered around the coach.

But strictly it is not a town, since the normal range of urban features (shops, banks, workers' housing, street sellers, beggars—above all, people) were hardly in evidence. The accommodation buildings lining the single street were all new and in varying degrees monumental. The traffic was almost exclusively tourist coaches, and the people on the streets trippers, overwhelmingly Chinese.

We were deposited in a middle-ranking hotel staffed by Tibetans in ethnic garb, barely any of them familiar with another language. Then after dinner it was off to a nearby theatre where booked seats awaited us, for an overlong program (for us outsiders) of brilliantly garbed singers and dancers (the gorgeous women twirling hugely long sleeves), clowns and acrobats, all accompanied by traditional music played by the orchestra, and all captured on a DVD presented to us later.

Whether the long day's travel or the altitude—or excitement at being the only Westerners in the party—or maybe the sheer exoticism of the spectacle, but ninety minutes sufficed before we were nodding off and finally sneaked out shamefaced to our quarters for a comfortable night's sleep, in profound silence at an altitude above Australia's highest peak, though once or twice I had recourse to the oxygen cylinder lying between our pillows.

Astir early next morning and officially checked out through the monumental gate, our coach headed up the Valley of the Nine Villages rising from 6,000ft to 14,000ft, laced with three rivers (including the headwaters of Chongqing's Jialing) tracing out the path of an ancient glacier with its legacy of enchanting lakes. Sitting near us we discovered a couple, the wife a medico, who could actually speak some English, having recently visited their daughter in Hobart, and who providentially 'adopted' us to explain the gist of the guide's commentary.

Minshan Range

But truly, as we made for the snow-covered peaks on the horizon the valley's glory spoke for itself. Bypassing the nine Tibetan villages (off the new road) we would halt from time to time, now to take in a memorable landscape, now to walk down to a lakeshore and follow paths or boardwalks affording splendid views of a lake in its total harmony of setting. Again the varying colours were magical but no two lakes were the same, not in size nor character nor feel.

Some were linked by teeming white cascades, or sundered by deep and rocky waterfalls—mini-Niagaras roaring away in the uncharted forests. Others were of great and dreamy depths, with sandy bottoms sharply visible, ribbed with ancient fallen tree trunks. Others again, tightly hugged by deep forest glades in autumn shades and set over against the pale blue of a cloudless sky, produced such idyllic reflections as to defy which image was the original. In the presence of such grandeur we were at times overcome with awe: small wonder that the original Tibetan tribes held it all to be holy, the dwelling place of gods and goddesses. Silently we exulted *"Let the mountains sing together for joy! Sing before the Lord"*[79].

Resort of pandas

After lunch in a showplace of contemporary *décor*, but crowded and noisy with coachloads of visitors, we pressed ever higher up the lake-studded valley to a point where we forsook lake for forest—our ever-present companion. Now a boardwalk wound among giant primeval trees of multiple *genera* forming a dense cloud-forest, habitat of the iconic giant panda and the snub-nosed golden monkey—both of them threatened species (but significant absentees that day). The area had recently been declared a UNESCO 'Man and Biosphere' preservation zone because of its wealth of precious but dwindling species of plant and animal life.

In a Tibetan village

The return drive to our base now took on a new character, assuming an anthropological rather than topographical perspective. We were in the heart of Tibetan territory, among mountain tribes for centuries holding aloof from the Chinese state, proud and self-sufficient. But in the past decades 'development' had overtaken them, co-opting them into the national economy as workers in the new tourist industry. There was said to be a population of 1000 Tibetans in the valley, living now in only six of the nine villages—and others away from home in the new 'urban' centre. Maybe the people's souls feed on the beauty and richness of their virgin wilderness as their 'mother'?

We turned off into two or three of the colourfully timbered villages picturesquely located and charming in their aspect, greeted by brilliantly-coloured flags and pennants flapping in the breeze whose function was, like the water-wheel steadily turning at the village portal, to generate continual prayer. As we fanned out along the main village laneway where local craftwork in wood and metal and cloth was on offer everywhere, I escaped into a shop a step or two below the street level, to find myself in a tiny Buddhist house of prayer, though deserted and affording the opportunity to examine the religious features with interest. Clearly the remote people had long lived in touch with their religious sensibility and in sustainable harmony with their pristine environment. I wondered how much longer such harmony could be sustained in the continual presence of rank yet rich outsiders with the power to put a price on everything—while maybe appreciating the value of nothing.

The point was borne out next day on our return journey to Huanglong airport

---

79 Psalm 98:8

when, without warning, the coach drew into a commercial establishment in vulgar contrast to its rural Tibetan setting, to usher us into an inescapable lecture by a *Chinese* guy in a white coat on the value of alternative medicines for maintaining health. When we finally escaped I asked our friendly doctor-interpreter what value did she attach to the claims. *"Absolute rubbish"* came her frank reply.

Our flight back to Chongqing through azure skies offered an aerial geography lesson on human settlements in river valleys and the function of roads and railways, as we followed the Jialing River valley southwards. From above, even in its dense urbanisation, China (if the atmosphere is clear!) offers a prospect that pleases. I longed to see more and more.

Double Aussie team at CQIT

We didn't delay: the following year 2006 was to see us again on the wing, having been assured by CQIT's International Office that we were more than welcome to repeat our small-group tutoring program. The internet booking I made for two days in Kowloon, on the mainland beyond Hong Kong harbour, turned out to be in a downmarket lodging of scant repute, where the bedroom consisted of a double bed literally covering the entire floor area, while the 'bathroom' shower fell directly into the toilet bowl as you perilously straddled it.

Our guardian angel was Samantha, a girl from St Michael's who insisted on accompanying us as though *ingénues* (although actually it was my fourth visit to Hong Kong), while taking the opportunity to visit her family. Then together we took a fast train to Guangzhou (the former Canton), third metropolis of China and cradle of the Cantonese spoken across south China, as well as of the celebrated cuisine which we know in Australia simply as 'Chinese', though actually it is only regional to that area. Practically all the Chinese who came to Australia in the goldrush days had come from the Pearl River delta in the Guangzhou region, especially from the See Yup area (*'Four Districts'*). During my National Groups Survey nearly 40 years earlier I had interviewed some of their Melbourne descendants.

Though we stayed in a cheap hotel in Guangzhou we were squired about by Samantha and later called in on her relations living in a down-at-heel apartment off a filthy back alley in a poor quarter, a rare exposure for foreigners to the lifestyle of tens of millions of Chinese. But one relation owned a down-market diner nearby where we had the run of the menu!

Then once again ensconced in our Chongqing habitat, our conditions of residence, lifestyle and educational roles were a repeat of the previous year but this time we abounded in confidence, drawing on a solid base of familiarity with living in China and relating warmly with the International Office. We took it all in our stride—great to be appreciated! But now everything was relocated to the new and attractive high-rise library building with its impressive marble foyer and escalator, and many floors of classrooms and teachers' studies accessed by fast lifts. (Built in what had been a duckpond the previous year!) It was there that we led our discussion groups, the 12th floor affording splendid views of the tops of fog-shrouded buildings around. Never in Australia had I seen such a palatial building on a university campus, though maybe it was built to commercial specifications envisaging the old campus being sold off as prime development sites.

Some weeks later we were joined by our old Sydney University, Canberra and Minden modern language teaching mate, Laurie Wigney and linguist wife Margaret, and enjoyed sharing with them our hard-won understanding of sinology. With them we spent a weekend in a guesthouse atop the range overlooking the satellite town of Bei Bei, the only Westerners there, sharing the off-putting meals. We wandered through veritable forests of bamboo, ancient and immense, as tall as trees with stems the width of a man's thigh. We clambered up rugged trails to the five-storey yet non-religious pagoda built by the PRC[80] regime to crown the tourist site. We closely checked out the unpatronised Taoist temple below, finally for an hour and more hanging around the bushy bus terminus hoping the last bus of the weekend had not already left—normally competent foreigners reduced to the helplessness of children. Doubtless a salutary experience.

Xian's terra cotta warriors

Three months later at the end of our second stint at CQIT, we flew from Chongqing to Xi'an in the northern inland province of Shaanxi, to admire the fabled Terra Cotta Warriors, claimed as the greatest archaeological find of the 20th century. Again we were able to stay in an academic guesthouse, at the Xi'an International Studies University teaching no less than 12 foreign languages, European and Asian. Our host was Rosemary Box, my secretary during the diocesan Review of Multicultural Ministry and Mission in 1993 and a former missionary in Tanzania, now an ESL teacher sponsored by the international mission group, Care for China's Children.

For many centuries of its 3,000 year history Xi'an was capital of China, previously named Chang'An *('eternal peace')*, at the eastern end of the Silk Road to Alexandria and Constantinople—linking Orient with Occident. Reflecting this history, today's city of six million has an age-old Muslim quarter with mosque and a street of restaurants offering Middle Eastern cuisine, hailed by us as a blessed relief. The ancient city walls are largely intact, pierced and surmounted by the dual architectural wonders of the Lantern Tower and the Bell Tower. Walking along the top for some distance, our advent at the Lantern Tower coincided with a splendid recital on traditional instruments in the tower room.

Among Rosemary's students whom we met was a young Catholic sister serving incognito in 'plain clothes', the only member of an Order that we ever encountered in China, and on Sunday we joined with an international worship group to which John and Marie Beatty, old Canberra friends had belonged when working there with *'Care for China's Children'* focusing on rescuing abandoned (sometimes disabled. or simply girl) babies unwanted under the one-child policy.

---

80   People's Republic of China

But of course for us the area's prime attraction was the amazing contents of the lost mausoleum of the first emperor, Qin Shi, dating from about 200BC, accidentally rediscovered in the 1970s by farmers ploughing the land a few kilometres outside the city. Originally the mausoleum complex had covered hundreds of square metres, featuring an army of some 8,000 life-sized pottery warriors, horses and chariots standing guard behind each other in long serried ranks, each face individually figured, but centuries later it had all been buried and forgotten. In 2008 the laborious work of digging them free from the clay in long parallel pits was continuing, now entirely covered by a large building erected over the site, around the inside galleries of which tourists walk to look down into the pits. Originally the figures had been lacquered in strong colours but this has long since worn away leaving grey-buff surfaces. Many artefacts and weapons had also been unearthed: actual swords and battle-axes. The whole site has now been landscaped and amenities created. Though fascinated at the quality of the figures and their infinitely different expressions we resisted the touts offering small sets of miniature figures on sale until we succumbed at the exit gate—for a fraction of the prices inside.

37
Heart-wrenching Partings

Two years later, in the early northern summer of 2008, once more we were on the wing and succumbing to the call of China. But this was to be our swansong—not tutoring but pursuing a round of visits with friends known from the CQIT (now the Chongqing *University* of Technology) and scholars from around China known from our English tutoring at St Michael's Church and Deakin University—and all in response to warm invitations, stemming doubtless from the twin social factors of our status as their teachers, plus the respect due to our age. Again, the Chinese culture of reciprocity. But along the way we had a call to make.

To China—*via Turkey*!

Our roundabout journey to China was to prove an epic one: via Kuala Lumpur for a 36 hours' free stopover, followed by a time in Turkey. In Istanbul we stayed with daughter-in-law Esma and our two grandsons, Raphael nine and Gebran six.. To our distress their parents had separated by mutual consent during a visit to Turkey. We had been desolated that we may never see our only grandchildren again. But on arrival we were made welcome in her newly rented apartment in Kısıklı above Ümraniye, busy suburban centre on the Asian side of the Bosphorus, and stayed for three memorable weeks.

On schooldays we would walk with the boys a couple of kilometres to and from the International School with its English-medium curriculum, which they attended at Christopher's expense. After a while we developed a warm (if necessarily) tongue-tied relationship with an elderly man who kept a stationery shop along our route. My Turkish was sufficient for him to grasp a rudimentary idea of who we were and why we were there—we found the Turks very empathetic.

But Marjorie, returning to Europe after 43 years, found herself enthralled at her first contact with a beautiful and historic country, with attractive and kindly people of exotic language, customs, Ottoman culture and Islamic faith, however nominal. Before first light every morning we would be woken by the symphony of amplified calls to prayer ringing out from minarets around the horizon, concluded by the delayed but deafening call from the small prayer house a few metres away.

Apart from criss-crossing the Bosphorus from Üsküdar to do the sights of Istanbul, especially the Topkapı Palace of the Ottoman Sultans, the ancient Hagia Sophia *(Holy Wisdom)* Cathedral, the Blue Mosque and Grand Bazaar, we took a few days' break in the small, traditional Black Sea fishing port of Şile, apparently the only non-Turks in town.. Later with Esma and the boys we travelled by suburban electric down the eastern Marmara shore and then by hydrofoil to an upmarket Islamic coastal resort featuring a heated indoor pool with huge water-slide, dodgems and motor bikes for children, and with a snow-capped mountain range just visible across the sea on the western horizon.

Towards the end of our stay, to our immense relief and utter delight, Esma announced her life-changing decision to return to Australia because of the better prospects open to the children in later life.

But our departure by air for Mersin was to prove a personal disaster for me because of my perverse impulse of taking the new city light rail to Atatürk Airport, however depositing us on the wrong side of the complex for domestic flights. By the time we wheeled our considerable luggage through interminable underground corridors we arrived at the counter just as the flight closed. It had been a special bargain fare which we had to pay a heavy excess to change. Justly my popularity sank to a historic low.

Arriving at Adana airport, we were met by Tolga Yavuz and driven westwards along the coast of the New Testament Cilicia (though never glimpsing the Mediterranean) via St Paul's home town of Tarsus to Mersin, a modern seaport sub-contracted to the Singaporean company for whom he was working.

As an overseas student in Melbourne but a disillusioned Muslim, Tolga had become a Christian and I had been privileged to play a part in his baptism by full immersion. Subsequently he studied theology at the Wesleyan seminary where we met monthly for mentoring. Once we had driven to Mildura for him to speak of his new faith with some of the Sunraysia Turkish community. Only as we stood in a supermarket queue after arriving in the town had it dawned on me that we had no address for the ministry couple sponsoring our visit. At that moment the lady behind us murmured, *"So you're Jim and Tolga."* In the face of my blundering God's impeccable timing!

Tolga had since returned to his country and married a lady from an evangelical Assyrian background Now they had a toddler Onur. The couple and Tolga's parents were the soul of hospitality (though only Tolga could speak English) walking us for kilometres along the splendid seaside esplanade featuring the most modern play-cum-exercise equipment to be seen outside a gymnasium, and driving us into the hinterland to a mountain reservoir and to Tarsus, where the only hint of St Paul was a kitschy 'St Paul's Well' attributed with magical powers. Despite its tourism aspirations I was continually struck by the country's wilful ignorance of the fourteen long centuries of its Christian history. . .

Indeed on Sunday we worshipped with the small evangelical community church led by a *Turkish-speaking Korean* missionary! After America, Korea is said to have sent the second-highest number of missionaries all over the world. Both Tolga and his wife Yasemin played leading roles in the service. Afterwards we took the (English-speaking) pastor to lunch and I was moved to make a sizeable donation towards his ministry.

Our pre-dawn departure next day was tinged with sadness that we would never see Tolga again in this life—though our flight by an amazingly dilapidated charter plane taking Turkish guestworkers back to Germany had us musing whether that might turn out to be rather sooner than anticipated! We had of course concluded that we should not fly to China without visiting our Minden family in Germany on the way, followed by a relaxing two-week holiday in the German twin-town of Annaberg-Buchholz in the Erzgebirge (Ore Mountains) on the Czech border

German holiday delights

From Hanover we entrained for Marjorie's first reunion with our Minden family in 43 years, though over the decades all our children had visited. Again I was amazed at her readiness to launch into speaking the language, gaily and with serious disregard for grammar, but comprehensible withal. If they thought how cute it sounded they didn't reveal it.

Sheer delight was brought by the following two-week holiday break in the German twin-town of Annaberg-Buchholz near the Czech border, selected on-line in Melbourne with some apprehension about its actual potential. But we had hit the jackpot! I was in my third heaven, being on a relaxing holiday with my beloved in a remote, unknown but beautiful part of Europe, indulging my wanderlust and speaking German! Our bed-and-breakfast host, Frau Schmidt, spoilt us by monumental and memorable Teutonic breakfasts sufficient to provide also for our lunch. Walking everywhere, on Sunday I went to a service in each town's Lutheran parish church: the very *korrekt* 18th century bosses' church in Annaberg (*Mt Anne*) and the mediaeval Gothic labourers' church near our lodging in Buchholz (=*Beechwood*). Of course the 44 years of living under Communism in the workers' paradise of the so-called German Democratic Republic had blurred the social distinctions, though vestigial remains were still in evidence. For instance, on one hand I was impressed at the stateliness of Annaberg's Georgian architectural heritage and streetscapes, reminiscent of wealthy English provincial towns like Bath, but on the other hand (being in the Ore Mountains) we discovered that in the town centre, literally under the main bank, was a deep silver-and-tin mine now open for tourist inspection (no free samples). Only in comparatively recent centuries had these ores been found under the town, throughout the mediaeval period simply an agricultural region. A relic of that time was the celebrated Frohnau Hammer, a massive and ancient hydraulic blacksmith's hammer for working molten metal, operated by a large and rugged wooden water-wheel. At first encounter its primitive power, gushing water (and noise!) were positively scary.

Finally came a sunny day when we took to the mountains, travelling in a narrow-gauge train hauled by an old but powerful steam loco, heading due south to skirt the Czech border and finally climb to Germany's highest town, the picturesque Oberwiesenthal at the foot of the Fichtelberg, ski resort at 1,200m. Through gorgeous knee-high summer grasses studded with yellow flowers we hiked over the range into the Czech Republic through an untenanted customs checkpoint, to lunch in a Czech roadhouse before returning to scale the highest point of the Erzgebirge by cable car, at the head of the long but grassy ski runs.

Another day we took the *Deutsche Bundesbahn's* stylish, modern diesel railcars from Annaberg-Buchholz right to the end of the line, actually beyond the Czech border in the unpronounceable Vejprty (German *Weipert*), to find the streetscapes quite down-at-heel compared even to the former East Germany, but clamorous with (Czech-speaking) *Vietnamese* stall-holders—in such a remote border town already straddling two cultures!

On the aerial Silk Road

The idyll all too soon past, we took an express to Frankfurt Airport, finally to span half of Europe and the whole extent of Asia in the world's longest overland flight. Heading for Beijing by Great Circle route across the Arctic, at high altitude and with night closing in over the Baltic Sea, the 'aerial 3D atlas' allowed me to discern on the left the Swedish coast and island of Bornholm and on the right the coast of Estonia. We settled in for the night haul but seemingly all of five minutes later we were drifting in for a wet and smoggy dawn landing in Beijing.

Late in the afternoon we were picked up in a minibus from the Mining & Technology University of Tangshan in Hebei province, north-east of the capital, as guests of a married couple of lecturers who at the end of the Cultural Revolution had been in the first cohort of students to be offered tertiary education places on merit, by a China-wide examination. In the horrendous 7.8 earthquake of 1976 (the most powerful of the 20th century) a quarter of Tangshan's population had perished and the whole city was laid waste, including the recently completed university library, to this day a grim memorial. left in ruins. We were shown around the university and next day taken by minibus over 100km into the countryside, to the imperial mausoleum complex of the Ming and Qing dynasties, the largest and most elaborate in China, dating from the mid-16th century, with subterranean marble vaults richly decorated in Buddhist imagery.

Creative traffic anarchy

The return drive was remarkable for the most heinous defiance of traffic regulations ever experienced anywhere in the world—so memorable that I wrote an article about it for publication in the journal of the Royal Automobile Club of Victoria, entitled *Fun on the Antheap*. Some excerpts:

> "Did you know that China has the world's fastest ants? They don't need segregating into lanes—inbound and outbound, slow and fast, for turning or through traffic. No, they just pour steadily along. That's how it is with Chinese city traffic.
>
> Every day, world's best practice is on display in the Chinese metropolises. It is the sheer exuberance and sense of unfettered freedom that makes such a strong appeal.
>
> Why are we so hung up on the fiction that you should only use one side of the road in going places? Mature ants and Chinese

drivers eschew such soul-destroying conformity. They opt instantly and with split-second timing for their own best path. They are creative. And they are right—not left behind. Goods get delivered, people arrive safely, the community's work goes on apace.

During our most recent safari into enlightened China, our traffic adventures in taxis and minibuses were a source of constant delight. Gone the quaint notion that the centre line is inviolable. Viewed from a high-rise 35 storeys above, the twirling yellow ribbon of taxis yawing and sashaying down the broad avenues must be a veritable ballet de wheels, weaving patterns of intricate beauty.

Who needs lanes when you've got a whole road? The temptation to power is irresistible. And the rewards are tangible. Enterprising drivers will always out-manoeuvre the pusillanimous. We have seen a fast bus overtaking a car being itself overtaken by a faster bus with a more enterprising driver not overawed by the double centre line.

But how shall we forget the crowning glory of our traffic adventures: in a university minibus we were once driven for fully five minutes along a six-lane divided highway on the wrong carriageway. Our minds ran the range of emotions from amusement to unbelief, from panic to terror, from despair to resignation, from wonderment to admiration—not for our liberated driver, but for the legitimate carriageway users coming towards us three abreast at a rate of knots. In the five glorious minutes only two oncoming drivers flashed their lights! Unsurprised? Even-tempered? Indulgent? Or just patient worker ants? At least they weren't bulldog ants."

Chinese surf beach

Next stop Qingdao, port city of five million in Shandong province on the Yellow Sea opposite Korea, via a day-long journey by 'ordinary' long-distance train where we encountered some extraordinary sharing and kindness at the hands of the travelling public. At one point (for fifteen minutes?) we traversed a landscape solely of long plastic greenhouses on both sides of the line. Twenty kilometres of tomatoes? So much for Australia's aspiration to become the 'foodbowl of Asia'! Qingdao is a resort city with a string of sandy beaches (creatively distinguished by numbers rather than names!), impressive buildings along the front and during our summer visit calling to mind the antheap—with the sand obscured by relaxing worker-ants—virtually none of whom ventured into the water. Some lazed about in the smoggy sun, some flew kites bought from a vendor (one of which we too acquired for our grandchildren), others paid for children's donkey-rides. All appeared deliriously happy. Chinese actually taking time out!

Our hosts were Margaret, an English teacher at the Oceanographic University and her husband, a distinguished architect to whose recent achievement we were proudly introduced: a fine civic square behind one of the beaches. To our surprise the small private hotel where they booked our accommodation was located in a sort of European-style suburb with tree-lined streets and separate two-storey homes set in their own grounds. I had never imagined such a feature could exist in China. But when we discovered in the commercial centre a large late-Gothic Catholic church the *pfennig* dropped: around the turn of the 20th century Qingdao had been a Prussian (later German) concession and of course the architecture and orderly streetscapes reflected this.

Quietly inspecting the church where a well-attended Sunday mass was in progress, we were informed that it was in Korean, the language of a sizeable minority in the city, strongly Christian. But it was also the university that impressed us with its charming ivy-covered buildings and pleasant perspectives interspersed with excellent sportsgrounds and facilities. At a festive dinner that evening we met a colleague of Margaret's whose English was even more superlative than hers. Without further ado I appointed Qingdao as my favourite Chinese city (at the time not knowing that it is also rated as China's *'most liveable city'*).

Farewell to Chongqing for ever

But from far inland, Chongqing was calling, certainly less liveable but more dynamic—despite the brewing corruption scandal soon destined to engulf its Communist leadership. Above all it was our home base in China, where we had so many friends maintaining e-mail contact. One of them, Deborah, a Christian working as an air traffic controller, met us at the airport and drove us to Yangjiaping, where in a kindly gesture the International Office had booked us for a week into a modest hotel outside the university's main portal. It was there that we invited many friends, both lecturers and students (some now graduates working in the community) to join us and share our lives. Not being on Party ground as in the university, we were free to raise Christian issues and were to enjoy some stimulating conversations. Subsequently one new graduate would come to Queensland for further study and become a Christian, later moving to Melbourne where we had an ongoing discipling relationship with her.

On our last evening in Chongqing the staff of the International Office hosted a farewell dinner expressing final votes of appreciation for our contributions over the three years—and marking the close of our association—reinforced next day by taking us in the minibus on the long drive to the airport.

It also represented the close of our 'China era' which had immeasurably enriched and deeply humanised our post-retirement years by setting robust—though manageable—challenges to heart and mind. In our mid-70s an opportunity rare indeed. In the process we had developed a love for the Chinese and their vibrant country with its age-old and amazing civilisation. In my case, the lifelong trajectory of understanding was traceable from my parents' dismissal of the Chinese market-gardeners of Moorefields in the 1940s as barely human, to my friendships with post-doctoral fellows in universities, sharing insights in my language now become the *lingua franca* of the planet. Some pilgrimage!

In tropical China

Our next call was to Nanning in the tropical south, capital of the Guangxi Semi-Autonomous Region of many ethnic minorities but particularly the *Zhuang*, and known as the most beautiful city of China for its broad boulevards and fine streetscapes, its public gardens cradling an attractive lake—and with a relatively clear (albeit humid) atmosphere! Our host was an English teacher and Director of the Library at Guangxi University, housed in a resplendent building just opened and by its marble splendour unimaginably eclipsing any Australian counterpart. Her charming husband was a Zhuang, a researcher in social development, internationally promoting his invention of a sanitation system for remote-area villages, an altogether inspirational man (invariably cooking us fried eggs and bacon for breakfast).

On a warm evening the four of us joined the throng promenading around the elongated garden-fringed lake, brilliantly lit in ever-changing colours and patterns of light. One day, though preoccupied with the triennial inspection of her department by a team of Beijing functionaries, Lily was kind enough to take us on a city-walk to an ethnic minorities museum by a small stream spanned by a traditional wood-carved and roofed arch-bridge where a man in Zhuang traditional garb was playing a native stringed instrument.

Our final impression of Nanning came from a longish drive through the countryside to the brand-new airport—one of dozens built in the past few years under the tremendous infrastructure-development program for the major cities. Along the way for kilometres we traversed a burgeoning forest of Australian bluegums! Did it betoken a future for our two countries jointly committed to a deepening and mutually gifting relationship?

Farewell to China forever

Finally flying north-east to Guangzhou in Guangdong Province we were guests of Joseph and Lisa, then buoyed with expectation and living on site with their workers in the spa bath factory compound, a typical small business in the Pearl River delta, the '*workshop of the world*'. But (predictably) they booked us into a large hotel[81] in the nearby city of Foshan—the only Westerners there—showing us over the factory operation and later through a large Taoist temple complex before driving us far out into the Guangdong countryside to the tourist attraction of Seven Star Crags. The famed nature park focuses on a large, dark-green lake divided into several sections by traditional causeways and bridges, all dominated by towering limestone outcrops featuring many caves and Buddhist inscriptions, with paths leading to

---

81   Memorable for the notice in the bathroom '*Fall Carefully*' and above the escalators in a department store '*No fling here*'

some of the summits and around the lake. Cherishing the precious time in such a beautiful setting with our adoptive nephew and niece, despite the afternoon heat we completed the path around the lake. Next day they drove us across the Pearl River delta by a maze of interlocking freeways to the embarkation point for the hydrofoil to Hong Kong's airport (now relocated to an island boldly reclaimed from the South China Sea) to join our Melbourne-bound flight.

We came home convinced, card-carrying Sinophiles committed to sympathetically monitoring China's unfolding future, and to praying for our fellow-believers whose numbers are said to be growing rapidly, notably among well-educated and professional people. Some Western estimates claim that there are now some 120 million Christians in the country, in both the officially sanctioned Protestant and Catholic churches and in the 'underground' congregations, some of whose leaders are no strangers to imprisonment.

If these numbers warrant credence and if, as reported, Christians are in earnest about living out their faith, it could make China already home to the world's largest *'real Christian'* community, destined not only to impact on the life of their nation but even to influence world history, for example through the visionary *'Back to Jerusalem'* movement committed to re-winning the Central Asian nations to the faith they once professed.

May this ancient nation, creator of so many artefacts and processes now held to be universal[82]—and with the sorry decline of faith in the once-Christian West—yet prove to be the bastion and powerhouse of world evangelism.

---

[82] Simon Winchester's book *Bomb, Book and Compass* identifies many such, as typified by the particular significance of gunpowder, printing, and navigation aids.

38
A New World a-Birthing

The world into which we were born is no more. Many things, visible and invisible—both cherished and disdained—have passed away, some now even characterised as 'museum pieces' (as we doubtless rate also). Others have been transfigured through innovation, while unimaginably new creative solutions have emerged. The ever-shrinking world, instant communication, the digital age, space probes, the explosion of scientific knowledge, including of vastly expanded medical care, cures for once intractable diseases, widespread affluence and financial security, social media, creature comforts beyond credence, even ten more years' of life expectancy. Impressive catalogue reflecting a single lifetime!

In such a rapidly evolving world, what are the underlying factors that have primarily shaped the climate within which Marjorie and I have lived out our lives? What are the competing values systems under which we have sought to find our own personal meaning: how do we think about ourselves and our world? These span the physical, economic, social, artistic and spiritual dimensions—all of which have been transformed during our now longish lifetimes. Eighty years confer a useful vantage point for observing gains and losses, and assessing trends.

Elegy for a lost world

Firstly: the economic and social dimension—the most tangible for our daily existence. Compared to our childhood and the lean post-war years, the 1960s and 1970s had seen the progressive transformation of our society through sustained prosperity, with the advent and maturing of the welfare state and the humanising of service provision to meet the needs of the whole community. Australia was sometimes hailed as the most egalitarian nation on earth.

But unbelievably, in the 1980s history would go into reverse, as hard-nosed economic rationalists would take power in the UK and later in Australia. A new economic model would be developed *by* the economic élite to *benefit* the economic élite. Since that decade we have been subjected to the sweeping triumph of neo-liberalism and globalisation, embraced by both sides of politics, swamping the wellbeing of whole sectors of the community and—like the emergent neo-capitalists of Russia and the socialist bloc on the fall of the Berlin Wall—daring to purloin and sell the people's crown jewels: our public utilities providing water, electricity, telephony, public transport, public works and infrastructure, airports, port installations, hydro-electric projects, the people's bank, our systems of personal services, health insurance, even our medical research institute, while privileging private schools and private hospitals over public.

All justified by invoking the primacy of private ownership, while claiming to be responding to a concocted phobia of deficits and indebtedness. But such debts had ever been the universal norm—whereby each new generation would benefit from the services it inherited and make provision for the next generation, for instance by building significant infrastructure (by *Public* Works Departments) without invoking private enterprise with its profit motive. A functional system—and well worth paying for.

Indeed, an eminent economist has recently given the lie to the current economic fad:of neo-liberalism, pointing out that the consistent surplus budgets that are so extolled actually *entrench unemployment*, put the brakes on *real wages growth,* and ultimately *shackle* the economy. Of course this serves the moguls, the real 'owners' of the world economy, further entrenching their neo-liberal system. And sadly, there is no lack of politicians of all stripes happy to do their bidding by conniving at their '*debt-phobia*' (as common-sensical as it may sound to the layman). But what is the nation-state for, if not to protect us and our culture from enemies without *and enemies within*? By 2016 the 'little people' of the UK, disillusioned and cynical, would have their say in voting down supra-national economic structures such as the European Union and worldwide elitist blocs.

But in the 1980s a harsh new phase of imperialism was exploiting Third World economies, often with the connivance of corrupt local élites. Though resisted by the masses, crony capitalism reigned everywhere: unrestrained free-market rule polarised society. As the social gains from decades of progressive politics in the West faded, America itself came to exemplify '*private affluence but public squalor*', at the cost of medical care, hospitals, education, infrastructure and the erosion of welfare rights. Home buyers found their mortgage payments impossible to sustain and all over the country homes were being abandoned or repossessed by the banks, owners often forfeiting their life-savings in the process. Amongst middle-class families deprived of income a new homelessness arose, with people living 'in the woods' and medical care becoming inaccessible. The shocking story is narrated in a comprehensively documented study *Some Place like America: Tales from the New Great Depression.*[83]

Local impact of economic rationalism

In the 1980s Australian local jobs were exported by the thousands to China, India, Bangladesh and other Asian countries with low-wage economies. With the removal of tariffs whole industries closed, notably the footwear and garment industries in Melbourne's inner north. In Victoria at one stroke Coalition Premier Jeff Kennett cut the public payroll by sacking 10,000 teachers! And closing schools galore—*three* of them in our long-suffering parish of Dallas, a heartless assault on Australia's poorest suburb!

Civil society became increasingly undermined as the arena of big business expanded exponentially, unchecked, untameable. Competition ruled, profits

---

83 By academic Dale Maharidge, with photo gallery by Michael Williamson and Foreword by Bruce Springsteen, University of California Press, 2011, 244pp

soared and affluence increased for some, while stress levels rose for many from threatened unemployment and forced early retirement, especially in the Public Service I had known, now decimated by the outsourcing of

projects (and hence jobs). Security of employment fell dramatically as workers were all too often pushed onto contracts making them no longer employees with rights protected at law, thus creating many areas of precarious, insecure work as inexperienced 'contractors'. All of which outflanked the role of trade unionism with its traditional mantra of *'unity is strength'*, by putting a largely non-unionised workforce at the mercy of management's drive for increasing productivity and profits. *'Divide and conquer'!* This factor alone has undoubtedly multiplied social stress and undermined community confidence and cohesion. We have all paid the price in a heightened struggle for personal meaning.

Simultaneously we have lived through the progressive decline of *service* as the traditional mode of interaction within our society, in favour of privileging competition over co-operation while discounting age-old areas of expertise. Many respected skills and occupations have disappeared, replaced for example by serried ranks of shelving in warehouses of technology offering a bewildering array of products of which the scant (and often junior) staff seem to know little of anything they are selling. The DiY revolution, now universal at supermarkets and petrol stations, as well as in department stores, has seen the end of being *'served'* as a right. Business had pulled off a massive coup by recruiting the customer as an honorary staff member—of course pocketing the savings as corporate profits!

Other social indicators told the story as society became more stressed: in Broadmeadows unemployment amongst non-English-speaking migrants sky-rocketed. Entire sectors of society were threatened with becoming superfluous, jeopardising community wellbeing and inducing despair. For those still working, job pressures grew and hours of work lengthened. At 7 o'clock in the evening suburban trains were now crowded by home-going office workers, many having worked unpaid extra hours.

Family life came under threat; leisure in decline and commercialised—you could no longer ride a bike to the gym without a proper lycra tracksuit! Elite sport was professionalised. Community organisations of all kinds went into a tailspin; we became a nation of non-joiners, including of the Churches. By way of dulling the pain the commercial media peddled trivia and soporific entertainment.

Unchallenged, from its Temple in Wall Street, Mammon was exacting a terrible price from its rabid worshippers. Under its compelling Articles of Faith—*'Making Money at All Costs'*—business had triumphed over humanity and decency, common sense and personal meaning, scornfully dismissing co-operation in favour of competition.

To be sure, a tiny élite had entered into wealth unimaginable: 85 mega-rich individuals now owned more than the rest of the seven billion put together![84] But

---

84   According to the head of the International Monetary Fund, Christine Lagarde, 2016

the most recent OECD figures show that, while in the past two years Australia has ranked as the world's richest country in per capita wealth (largely because of our high rate of home ownership—now in sharp decline), one in six children are living below the poverty line! Wasn't Australia traditionally *'the land of the fair go'*?

> "From those forever shackled to what their wealth can buy,
> the fear of lost advantage provokes the bitter cry:
> 'Don't query our position! Don't criticise our wealth!
> Don't mention those exploited by politics and stealth!'
> To God, who through the prophets proclaimed a different age,
> We offer earth's indifference, its agony and rage:
> 'When will the wronged be righted? When will the Kingdom come?
> When will the world be generous to all instead of some?[85]"

Counter-balance: the legitimacy of business

On the other hand it must be soberly acknowledged: with private enterprise *per se* we need buy no argument. Undoubtedly it is the oldest mode of social interaction on earth since hunters exchanged meat for vegetables (cf. the Cain and Abel episode in the Old Testament at the dawn of time)[86]. Business has saved us from living as hunter-gatherers, has pioneered sociality, has engendered the town, has trained us in relational skills, has generated profits as the basis for expansion and diversification, has fathered exploration, innovation, progress, technology, the arts and culture. Business is simply humans seeking reward for their efforts in serving the needs of a reciprocal society, whether for the very elements of life itself or for its adornment.

As Pope Francis would write in his 2015 Papal Encyclical *Laudato Si'*,

> "Business is a noble vocation, directed to producing wealth and
> improving the world. It can be a fruitful source of prosperity for the
> area in which it operates, especially if it sees the creation of jobs as
> an essential part of its service to the common good.'[87]

And moreover Jesus did not disapprove of business activity as such. Among the characters in his teaching illustrations (parables) was on the one hand the shrewd manager commended for putting his master's funds to productive use rather than settling for mere security, and on the other Dives (Latin for *'rich man'*) scorning the needs of the poor but reaping his eternal 'reward'. But the young plutocrat seeking to join the band of disciples would withdraw sadly on learning the affiliation fee: divesting himself of his wealth for the benefit of the poor. And Zacchaeus, the stumpy little tax collector hoping for a glimpse of Jesus from his perch in a sycamore tree, would spontaneously respond by offering fourfold

---

85	From a contemporary hymn by John Bell in *Together in Song: Australian Hymn Book II*, hymn no. 674
86	Genesis 4: 1–15
87	Catholic doctrine mentioned by the Pope with approval in his 2015 Encyclical *Laudato Si'*.

restitution for his ill-gotten gains. Already another tax collector, Matthew, had forsaken his toll-booth to join the wandering preacher as a disciple (= *'little learner'*), later recording his experience of the three years with Jesus in the Gospel that bears his name.

Today as ever, at the heart of our economy are the small business enterprises that employ the most workers, some of them actually associated with progressive politics promoting *'capitalism with a human face'*. The reality is that we all depend on business for our daily bread as well as to safeguard and grow our money. Indeed over the millennia no other durable option appears to have been devised. Rather, talented entrepreneurs have made their mark in shaping the Western world by their energy, flair and enthusiasm. By contrast, the dismal two-generation Communist experiment of state-ownership of everything simply did not work: for me its failure was on display in the lavish staffing of the large GUM department store in Moscow (with its half-empty shelves) where a mere customer stood around awkwardly until the shopgirls finished their absorbing conversation!

Commercial business actually works for the benefit of all involved in it, whether as manufacturers, suppliers, distributors, sellers or customers, and the creative energies released can be explosive agents of progress. Further, the wise investment of surplus profits meets emerging needs and strengthens the system for all.

But this is a far cry indeed from the 'gnomes of Zurich' playing with other nations' currencies—and futures, or American investment banks collapsing from frenzied trading in tranches of worthless loans. It is the very *inhumanity* of the rapacious 'Wall Street' capitalism, unable to resist the temptation to greed and megalomania that I have learnt to deplore—as does the Pope! Not to mention the perennial issue of corruption.

Papal infallibility?

The current Pope Francis sees it as intolerable that whole economies are being reshaped to serve the interests of financial markets, accumulating immense wealth in the hands of relatively few while depriving millions of a decent livelihood. He rejects the neo-liberal notion that the market of itself will resolve moral dilemmas and reward people appropriately, with governments playing only a very minimal role. Far from social equity being a subversive or communist notion, he appreciates its potential for promoting rapid social uplift for whole populations.

Even more comprehensively has he spoken up for millions of people across the developing world in *Laudato Si'*, his 100-page Papal Encyclical[88] in 2015, protesting the current unfairness in economic outcomes, the destruction of the environment, and the prospect of global warming hitting them the hardest.

---

88 *Laudato Si'* (the words from the mediaeval Italian dialect of St Francis of Assisi meaning *Praise Be*) is subtitled *On Care for our Common Home*. Pope Francis critiques consumerism, irresponsible development and laments environmental degradation and global warming, calling all people of the world to take 'swift and unified global action'.

It is not socially responsible forms of capitalism that the Pope is targeting, but the neo-liberal versions of economics now dominating conservative circles. He is not opposed to the free market, but insists that it be regulated to ensure social justice for all and to enhance social equity and cohesion. He has repeatedly appealed for investors and business people to help eradicate global hunger and severe poverty, to lift living standards, create opportunities and to restrain excessive consumption in order to secure a more equitable and sustainable future. And he does so in forthright terms wherever he travels:

> "Once capital becomes an idol and guides people's decisions, once greed for money presides over the entire socio-economicsystem, it ruins society, it condemns and enslaves men and women, it destroys human fraternity, it sets people against one another and, as we clearly see, it even puts at risk our common home—sister and mother earth.
>
> The first task is to put the economy at the service of peoples. Human beings and nature must not be at the service of money. Let us say 'NO' to an economy of exclusion and inequality, where money rules, rather than service. That sort of economy excludes. That economy destroys Mother Earth.
>
> The economy should not be a mechanism for accumulating goods, but rather the proper administration of our common home. The economy should serve human beings and nature and ensure a decent life for the poor and respect for the environment.
>
> Working for a just distribution of the fruits of the earth and human labour is not mere philanthropy. It is a moral obligation. For Christians, the responsibility is even greater: it is a commandment. It is about giving to the poor and to peoples what is theirs by right. It is a reality prior to private property. Property, especially when it affects natural resources, must always serve the needs of peoples. I ask you, in the name of God, to defend Mother Earth."

Finally, over the heads of finance ministers and governments, he appeals directly to the people to struggle for an order that will bless both the natural world and its poor. At the Vatican he has brought together the mayors of 60 world cities and at another time Police Commissioners, in what he terms *'communities of conscience'*, simple but unique initiatives to foster the civil society. He recognises that any structures built on these principles will require personal conversion if they are to be sustained.

But this is not a new departure in Catholic social teaching. Already in 1993 Pope John Paul II had rejected 'neo-liberal' capitalism, saying that the Church had 'always held capitalist ideology responsible for grave social injustices' and for 'placing intolerable burdens' on poorer countries. Later, Pope Benedict had also warned against the widening inequality and the 'ruinous exploitation of the planet'.

The article *'Of the 1%, by the 1%, for the 1%'* by Nobel Prize winner Joseph Stieglitz helped spark the 'Occupy Wall Street' movement of 2011 during the Global Financial Crisis. The top 1% had accumulated astronomical wealth, with which came unprecedented political influence and power, leading to growing inequality and economic instability.

In an earlier interview with a Spanish newspaper's Vatican correspondent, Pope Francis, then newly elected leader of the world's 1.2 billion Roman Catholics, had launched a scathing attack on the world economic system, saying it discarded the young, put money ahead of people, and survived on the profits of war. Some countries had a youth unemployment rate of over 50 per cent, with many millions in Europe seeking work in vain. He proclaimed:

> "In this system devoid of ethics, we have now fallen into the sin of idolatry of the god 'Money'. Money is in command! Money lays down the law! We must say we want a just system. We must say, 'We don't want this globalised economic system that is doing us so much harm.' As God desires, men and women must be at the centre—not money."

No wonder the editor of *The Australian*, the right-wing Murdoch flagship, felt constrained to openly attack his Church's leader, even though in an Encyclical he was speaking infallibly *ex cathedra!* His frenzied opinion piece accused the Pope of being an 'environmental populist', an 'economic ideologue', a 'quasi-Marxist', of employing 'hysterical' language, and of 'profound intellectual ignorance'. In the face of *infallibility,* quite a catalogue!

Today my heart sinks at the ultimate triumph of globalised capitalism over the interests of the world's people. I find little of grace, mercy or common humanity on public display—but rather a world conspiracy of ruthless greed. As the New Testament notes, *"The love of money is the root of all evil"*, and elsewhere, *"The whole world is under the control of the evil one"*. So we are actually confronting the perverse power of cosmic forces, against whom Jesus tells us to pray *"Deliver us from the evil one"* while St Paul adds *"We struggle not against flesh and blood but against the powers of this dark world and the spiritual forces of evil"*[89]. So in the Christian understanding of greed, the gloves are off. But in a finite world—the only one we have—materialism blindly pursues the folly of endless growth, raping the planet's dwindling resources as if there were no tomorrow.

Global environmental crisis

Thus against this turbulent on-stage action looms the backdrop of impending environmental crisis, hastened by our society's inability (or even refusal?) to share in the global action required to impede the warming of the planet towards the point of no return: escalating climate change, rising sea levels, deforestation, desertification[90] loss of species[91], and inevitable food and water wars (a dimension of

---

89　I Timothy 6:10; I John 5:19; John 6:13; Ephesians 6:12

90　In a penetrating insight Pope Francis has written that it starts with the *'desertification of the human heart'*.

91　The ABC Radio National's 'Science Show' claimed that one third of all species of wildlife animals are now threatened with extinction (2014), while the BBC has indicated that the greatest extinction since that of the dinosaurs 65 million years ago is in view, with so many species of wild animals now among the 'walking dead'.

a looming Armageddon?). In our earlier adult years it would have been dismissed as the over-fevered imagination of science fiction writers. But a recent ABC Radio National program put it that the central challenge would be to produce food enough to feed an extra nine billion people by 2025 given the annual loss of arable land and with declining water reserves.

Yet despite the near-unanimity of scientists worldwide on the inescapable crisis, backed by irrefutable empirical data, there seems little apparent interest on the part of Wall St and their close cohorts [92] to turn aside from the main game (*'the only game in town'*) of maximising profits. Their tiny coterie of billionaire corporate moguls from the extractive industries (coal, oil, coal seam gas, tar sands) and their bankers, together with the arms manufacturers trading in human flesh, and all of them facilitated by conservative political leaders and their suppliant media—though actually only in a few key Western countries—are holding the planet's future to ransom.

Commenting on this recently, Pope Francis proclaimed that the Earth is "frequently exploited by human greed and rapacity" and that "humans have slapped nature in the face. Well might we ask *'How is it possible that the most intelligent creature ever to walk the face of the earth is conniving at its destruction? We are standing on the wrong side of history'.*" [93] Again, until recently, an unbelievable proposition.

Yet a group of climate experts examining world governments' submissions to the 2015 Paris climate talks concluded that pledges to cut emissions would fall short of the minimum 2° rise in world temperatures that the Earth could tolerate without risking catastrophic changes to food production, sea levels, fishing, wildlife, deserts and water reserves. Even if rises were pegged at 2°C, scientists said this would still destroy most coral reefs and glaciers and melt significant parts of the Greenland ice cap, bringing major rises in sea levels.

Taking people power seriously

Yet hope springs eternal in the human breast, as ever, linked with the latent power of the people. The quest for a common understanding of the issues and the possibilities of unified resistance lies before us all. As Marjorie and I have at times rhythmically chanted at demonstrations, *"The people, united, will never be defeated"*. In a film screened here recently by a local civil society group, *'The Wisdom to Survive—Climate Change, Capitalism and Community'*, we learnt that lateral thinking, ingenuity,

---

92   I use the term to describe the unrestrained web of banking and multinational corporations that ultimately control 'big business' worldwide, averse to public opinion, not answerable to governments, paying little tax, scorning democracy [*demockracy*?],while breeding widespread cynicism and alienation.
On the other hand, for many years we two have held a productive ethical investment portfolio. I use the term to describe the unrestrained web of banking and multinational corporations that ultimately control 'big business' worldwide, averse to public opinion, not answerable to governments, paying little tax, scorning democracy while breeding widespread cynicism and alienation. On the other hand, for many years we two have held a productive ethical investment portfolio..

93   From an ABC Radio National broadcast in August 2014.

humour, the power of the arts, and above all widespread collaboration can outwit the dire predictability of the boardroom planners.

For a Christian this may be identified as Jesus' strategy when confronted by the overpowering legalistic code of the Jewish establishment under Roman hegemony, comprising the pedantic Pharisees and the collaborationist Sadducees. Not only did he go way downmarket to the *'common people who heard him gladly'*[94]— by his message of hope and love identifying with the suffering and the rejected— but personally he also exemplified a life of chosen poverty, once observing that he *'had nowhere to lay his head'*. Neither did he shrink from speaking truth to power, costly as it would prove. In the courts of the Jewish Temple in Jerusalem he staged a one-man demonstration against commercial greed in a sacred space by overturning the money-changers' tables and driving out their stock-in-trade. But the stakes against him were high—as they are in our world situation today.

Yet actually today's environmental issues are not so complex: either planet earth is in dire trouble and needs help, or else we can carry on blithely as if all is well. For instance the first course would identify with the common people in their impending plight (e.g. the people of Tuvalu and Kiribati in the Pacific with the ocean lapping ever higher on their shores).[95] The alternative is to blindly pursue higher profits. In the ludicrous words of Louis XV as the French Revolution smouldered: *"Après moi, le déluge"* (Hang the future!).

The options are stark: while rapacious capitalism focuses on the self-interest of relatively few powerful individuals, Christian social teaching (after Jesus) focuses on the wellbeing of the whole community, particularly of its weakest members. Or in the sharper words of a pastor friend identified with the struggle to preserve workers' rights, *"Christians need to decide whether to sit with the bosses or stand with the workers"*. No doubt about where Jesus would be found.

Joining in public resistance

In the past few months, at the tender age of 82, Marjorie and I have taken to the streets in four demonstrations: resisting the Coalition Government's dismantling of environmental provisions (an action unique in the world); opposing the disproportionate impact of the deceitful 2014 Federal Budget secretly sprung on needier people; with 60,000 Melbournians calling for real action at the Paris Conference updating the Kyoto Protocol; and appealing to the Government to offer refuge to the Christian community resident since 100AD in northern Iraq but now being driven out or murdered. On such public issues of conscience, as long as we are able, we aim to offer our mini-contribution.

From the first paydays of our respective careers, we have rigorously given one tenth (the biblical *'tithe'*) of our income to the work of God, inside and outside the church. As we have become more prosperous (*'You can't outgive God'*) we have

---

94 Mark 12: 37
95 The President of Kiribati has said, *"If nothing is done, Kiribati will be the first country to go under water. By about 2030 we start disappearing.* **We will not survive.**"

exceeded this proportion. From our family-raising years and until the present day, we hsve contributed to the support of several orphans allocated under sponsorship schemes. Now it all happens under direct-debit arrangements that have even replaced the collection-plate in church.

A few years earlier, taking part with Nick in a mobilisation against the meeting in Melbourne of the world trade cartel, during a rowdy pushing match between demonstrators and police, I was felled and feared being trampled to death. The view of a demo *from below* is not for the faint-hearted!

Global insecurity: extremism and terrorism

In the wider world, in the face of glaring disparities of wealth and poverty, now enter a new factor: the frightening rage of militants and armed insurgents, the advent of Islamist extremism and ready recourse to terrorism—explicable by the perceived American hubris and depravity fuelled by the unholy alliance of Wall Street and the military-industrial complex, climaxing in the perverse search for 'weapons of mass destruction' in Iraq (which reputedly led to the death of some 500,000 Iraqis!) and other ongoing incursions into the Middle East. In 2001 the September 11 airborne attack on New York City had lain low the corporate Twin Towers at the cost of 2,996 lives, including of the 19 hijackers.

But as contended by its own 'peaceniks', from its earliest beginnings—despite its concomitant identity as 'God's own country' with a deep commitment to Christian faith both in public and private life—the USA's history of waging war has been virtually incessant. The society seems fascinated by bearing arms and making war—what of the perversity of the 'gun lobby'? Already the Republican hopefuls for the next Presidency are campaigning for a smaller bureaucracy and a growth in the military. Yet since the Allied victory of 1945, major US wars in Korea, Vietnam, Iraq (two) and Afghanistan have all failed to achieve their objectives, on the contrary slaughtering and maiming millions, alienating whole populations and stoking the fires of hatred against the 'Christian' West. For instance in Cambodia to this day the myriad unexploded American bombs still lying hidden in the soil exact an appalling annual toll. Unbelievably, during the war in Vietnam the Americans had dropped more bombs on that small country than over the whole of Europe during World War II!

"Blessed are the peacemakers, for they shall be called the children of God". But what of the warmongers? Especially in an age when nuclear weapons are stockpiled by the USA, Russia, the UK, France, China, and almost certainly Israel, with active aspirations by Iran and North Korea, and have most recently been developed by both India and Pakistan (proudly proclaiming *'the Muslim atomic bomb'*—sending shivers up and down my spine). A recent ABC Radio National *'Science Show'* on the ongoing challenge of nuclear disarmament claimed that in an atomic war, only 43 atom bombs would render the planet uninhabitable!

With 2014 marking the beginning of the four-year commemoration of the 'Great War' (World War I), we are doubtless destined to be bombarded by the war propaganda machine (admittedly for the moment decently sheepish about the indeterminate reasons for the outbreak of that landmark bloody conflict), but as ever determined to 'remember' everything but learn nothing. Moreover our young people continue to be exposed to a diet of computer games, cinema and DVDs normatising and indeed glorifying war and violence, e.g. the egregious *Call of Duty* where the young player is challenged to develop his skill by maximising his personal 'kill'. Baroness Susan Greenfield, professor of physiology at Oxford, maintains that young people involved in a heavy diet of such war games are exposing their brain to permanent neurological damage. Even the incessant use of mobile phones is now being queried by science as likely to threaten brain cancer.

The conclusion seems to be that, beyond the end of the Cold War—hailed by Francis Fukuyama as heralding 'the end of history' and the triumph of the civil society—today's world is actually more fraught with violence, suffering and despair than at any other point in our lifetime, except between 1939 and 1945. I have just read that *'the world is full of tears and blinded by hate'*. Certainly there are now millions more refugees in the world (over 60 million) than ever in human history (two million of them Syrian *children*), because there are more armed conflicts using ever more sophisticated weapons, in more ruthless hands and backed by more ruthless ideologies—ultimately thanks to the arms dealers, evil princes of world capitalism. And now we are living with the advent of an over-arching ideology to motivate alienated young Muslims in the West in many lands by the vision of a worldwide Caliphate, serving Allah by spreading Islam through *jihad*.

Where is the good news?

Paradoxically, at the same time we read of the ongoing spread of Christian belief, especially across China, parts of Africa and in Latin America. There are even reports of Muslims at many levels, including imams and sheikhs (and now two members of the ISIS 'death cult'!) currently embracing the Christian faith and braving ignominy and death. As a result the fault line of the Tenth Parallel marking the Muslim and the Christian zones of Africa (and even east to the Philippines) is now traced in blood.

The clash of values implicit between the extremes: local libertarian nationals in the West eschewing any religious faith and strict *jihadis* bent on imposing a mediaeval-style behaviour code may well ultimately imply civil strife conceivably morphing into a worldwide apocalyptic conflict, with the Israel/Palestine flashpoint ever the focus of angry international division.

Thwarting God?

But there is another side to the coin. Thank God, all is not doom and gloom. Though today our cheeky brat of a society has *"turned God's glory into shame"*[96], it is still God's world that we live in, despite some of our less savoury companions on

---

96 Psalm 4:2

the journey. And that world a mere pinprick in a cosmos where a new sun explodes into being every tick of the clock! As an Aboriginal tribal elder in remote north-west Australia observed on-line recently, "He's a big God—and He loves you."

"*God cannot be mocked. A man reaps what he sows.*"[97] Despite the media's assiduous reporting of crime and sleaze—tending to obscure the presence of decency and kindness, and even normality in the world—over our lifetime real progress has been made by the civil society in 'humanising' the Western world: liberating multitudes from past inequities, expanding social welfare coverage, defining and extending human rights, combating discrimination on many grounds, identifying and countering racism, caring for the disabled, guaranteeing freedom of conscience and generally making the rule of law more comprehensive. Significantly, this liberal breakthrough had never been on the capitalist agenda, preoccupied as it has ever been with ignoring the injustices of the status quo while focusing on higher profits.

Surely it has been God's Holy Spirit inspiring such advances (all of them reflecting compassion and historic Christian insights at the local and the international levels), as exemplified particularly in the emergence of the United Nations system of global co-operation and solidarity, backed by international specialist agencies *(inter alia)* for health, food and agriculture, education, science and culture, labour relations, human rights, refugees and the environment. Yet an early Secretary-General of the United Nations Organisation, Dag Hammarskjøld, a devout Christian, is believed to have been murdered (martyred?) in 1961 in an unexplained plane crash in the Congo.

Moreover at the opposite end of the scale of power and fame, throughout the Third World large numbers of young Western expatriates daily brave fearsome hazards in seeking the wellbeing of disadvantaged people and communities. Many of them are Christians. Without their presence some of the Western macro-level financial aid programs would be unworkable.

Indubitably, today's is an immensely complex world, unrecognisable from the one we lived in at the height of the Cold War in the mid-'50s (despite all its uncertainties)—though there is still far to go in countering poverty and inequality.

And more than ever, today looms the new challenge of military violence around the world: maybe portending an Armageddon triggered by the wide perception of our Western 'superiority' (read godlessness).

Back home: what of race relations?

Tragically, in our own wealthy country we still see too many of our 'First Nations' people deriving too little benefit from the advances we celebrate. But at a commemoration in Sydney in 2015 of 40 years of the federal *Racial Discrimination Act*, to which I was invited as one of the speakers, sharing my memories of the Fraser Government's indifference during the early years, the proceedings opened

---

97   Paul's Letter to the Galatians 6:7

(as customary by then) with a *Welcome to Country* by a descendant of the Aboriginal people of the area—around Sydney!

By then his people nationwide owned over one third of the total area of the Australian landmass, thanks to the powers of the *Racial Discrimination Act* being upheld in 1992 by the High Court of Australia in the Eddie Mabo land rights case, focused on unbroken possession of Murray Island (Mer) off the tip of Cape York Peninsula. The subsequent enactment of the *Native Title Act* by the Keating Government had applied the ruling throughout Australia wherever unbroken possession could be proven. Many further claims are pending. But to our shame, it had only been with the passage of the *Racial Discrimination Act* by Gough Whitlam in 1975 that Aborigines were first formally recognised under Australian law.

Yet this *legal* reality does not necessarily affect the daily lives of Aboriginal people as lived in the rest of the continent, which includes all cities, towns and areas settled by non-Aborigines. Less than one third of all Aborigines live on the land to which they have native title. Of the total Australian population Aborigines comprise only 6% and in Victoria a small remnant of the original indigenous population survived European settlement, today numbering less than 50,000. For over 35,000 years they had occupied the land, and their Dreamtime stories included accounts of volcanic eruptions and the rising sea levels cutting off Tasmania and filling Port Phillip Bay.

However in the closely settled parts of Australia, the 'bran nue dae' that the Aboriginal musical road film evokes is reflected in real progress made towards social equality in our richly multicultural society. Today there are many Aboriginal teachers, community workers, lawyers, artists, film makers, doctors and a surgeon, a number of academics and politicians, one of them a former national president of the Labor Party and another a Minister in the Turnbull Government, while acclaimed sportsmen and women abound. I would like to think that the intensely multicultural pattern of our cities has also boosted Aboriginal stocks by breaking down the local WASP[98] stereotype that had long prevailed as the norm for holding power.

Equally encouraging is the broad measure of peace, harmony and mutual respect achieved within our multicultural society, though one of the world's most diverse. Probably this is the greatest single achievement during the fair slab of Australian history that we have lived through, and compared to the prevailing social attitudes of our childhood, it is nothing less than dramatic. And to have an awareness that I had the privilege of some involvement in shaping this movement brings the utmost satisfaction.

---

98   White Anglo-Saxon Protestant

39
In Search of Meaning

Beyond the values of capitalism, where else shall we seek meaning in our materialistic society? Can we invest our energy and talents in the service of humankind? The prospects are legion, some of them perennial and some very contemporary: home making, cooking and serving meals, tending babies, caring for the young, raising children—and blessing the old.

But also the service of the wider community, providing health care, education, and training in skills and learning. Fostering science and technology—whose bounds are advancing by the hour offering endless prospects of research geared to the wellbeing of society beyond personal gain. Involvement in government, the administration, the law and justice, in planning, construction, communication. And much of this activity can be self-funding: growing things, building things, making things, distributing things.

And what of the non-material realm: the search for meaning, for wisdom and contentment? And in the realms of education, the arts, entertainment and of philanthropy? What of the quest for God's truth, offering a focus for meaning and connection, and hope in the darkness? The proclaiming of God's message for human existence, and the *'cure* (=tending) of souls? Whereas there is adequate wealth in society for all these realms, capitalism is serving up a thin gruel indeed, a starvation diet for the soul.

But as Robert Louis Stevenson famously enthused,

> "The world is so full of a number of things,
> I'm sure we should all be as happy as kings".

Ever since schooldays the adage has rung in my head, with its *'go find'* promise of new hope and the hint of better things to come, a counter to the tyrannous preoccupation with merely earning a living. Transcending the humdrum daily struggle, evoking far horizons, half-glimpsed dreams, looking outwards and up. It offers a rich context for exploring personal meaning. Cherishing it as I do, I have tried to instil it into our children, I would like to think with a measure of success.

Place of the arts and culture

And what of the potential of the arts and culture for enhancing meaning in our lives? Unfortunately the home I grew up in placed little emphasis on high culture, beyond that occasionally encountered on the radio (then 'wireless'). In Sydney the ABC had two radio stations: 2FC for everyday information and entertainment and 2BL for highbrow culture, but our mother favoured the commercial stations with their inane chatter, lowbrow music and trite advertisements: 2GB, 2UW, 2UE, 2KY, 2CH (for Church, Protestant) and 2SM (St Mary's, Catholic). After coming home from church on Sunday evenings I would turn to 2CH, but of course (ever so broad-mindedly!) we boycotted 2SM altogether.

Apart from my adventures in learning the violin from Mischa Dobrinski in the city in 1942, aborted by our move to the philistine outer suburbs, I first encountered classical music in an accessible form in two Gilbert & Sullivan operas at the Theatre Royal, attended as matinees at the ages of 11 and 12 by our Opportunity C Class at Hurstville in 1943-44, and also the memorable demonstration of the instruments of the orchestra under Sir Bernard Heinze at a schools' concert in Sydney Town Hall after which they played *The Sorcerer's Apprentice* of Dukas. Then I had to wait till my student days in the 1950s to attend the heavily subsidised ABC Youth Concert series in Sydney Town Hall in the early evenings, mostly with the maestros Sir Bernard Heinze and Sir Eugene Goossens presiding over the Sydney Symphony Orchestra.

Classical music

Captured for life by the majesty and power of a symphony orchestra in full voice, in later adulthood I would satisfy the craving by always holding season tickets for concerts of the Canberra and later the Melbourne Symphony Orchestras, and the years have brought untold musical delight in the darkened recesses of the Llewellyn Hall and the Hamer Hall. I have probably imbibed a good deal of the entire classical repertoire—although at times affronted by contemporary cacophonies. (A quirky memory of Canberra concerts was the night Ernest Llewellyn himself, conducting a symphony, lost control of his *bâton* which soared backwards over his head, to be passed up the rows again and ever so discreetly handed back to the maestro, all without his missing a beat!)

Sometimes in retrospect I have taken to wondering whether my truest calling might not have been to music in some form. Certainly I had made a good, if precocious start—but it petered out for lack of funds and teachers. But I am very focused on music: I could not contemplate living without it; somehow the wellbeing of my soul is intertwined with it. Moreover my whole Christian experience has been expressed in music: hymns, modern songs and choruses, both words and music forever coursing through my brain. Thank God I was not born in a Muslim land devoid of musical worship! And invariably I write against a background of classical music playing (now) on FM radio, switching between ABC and the public MBS-FM to which in more affluent years we paid our annual subscription.

But sad to say, today classical music seems to be in steep decline, rarely if ever presented on television or on commercial radio—hence never encountered by the bulk of the population, but particularly the younger generation. This gloomy prognostication is backed by the current inability of the Melbourne Symphony Orchestra to woo a full house to the splendidly refurbished Hamer Hall on the Yarra bank where 25 years ago the symphony concerts would have been booked out, admittedly mostly by silver-haired patricians and matrons, whose grandchildren must now have other musical tastes. The threatening demise within one lifetime of European musical traditions spanning five centuries is quite shocking. And what does the future hold for choral singing when young people seem to be mostly tone deaf?

Doubtless the realm of music provides something of a barometer for the changing social climate: is there some parallelism now between ethical and aesthetic anarchy—both dimensions having lost their rootedness in the classical norms practised in the West for centuries and profoundly undergirded by Christian values? Today the universally humanising component of melody seems to be under siege from disharmony, with the overwhelming domination of percussion ('noise') broken occasionally by snatches of melody. No longer are pop songs whistlable. And what can be more cringe-worthy than hearing the cacophony of a victorious football team 'singing' its club song on a tuneless monotone, or a crowd 'singing' the national anthem?

Ironically, under the onslaught of the insistent *now* of global commerce, it is only 'world music' that retains its melodic charm. The other traditional arena, church music, has largely succumbed to the power of canned music so that hymns or worship songs are barely 'sung' in church any more but rather swamped by the electronic power of a band's booming percussion.

Church music

Moreover in the mainline churches an irreconcilable gap in musical tastes has opened up across the generations between hymn *singers* and band *listeners*. The poetic beauty and spiritual profundity of the classical hymns reflecting almost two thousand years of the life of faith have been replaced by tuneless ditties clothing trite (and often surprisingly archaic!) spiritual clichés rather than the full sweep of theological truth. In most churches the inevitable response has been to corral the older generation apart from the younger ones into separate worship services (earlier, of course) but this offends against the universal vision of the one worshipping people of God. Again it reflects the uniquely fractured nature of Western society, in which we are united only in our brokenness.

However in our current parish base at All Saints' Greensborough, with one of the best modern organs in Melbourne and a master organist presiding, early on Sunday mornings a virtual churchful of older worshippers sing not four but five traditional hymns reflecting the biblical theme of the day, and the 'professional' choir leads the chanting of an ancient Jewish psalm.

Indeed as I ponder it all now I am amazed at how profoundly in one lifetime has the macro-societal situation changed, and at a pace unprecedented in recorded history. So much so that critics of my musing will be tempted to dismiss them as nothing more than the jaundiced maunderings of one who has outlived his cultural day. To be sure I do struggle against the negativity of so much around us in today's world: brutal reality or merely media projection? But again, in defence of the longer, comparative perspective it can well be asserted that *'You'll never know what you never knew'*. And of course it reflects that dimension of awareness that only older people can possess, having lived through some of 'the past' not shared by younger generations.

With the other fine arts regrettably I have little experience, other than one play in London's West End about the Irish 'Troubles' and a few visits to operas— *Parzifal* in Germany and in Canberra occasionally Aboriginal drama and dance performances recommended by Dave from his wide contacts. Of course we have also frequently attended his own performances. Once during a work assignment in Brisbane I went with a colleague to the classical ballet *La Fille Mal Gardée*, charming but more for the music than the dance.

Galleries and museums

But the visual arts (other than utterly abstract works) make a huge appeal—perceiving reality mainly through the eyes as I always have. I recall lengthy visits to Le Louvre and to the Musée d'Art Impressioniste in the former Gare d'Orsay railway station in Paris, to the Neue Pinakothek in Munich and the Museum of Art History in Vienna, as well as to galleries in London and Istanbul (and of course in most of the Australian capital cities). Of even stronger appeal have been museums spanning the arts and history and cultures. Many have been the hours lost in wonderment in memorable museums: the Victoria & Albert in London, the Museum of Wales in Cardiff, the 'Spanish Riding School' in Vienna, the Pergamon Museum in East Berlin, and many a museum of archaeology: in Cairo, Istanbul, Ankara, Budapest, Quito and Chongqing, plus the traumatic commemorations of devastating bombing attacks on Hiroshima, Nagasaki and Würzburg. Together they present the fruits of peoples' and cultures' and nations' search for meaning worldwide down the centuries.

Not to speak of the splendid royal and imperial palace complexes in Windsor, Versailles, Vienna, Potsdam, Hanover, Dresden and Stuttgart , as well as in Istanbul and Beijing. In fact it is the architectural glories of Europe that have captivated me the most. A huge proportion of the countless colour slides and photos taken around the world turn out to be of impressive buildings: cathedrals, castles, marketplaces, half-timbered houses, urban vistas. Nor to mention world-famous sites such as the Pyramids and Sphinx, the Suez Canal, Mt Vesuvius and Pompeii, the Colosseum, the Catacombs, the Acropolis, Ephesus, Troy, the Holy Land: Jerusalem, Bethlehem, Nazareth, the Sea of Galilee; Holy Mt Athos, the Pont du Gard, Hadrian's Wall, Stonehenge, the Mexican pyramids, the Great Wall of China, the Kremlin and Red Square, and of course Machu Picchu. All of them meccas of tourism proffering memories to cherish lifelong.

Of immense satisfaction has been the relationship between the range of these worldwide travels and the minimal outlays on creature comforts. Who has seen and done so much while expending so little? Childhood dreams fulfilled beyond all imagining. Truly the Botany Bay Heads beckoned to a captivating world.

Sports spectator

On the other hand, of merely passing interest was the Australian passion for spectator sports which lend meaning to the life of so many compatriots. Never again would I attain the degree of loyalty and commitment felt at the age of 15 for Canterbury-Bankstown Rugby League team (today's Bulldogs) when on wintry Saturday afternoons I could regularly be found at Belmore Oval with a mate from school clamouring for a local victory or occasionally at the Match of the Day at Sydney Cricket Ground. One year we got as far as the Grand Final. Then in 1948 I went to see the Sydney Test match against the first post-War English touring cricket team, with our 'Invincibles': Don Bradman, Keith Miller, Arthur Morris (an old Cantabrian), Sid Barnes, Neil Harvey, Ray Lindwall *et al.* and the following year a match against India with Mankad and Armanath (who like me bowled off the wrong foot). In later years I would watch soccer matches at the Melbourne Olympics of 1956 and the Sydney Olympics of 2000, but among my passions sport never rated highly.

'Sportsman'

On the other hand in my early days, with no great distinction, I did enjoy involvement in team sports: cricket, soccer, hockey and one unmemorable season of baseball, with church teams in Sydney and club teams in Wagga and Canberra. From my twenties I also had a good bicycle, which accompanied me to Muswellbrook, Wagga and Canberra. In Melbourne I invested further and to this day (at 83), closely consulting my pedometer/speedometer. I try to ride up to 25km per week around the bike paths beside the Yarra and Diamond Creek, which joins it at Eltham. Naturally, a few spills have heightened the challenge.

A richly diversifying society

Part of my quest for meaning and fulfilment, intensifying over the decades, has been my interest in monitoring the evolution of Australia within the broader world, as our population has quadrupled from six to twenty-four million in my lifetime! Apart from the endless frustrations (and occasionally the triumphs) of party politics, my interest has been excited by the physical environment, architecture, the townscapes, town planning and the urban scene, the development of public transport, motoring and aviation, rather than the boring, underlying (but indispensable) technology—not to mention the economy—which remain closed books.

But beyond all this, my sharpest focus has been reserved for the human context of our national development: who are we Australians? In my childhood, from coast to coast the answer would have been unequivocal: people from British backgrounds. Later censuses would show that this was the least multicultural period since the First Fleet. In my schooldays I only knew one boy who was half-

Chinese, two Jews, and one classmate with an Italian-sounding surname. Only at university would I meet holocaust escapees studying (of all things) German!

And of course I was barely aware of the scope of the White Australia Policy for excluding Asians ('coloureds') from the country—rather, we sensed we were a branch of the British Isles somehow transposed to the Antipodes and with no local regional connections at all. Yet the great romance of my life would become bound up with facilitating the diversification of cultures destined to create the Australia we know today, where every second Australian is overseas-born or has one or both parents born overseas—including all four of our grandchildren!

And of course we have all enjoyed the great good fortune of living our lives in a stable and secure society far from the world centres of conflict marked by the arms race, the Cold War and the balance of terror, and now the Islamist excesses. Beyond our parents' soul-destroying experience of two dreadful wars interspersed by the near-total collapse of national economies, our generation in Australia has been privileged to live through an era of peace and reconstruction, with full employment, growing prosperity and social mobility. And in later years through an amazing technological evolution which has transformed human existence in the West, although within which there was still some continuity of earlier moral and religious values.

Thus we have living memories of a church life that for so many Australians claimed centre stage, both in the public realm and in satisfying the personal quest for meaning through offering a faith to live by. The stability conferred on our lives by these factors stands in stark contrast to the sense of multi-level crisis that seems to pervade the community today, casting a long shadow over our future.

The domestic scene

In retrospect, it seems that the travel motif has been symbolically incarnated in the three serial forays of my working life: into education and teaching, into public service research and community development, and into Christian ministry. All three of them focused on human betterment rather than competitive or commercial gain—a tremendous privilege which I never foresaw, let alone sought. In the ongoing pilgrimage there was always a sense (if at times only dimly perceived) of a divine guide quietly unfolding purposes for my existence in his world. *Very rarely has regret tinged the onward way.* Thank God!

And how much have I treasured the understanding, support and love of my life-partner Marjorie, despite the changing scenes we have explored together and the burdens I have laden her with. Her patience and loyalty in the face of misgivings, her courage in venturing out into the unknown, and the diligence of her physical caring for our family is all exemplified in the portrait of the remarkable wife and mother whom we meet in Proverbs chapter 31 in the Jewish culture of the Old Testament:

> "A good woman is hard to find and worth more than rubies. She's diligent in

home-making, quick to assist anyone in need, reaches out to help the poor. When she speaks she has something worth hearing and she always says it kindly. Her children respect and bless her. Many women have done remarkable things, but you've outclassed them all!"[99]

But of course she has also led her own creative life both within and beyond the domestic setting, bringing her finely honed skills to the task of counselling and blessing people, always within a community development context, as well as raising and nurturing four children, often under the testing circumstances of my frequent and at times lengthy absences on demanding work commitments. And in our ministry phase she was in reality 'co-vicar', humanising the parish by being ever available for all, initiating creative activities for all ages. In recent years she has become active in spiritual direction *('soul companioning'* or *'holy listening'*), completing a three-year diploma and working with her mentorees under the close supervision required of practitioners.

Beyond this she is currently the co-ordinator of the women's network of Renewal Retreat Ministries in Victoria which sustains women in professional ministry by offering mutual support over a three-year cycle of residential retreats.

In 2016 we hope to celebrate sixty years of our life together. As someone had ever so tactfully observed at my 80th birthday celebrations with Sydney family and friends, *"She deserves a VC"*. Indeed she does. But at this remove, mulling over what it has all meant during a lifetime, maybe I can claim to have seen the scriptural promise fulfilled, that those who seek shall find. I have indeed *'found'*: peace in my home and among my family, a faith to live by and the prospects of eternity, the joy of belonging to God's people and using my gifts for serving among the worldwide company of believers, the pleasure of children launched into the world and our four dear grandchildren growing apace in a land still marked by hope, despite many indications of gathering darkness.

And on every hand the enticing wonders of creation, the promise of every new dawn—and peace at the end.

---

[99] Excerpts from Proverbs chapter 31 in *The Message: The Bible in Contemporary Language* translated by Eugene H Peterson

40
Core of my Heart

Throughout the story it is manifestly the realm of the spirit rather than the mind that has endowed my life with meaning, both in scope and in depth. Unsurprising this, given the concept of a Creator who *"made the world and everything in it, and gives to everyone life and breath and everything else, and in whom we live, and move, and have our being"*, as St Paul put it to the philosophical dilettantes in Athens[100]. We were created as spiritual beings.

Halting journey into faith

But it has taken a lifetime to get my head around the unfolding implications of living in and by faith.. Yet along the path, the God dimension has increasingly taken hold of my imagination, as everything else has fallen into perspective. Without such an ordering principle life would remain inexplicable, maybe meaningless. As a teenager responding to a call in Sydney Town Hall to *'come to Christ'*, my discovery was that God is for real, that he has taken the initiative of self-disclosure, and may be accessed by us mortals. Encouraging news to one who had already learnt in Sunday School many of the Bible stories and the facts of Jesus' life—but how did that relate to my life 2,000 years later? What new conclusions were to be drawn now? How should it affect my ongoing behaviour, my goals—and my dreams?

During the next decade, though blessed with opportunities for education unheard-of in my extended family and the opening up before me of professional life—not to mention the joys of friendships and ultimately love—I seem to have been a slow learner. (Is that why I have been granted so long a life?) I could never quite grasp that a Heavenly Father *loved* me and (to invoke transactional analysis terms) *that I was 'OK'*, indeed pleasing to God as his redeemed child. So I was ever looking for subjective experiences of God as others claimed to enjoy. Beneath a certain bravado, at times I even feared to be something of a fake.

From a vantage point 65 years down the track I suspect the underlying issue had been the lack of any firm sense of my own personhood. I cannot remember being purposively *'raised'* by my physically present though emotionally absent parents. Rather I seem to have been left to myself to make what sense I could of my own existence. In those difficult times around the Great Depression, perhaps they were simply too preoccupied with survival to understand that their children needed a positive investment in their formation and an emotional education beyond well-meaning physical care. For instance, I cannot recall ever *hearing* that I was loved, though probably the care I received would have been evidence enough.

Nor do I have any memories of life-related issues ever being discussed—or even commented on—in our home. Indeed I never knew what anyone thought

---

100   His exposition is summarised in Acts 17: 16–34

about anything. Or even whether there were things to think about beyond your inner preoccupations. So the only ethical code I internalised was my mother's peculiar commitment to pursuing respectability and waxing irrationally critical of those who failed her test. My instinctively leftist father never ventured an opinion on anything, thus keeping the peace in a divided household under the stern eyes of the dour, conservative patriarch—from which I internalised that 'nice' people don't hold opinions about anything, but simply pursue being *good*.

With so little of anything significant addressed to me—and having no contacts with playmates outside school hours—it was little wonder that I would grow into a painfully shy, rather taciturn child, withdrawn and inwardly absorbed. In my adolescent years I never knew how to converse with peers: I would agonise that I had nothing to say, and would muse on how other people engaged in meaningful conversations. On this unsatisfactory basis I had bumbled through the passage from childhood to manhood (teenagers not having yet been invented) without succumbing to the temptations then just starting to be held out by the media and the profiteers. Certainly today it has become harder to maintain an even keel through adolescence, given the ubiquity of the media and the cyber world with their distractions and temptations—and their hidden agendas.

Only decades later, through involvement in personal growth groups, would I grasp the basic (and obvious) principle that meaningful encounters flow from tuning in to your conversation partner's life and concerns as well as being preoccupied with your own. Walk a mile in their shoes! Sadly, until then my approach to parenting adolescent children, particularly the boys, had unwittingly reflected my own non-purposive upbringing, undergirded and justified by the naïve new rationalisation of the 1970s social revolution that all the traditional conventions and didactic measures were now invalid, replaced by an exciting new world of non-directive relationships and personal discovery. There was even a modish theology around suggesting that Christians should never 'name the Name' but let their own integrity and inner wholeness carry the day. (In retrospect, this probably meant that for the most part nobody noticed anything!) I feel sad about having acted out this misguided approach to parenting adolescents, in essence weakening the essential link between faith and life.

Moreover, it was only after internalising the belated insight about focusing on others that the possibility of involvement in Christian ministry could start to become thinkable. As it happened, years afterwards and beyond professional training, as a parish minister I did seem able to invest myself in people and to handle pastoral care with competence and warmth. Indeed I can claim to have actually grown into enjoying it. But it had taken all of 55 years!

As a young adult what I hadn't adequately grasped was the veriest core of the Gospel: the almost unbelievable truth about the scope and plenitude of God's grace (goodness, kindness, generosity)—of course undeserved—and the perfect efficacy of the redemption purchased for humanity once for all on the Cross and offered to us freely through a love-relationship with Christ. To be accessed simply by our identification with it (taking God's promise seriously and accepting it inwardly). And even that act of faith on our part also a gift of God's love: the ability to internalise the liberating notion that Christ had done it all and offered us the unspeakable gift of God's friendship and guidance throughout life. And over the years moderating any legacy of the Aspberger's syndrome.

The social setting for these early struggles of heart and will had been the hothouse atmosphere of the Sydney University Evangelical Union and subsequently Methodist (later Uniting Church) parishes, supplemented by the broader experience of churchgoing in England (Anglican and Plymouth Brethren) and Germany (Lutheran and Methodist). Along the way had come the dawning awareness of the dualistic character of Christian belief—personal faith *and* commitment to others, especially the neediest. Of course the two dimensions are intertwined, because discovering the reality of God immediately implies relating with our local fellow-believers in fellowship and worship. The pity is that this fellowship can so satisfy us that we may not take the next step of 'serving the present age', as Charles Wesley's programmatic hymn *A Charge to Keep I Have* puts it:

> To serve the present age, my calling to fulfil,
> O may it all my powers engage, to do my Master's will".

Throughout church history, times of renewal and revival have been marked by the rediscovery of this dualistic message: God's favour *proclaimed* with new conviction but also *demonstrated* through relevant social action, e.g. in the combat of poverty and industrial exploitation, slavery, child labour, treatment of prisoners, discrimination against women and the disabled, opposing racism, war, the arms race and nuclear armaments; and seeking justice for indigenous people, refugees and asylum seekers—besides the wellbeing of the environment within which it all happens.

God's worldwide strategic initiative—the 'charismatic movement'

Twenty years later, in Canberra (jaded and struggling to hold our lives together, both of us in demanding jobs and parenting four lively children) we were to encounter a new liberation—the heart-softening and praise movement, as though we had all just broken through into a fresh dimension of intimacy with God—and pleasure in his family. We rejoiced to be living in an age of such unexpected and refreshing newness. What would God do next? It was to usher in the third and decisive phase of our professional lives.

Many of our fellow church members sensed a call to fulltime ministry for the Kingdom of God and moved off to Sydney and Melbourne for training. Others became involved in parish initiatives in community welfare, outreach and the founding of a Christian school accessing federal funding. One initiated an embrace of politics, ultimstely leading to his becoming Prime Minister!

But Marjorie and I sought to integrate our weekday secular activity with

Kingdom insights. Only with my professional world under terminal party-political attack some years later, and finally through my adventure with once-lethal tuberculosis did the blurred prospect of Christian service begin to assume sharper outlines, finally to be grasped in response to an invitation to embrace a two-year ecumenical project in multicultural clergy education in Melbourne ... *et nous voilà aujourd'hui!* [101]

Amidst the social upheaval of the '60s and '70s God was the Prime Mover, arguably to be seen (in retrospect) as preparing the Western church for the coming age of tribulation that we call the 21st century—yet within two or three decades a church to be widely (and justly) reviled and shamed for its public sins and its traditional hubris. Does it betoken a countdown to the scriptural promise of Christ's appearance at the end of the age in a welter of apostasy, confusion and conflict?

Recently I encountered the shocking claim that the 20th century had witnessed more persecution of Christians worldwide than the previous 19 centuries put together, with no less than 100 million victims! The pace of the countdown is quickening. A bloody persecution of Christians is now escalating in many parts of the Muslim world and in North Korea—with scant succour (or even interest) from the once-Christian West. Is that also an end-time marker?

Forsaking the faith

Certainly within my lifetime, in Western society, the widespread abandonment of virtually two thousand years of Christian belief has come about at a bewildering pace and at terrible cost, in little more than one generation—leaving a void of purpose, a vacuum of values, and a legacy of libertarianism, confusion and anomie. Not to speak of rampant evil manifest across our society and throughout the world. I am desolated at the accelerating rate of abandonment of the core verities underlying Western civilisation.

A recent survey found that 49% of Australians now hold that there is no God. In the context of post-modernism, what might now offer a meta-narrative for exploring the meaning of life, in place of the belief in a loving Creator seeking our good? But with both the motivations and sanctions of religion lost, the search for personal meaning becomes a daunting challenge, perhaps inducing confusion and despair or leading to a headlong embrace of provocative or self-destructive behaviours reflecting social disintegration and nihilism. Welcome to today's Western society!

A gathering gloom

At the personal level, to spurn a faith to live by and the guidance it provides for discerning good from evil, and to ignore God's indwelling Holy Spirit who empowers daily living, seems to amount to serious acts of folly. But when such

---

101   'and here we are today!'

acts are widespread across society it must trigger an erosion of moral and ethical standards once perceived as normative, but now more likely to be ignored, even derided. Further, when this drift occurs within one single generation—as we have experienced—it amounts to the society losing its moral compass, to become the plaything of sinister forces bent on sidelining the rumour of God and actively encouraging agnosticism or even atheism. *"No God, no master!"* rang the catchcry of rebellion in the 1970s. In the Western world the all-pervasive media and entertainment colossus, whether intentionally or subconsciously, has moved into a new crusade to dismiss God from his creation and subvert residual Christian ethics by libertarian campaigning. Its success is attested by the current generation's scepticism of religion as simply irrelevant to living.

Society under siege

So what are the most serious areas of distress apparent in our social and community life today? What are the losses, resulting from these trends, that spawn new challenges to societal wellbeing—not to speak of personal meaning and contentment?

- **Eclipse of marriage**
  Society is paying dearly for the wholesale disdain of the timeless and universal bond of matrimony—*a committed lifelong partnership with a religious or social sanction.* The worldwide concept of the family as the nest for raising the young is in retreat. One recent media report acknowledged that the majority of cases of violence against women occur within non-marital relationships. One unintended outcome of this is the later age at which many people ultimately marry– if indeed they do. *('Why buy a book when you can join a library?')*—leading to later problems, for instance constricting the years of grandparental support. Not to be wondered at is the escalating number of disgruntled, angry and sometimes vengeful ex-partners, maybe from serial relationships—and sad, lost children.

- **Epidemic of domestic violence**
  A perennial barometer of the level of distress is the abuse of alcohol, identified now as a cardinal factor in fuelling the epidemic of *domestic violence* ('family terrorism') declared by the federal government to be a 'national crisis'. One in four Australian women experience it: across the continent every two minutes there is a call for police intervention. Every week two women (partners/ex-partners) are murdered, and three women are hospitalised with brain damage. And among Aboriginal communities the rate of alcohol-fuelled violence is no less than *forty times* the rate for Australians as a whole! Today's news bulletin hails the allocation of no less than $100 million by Canberra for nationwide counter measures. Both NSW and Victoria have a 'Minister for the Prevention of Family

Violence' and in Victoria a Royal Commission on Domestic Violence has opened.

- **A new 'ice age'?**

Before the 60s, 'recreational drug-taking' was unknown, the drugs of choice being alcohol and nicotine. I had never tasted alcoholic drinks and my only brush with nicotine resulted from the offer of a cigarette to me at the age of *nine* by, of all people, a trainee minister at Dulwich Hill Presbyterian Church. The resultant splutter put me off smoking for life. Maybe he did it with good intentions?

But in recent times we have witnessed a veritable explosion in the use of crystal methamphetamines (*'ice'*) triggering crazy, destructive, even fatal episodes currently beyond the scope of the ambulance services in Melbourne to handle, with children as young as ten addicted

- **Gambling addiction**

A further indicator of social distress is the addiction to gambling, particularly through the ubiquitous poker machines in suburbia and country towns with their deliberately contrived capacity to addict players, so that entire family budgets can come under threat. But all attempts to seek restrictions come to naught because of advertising on television (and particularly at sporting venues, with instant opportunities at every second kick or cricket shot)—and governments' addiction to the revenues at stake.

- **Mental health concerns**

Not unrelated to these challenges is the growing incidence of *depression*. In a 'Q and A' program for Mental Health Week, the web of contributing factors were explored, as experienced in the lives of *45% of Australians*—three quarters of them men—and among Aborigines *double the rate* of depression. A raft of concerns were identified: biological/genetic, drug and alcohol or gambling addictions, isolation, loss of employment heightened by hopelessness, as well as the intensity of brutal competitiveness—but also by the loss of the 'scaffolding' in our society and the general lack of a belief system other than holding money as the chief good (*god?*).

- **Suicide rate**

For Australians under 44 suicide has become the commonest cause of death and among people under 22 now accounts for one third of all deaths—among young Aboriginal people a veritable epidemic (recently a girl of ten!) It seems clear that the moral fabric of our society is starting to fray—if not unravel—at an accelerating rate. An American magazine reports that the children of parents caught up in the '60s sexual revolution with its flouting of boundaries are becoming a generation killing themselves in unprecedented numbers. And today comes a call for all teachers to be trained in suicide prevention.

- **Pornography and children**
  Changes in the realm of sexual ethics, linked with the upheaval of the '60s, the permissive society of the '70s and today's explicitly *sexualized and violent society*, make pornography virtually inescapable by children from primary school level, thus subverting parental responsibility. In response there have been commissions of enquiry in the UK, Scotland, the European Parliament and in the USA. In 2006 a Senate Enquiry in Australia on the Sexualisation of Children in the Media proffered strategies for countering the outcomes of such advertising but no action appears to have resulted. On the contrary we have witnessed the advent of the civil libertarian *Sex Party* in the Victorian Parliament with the express purpose of countering 'the *increasing influence of religion* in Australian politics'!

Ambivalent role of the media

The cynical role of the commercial media has recently been highlighted in its conniving with predatory capitalism to *undermine public health* through unconscionable advertising of food products reeking in sugar known to promote obesity with all its attendant ills. Our expanding silhouettes tell the story. Two-thirds of Australians are now over-weight or obese, and this is rapidly becoming a major health concern worldwide, clearly related to dietary intake. In a series of recent ABC television programs these strategies were clinically dissected, revealing the shameless behaviour of captains of commerce, actually *backed by* conservative governments—although their refusal to act in defence is bringing about ever higher budgets for health care.

By way of a juicy conspiracy theory, one might even premise that a principal function of the *commercial* media is to breed cynicism in order to devalue people's identification with ideologies or faith. Traducing truth for trivia. Buy, BUY! Conform, CONFORM! (that is, to the media's take on issues precluding any other opinion). Why? Maybe to dumb down the functioning of a discriminating, citizen-based civil society by substituting the bread-and-circuses mentality? Of course the 'circuses' today are the products of a highly professional, ingenious, appealing entertainment industry, spinner of dreams of which we are all incessant but passive consumers in our own homes. one of the leading figures an (ex)-Australian media mogul sometimes cited as the world's most powerful figure, to whom even leaders of nations defer.

As an insightful comment in the preface to a contemporary autobiography put it: "The media today is obsessed with the moment, so memories get cancelled out in a generation". This factor could account for the astonishing loss of Christian insights about how we might publicly address the intractable dilemmas of our day.

By its unrelenting negativity, carping criticism and intentional neglect of other ideological standpoints (especially with a religious sanction) the media contribute to a growing contempt for democracy (or is it *murdochracy?*), with politicians shrinking from moral leadership but merely acting in the role of managers. It is the media that ought to be under the spotlight. But for all their self-obsession, media operatives seem incapable of self-criticism.

Silence—or connivance?—of Church hierarchy

Sadly, Christians have to admit that the '*household of Faith*' has also lost its innocence, and has made its own not insignificant contribution to public disillusionment. High-level public enquiries across the Western world have brought to light the appalling incidence of paedophilia and reprehensible (not to say hypocritical) high-level cover-ups over several generations in institutional settings both Christian and secular. In response the libertarian lobby, spearheaded by the emergent atheism movement and favoured by the media, is pushing for ever greater marginalisation of God and his believers, currently declaring schools the new battleground: '*in a secular society religion should be declared out of bounds in public*'. But this is to act on a misunderstanding of the key stipulation in the Public Instruction Act of NSW in 1880 (and in other States around that time) that public education had to be 'free, *secular,* and compulsory'. At the time the meaning of the word 'secular' was not 'non-religious' but 'non-sectarian', i.e. not supporting any one particular Church or denomination. Since society then saw itself as Christian, to be non-religious would have been meaningless. Hence there is no historical basis in law for such campaigning, as legitimate as it may be in other respects, e.g. the right to freedom of speech.

Re-writing history

My own experience in the Commonwealth Office of Education, the federal Department of Education & Science, and the Schools Commission—not to mention earlier Dip.Ed. studies—plus teaching for nearly ten years in three different countries, has left a legacy of awareness of the *social significance* of the curriculum taught as well as how best to teach it. Against this background I have become wary of the values to be transmitted to the present and future generations of young people through a new national curriculum. All Christian emphases and even the record of past Christian leadership in society have been watered down or completely relegated, ostensibly in the interests of the multicultural society (maybe read: the *sensitivities of Muslims* who comprise no more than 3% of the population—less than Buddhists—a tiny tail wagging a considerable dog!). It recalls Karl Marx's observation about the effectiveness of blocking the transmission of values, morals and beliefs to the next generation.

'Post-God Nation?'

In a new and well argued book former barrister Roy Williams[102] refutes the wilful blindness of the narrative taking shape under modern libertarian secularism, as reflected in the new national curriculum, which claims that Christianity has exercised only a minimal or even malign influence on Australia's development. Without overlooking the many failings of Christians and the Church, Williams meticulously catalogues the cavalcade over two centuries of men and women explicitly motivated by their faith as they contributed to the leadership of every significant area of Australian community life—*"Today far more common than atheism is an agnosticism among a population that is religiously 'tone-deaf', lacking any sense of the numinous and trying to ignore their own mortality."*

He demonstrates that the first settlement was devised in England by strategically placed Christians, and early Governors were almost invariably devout men, particularly the evangelical Anglican, Governor Lachlan Macquarie, who with his far-seeing vision led NSW from penal colony to free society.

> "All social welfare, healthcare and education was done by the Church and Christian volunteers. Without people motivated by their faith the early colony could not have survived. Though rough and irreverent, the colony would not have got through its early years without descending into impoverished barbarism. And over this period, saving the indigenous people from total extinction may be the Churches' most important achievement, though much evil was perpetrated on its frontiers."

Roy Williams spells out how the later colonial legislatures brought together many Christian men in leading roles imbued with the ideal of service rather than personal advantage, while Christians also played crucial roles in the discussions leading to Federation. Since then the Churches have played a vital role in shaping modern Australian society. Meticulously recording our 200-year history, he challenges atheists, agnostics and believers to a genuinely open debate about the power of Christian faith to change society. But he warns that there is a limit to how long our society can go on drawing down its Judaeo-Christian patrimony. He suggests that Churches would find more allies on the Left because that is where the more well-meaning idealists reside, while the Liberal Party, once the preserve of the 'moral middle class', has been hijacked by neo-liberals to become the populist party of the super-rich and the go-getters, with its senior ranks dominated by shallow, market-driven secularists and selectively doctrinaire Catholics who endorse the Vatican on narrowly dogmatic issues but not on the macro-level issues of war, the

---

102 *Post-God Nation? How religion fell off the radar in Australia—and what might be done to get it back on*, Harper Collins, Sydney, 2015, 406pp

environment, social justice, or refugees. In the process the Liberal Party has become less benevolent and much less Protestant.

Of course Williams does not refrain from acknowledging that the Churches have also lost influence through such societal issues as prosperity, scientism, nationalism, war, sex and gender but claims that, if they could become more open to change, they could yet restore their tarnished image and project an attainable moral vision for Australia. Though there is little doubt that it is becoming harder to be a Christian in our land.

Christians in the contemporary debates

On the other hand, among some more reactionary Christians concern has surfaced over the campaigning for wider individual rights, such as liberating women from stereotypical roles, for gender equality and for gay marriage—ranked by some as above more traditional notions of responsibility, duty and virtue as the foundations of a good society. To the extent that the newer reforms are viewed as reflecting 'God's agenda' many Christians lend their support. For me this has been something of a journey because of my somewhat schizophrenic commitments both to traditional Christian insights and to social liberalism, proffering the temptation to run with the hares while hunting with the hounds. I was not alone: Prime Minister Kevin Rudd sought to be acceptable in both camps and ended opting for the radical posture, perhaps contributing to his ultimate electoral rejection in 2013. Not having to confront such a moment of truth I enjoyed the disreputable luxury of holding aloof from strict logic or consistency over some of the more radical issues.

Gender equality? Why not? The case for equality has been well demonstrated, accepted and now safeguarded under anti-discrimination legislation, and is also the established norm in virtually all Protestant Churches with their women clergy and bishops. But in the Catholic Church and the Orthodox Churches women priests are still unthinkable, reflecting a patriarchy not known in the original New Testament churches[103] and not universally proclaimed until the eleventh century! Nevertheless under the present liberal-minded and reformist Pope Francis, review even of the issue of clergy celibacy appears conceivable.

While endorsing equal rights for homosexuals, including access by couples to civil unions, I baulk at the concept of same-sex *'marriage'*, because this entails draining the word of its age-old worldwide meaning: a union of a man and a woman as the universal setting for the begetting and nurture of children—and seen by Christians as ordained by God—in order to score a political point by the semantic *tour de force* of invoking the term 'equality'. But the losses for the whole society must immeasurably outweigh the nominal gain for a tiny but vociferous minority, the darlings of the media, a whole 1.7% of the Australian population (the Aboriginal population is four times larger!).

---

[103] Paul writes in his Letter to the Galatians, 3:26–27: "You are all children of God through faith in Christ Jesus... There is no longer Jew or Gentile, slave or free, male or female. For you are all Christians—you are one in Christ Jesus."

Indeed at the world level the issue turns out to be rather insignificant: 91% of the world's population have been said to oppose it, and 193 of the 214 Member States of the United Nations[104]. Further, a high proportion of Australians from ethnic backgrounds and from other world faiths beside Christianity maintain their age-old commitment to marriage as they have always understood it—as primarily for the nurturing of children by their biological parents. These children's rights—and the rights of the overwhelming majority of the population in all its cultural and faith diversity—also need to be safeguarded.

Moreover a disturbing and illiberal trend has already become clear in overseas societies now embracing 'marriage equality' that, in its favour, other social freedoms may be restricted, even verging on the freedom to practise religion, a prime achievement of the secular West and an inalienable human right. Recently the Catholic Archbishop of Hobart was cited to appear before an anti-discrimination tribunal for daring to publish a booklet defending the Church's teachings about marriage. Marriage as discriminatory behaviour?

Naturally, in the generalised debates over current social issues, while appreciating the relative virtues of both the Christian and the secular-humanist camps, I tend to opt instinctively for the Christian commitment where there is a good case to be made. However, more important for me than a reactionary preoccupation with the 'bedroom issues' espoused by the newer Christian political parties, is the ongoing worldwide struggle for human rights and against poverty, racism, ignorance and disease[105].

---

[104] From the blog *Family Voice* of June 2015, citing a letter to the Australian Prime Minister sent by 40 faith leaders [from several major world faiths] calling for marriage to be upheld as the mutual love of a man and a woman, open to the gift of children.

[105] In April 2015 I wrote to the Australian Christian Lobby (ACL) in Canberra: "It is important to express Christian viewpoints on the news, but it does pose the dilemma of what stance to take as Christians. We will have a political viewpoint as well as our theological viewpoint, and I am always sad to observe that ACL's political stance is to the right of centre, as though viewpoints to the left of centre are not so Christian. This is idle, since Bible-believing Christians cover a wide range of political orientations. My reading of the Gospels leaves no scope for aligning Jesus' ministry with the Establishment of his day. Invariably he was on the side of the little man, the underdog, the powerless, often the outcast. Never the system. So why would ACL support parties dedicated to the maintenance of power by the corporate lobby (=Zacchaeus *unconverted!*)? As a Christian minister I share absolutely no identification with the concerns of big business or the political parties they have created to further their interest in the great god Mammon.

But I do have ongoing interest in the wellbeing of ordinary people, the great majority of the community. Clearly their lives are often disadvantaged by the failure of conservative governments to allocate sufficient resources to improve their quality of life. Or the failure of employers to grant wage justice. Instead ACL's resources seem disproportionately devoted to concerns that business people lobby for. At worst this process can become quite anti-social—and I do not believe that Jesus would have endorsed that.

Further, by appearing naturally to favour the Right, ACL forfeits the support of large numbers of Christians in all the Churches. But even more seriously, it gives the world the impression that Christians are basically not on their side, but lack understanding & compassion for their needs, instead following some incomprehensible agenda for impeding social progress. This does not honour the Lord. The great issues of our day are not limited to the bedroom, and I can't remember Jesus ever giving such an impression. The Kingdom of God is about righteousness—the same Hebrew word as 'justice' (not a word ever heard on the lips of the Establishment). Read the 'Micah Challenge', look at Isaiah and the minor prophets again. Even the care of the earth is a commandment—are the Greens to be dismissed because of some of their social views?

It's all about perspective. I ask you again to consider the broad picture of our society's needs—and our need to be relevant and compassionate, in Christ's name. '*Seek first the Kingdom of God—and all these things* (what are they?) will be added unto you' (Matt. 6: 33)."

Worldwide Christian expansion

Yet despite the current decline of Christian faith in Australia and the West, statisticians of world religions envisage Christianity still being the globe's major faith in 2050, with the overall percentage of *'unbelievers with no religion'* actually in decline! Of course it must be noted that today it is only in the secular West that Christianity is in such sharp decline. Recent decades have seen millions turning to Christ in Africa and Asia and Latin America, which remain unaffected by Western post-modernism and hedonism, so that today the dynamic in world mission is coming from countries like Korea and Nigeria. For instance, in Nigeria there are more *Anglicans* in church on Sundays than in England, America and Australia combined! Today many of them are putting their lives on the line at the hands of the Islamist terrorist movement Boko Haram *('Education is Sinful')*. Across the world it is a similar story of risking persecution in many countries where Christian missions have planted churches.

And academic estimates by leading Chinese universities put that country's Christian population variously between 54 and 120 million. Difficult to substantiate because of the explosive growth of the *'underground churches'* gathering in farms and rural villages out of the public eye. A recently published statistic puts the number of Christians for the first time as exceeding the national membership of the Communist Party (88 million), triggering random localised reactions such as the forcible removal of crosses from the roofs of 21 church buildings and the bulldozing in 2014 of a newly built Catholic cathedral in Wenzhou in Zhejiang Province.

Indeed overall the decline of Christian faith in the West, balanced by its growth in the non-Western world, may effectively dissolve the European captivity of the Gospel: from the beginning the faith was not a Western phenomenon, although early in Christian history it had become domesticated under the centralised power of Rome and later of New Rome (Constantinople), and subsequently it informed European history and culture for a thousand years, culminating in the missionary movement from the 16th to the 20th century within the framework of colonialism which made the Christian faith the world's foremost religion—the only one practised in every land on earth.

So today's Western scepticism stands in sharp contrast to the norms of Christian religion across the face of human society throughout all ages—its ubiquity, its devotion and its intensity. Particularly its capacity for offering devotees, in an often meaningless world, a sense of belonging. My recent reading of several modern scholarly novels set in classical antiquity has confirmed just how drenched with religion that society was, despite the disdain of its élites. So it is scarcely surprising that Christianity's decline in the West is not matched elsewhere. Nor by rejection of any of the other great world faiths in their homelands e.g. of Islam in the Middle East, Hinduism in India, Buddhism in Tibet, or even Confucianism and Taoism in Communist China. Nor among their settler groups in Australia.

It is even claimed that the rest of the world is becoming more religious—

ominously so in parts of the Middle East! The West may yet wind up as an effete push-over for looming religious militancy beyond its borders.

So why the decline in the West?

Of course already, from the period of the 18th century Enlightenment and more intensively in the latter half of the 19th century, most western European philosophers, political thinkers and scientists were positing a new scientific-rationalist understanding of life and society which dispensed with the need for a divine creator or agent of 'progress'. To many, modernity and humanism offered appealing alternatives. So for the first time the educated élites largely grew up without the rumour of God or the sanction of his holiness—or the power of his love.

Today with the new factor of the silencing of Christian opinion in the media and often in academia—and the feckless abdication on the part of so many of us Christians—God seems to have been written out of his creation, including by cosmologists: it's all too big—and expanding at an incomprehensible rate! Or is it that the human mind has been rendered the smaller?

Conceivably the decline of Christian faith during the 20th century in Europe (reflected in Australia and New Zealand) is attributable largely to the crises of competing capitalisms masquerading as nationalism, which triggered unprecedented conflicts, killing some 80 million human beings in two barbaric World Wars (the most bloodthirsty in human history) and demoralising entire populations. On both sides the majority of Church leaders allowed their national loyalty to eclipse their loyalty to the Prince of Peace: where was God when both sides were claiming a monopoly on him? Why had he not responded to the heart cry of millions, especially the mothers? Or had he too wept over such freely chosen human wickedness culminating in the Holocaust[106] that smote the descendants of the 'Chosen People' with the genocide of six million?

Understandably over the post-war generations the drift from the Churches of the West would grow into an avalanche. Would this amount to the greatest (and *swiftest*) mass apostasy from any faith in human history? Certainly it seems unprecedented!

Yet the scientific humanism and modernity which Western wiseheads have substituted for religion do not enjoy universal esteem, even within some technologically advanced societies. For instance the ex-Communist bloc of eastern Europe, for 70 years predicated on a Marxist understanding of scientific humanism and the suppression of religion, has re-endorsed Eastern Orthodoxy as the religion of the State, which is paying for the restoration of the churches. With the current explosion of interest in Orthodoxy, Russian churches are struggling to keep up with the pace of growth as the younger generation rediscovers faith. We read that churches are now packed, at times seeing parishioners queuing up outside, waiting

---

106   The Hebrew word for 'burnt offering'

for someone to leave so they may enter. And today denominations other than Orthodoxy are also sanctioned. I have just heard of a minority ethnic group of traditionally animistic reindeer herders in far NE Siberia becoming Christians, as are large numbers of nominal Muslims across the various 'stans, and now forming new churches.

The contrast between this situation (arguably purchased by 70 years of oppression and persecution of Christians in the former USSR) and the dwindling role of faith in public life in our country is stark indeed. Maybe we've had it too easy: has no one much noticed our presence, or valued our contribution? Or have we become such a stench that our faith is not perceived as desirable, let alone compelling? It saddens me that by and large we appear to have become

unprofitable servants of our Lord—yet who among us could dissociate themselves from this sorry reality? Or are the issues now so cosmic that not even the most faithful of us can make the slightest impact on our communal environment of disbelief?

Humanism vs Christian faith

Hence the massively subjective turn of today's Western culture, with its focus on individualism and self-actualisation, has at best led to a *'believing without belonging'* but more commonly to a scepticism about God expressed in a brutal materialism portending the end of civility and the widespread rejection of authority—replaced by the search for authenticity, expressivity and self-fulfilment, all reflecting the increase in prosperity and the benefits of the welfare state, as well as consumerism and greater social mobility—all of them manifestations of modernity and in some cases actually Christian gifts to society. But it has all come at a price: a collective amnesia threatening the loss of our history, our identity, and our destiny.

> "It is important not to be deceived by the secularisation process which denies the sovereignty of God in history... Christians of Australia can rejoice in the contribution of our Christian forebears and confidently step out in faith aware of God's intentions for our great island continent".[107]

The Cosmic Christ

The recent identification of a possible counterpart of Earth in a galaxy some 490 light-years away, graced with the fetching name of 'Kepler 186f', is said to have further shifted the goalposts. Travelling at the speed of light, we could circle the earth seven times in one second. So sailing through space at that speed (300,000 km per sec) since his 15th century lifetime a Columbus would now be nearing his Kepler destination. I wonder how he would have whiled away the centuries while covering the nine trillion kilometres.

It must surely take a robust 'faith' to hold that life on earth in all its intricacy,

---

[107] Dr Graham McLennan, *Australia's Christian Foundations and Heritage*, 2014

complexity and beauty, with 8.7 million species identified (and still counting!)—from single-cell organisms to the human brain with its infinite inventiveness, within the context of an inter-dependent world of wonder and delight on a planet spinning through space within a solar system of impeccable timing—all this simply materialised out of nothing? *Nothing?*

The Orion Nebula, 1,500 light years from Earth

The very notion that God would even conceive of the idea of *creating* seems mind-blowing, not to speak of the implication that without the Christ *"nothing was made that was made"*[108] So it must take a truly robust 'faith' to hold that life on earth in all its intricacy, complexity and beauty, with 8.7 million species identified (and still counting!)—from single- cell organisms to the human brain with its infinite inventiveness, within the context of an inter-dependent world of wonder and delight on a planet spinning through space within a solar system of impeccable timing—all this simply materialised by chance out of nothing? Nothing? Our basic instincts rebel against it:. It all just happened by chance, with no place for a Cause or an Intelligence? Let alone a Maker of infinite power and majesty?

Or even to hold that such a Creator has no interest in his human creation, loftily indifferent to its fate? Most ordinary Australians are not so sure. Too often we are overtaken and held spellbound by the morning magic of a misty glen, the riotous greens of a rainforest, the wonder of a desert night sky, the soaring harmonies of a symphony, the glory of a life laid down for another.

Manifestly, by definition God must be *unimaginable, indefinable, incomprehensible*. Is theology then foolish in even essaying to corral God into the constraints of human thought? But if indeed God exists and created everything for his own pleasure, then clearly he is invested in his whole creation—including

---

[108] John1:2

us and our environment—and must be granted the equally incomprehensible condescension of disclosing himself by seeking us out for a conscious love-relationship. If God chooses to reveal himself to humankind through wrapping himself in the human clay he had created, is it folly to explore—and embrace the offer? Doesn't the alternative of dismissing the claim unexamined (on what credible grounds?) which might make sense of our human condition, seem hubristic—to say the very least?

God's future—and ours

But it is not what we humans think of God that counts, but what the holy, infinite, all-loving and self-revealing God purposes to do in the ongoing story of his world, let alone his cosmos. What we learn of God through his self-disclosure might lead us to understand that he is not fazed by hard human hearts as much as grieved because so many lost people decline to be *'found'*. What might God's intentions be? And what sort of future could this betoken for the West? Where is hope? And how well grounded?

The only certainty can be the future outlined in the Christian Scriptures: that the Reign of God, from the beginning of the Christian era growing in the world in embryonic form among the *'household of faith'*, will be publicly vindicated and universally ushered in by the personal return of Jesus the Christ in triumph, in an era of cataclysmic worldwide conflict (nuclear?) termed Armageddon, beyond which God's values and God's truth will reign. Hence we pray in the Lord's Prayer, *"Your Kingdom come, your will be done"*. From as far back as the widespread persecution of Christians in the Roman Empire the Church has looked and yearned for the 'Day of the Lord' to come soon, expressed in the traditional sigh of prayer in Aramaic, the language of Jesus: *Maranatha*: 'O Lord, come'. Come quickly.[109]

This is the one hope that unites and sustains Christians around the globe, including many Syrian and Iraqi Christians facing death at the hands of enemies hell-bent on their eradication, and also us beleaguered ones in the West held in the thrall of a godless affluence. While secular Westerners in general may view our 'civilisation' as the apex of human achievement, God's schedule relates to a universal scenario and indeed favours the 'insignificant' parts of the world: according to Jesus' timetable: "The Good News must *first be preached among all nations* [people groups] before the end shall come."[110]

Only in our time has this condition come close to being met, with churches or missionary activity now found in every land on earth (even including Saudi Arabia) and Scripture translations being made into tiny minority-group languages worldwide.[111] So the times may be steadily ripening towards God's promised intervention in history.

---

109 Both 'soon' and 'quickly' are implied in the word.
110 Mark's Gospel, 13:10 and Luke 24:47.
111 It is significant that, around the world, the Wycliffe Bible Translators alone initiate one new translation into minority group languages every week.

But of course contemporary Western scepticism scorns God's perspective that humanity is fatally flawed, dogged by evil without and sin within—the latter term cringe-worthy indeed to our enlightened belief in human perfectibility through knowledge and education (despite the verdict of history and this morning's newspaper). However such scepticism also precludes the acceptance of God's redeeming love-initiative: his amazing condescension in visiting our planet divinely wrapped in human flesh, bringing the sublime ethical insights offered our race with their potential for creating one worldwide family. To spurn God's love-initiative is to defer to the powers of evil—sadly, an ongoing reality in our world.

> "Lord, for our world where men disown and doubt you,
> loveless in strength, and comfortless in pain,
> hungry and helpless, lost indeed without you:
> Lord of the world, we pray that Christ may reign."

In later years, in our ever-darkening world of tears and fears still doggedly dismissive of God's solution for human brokenness, at times I struggle to maintain hope. I find it truly saddening to think of militant atheists and honest agnostics despising the love of Christ on the cross as he whispers, *"Father, forgive them. They know not what they do"*. Yet against this backdrop of human unbelief reigns the unchanging, eternal God, throughout and beyond the cosmos. Irrespective of human scepticism his Son still offers our conflicted world the unique hope of reconciliation with God—and with each other across all barriers of hate and fear. Of course only God's Holy Spirit can soften hearts and open closed minds, to comprehend and receive such love.

> "You know how full of love and kindness was our Lord, Jesus Christ: rich as He was, He gave it all away for us, so that by His poverty He could make us rich."[112]

From my late eventide perspective I offer my gratitude for God's sovereign initiative in loving, calling, forgiving and receiving me. And for his ever-patient companionship during *the ride of a lifetime:* his steadily unfolding purposes for my life, his gifts of health, home and family love, of work callings, of adequate resources, of friendships, of encouragement in perplexity, in worldwide travel adventures and dramatic rescues. And for the assurance, as Jesus has explicitly promised[113], that he has prepared a place to be where he is.

So in the face of my despair at the world's rampant evils, the challenge comes to continue to watch and pray, both for the world's little people suffering at the hands of the ruthless, the cruel and the greedy, while also pondering our Lord's incredible challenge to forgive—and even pray for our enemies.... ISIL!

'The Kingdom' was the unifying focus of all Christ's teaching: prophesied in ancient Jewish writings over the previous five hundred years, the Reign of God (in Jesus' words characterised as the *'Kingdom of God'*) would be ushered in through

---

112   II Corinthians 8:9
113   John 14: 1–4

the Messiah's birth,[114] his sublime teachings, his peerless life, his atoning death, his wondrous resurrection and his exaltation to glory—the pivot of world history. For the whole race, reconciliation achieved through the Cross: this world matters—*love has won!*

But while God's rule is not yet manifest as a visible reality in the world, nonetheless over the past two thousand years of His grace, His unfailing love and His patience, it has been inwardly experienced in myriad human hearts. To conventional thinking the values of God's Kingdom will prove upside-down: status hierarchies reversed—*"putting down the mighty from their seat and exalting the humble and meek"* so that *"the first shall be last, and the last first"*. The coinage of the Kingdom will not be wealth and power but humility and love. No wonder during Jesus' public ministry *'the common people heard Him gladly'*.

So the Kingdom of God that Christ has brought into the world is 'already—but not yet': that is, ineradicably planted and in embryo growing over the past 2000 years, now finally spanning the globe but yet to be made manifest in majesty and awe at the revelation of Jesus as the cosmic Christ, the Lord of all creation, and the Judge of all the earth who *"shall reign for ever and ever"*.

Until that great day, Christians dwell simultaneously in two worlds: the so-called *'real world'* and the unseen, inwardly experienced world of the Spirit, living in daily communion with Christ.

His appearing will spell the defeat of evil and the vanquishing of death, bringing renewal of the creation, with a new heaven and a new earth finally restored in harmony with their Creator. So God *"will be all in all, and His Kingdom will have no end."*[115]

Until God chooses to fulfil that enticing vision, the bidding of Jesus rings down the centuries to make disciples among all nations. And to strive to be hope-bearers in a world marred by violence and the worship of the 'Golden Calf'. *"Occupy till I come"*.[116]

Meanwhile to be grateful for living in God's world of beauty and wonder. To be loving, to be trusting. To be watching and praying.

Maranatha—"Come, Lord, come quickly!"

---

114 *The Messiah* (in Hebrew) or *The Christ* (in Greek) was long prophesied in the Old Testament as God's Anointed and Chosen Leader—of Israel and of the human race.

115 I Corinthians 15: 28 and Luke 1: 33

116 Luke 19:13 (King James Version)

EPILOGUE

So there it is. The ride of a lifetime. But what is a life? At heart, a mystery. But also a sublime gift of God, to be lived out reverently and gratefully. A journey, a pilgrimage. And pilgrimages have a goal, an end to the rigours—as well as the delights of the way.

Doxology

God's love, joy and peace are perhaps best evoked in the treasures of hymnody that have graced and sign-posted my life:

> This, this is the God we adore,
> our faithful, unchangeable Friend
> whose love is as great as his power,
> and neither knows measure nor end.
> 'Tis Jesus the first and the last,
> whose Spirit shall guide us safe home,
> we'll praise him for all that is past,
> and trust him for all that's to come.

And since the Good Shepherd has been the unseen but ever-present companion of the way, the final verse of a hymn based on the universal favourite, Psalm 23, says it all:

> And so through all the length of days
> Thy goodness faileth never;
> Good Shepherd, may I sing Thy praise
> within Thy house for ever.

Perhaps my expectant hope is best captured in the triumphant final verse of the modern hymn set to the melody of the *Londonderry Air*, which I have dared to turn into a prayer:

> I cannot tell how You will win the nations,
> how You will claim Your earthly heritage,
> how satisfy the needs and aspirations
> of East and West, of sinner and of sage.
> But this I know: all flesh shall see your glory,
> And You shall reap the harvest You have sown,
> and some glad day Your sun will shine in splendour
> when You the saviour, saviour of the world are known.

"Come, Lord, come quickly!"

Maranatha

FINIS
Book Two

BIOGRAPHICAL NOTES

James Houston was born in Sydney in 1932. He studied languages at the University of Sydney leading to a career as a school teacher of French and German in Australia, England, and Germany.

On return to Australia he joined the Commonwealth Public Service and pioneered the concept of multiculturalism based on field research within ethnic communities nationwide.

Ordained an Anglican priest in later life, he served in a poor, multicultural parish, as well as in various positions for the Anglican Diocese of Melbourne, including as Director for its Multicultural Services.

He was awarded the Order of Australia Medal in 2001. James is married to Marjorie, and together they have cared for four children and four grandchildren.

www.ingramcontent.com/pod-product-compliance
Lightning Source LLC
Chambersburg PA
CBHW061402160426
42811CB00100B/1431